W9-CPF-618

# THE REVOLUTION IN VENEZUELA
## SOCIAL AND POLITICAL CHANGE
### UNDER CHÁVEZ

Edited by Thomas Ponniah and Jonathan Eastwood

Published by Harvard University
David Rockefeller Center
for Latin American Studies

Distributed by Harvard University Press
Cambridge, Massachusetts
London, England
2011

Library of Congress Cataloging-in-Publication Data

The revolution in Venezuela : social and political change under Chávez / edited
by Thomas Ponniah and Jonathan Eastwood.

p. ; cm.

Includes bibliographical references.
ISBN: 978-0-674-06138-5

1. Venezuela—Politics and government—1999– 2. Venezuela—Social
conditions—1999– 3. Revolutions—Venezuela—21st century. 4. Chavez Frias,
Hugo—Influence. I. Ponniah, Thomas, 1966– II. Eastwood, Jonathan.

F2329 .R48 2011
987.0642

# Contents

# Acknowledgments

This project began as a result of conversations between the editors while both taught in the Committee on Degrees in Social Studies at Harvard University, a wonderful program that provides a liberal arts education in social theory and social science to Harvard's finest students. Special thanks for their support are due to Richard Tuck, Chair of Social Studies, and Anya Bernstein, Director of Studies. Thanks also to Sarah Champlin-Scharff, Undergraduate Program Administrator and Department Administrator, as well as to Staff Assistants Kate Anable and Katelyn Greene, Assistant Director of Studies Nicole Newendorp, and Head Teaching Fellow Nicolas Prevelakis.

Many people have contributed to the development of this project. We would like to thank our chapter authors, who were patient with revision requests and generous with their time and effort. We would also like to thank Merilee Grindle, Director of the David Rockefeller Center for Latin American Studies (DRCLAS) at Harvard, for her encouragement and support. Further thanks are due to June Erlick, publications director overseeing DRCLAS' book series, as well as the anonymous reviewers, who made a number of important suggestions and criticisms. Following and resolving them improved the book. Likewise we are grateful to Anita Safran for her excellent work on the manuscript. Thank you to Professor John Coatsworth, former Director of DRCLAS, for first encouraging us to pursue this project via Harvard University.

The work was greatly aided by a Research Conference Grant from the David Rockefeller Center for Latin American Studies at Harvard University, supported, in turn, by the Cisneros Foundation. This enabled us to hold a conference in December 2007, at which some chapter authors shared their work. In addition, several outside scholars at Harvard and elsewhere joined in our proceedings and offered important suggestions and critiques. Here we would like to single out Merilee Grindle, Steve Levitsky, Chappel Lawson, and Arachú Castro for special thanks. We would like to also recognize the important participation of Carlos Blanco and Gerver Torres in that conference. We are also grateful to Ramón Piñango, Alex Campos, and Leslie Gates for their contributions to this project.

Work on the book was aided by a Fulbright Grant that allowed Jon Eastwood to travel to Venezuela in the summer of 2007, as well as Glenn/Lenfest Grants from Washington and Lee University in the summers of 2007 and

2008. Support from the Office of the Provost at Washington and Lee University is gratefully acknowledged. Elissa Hanson, a student atWashington and Lee, helped with references and the consolidated bibliography. Some of the core ideas of the introduction were developed when Eastwood gave the Sherman Emerging Scholar Lecture at the University of North Carolina, Wilmington, in October 2007 and at a paper presentation at the colloquium of the Department of Sociology at the University of Virginia. Eastwood's thinking about theories of revolution—and where recent events in Venezuela fit in relation to those theories—was developed through teaching seminars on social revolutions in 2007 and 2008 at Washington and Lee, and he would like to acknowledge his students here.

For Thomas Ponniah, work on the book was aided by funds from the Committee on Degrees in Social Studies at Harvard University that allowed him to travel to Venezuela in 2006. Some of the key ideas of the conclusion were developed when Ponniah was invited to give lectures on Venezuela at Harvard University, Brown University and Pace University in the spring of 2008 and 2009. Ponniah's reflections on modernity, progress, revolution and development were greatly by aided by his students' and colleagues' comments in his teaching seminars on modern social theory, globalization and development, and the philosophy and methods of the social sciences.

Finally, we would like to thank our families and friends.

Thanks to the Ponniah family and to Robin Browne, Marva Major, Jaedon Browne, Kasai Browne, Kim de Lallo, Kim Elliott, Benjamin Diop, Laila Smith, Andrew Wood, Barbara Feldman, Lucas Feldman,Tom Johnson, Shanti Thakur, Anurima Banerji, Ngaire Blankenberg, and to James Parker, his partner Barbara and his daughters Chelsea and Billie for their support.

María Emilia Nava deserves thanks for being so supportive throughout the process and for consistently being willing to discuss contemporary Venezuelan life. Gabriela and Samuel Eastwood have been wonderful sources of distraction from work. Eastwood would also like to thank his family and *suegros*, even as he knows that not all of them will agree with everything said in the book.

Finally, this book is dedicated to the memory of James Ponniah (1935–2009).

# Introduction: The Revolution in Venezuela?[1]

*Jonathan Eastwood*

During the mid 1990s, it was possible to imagine that revolution was dead.[2] Memories of the political revolutions in Central and Eastern Europe, as well as the transition from apartheid in South Africa, had not faded, of course. Yet one could view all of these "revolutions" as contributing to the institutionalization of a non-revolutionary era.[3] Liberal-democratic and capitalist triumphalism seemed to meet little criticism when its observers declared obsolete the tradition of radical social revolution that had emerged in the 19th century and animated so much of 20th century social conflict. In Latin America, this story took the form of the much-discussed Washington Consensus.[4] This consensus defined the possibilities for organizing social life in the hemisphere quite narrowly: not only was the revolutionary tradition, temporarily represented only by Cuba in the Americas, viewed as clearly anachronistic—its demise just a matter of time[5]—but even social democracy was suspect. State services were to be privatized, presidentialism and centralism to be reduced through federalism or some other form of decentralization, and liberal regimes to be consolidated.[6]

Viewed now—a decade into the 21st century—things look very different. Many judge statist development strategies to have been vindicated.[7] Others are skeptical about "one size fits all" approaches to political democratization and democratic consolidation.[8] Equally notable, the idea of revolution, or the "revolutionist tradition,"[9] has achieved a new lease on life. Hugo Chávez and Venezuela's Bolivarian Revolution have played a key role in these major shifts.

But is the Bolivarian Revolution truly revolutionary? This is a contentious question, and a difficult one for social scientists to answer definitively. It is contentious because the answer to this question is bound up with efforts by some actors to legitimate and others to delegitimate the Chávez government.[10] For some, the government's revolutionary status is its greatest selling point, and for others, it is evidence that the government and its programs are doomed to fail. For others still, the *problem* with the government is that it is not in their estimation *authentically* revolutionary. This latter critique, interestingly, comes from both the political left *and* the right.[11]

The question is difficult definitively because social scientists don't agree about how to define revolutions.[12] Positions on this question range widely. Some define revolutions quite narrowly.[13] Others treat revolutions as shading into other types of "contention" such as social movement activity or insurgencies.[14] Still others deny that the concept of revolution can be clearly defined at all.[15] Revolutions are extraordinarily complex social processes, and this complexity contributes to analysts' difficulties in coming to consensus about how to conceptualize and explain them. In the first place, revolutions seem to require the weakening or even collapse of existing political institutions and structures that hold in place the ongoing distribution of resources.[16] Research reveals that absent such weakening, the success of revolutions is highly unlikely.[17] Revolutions further require the presence of disaffected groups with sufficient clout so as to be able to take advantage of political opportunities made available by the weakening of existing institutions.[18] Typically, multiple social groups, including both subaltern and elite actors, must be involved, and the coordination of their activities is itself typically a matter of extraordinary complexity. Revolutions also depend on the presence of sufficient potential organizational capacity so that these groups can be mobilized.[19] Furthermore, they depend on cultural resources, whether conceptualized as "collective action frames"[20] or as "political cultures of opposition,"[21] that channel disaffected groups toward revolutionary mobilization rather than quiescence. It is clear from history that while ideals and goals derived from such cultural resources are important motivators for revolutionary activity, revolutions do not typically take the paths intended by their would-be leaders.[22] In other words, they exhibit their own logic or pattern of change, and are extraordinarily difficult, if not impossible, to steer.[23] While there *may* be common causal patterns operative in revolutionary processes across different types of societies, it is quite clear that these factors vary considerably across time and space, further complicating the study of revolutions.

Scholars are well advised to proceed cautiously when analyzing putative revolutionary projects, yet students of contemporary developments in Venezuela—and Latin America more broadly—cannot wait for scholars of revolution to come to consensus about how to conceptualize and define this key term before we proceed to analysis.

Although scholars of revolution have not achieved consensus about definitions, there is one key feature of revolutions about which many of them agree: revolutions dramatically alter *social stratification* and the perception of stratification. Some may do so through reconfiguring formal and informal power, some may do so through reconceptualizing status relations, and some may do so through transforming *class*.[24] In this volume we aim to assess the Bolivarian Revolution against this background. To what extent have events of the last decade-plus transformed the experience of class, status, and power in Venezuela? In other words, how substantial has *social change* been under Chávez?

## Class

Revolutions typically claim that they will transform class structures, and the Bolivarian Revolution is no exception. The discursive categories through which class is conceptualized in the revolution vary, in part, because *nationalism* rather than traditional Marxian *revolutionism* was the principal official discursive frame of class relations for much of the time that Chávez has held power, yet this has begun to shift, gradually and partially.[25] Typically, class relations have been discursively presented in *binary* terms: *el pueblo* versus *la oligarquía*.[26] From the point of view of the revolution's discursive *strategy*, this makes sense.[27] Nationalism has been well established as the fundamental frame for Venezuelan politics since the 19th century.[28] The designation of the nation as *el pueblo* or *el soberano*, moreover, has the advantage of ambiguous inclusiveness:[29] many potential constituencies, even including those who would be conventionally judged as upper class or middle class, are likely to identify themselves as part of *el pueblo*.[30] The other class designated in this binary pair, the oligarchy, is one with whom very few (even those we might consider oligarchs) would identify. In other words, the oligarchy is an ideal discursive target. Since it has no clear referent, consensus across wide social divisions can (in principle) be achieved by a discursive strategy that presents the state's interventionist and redistributive actions as targeting this treacherous oligarchy on "the people's" behalf.[31] This discursive strategy likely contributed to Chávez's *early* electoral victories (e.g., the 1998 presidential election), in which socioeconomically heterogeneous groups supported him.[32]

Since 2005, however, Chávez has officially declared his government to be "socialist."[33] From then on, official discourse has increasingly used a partially distinct frame for conceptualizing class relations, one embedded in the broader frame of socialist revolutionism. These overlapping ways of speaking about class now exist simultaneously. The group previously labeled the oligarchy is increasingly referred to as the bourgeoisie.[34] This signals an official discursive move towards a more traditional, Marxian, conceptualization of class relations. Note that the concept of the bourgeoisie can serve as a rough functional equivalent to the oligarchy (in terms of its ambiguous *exclusivity*), since very few Venezuelans would self-identify as bourgeois (it is therefore an ideal label to ascribe to others). Yet part of what is happening here is an effort to gradually reframe the official discourse of class, because different discourses of class have embedded in them (a) different critiques of the old class order and (b) different prescriptions for the future. The binary pair, "the people" versus "the oligarchy," suggests that the treasonous corruption of a few is the fundamental source of social problems. Even as the government aims to establish a linkage with an "invented tradition"[35] of Venezuelan revolutionism that reaches back to historical precursors like Simón Bolívar and Ezequiel Zamora, to pursue the socialist vision it aims to achieve it needs to transcend the essentially *liberal* critique of the social order in the service of which so many of these figures labored. The government and its supporters appropriate the liberal slogan *¡Oligarcas temblad!* The completion of that 19th century refrain *¡Viva la libertad!* must either be underemphasized or its meaning transformed.[36]

Thus the government turns to an alternative discursive framing of class relations, one rooted in Marx and the revolutionist tradition inspired by his work. If the class that represents the interests of the old order is not just another oligarchy but the bourgeoisie, this suggests that their exploitation of the majority is not just political but fundamentally economic. Revolution must not just replace corrupt oligarchs but rather achieve dramatic social structural change, emancipating the proletariat from the economic exploitation of the owners of capital.[37]

The process of shifting discourse in this way is a complicated one. On the one hand, it is unclear just how *strategic* this discursive shift has truly been. In other words, while it would serve the strategic purposes that I identify here, it is possible that the change is less intentional and strategic and more a consequence of shifting influences within the inner circle of the Chávez government,[38] or a consequence of the unfolding path of radicalization discussed by Corrales in his chapter in this volume. On the other hand, strategic or not, discursive shifting of this kind is politically risky. As noted above, the distinction between the people and the oligarchy was well established in Venezuelan political culture before Chávez. This discourse cut across many social divisions and gained legitimacy by virtue of its close association with the idea of the Venezuelan nation, which resonated with the vast majority of Venezuelans. The "bourgeoisie-proletariat" frame is potentially much more divisive (this is even true, though less so, of the hybrid "bourgeoisie-pueblo" frame).[39] Perhaps for this reason, these two official discourses of class now exist alongside each other. Chávez himself weaves them together, despite the apparent contradictions between them.[40]

Class, of course, is not just discourse, and efforts to change the discourse of class should not be conflated with efforts to transform so-called "real" class relations. In other words, we might ask the question that Marx him-self would ask of this "revolution." Has it transformed the objective eco-nomic conditions of the major groups that make up this society? Moreover, have any such transformations been *systematic* and *progressive*?

The government's broader strategy has been to use spending of oil rev-enues, especially social spending, to increase aggregate demand, yielding high levels of economic growth between 2003 and 2008.[41] This, rather than being revolutionary, is a variation on a traditional Venezuelan approach to state-led development.[42] However, the government's efforts to target and institu-tionally structure its spending depart to some extent from prior practice. The government could have attempted to work directly through existing state bureaucracies (e.g., the public health system, social security) while reforming them, rendering them more efficient and, at the same time, expanding their resources and power. This strategy would have been politi-cally costly and its success less than certain. The government instead chose to construct *new* institutions for the delivery of social services, the "missions" (discussed in several chapters below). Unlike the existing bureaucracies, these could be built largely from scratch. This meant that they could be rolled out quickly, they could be targeted at specifically identified social problems, they could be flexibly adjusted to emergent problems or to changes in the nature of existing problems, and they could be staffed with loyalists.[43]

These efforts notwithstanding, it is hard to argue that the Bolivarian Rev-olution has, so far, decisively transformed the class *structure*.[44] That is, most of the same economic groups found in Venezuela in the 1990s (e.g., rural workers, urban poor, the middle class, upper-middle class, and the wealthy) still exist today. Despite the increasing pace of nationalizations, there are still many thriving capitalists in Venezuela and many working-class labor-ers in industrial settings controlled by those capitalists (as well as those con-trolled by state-owned enterprises, of course). There are still many poor workers in the informal economy, and many who work as domestic ser-vants in the homes of wealthy and middle-class Venezuelans. For a time it seemed possible that novel economic arrangements such as the proliferation of state-supported cooperatives would change this, but the success of such efforts so far is unclear.[45] It is also possible that the government's more aggressive use of nationalizations exhibited in recent months will have a more pronounced influence on the class structure in the future.

Data from the United Nations Human Development Reports allow us to gain a rough sense of the degree of changes in levels of inequality in recent years.[46] The 2001 report lists the Gini index (the most common statistical measure of income inequality, with higher figures representing higher inequality) for Venezuela at 48.8, and notes the income ratio between the top and bottom tenths of the income distribution at 24.3.[47] According to the data in the 2009 report, the Gini index had fallen to 43.4 and the ratio of the incomes of the richest to the poorest tenths of the population to 18.8.[48] According to at least some figures, Venezuela has the lowest Gini index level in the region.[49] By any definition, this is progress. However, it is worth noting that during the same period the Gini index fell in Brazil from 59.1 to 55, and in Mexico from 51.9 to 48.1.[50] The ratio of incomes of the highest to lowest tenths of the income distributions in these societies fell as well, from 48.7 to 40.6 in Brazil's case and from 26.4 to 21 in Mexico's case.[51] The question of whether global income inequality in this period has been rising or falling is debated,[52] but Venezuela's performance in this regard does not seem to be exceptionally "revolutionary" in comparison to others in the region. Income inequality has been reduced—indeed, according to Sebastian Edwards, data point to a reduction in inequality in Venezuela exceeding that of any other Latin American country, at least from 2002–2006[53]—but so far at least probably not to the extent that we would expect from a social revolution.[54]

A number of changes have been deemed more substantial, however.

The first is the relative size of some of these social groups, as well as, to some extent, their specific composition. Much has been made of the rise of a "new elite" group, derisively dubbed the "Boli-Bourgeoisie," which benefits from preferential relationships with the government.[55] Yet these individuals are capitalists practicing business via the sorts of ties to the state that have been characteristic of Venezuelan economic activity for decades.[56] Thus some individuals have experienced mobility, but the *structures*—the "hotel" rather than the "occupants" in Schumpeter's famous metaphor—are still in place.[57]

Along similar lines, a second major change is that poverty was reduced considerably, at least during the 2003–2008 economic boom (though again, without a basic transformation of the class structure).[58] While some in the Venezuelan opposition deny it, virtually all scholarly commentators agree about this reduction, independent of their political leanings. Where they *disagree* is over questions of (a) the *extent* of this poverty reduction; (b) the degree to which it is a consequence of government policies or just a function of economic growth produced by high oil prices (perhaps even in spite of government policies); and (c) the sustainability of the Bolivarian model of macroeconomic management and the way in which it is integrated with social policy.[59]

A third major aspect of change is that evidence suggests than many poor Venezuelans feel that their status and power positions have improved as a result of the Bolivarian Project.[60] Thus how one judges the relative revolutionary status of the government in this area will depend on how one defines revolution and what components of stratification one considers fundamental. From a traditional Marxian point of view, this has clearly *not* been a revolution, at least so far, because it has not radically transformed the class *structure*. Yet if the process is sustained for years—and if the increasing pace of expropriations continues—it is possible that more pronounced social-structural changes will take place.

## Status

Our first thought when we consider the impact of a putative revolution on status relations concerns the *internal* status hierarchy of a society. That is, we think of the impact of the revolutionary process on the system via which status is ascribed to elements of the population.[61] Yet there is a second important way in which revolutions, particularly those in the developing world, can affect status-relations: that is, in terms of their effect on the geopolitical status hierarchy. This global status hierarchy arranges societies and their populations in relation to several indices, such as "development" or perceived "modernity."

These status hierarchies are, of course, connected.[62] In much of the developing world, elites identify (indeed, increasingly so) with a so-called global culture that is itself a key feature of the geopolitical status hierarchy.[63] These very relationships have been bound up with the construction and promotion of expertise that has influenced the policies and directions of states in recent decades.[64] At the same time, the geopolitical status hierarchy forms the context in which many intellectuals in the developing world aim to define their status positions *against* this order.

Thus the Bolivarian process (*El Proceso*) should be seen as acting upon a complex status hierarchy that has both internal/domestic and external/geopolitical components. The internal component defines social status largely in relation to class, but also in relation to race, gender, and other such categories.[65] As in all stratification systems, there are many gradients to status in Venezuelan society (and the more microsociological the lens, the greater the visibility of fine gradients of status difference).[66] However, at the most *fundamental* level, status differences in Venezuelan society separate those who aspire to or perform middle-class or elite status from those who experience a subaltern or "marginal" status.[67] Perhaps not surprisingly, this difference mirrors closely the political polarization that has characterized the Chávez years in Venezuela. Thus, on the one hand, this process seems to have exacerbated and made more rigid existing status relations.

On the other hand, status relations have indeed changed in certain respects. Social status involves both external ascription and internal self-definition.[68] While the existence of major status groups within Venezuelan society has not been radically altered, the possibilities for status identity, particularly among subaltern groups, have shifted. Perhaps most notably, the poor in Venezuelan society have been symbolically elevated. Official discourse regarding race and gender has shifted as well. Indigenous and Afro-Venezuelan figures from the past have been placed—literally and figuratively—in the national pantheon, and re-evaluated by the government and social movements alike.[69] Likewise, the 1999 constitution used gender-neutral language, and this practice has found its way into the public speech of many prominent Chavistas as well.[70]

At the same time, the Venezuelan state's position in the international status hierarchy has shifted. As discussed in detail by Mark Williams and Mark Weisbrot in their chapters below, Venezuela in the Chávez era has adopted an ambitious and much-discussed foreign policy agenda, one which departs in both substance and style from previous Venezuelan approaches to foreign policy.

Symbolically (and all status is *symbolic* in character), this change in position is a major realignment. During the Cold War, Venezuela was a "good example" from the point of view of U.S. policymakers. As has been much discussed—and recently much criticized—Venezuela was often identified as a "model" or "exceptional" democracy, meaning that it was taken to have demonstrated that U.S.-style liberal democracy was a viable political choice in Latin America.[71] Its guerilla insurgency in the 1960s had failed, and it had consolidated a two-party liberal democratic system. Moreover, throughout the 1990s, under the influence of Luis Giusti, Venezuela's oil policy was aligned with the interests of the United States.[72] Perhaps more important, at the symbolic level, Venezuela was perceived by many as culturally close to the United States.

Under Chávez, Venezuela has repositioned itself as one of Washington's chief strategic opponents. At the symbolic level, Venezuela under Chávez has been placed in the vanguard of an effort to restore the left and to emancipate Latin America and the rest of the developing world from the domination of the developed world and the multinational organizations largely controlled by that world.

The impact that this has had on internal or domestic status is complicated. But at the risk of oversimplification we note that the attitude of many subaltern Venezuelans to the international or geopolitical status hierarchy has been partially reframed through the discursive work of the government and its allies. The new frame is one of anti-imperialism. A classic transvaluation pattern is evident.[73] The old/existing geopolitical status hierarchy asserts the social superiority of so-called developed societies, but Chavismo redefines them as imperialist oppressors: solidarity and equity are held up as alternative indices of international status; development itself is redefined so as to build on these values.[74] It is apparent that the symbolic elevation of the poor and the official reconsideration of the geopolitical status hierarchy are connected.

## Power

Of the three major dimensions of stratification, it is perhaps in the domain of power where social relations have changed the most over the Chávez years. Much has been written on whether these changes are democratic or antidemocratic and authoritarian.[75] These are without doubt important issues, and the chapters below examine them and provide contrasting interpretations. Yet if we wish to consider the Chávez government's revolutionary status, we should first assess whether and to what extent structures of power have been transformed.

Certain conclusions can be clearly drawn. As others have noted, the representative democracy of the period preceding Chávez's election had decayed. Pactism had rendered democratic participation for members of subaltern groups limited at best.[76] As economic problems mounted and the state was unable to address them, the failures of the old political system became clearer to all.[77] Even had the Chávez government not built new institutions and constructed new arrangements for organizing power, the decline of COPEI (Comité de Organización Electoral Independiente) and AD (Acción Democrática) in the 1990s represented a major shift in how power is structured in Venezuela (if this is thought a revolution, these developments must also be considered part of the process).[78] Likewise, it is important in this context to consider the state's difficulties—emergent in the late 1980s and 1990s and growing under Chávez—to manage street crime, suggesting that not only the formal rules of political competition of the old regime collapsed, but that state capacity and the rule of law declined as well.[79]

Since then we have seen more radical changes in the power structure. The 1999 constitution promoted some limited recentralization, and the process of political recentralization has proceeded since. Recent years have witnessed the Chávez movement's total dominance of all branches of the Venezuelan government (though it must be acknowledged that in the case of the National Assembly the *extent* of this dominance was a function of the opposition's refusal to participate in the 2005 elections).[80] At the local level—as explored by Greg Wilpert in his chapter below—a variety of experimental forms of participation have been developed, though there are debates about their effectiveness, fairness, and long-term viability, as well as about the extent of their compatibility with liberal, representative, or pluralist democracy.

The 2007 constitutional reform process would have radically altered power relations—installing, in Chávez's words, a "new geometry of power"—but the proposal lost by a narrow national vote. Yet a number of its provisions have subsequently been enacted or otherwise attained, and in the last several years the Chávez government has used a widening range of tools to expand its power position vis-à-vis opponents. For example, the presidency and other offices are now open to indefinite re-election. As noted above, the government has had some success in achieving recentralization, notably in taking over control of the ports, which had been a key responsibility and revenue source of state-level governments, some controlled by the opposition. When opposition figure Antonio Ledesma was elected mayor of Caracas, the national government not only did nothing to back him when its supporters took over the mayor's office, refusing to let him and his staff enter: instead, the government placed Vice President Jacqueline Farías in control of most of the city, dramatically cutting the elected mayor's funds and responsibilities. The new Federal Council, established in May of 2010, seems certain to undercut the power of governors and mayors more generally, though government supporters stress that it includes communal council representation.[81] The government has moved to bar prominent opposition candidates from running for office on the grounds that they have been accused of corruption (though often government officials present little direct evidence of this, and though the law seems to suggest that a conviction, and not just an accusation, would be needed). Other prominent opposition members—including Manuel Rosales, who opposed Chávez in the 2006 presidential elections discussed by López-Maya and Lander below—have fled when charged with corruption, while some opponents, such as former ally General Raúl Baduel, have been jailed. To regime critics, such moves—perhaps best exemplified by the Chávez-ordered jailing of a judge, Maria Lourdes Afiuni, who freed another individual accused of corruption (the banker Eligio Cedeño) and by the arrest of opposition figures like Oswaldo Álvarez Paz and Guillermo Zuloaga for speech crimes in 2010—signal a steady turn away from ostensible respect for liberal conceptions of the rights of individuals that some judged consistent with policies and behavior of the government in earlier years. Indeed, these developments have led critics such as Teodoro Petkoff, while noting that there is still a vibrant opposition operating with considerable freedom in Venezuela, to label the Chávez regime a "quasi-dictatorship,"[82] a designation that seems to me at the time of this writing to be increasingly apt, though many of the authors of chapters in this volume do not share in this assessment.

Defenders of the government argue that individuals like Baduel, Afiuni, Álvarez Paz, and Zuloaga are indeed corrupt or have participated in one or another illicit activity, and that the government or the revolution needs to protect itself. They also charge that the focus on these issues and abuses only tells half of the story. The more important part of the story, they suggest, is that the government has *empowered* subaltern populations. It is important to distinguish this claim from the one noted above, that subaltern groups have been *symbolically elevated* by the Bolivarian process. It is indeed quite possible for a group to be symbolically elevated without being handed power.[83] These issues are taken up by a number of the authors below and by Thomas Ponniah in the Conclusion.

## Explaining the Bolivarian Revolution

It is not the primary object of this volume to explain causally the social and political change that Venezuela has witnessed in recent years. Others have made important contributions to answering this question,[84] and here we are more interested in analyzing the nature and implications of these changes. I will therefore provide only a brief, synthetic summary so as to contextualize the chapters that follow. The process that brought the Chávez era has unfolded in three basic stages. First, a marked decline in living standards for Venezuelans of different class backgrounds in the 1980s produced increasing discontent. Second, a variety of actors—again, from different social locations—articulated critiques of the existing political system that undercut its legitimacy. At the same time, the state's ability to function and provide basic services declined dramatically. Finally, mobilization for social change took place *through* electoral politics.[85]

After many years of championing Venezuela's alleged "exceptionalism" and democratic political culture,[86] scholars concerned with changes in Venezuelan democracy came to focus on weaknesses in what is sometimes called the *Punto Fijo* system in Venezuela.[87]

As Karl has persuasively argued, Venezuela's heavy dependence on oil left it in a vulnerable position, helping to engender a state in which "rent seeking" was "the central organizing principle of its political and economic life, and the ossified political institutions in existence operated primarily to perpetuate an entrenched spoils system."[88] Focusing more on how the Venezuelan state's oil dependence interacts with identity (and thus with the perceived legitimacy of the state), Coronil has argued that Venezuelans have conceptualized the state as possessing the "magical" ability to distribute rents from oil, a resource which, he claims, is itself conceptualized by Venezuelans as the nation's "natural body."[89] On this line of analysis, when perceived obligations of the state vis-à-vis its citizens were no longer delivered, the political class that controlled the state delegitimized itself. Political scientists and others have documented the clientelism of the "partyarchy" that developed in the later years of the *Punto Fijo* system.[90] Embedded in this clientelism and partyarchy were further vulnerabilities, since support for the existing regime depended upon the state's ability to offer both economic and political patronage. Smith and McCoy point out that the Venezuelan state experienced "three related crises": "the fiscal crisis of the state"; "administrative shortcomings associated with a bloated state bureaucracy"; and finally "a crisis of legitimacy of public institutions."[91]

The 1970s had been years of economic growth and exuberance, but this very expansion, on Karl's model, only served to reinforce the weaknesses that would follow.[92] After the devaluation of 1983, Venezuela saw times of low oil prices and poor economic performance.[93] As Susan Eckstein and others have noted, the 1980s were, throughout Latin America, a decade of protests, and many of these protests were fueled by discontent with at least the short-term economic consequences of structural adjustment programs.[94] However, in Venezuela, despite the significant, partial delegitimation of the state and the major political parties by the early 1980s, the currency devaluation of 1983, and the ongoing economic problems that plagued Venezuelan society in these difficult years, until 1989 there was no major, concerted street protest action of such intensity and organization as to threaten the state. The lack of potentially revolutionary street action in this period may be due to the fact that both the COPEI government of Luis Herrera Campins and the AD government of Jaime Lusinchi implemented only attenuated economic reforms and did so inconsistently.[95] It may be that, for a time, blame for worsening economic conditions was individualized, attributed to bad government but not yet, for many, identified with a *system* perceived to be fully corrupt. Moreover, the weakness of the state had not yet been revealed, and it had not yet acted to undermine its own legitimacy through extensive use of force against its own population and perceived weakness following the coups d'état of 1992. Throughout the entire period, when reforms did come, they were sporadic. The enervating turns from traditional policies to economic and political reforms, to promises of a return to the past, to a renewal of structural adjustment, can only have served as a stimulus to the commonly held feeling that more substantial changes were needed.[96]

There *were* persistent efforts at reform, and they were accompanied by a gradually increasing sense of dissatisfaction with the old order. In Venezuela, as in other cases of putative revolution, initial reform efforts often came from within elite sectors.[97] From early on, Naím and Piñango, among others, famously declared that Venezuela faced an "illusion of harmony" and that deepening social polarization was visible beneath the surface.[98] As Buxton notes, the Grupo Roraima, as well, began calling for political and economic decentralization from the early to mid 1980s.[99] The notion that what the country needed was a new constitution took hold early on among many.[100] In advocating reforms, elites tried to maintain power and the existing rent distribution system despite the changing fiscal and political environment.[101] Perhaps most important in this connection would be the establishment of COPRE (Comisión Presidencial para la Reforma del Estado) under President Lusinchi, the fulfillment of a campaign promise to work toward political decentralization.[102] This move only highlighted and exacerbated the perceived need for reform. However, as Buxton notes, Acción Democrática (AD) ended up opposing COPRE's recommendations, and "no effort to reform the political system was undertaken for the remainder of [Lusinchi's] presidency."[103] The country would have to wait for the second presidency of Carlos Andrés Pérez and the interim presidency of Ramón Velásquez for serious efforts at implementation to be made.[104]

The story of the reforms of 1989 and the *Caracazo* has been repeatedly told.[105] I will offer, therefore, only the most schematic of presentations here. Following the disastrous economic performance and the popular view that the governments of the 1980s had been hopelessly corrupt,[106] Venezuelans reelected Carlos Andrés Pérez, who had served in the presidency from 1974 to 1979, managing to nationalize the oil industry; expand the state bureaucracy; and leave Venezuela deeply in debt, despite—or, as Karl's analysis suggests,[107] perhaps "paradoxically" because of—the oil boom. The debt that the governments of Herrera Campins and Lusinchi inherited in the 1980s (continued, indeed, by Herrera), along with the suddenly much lower price of oil, sowed the economic and social problems with which these governments would have to reckon.[108] This meant that Pérez returned to office in 1989 attempting to undo some of his earlier legacy. He would play in the unfolding story a role that Buxton aptly labels "Pérez-Stroika."[109] It is likewise worth noting, with Buxton, that Pérez restored the status of COPRE and actually followed through on some of its initiatives, ending, for example, the practice of appointing governors and mayors directly and allowing, instead, for local and state elections to these offices.[110] As Myers, drawing on survey data, notes, Pérez's election raised public expectations considerably.[111]

A structural adjustment program was implemented quickly and, according to some of its architects, without sufficient communication and political know-how, leading to a situation in which both the populace and the political parties—including Pérez's own party, AD—were strongly opposed to the reforms and their costs.[112] Moreover, the implementation was imperfect.[113] Protests turned violent, looting took place, and for the longest time, the authorities essentially did nothing. After hesitating for days, Pérez used force, and hundreds were killed, many of them apparently innocent and a number extrajudicially executed.[114] As López-Maya has shown, participants in the *Caracazo* were drawn from heterogeneous social groups, including socially active students, working-class commuters, and marginalized members of "informal" sectors.[115]

The violence was a clear sign of social discontent, as López-Maya, Smilde, and Stephany have noted, and indeed was part of a growing cycle of protests and social organizing that continued throughout the 1990s.[116] The reasons for this discontent are many, but most fundamentally concern rising poverty throughout much of the period,[117] one immediately following an extended time during which expectations were greatly raised.[118] At the same time, the *Caracazo* should probably not be interpreted as revolutionary in and of itself. As many have pointed out, stores were the main targets of popular violence and looting was among the central activities. Considering the *Caracazo* a merely reactive event by an inarticulate mass of poor will clearly not do;[119] there were, in this period in Venezuela, many articulate would-be architects of social change, both within the more marginal national political parties—for example, MAS (Movimiento al Socialismo) and La Causa R—but also at the grassroots level.[120] What the *Caracazo* did accomplish, as many commentators agree, was to turn discontent into crisis, further eroding the now crumbling *Punto Fijo* order. At the popular level, this issued in an expansion of protest activity. At the elite level, it increased the sense of crisis and served as the final impetus for the implementation of some of COPRE's suggested reforms.[121] Among other things, repeated calls were heard for an assembly to establish a new constitution. The Chávez coup attempt of February 1992 and the subsequent coup attempt of late 1992 only furthered these developments.[122] Media assaults on the old order also played an important role.[123]

Carlos Andrés Pérez was impeached in 1993, and Ramón Velásquez served as interim president. Then Rafael Caldera was re-elected after renouncing COPEI as well as the entire political system he had helped to construct. He forged an alliance with some of those on the traditional left who had for many years been marginalized.[124] Caldera released Chávez from prison in 1994, around the same time that Chávez came into contact with Luis Miquilena.[125] According to several sources, it was Miquilena who convinced

Chávez to seek revolution through electoral means, and it was Miquilena who was, in many respects the architect of much of the project until his break with Chávez in 2001–2002.[126]

More generally, there were essentially three sources of potential revolutionary leadership: (a) military officers, and most notably junior officers in the military who had conspired for years in the MBR-200 (Movimiento Bolivariano Revolucionario 200)[127]; (b) representatives of the old civilian left, such as Miquilena and José Vicente Rangel; and (c) members of newly successful political parties whose rise to positions of local power was itself dependent on elite-led political reform from within the *Punto Fijo* order. However, at least four additional collective actors were of critical importance: (d) elite reformists, especially advocates of both political and economic decentralization, beginning in the mid 1980s, who articulated an ongoing critique of the *Punto Fijo* order and whose policy recommendations were adopted in several critical ways; (e) some business interests that played an important role in funding Chávez's initial electoral victories;[128] (f) the rural poor; and (g) the urban poor.[129]

These social groups interacted in ways that would have been difficult to predict. Both absolute and relative deprivation generated by economic problems of the 1980s and 1990s produced discontent across the social spectrum.[130] The middle class shrank as many within it were pushed into poverty. The informal sector of the urban labor force expanded dramatically. Social services decayed. The rural poor felt abandoned by political elites that had claimed to champion them. Virtually all citizens viewed the society as having entered into a crisis. Elite reformers correctly saw that political closure was an important aspect of the problem, since closure both led to subaltern groups feeling excluded from political deliberation *and* created the conditions that led the state to fail in responding to their concerns. However, they probably underestimated the degree to which socioeconomic concerns underlay the sense of crisis,[131] or at the very least they placed too much faith in the ability of neoliberal economic reforms to address poverty in the short term, failing to grasp adequately the political difficulties they faced as well.[132] Moreover, they were clearly too optimistic about the chances of solving such a crisis through reformist political opening and decentralization. Their efforts seem, in retrospect, to have only exacerbated the decomposition of the old regime. Indeed, as Penfold-Becerra suggests, "the activation of federal institutions" was "a primary cause of the demise of the AD-COPEI duopoly in Venezuelan politics and paved the way for the rise of Hugo Chávez Frías."[133] Moreover, as López-Maya notes, the creation of new political space dovetailed with protest activity.[134] Importantly, reforming elites had competitors in the game of framing discontent in the form of the three groups of leaders mentioned above: disaffected military officers, old guard leftists, and representatives of newer left-leaning political parties. All of these groups were able to both draw on elite critiques of existing politics (emphasizing corruption) and to focus on socioeconomic problems more centrally, presenting novel economic reforms as continuous with traditional elitist exploitation.

Thus a number of the conditions typically used to explain revolutionary upheavals were present: declining state capacity, increasing absolute and relative deprivation, economic problems following a period of rising expectations, elites and intellectuals turning against the regime. Moreover, capable leaders of change with resonant ideological frames were available. The major question that remained was the problem of mobilization.

While there was indeed a great wave of protest activity in the early 1990s, it achieved little central coordination. As in all cases where the desire for dramatic social change is present, barriers to cooperation needed to be solved.[135] While there were many discontented actors, existing formal and informal structures, in particular the party system, channeled them in a non-revolutionary direction. How could disparate groups with their own interests and analyses of the situation be brought into a common cause? In this particular case, it was solved through participation in formal politics.[136] Chávez's advisers convinced him to seek power through elections, and a campaign was crafted that deliberately sought to appeal to most social sectors.

This approach had important implications for what followed. As the process accelerated, it would necessarily lead to conflict with groups with vested interests: for example, much of the business community, as represented by FEDECAMARAS, the upper-level management of PDVSA (Petróleos de Venezuela, S.A.) before the events of 2002–2003, and the remnants of existing political elites, including the major political parties and the unions attached to them.[137] As the process radicalized, it would also produce tensions with some Chávez supporters, particularly middle-class and elite voters, a number of whom supported Chávez when he was elected president in 1998. To maintain success, the government would need to mobilize greater and greater numbers of supporters it could reasonably expect to be loyal, those on whose behalf it claimed to be acting. As middle-class and elite supporters would fall away, it needed both new elites (to manage institutional zones from which opponents would be partially displaced, such as PDVSA and upper levels of the state bureaucracy) and, most important, a mobilized base of rural and urban poor to vote consistently for Chávez and his supporters. This strategy—which has depended on tactics including material improvements in the lives of these individuals and experimentation with a variety of organizational forms, first Bolivarian Circles and later voting "battalions" as well as community councils, urban land committees, and finally the PSUV (Partido Socialista Unido de Venezuela)—has been key to the political success of the Chávez government so far.[138]

## The Structure of the Book

The chapters that follow aim to analyze and evaluate the nature and extent of social change in Venezuela during the period in which Chávez has held power. Given the highly polarized nature of political debates in Venezuela, any effort to bring together scholars to analyze recent developments there has essentially four options.[139] First and second, one could draw together scholars who are either sympathetic to or opposed to Chávez and the government he heads. The problem with these approaches is that any collective work produced by them would be blind to much of what is going on in contemporary Venezuela. Alternatively, one could aim to put together a list of so-called impartial analysts: yet experience has taught us that with respect to contemporary Venezuela few are so impartial, and that much writing that presents itself as such nevertheless has an angle. The final strategy—the one we have pursued—is to construct the text so that it embodies the heterogeneity of scholarly views about contemporary Venezuela. Of course it is impossible to capture all voices, but we have included a wide range of scholarly perspectives from within and outside of Venezuela. At times, this might potentially be confusing: one author may argue that political polarization is a consequence of the strategic choices of the government, another that it is largely the intransigence of the opposition that has caused it. The chapter authors speak only for themselves; the book is a sort of experiment insofar as it aims to construct a narrative out of contrasting views. We believe that readers will be best served by reading these arguments—and surveying the evidence mustered to support them—for themselves. This is the state of debate—both popular debate *and* scholarly debate—about the Chávez government: things may look very different in later decades when passions have cooled, but at present the polarization of debate is inescapable. The same is true, of course, of the contested data on the basis of which much analysis of contemporary Venezuela is carried out.[140]

The book is divided into two main sections. The first, under the title "State and Society in the Chávez Years," focuses on what is often called the alleged state/civil-society divide, and is concerned with how state/society relations have developed over the years in which Chávez has held the presidency. Here, in part, we hope to contribute to still evolving efforts to understand both the origins of the Bolivarian Project and its trajectory over the last decade. The second section, "The Bolivarian Project," focuses more on specific arenas of policy formation and governmental performance. Here the core goal is to assess how the government has performed in a variety of issue areas. We focus on issues central to the government's claims to revolutionary legitimacy: its women's rights agenda, macroeconomic performance and social programs, and its efforts to craft a new global order and to encourage South-South development. This is, of course, by no means an exhaustive list of the issues that the government has taken on, but these are among the most important ones.

The first chapter, by Fernando Coronil, at first glance appears to be an effort to unearth the story of what took place during the coup d'état of April 11–14, 2002, that temporarily forced Chávez from power.[141] More than this, though, Coronil's chapter is an attempt to understand the nature of the contemporary Venezuelan state, and, indeed, the state itself as a political form. Drawing on his work in *The Magical State: Nature, Money and Modernity in Venezuela*, Coronil argues that Venezuelans have historically imagined their nation to have "two bodies": a "social body," the individuals who make up the nation itself, and a "natural body," comprised of Venezuela's oil.[142] He then analyzes the discourses of both the opposition and the Chávez government to show their intelligibility within a broader discursive tradition. This analysis reveals that while contemporary Venezuela is indeed deeply divided, key shared cultural features—ways of looking at politics and identity—lie underneath these differences. Further, Coronil argues that focusing on a coup d'état can allow us a brief glimpse into the performative process through which the state maintains itself.

In the second chapter, Javier Corrales provides an account of the sources of contemporary Venezuela's much discussed polarization. One view is that this polarization is a function of inegalitarian wealth distribution and the "pacted democracy" of the pre-Chávez years.[143] While Corrales does not disregard such factors, he argues that something else is at work, namely, deliberate efforts by the Chávez government to deepen political polarization. While it has often been noted that certain levels of in-group/out-group polarization engender solidarity among in-group members, Corrales, using a game-theoretical framework, shows that, given certain distributions of ideological preference, deliberate divisiveness can actually be an effective electoral strategy. He argues that this shows the electoral rationale behind Chávez's polarizing rhetoric and policies. However, Corrales acknowledges that his model cannot explain radicalization over the last several years, and he suggests that this ongoing polarization and radicalization is best explained via the concept of path-dependence.

In the third chapter, Gregory Wilpert considers political polarization as well, from a contrasting point of view. On his analysis, it is the intransigence of the opposition that explains the government's radicalization. Wilpert analyzes the Bolivarian Revolution's claim that its aim is to deepen "participatory democracy." He argues that active citizen participation in decision-making is at least as important to true democracy as voting in mass elections. He highlights the various ways in which the Chávez government seeks to foster public participation, ranging from local community councils to the participatory aspects of the missions and the "social economy" that the Chávez government seeks to establish. He closes with a discussion of some of the forces in Chavismo that may reduce the likelihood of success for this project, though he does not share the views of some critics who regard participatory democracy as essentially a façade covering a deeper, authoritarian project.

In the final chapter of this section, Margarita López-Maya and Luis Lander offer a close analysis of the 2006 electoral campaign between Hugo Chávez and Manuel Rosales. This election was an important one for many reasons. On the one hand, it represented a major change in strategy on the part of the opposition. The opposition had always been more heterogeneous than its critics assert, but important elements in it had favored confrontational and sometimes extra-democratic strategies before 2006. From this election forward, however, the opposition and its most powerful voices have focused on electoral and democratic methods. This election was also important because Chávez's decisive victory paved the way for the deepening of the Bolivarian Project. López-Maya and Lander briefly tease out some of the implications of these elections for subsequent events in Venezuela.

The four chapters of the second section—"the Bolivarian Project"—focus on specific policies of the Chávez government, how it has endeavored to promote social transformation. The issues treated here are, not surprisingly, among the most contentious in the volume, and the differences evident in the accounts themselves mirror the divisions of contemporary Venezuelan political discourse.

In chapter 5, Cathy Rakowski and Gioconda Espina assess what they take to be the ambivalent, though in some ways positive, record of the Chávez government with regard to a feminist social agenda. While much progress has been made in recent years on a number of issues, they argue, the picture remains murky. They focus considerable attention, however, on the question of the extent to which the Bolivarian process is responsible for the advances that have been made. They find that, while that movement has made important contributions, it has tended to take credit for developments that preceded it, and that it has alienated many of the "civil society" feminists whose ideas have served as the basis of various initiatives. Moreover, they note a dangerous tendency to identify Chávez as personally responsible for all feminist advances and to encapsulate rhetorical attention to women in a discourse that is, in certain respects, still *machista*. Finally, they remind us that not all of the Chavistas' proposals and plans have been implemented.

Mark Weisbrot, in the following chapter, takes on the issues of macroeconomic policy and performance. His is by no means a universal view, and ECLAC's 2009–2010 survey of regional development showed that Venezuela has so far lagged considerably behind the rest of the region, sharing with Haiti the dubious distinction of being among the two regional countries with negative growth projections for 2010. In his view, economic performance under Chávez's government has been very strong, and indeed, had it not been for the previous political instability caused, in his view, by the opposition, it would be even more impressive.[144] Though many see recent economic problems as a sign that the Chávez regime will soon fail, Weisbrot controversially argues that the Venezuelan economy is likely to emerge from the recession in the near future and that it might have avoided the recession entirely had the government responded more aggressively with increased stimulus spending.[145] According to Weisbrot, worries about inflation, though real, have been exaggerated. More broadly, he believes that Venezuela has taken advantage of high oil prices to open up a new development path, creating a possibility of a novel form of South-South development.

In their chapter, Muntaner, Chung, Mahmood, and Armada briefly analyze the history of the Latin American welfare state and associated public health policies, arguing that the neoliberal turn in the region had a dramatic negative impact on public health. Privatization of medical services and the imposition of fiscal austerity led to high inequities in health care provision and thus declining standards of care for the poorest populations. Focusing then on the Bolivarian response to these conditions—the Barrio Adentro Mission—the authors summarize what they take to be its main achievements, largely focusing on the period of its inception through 2006, arguing that it constitutes a truly transformative development. While the Chávez government has implemented many missions that seek to provide social services in a wide variety of needy areas, Barrio Adentro is perhaps the most highly touted.

Then Mark Williams analyzes the foreign policy of the Chávez government, finding that, despite occasional appearances to the contrary, it shows a clear, consistent rationale. That is, Venezuela seeks to make use of what international relations scholars call "soft balancing" to bring about a multipolar order. It is worth noting that this is part and parcel of the government's strategy of aiding in the development of an anti-imperial wave. This argument is an important corrective to widespread perceptions—often cemented by media accounts and even some scholarly treatments of the issue—that the Bolivarian foreign policy is simply a hodge-podge of irrational decisions and misspent funds.

Finally, in the Conclusion, Thomas Ponniah, building on the theoretical work of Max Weber and Nancy Fraser, contends that the government and its supporters, despite their dangerous internal contradictions, have undertaken a conceptual revolution that synthesizes decades of reformulation and activism by various progressive movements across the continent. Ponniah conceptualizes the Bolivarian vision of development in terms of participatory forms of redistribution, recognition, and representation—while also noting the shortcomings of the government's actual practice.

As readers reflect on these contributions and consider the destiny of this effort to implement social change, it might be helpful to focus on several key tensions present in the process so far.[146]

1. The **tension between the reduction of inequality, poverty reduction, sustainable development, and an oil-based economy.** Can the Venezuelan government sustain its commitment to social programs over the long haul despite fluctuating oil prices?[147] Can it move beyond oil-dependence and escape the "resource curse"?[148] Or will it merely replicate other periods of oil-fed development hopes? Results so far seem mixed at best, and the Venezuelan state more oil dependent than ever.

2. The **tension between participation and clientelism.** Is the discourse of participation an attempt at genuine public consultation, or is it a sophisticated strategy of extending state control over more spheres of society by creating interests that benefit from acquiescence?[149]

3. The **tension between participatory democracy and authoritarian centralism.** If the Bolivarian process aims to transcend the perceived errors of previous iterations of revolution, it will have to avoid the pitfalls of populism, personalism, and presidentialism.[150] This is not easily done, and scholarship on the subject again so far shows mixed results at best.[151] An important sub-question here concerns whether Chávez and his movement can resolve the tension between organization and charismatic leadership.[152] Can a proper balance be struck between what Eric Selbin calls "visionary" and "organizational" leadership?[153] Will the project be able to develop a set of responsive poli-

tical structures—both within the state, state-linked organizations like the missions, *and* formally independent organizational structures like the PSUV[154]—that are not entirely dependent upon Chávez's own charismatic authority, yet still able to maintain legitimacy?

While these are certainly not the only issues facing the Chávez government in Venezuela, they are among the most general and important ones. Moreover, they are open tensions: this book makes no concerted claim about if and *how* each of these tensions will be resolved in the coming months and years, preferring that readers draw their own conclusions based upon the evidence and arguments presented in the chapters below.

### Endnotes

* For complete bibliographical data for notes in all chapters, please consult the Bibliography following the book's Conclusion.
1. I thank Thomas Ponniah, Margarita López-Maya, Fernando Coronil, Javier Corrales, Mark Katz, Krishan Kumar, Nicolas Prevelakis, Mark Williams, Maria Nava, Michael McCarthy, Morten Wendelbo, and the anonymous reviewers for their helpful comments.
2. Lindholm and Zuquete, *The Struggle for the World*, 3–8.
3. Perhaps the most notable exponent of this view was Francis Fukuyama. See his *The End of History and the Last Man*.
4. Williamson, "What Washington Means by Policy Reforms"; see also discussion in Bulmer-Thomas, *The Economic History of Latin America Since Independence*, 357–363.
5. For a range of views on the likelihood of the collapse of the Castro regime over the time period concerned—earlier ones confidently expecting it and later ones seeking to explain why the regime had not yet collapsed—see the essays in the "Polity" and "Transition to Civil Society" sections in Horowitz and Suchlicki, eds., *Cuban Communism*, 533–836.
6. Indeed, the Chávez government has attempted to position itself at the head of what Mark Katz calls a "revolutionary wave." See Katz, *Revolutions and Revolutionary Waves*.
7. Krugman, *The Return of Depression Economics and the Crisis of 2008*. Stiglitz, *Globalization and Its Discontents*.
8. For example, see Markoff, "Where and When Was Democracy Invented?"
9. On revolutionism see Kumar, "Revolution"; Kumar, *1989: Revolutionary Ideas and Ideals*; Kumar, "The Future of Revolution: Imitation or Innovation." See also Arendt, *On Revolution* and Palmer, *The Age of Democratic Revolution*, 35–65.
10. Weyland, for example, argues that "no significant force in contemporary Latin America advocates a full-scale revolution" and that Chávez and those associated with him "invoke some of the slogans and symbols of the revolutionary tradition, put ambition ahead of prudence, and pursue fairly far-reaching goals

under current circumstances." Weyland, "The Performance of Leftist Governments in Latin America," 7–8.

11. From the right, see Rodríguez, "An Empty Revolution." From the left, see Douglas Bravo's critique of Chavismo. For example, Garzón and Barboza, "En Venezuela no hay Revolución. Es un modelo de economía mixta y de conciliación de clases" (interview with Douglas Bravo). http//:www.kaosenlared.net/noticia /Venezuela-no-hay-revolucion-model-economia-mixta-conciliacion-clases. Accessed May 28, 2010. In the end the question of the revolutionary status of contemporary Venezuela may be impossible to isolate from ideological discussions inside and outside of Chavista discourse, where, as noted, the term often serves to either legitimate or de-legitimate the process. I am grateful to Julie Skurski for discussion of this point.

12. The literature on this question is considerable. For introductory reflections on defining revolution see Calvert, *Revolution and Counter-Revolution*, pp. 1–5. Readers seeking a general survey of scholarship on revolution should see Sanderson, *Revolutions: A Worldwide Introduction to Social and Political Change*. See also Pincus, "Rethinking Revolutions."

13. Brinton, *The Anatomy of Revolution*; Skocpol, *States and Social Revolutions* and "Explaining Social Revolutions."

14. See, for example, Tilly, *European Revolutions, 1492–1992*, 8–9.

15. Kumar, "Revolution."

16. Tocqueville, *Old Regime and the French Revolution*, pp. 203–204, 207–208; Marx, "Manifesto of the Communist Party," 477–478.

17. Brinton, *The Anatomy of Revolution*, pp. 29–41; Gurr, *Why Men Rebel*, pp. 148–153; Skocpol, *States and Social Revolutions*, p. 285 and "Explaining Social Revolutions," p. 7; Lichbach, *The Rebel's Dilemma*, pp. 68–74; Goldstone, "Toward a Fourth Generation of Revolutionary Theory," 146–152.

18. Goldstone, "Toward a Fourth Generation of Revolutionary Theory," 150–152.

19. Tarrow, *Power in Movement*, 123–138.

20. Benford and Snow, "Framing Processes and Social Movements." Tarrow, *Power in Movement*, 16–18, 21–22.

21. Foran, *Taking Power*, 21–22.

22. Arendt, *On Revolution*, 51–52.

23. Brinton, *The Anatomy of Revolution*, 134–136, 151–159, 262–263.

24. "Class" too is a contested term. Some scholars follow Marx in defining social classes in relation to the "forces of production" to which they are allegedly tied. Others aim to define classes through empirically grounded groupings of occupations, with those groups organized in relation to varying levels of occupational prestige. Still others, proponents of an approach to class known as "gradationalism," deny that there are discrete classes at all. Most of these scholars, however, even those who deny that discrete classes exist, would recognize "class" as a dimension of stratification, one concerned with people's position in relation to the system by which goods and services are distributed. Note that the

broader conceptualization of stratification as reflected in the three dimensions of class, status, and power, widely accepted in stratification research, is rooted in Weber's classic "Class, Status, and Party." For a range of perspectives on these issues see the essays in Grusky, ed., *Social Stratification: Race, Class, and Gender in Sociological Perspective*.

25. For an explication of the concept of "frame" and of "frame analysis" see Goffman, *Frame Analysis*; Gamson, *Talking Politics*; and Benford and Snow, "Framing Processes and Social Movements: An Overview and Assessment." On the shifting ideological background of Chavismo more generally, suggesting a move from "revolutionary nationalism" to "21st century socialism," see Biardeau, "Del Árbol de las Tres Raíces al 'Socialismo Bolivariano del Siglo XXI.'"

26. For example, see Chávez Frías, *Palabras antimperialistas*, pp. 22–23. See also discussion in Biardeau, "Del Árbol de las Tres Raíces al Socialismo Bolivariano del Siglo XXI," pp. 62–63, 67. This feature of Chávez's movement causes many to label it "populist." See the penetrating discussion of these issues in Hawkins, *Venezuela's Chavismo and Populism*.

27. In focusing on "discursive strategy" here I mean to emphasize that we should not take the discourse of the government—or the opposition for that matter— as a direct reflection of underlying social changes. For example, the fact that the Chávez government claims to be making a revolution should not lead us to uncritically accept this claim. Political speech is a political act. The government and its supporters—again, like the opposition—have a wide range of messages that they aim to direct to a wide range of audiences, and distinct mouthpieces and media for doing so. This helps to explain some of the seeming contradictions present in official discourse.

28. Coronil, *The Magical State*; Eastwood, *Rise of Nationalism in Venezuela*.

29. In the language of semiotic theory, it is an "empty" or "floating signifier." Laclau applies these concepts to the analysis of populist discourse. See his "Populism: What's in a Name?" esp. 107–110. See also Hawkins, *Venezuela's Chavismo*.

30. For this reason the opposition in Venezuela sometimes appropriates these terms. This does not mean, of course, that such individuals do not also draw distinctions between themselves and so-called "popular sectors."

31. One possible *disadvantage* of this discourse is that the very ambiguous inclusiveness of the category "the people" allows others to try to appropriate that key term, defining *themselves* as "the people" and the Chavista government as a usurper of the people's rights. This, as can be clearly seen in Coronil's discussion below, has been a key discursive strategy of the opposition for a number of years now.

32. Cedeño, "Venezuela in the Twenty-First Century," 95.

33. Hawkins rightly points out that socialist revolutionism has not been a constant in Chavista discourse, unlike populism, but that they are now both evident. Hawkins, *Venezuela's Chavismo and Populism*, 52–53, 83–85, 246–247.

34. Chávez himself now uses these terms interchangeably. See Chávez, *Revolución Bolivariana, Año de Logros*, 16.

35. Hobsbawm and Ranger, eds., *The Invention of Tradition*.
36. Of course this is perfectly possible, and "non-liberal" conceptions of liberty have existed for centuries. See the classic essay by Berlin, "Two Concepts of Liberty." Moreover, historians debate Zamora's radicalism and the degree to which he could be considered a "liberal." I do not mean to suggest that Zamora cannot necessarily be considered a precursor to later radicalism.
37. Marx, "The Manifesto of the Communist Party," 484, 490–491.
38. On the distinct "currents" within Chavismo see Ellner, *Rethinking Venezuelan Politics*, 139–174.
39. As Biardeau notes, there is also less flexibility in the broader "socialist" frame than in the "national-popular-revolutionary amalgam." Biardeau, "Del Árbol de las Tres Raíces al "Socialismo Bolivariano del Siglo XXI," 102.
40. On the relationship between nationalism and Marxian revolutionism see Anderson, *Imagined Communities*, 1–3.
41. For an explanation of this strategy and a positive analysis of outcomes produced by one of its key architects see Giordani, *La Transición Venezolana, y la Busqueda de su Propio Camino*.
42. Corrales, "The Repeating Revolution," p. 39. For an overview of this approach to development see Karl, *Paradox of Plenty*. On development and policy formation in oil producing countries more generally—including discussion of this pattern—see Humphreys, Sachs, and Stiglitz, eds., *Escaping the Resource Curse*.
43. The effectiveness of the missions has been the source of some controversy. On the positive side of the ledger, particularly with regard to Mission Barrio Adentro, see especially the chapter by Muntaner, Chung, Mahmood, and Armada in this volume as well as Briggs and Mantini-Briggs, "Confronting Health Disparities: Latin American Social Medicine in Venezuela." See also Alvarado et al., *Mission Barrio Adentro*. Critics charge that the missions are often politicized, that independently collected data on their scope and effectiveness are unavailable, and that the government exaggerates their successes. For example, see Thanalí Patruyo, *El estado de las misiones sociales: balance sobre su proceso de implementación e institucionalización*. See also D'Elia and Cabezas, *Las Misiones Sociales en Venezuela*. See also España, "The Social Policy of the Bolivarian Revolution: Mission Tricks" and Ortega and Rodríguez, "Freed from Illiteracy? A Closer Look at Venezuela's *Misión Robinson* Literacy Campaign." Hawkins, Rosas, and Johnson find evidence that Chávez supporters benefit disproportionately from the missions but little evidence that explicit political conditions serve as barriers to receiving services. See Hawkins, *Venezuela's Chavismo and Populism*, 195–230.
44. There is a need for empirical work on both the "subjective" and "objective" features of class in Venezuela over the last decade. Oliver Heath's findings for the period preceding Chávez's presidency (into the very early years of that presidency) suggests fluidity and room for the shaping of class consciousness. Heath, "Explaining the Rise of Class Politics in Venezuela," esp. 191–193.
45. Ellner, *Rethinking Venezuelan Politics*, 130–131; Torres, "21st Century Socialism: Old Names, New Ideas?"

46. Antonio J. González Plessman, relying on data from SISOV, finds a pattern broadly similar to the one noted here. See González Plessman, "La Desigualdad en la Revolución Bolivariana," 193–195.

47. United Nations Development Programme, *Human Development Report 2001, Making New Technologies Work for Human Development* (New York: Oxford University Press, 2001), Accessed at: http://hdr.undp.org/en/media/complete-new1.pdf, 6/1/2010, 183.

48. United Nations Development Programme, *Human Development Report 2009, Overcoming Barriers: Human Mobility and Development* (New York: Palgrave MacMillan, 2009), Accessed at http://hdr.undp.org/en/media/HDR_2009_EN _Complete.pdf, 6/1/2010, 195

49. Latin American Weekly Report, "Regional Growth Rebounds But Persistent Inequality Arrests Development," July 29, 2010. http://www.latinnews.com /lwr/archive.asp.

50. United Nations Development Programme, *Human Development Report 2001*, 183; United Nations Development Programme, *Human Development Report 2009*, 195–196. The comparisons are provided only for illustrative purposes, as for methodological reasons they are not strictly comparable. See United Nations Development Programme, *Human Development Report 2009*, 198.

51. United Nations Development Programme, *Human Development Report 2001*, 183; United Nations Development Programme, *Human Development Report 2009*, 195–196.

52. Mills, "Globalization and Inequality."

53. Edwards, *Left Behind*, 203.

54. Weisbrot points out, in arguing for poverty-reduction in Venezuela, that a number of government services and benefits do not appear as formal income and thus would not be counted. This argument would apply to the case at hand as well. See Weisbrot, "Poverty Reduction in Venezuela: A Reality-Based View," 38. Some assert that income inequality has increased. See Corrales, "The Repeating Revolution," 45.

55. On "new elites" see González Plessman, "La Desigualdad en la Revolución Bolivariana," 179, 195, 197.

56. Gates, "The Business of Anti-Globalization" and *Electing Chávez*, 140–141.

57. Schumpeter, *Imperialism and Social Classes*, 165.

58. It is also worth noting that this poverty-reduction was dependent on the high levels of economic growth in Venezuela between 2003 and 2008. It is unlikely that poverty-reduction will be sustained if the Venezuelan economy does not experience a robust recovery from its current recession. At the time of this writing it remains the only Latin American country that has not yet emerged from the recession.

59. The most important debate has been between volume author Mark Weisbrot and Francisco Rodríguez. See Rodríguez, "An Empty Revolution" and "How Not to Defend the Revolution: Mark Weisbrot and the Misinterpretation on Venezuelan Evidence" and Weisbrot, "An Empty Research Agenda: The Creation

of Myths About Contemporary Venezuela" and "How Not to Attack An Economist (and An Economy): Getting the Numbers Right." See also Santeliz Granadillo, "1999–2009, La Economia en diez años de gobierno revolucionario"; España, "The Social Policy of the Bolivarian Revolution: Mission Tricks"; Torres, "21st Century Socialism: Old Names, New Ideas?" and Sebastian Edwards, *Left Behind*, 200–205.

60. One gains a clear sense of this from Sujatha Fernandes' discussion of social movement activity among the urban poor in *Who Can Stop the Drums?*

61. This is partially a consequence of what some scholars have called "methodological nationalism." See Wimmer and Glick Schiller, "Methodological Nationalism and Beyond: Nation-State Building, Migration, and the Social Sciences."

62. Wallerstein, "Class Formation in the Capitalist World Economy."

63. See discussion in Sassen, *Territory, Authority, Rights: From Medieval to Global Assemblages*, esp. 298–303.

64. Markoff and Montecinos, "The Ubiquitous Rise of Economists"; Centeno, *Democracy Within Reason: Technocratic Revolution in Mexico*, 24. Domínguez, ed., *Technopols: Freeing Politics and Markets in Latin America in the 1990s*. Francesco Duina notes, however, that the homogeneity of these developments has been exaggerated. See Duina, *The Social Construction of Free Trade*.

65. On the history of race in Venezuela see Wright, *Café con leche*. For some discussion of race in contemporary Venezuela see Herrera Salas, "Ethnicity and Revolution"; Cannon, "Class/Race Polarization in Venezuela and the Electoral Success of Hugo Chávez"; Fernandes, *Who Can Stop the Drums?* 1–2, 87–88, 118–120, and passim; and Ellner, *Rethinking Venezuelan Politics*, 183–184.

66. For example, while I treat "elite/middle-class" and "subaltern" as basic status categories here, a micro-sociological study of any of these groups would reveal many fundamental internal divisions. Among elites in Caracas, for example, there would be important differences between those who are members of the Caracas Country Club and those who join other, less exclusive, clubs; between those who vacation in Europe, those who travel to Miami and related sites, and those who vacation domestically; those who attend traditional elite Venezuelan schools and those who attend German, British, and U.S.-linked international schools; and so forth. Such distinctions are sociologically quite important but not *as* important as the more fundamental dichotomous distinction between elite/middle class and subaltern.

67. These distinctions are mirrored in the geography of Caracas. See Smilde, *Reason to Believe*, pp. 18–21. See also Garcia-Guadilla, "Social Movements in a Polarized Setting," 145–147.

68. Mead, *Mind, Self, and Society*; Shils, "Deference."

69. Fernandes, *Who Will Stop the Drums?* 84, 148–157.

70. Nevertheless, Venezuela remained, with Cuba and Nicaragua, at least as of 2007, one of the Latin American societies with the greatest loss of HDI due to gender inequality. Programa de las Naciones Unidas para el Desarrollo (PNUD), *Informe Regional sobre Desarrollo Humano para América Latina y el Caribe 2010: Actuar*

*sobre el futuro: romper la transmisión intergeneracional de la desigualdad* (New York: Programa de las Naciones Unidas para el Desarrollo, 2010), www.idhalc-actuarsobreelfuturo.org, 27–29.

71. See, for example, Alexander, *Romulo Betancourt and the Transformation of Venezuela* and Martz, *Acción Democrática: The Evolution of a Modern Political Party*. For a recent critical account of such views see Ellner and Tinker Salas, eds., *Venezuela: Hugo Chávez and the Decline of an 'Exceptional Democracy'.*

72. On the approach to oil and development in Venezuela of Giusti and others see the interviews conducted by Fernando Coronil in the section "Oil and Revolution" in the fall 2008 *ReVista* issue ("Venezuela: The Chávez Effect"), 19–33. On the oil industry and its social and political effects in Venezuela more generally see Tinker Salas, *The Enduring Legacy*.

73. On ressentiment and transvaluation see Nietzsche, *On the Genealogy of Morality* and Scheler, *Ressentiment*. Liah Greenfeld has brought the concept of *ressentiment* back to social science. See Greenfeld, *Nationalism: Five Roads to Modernity*, 15–16.

74. Thus Chávez appeared to celebrate the poor economic indicators for the first portion of 2010 on the grounds that they showed the failure of capitalism. Latin America Weekly Report, "Venezuela: Chávez Unfazed by Economic Slump," June 3, 2010. http://www.latinnews.com.

75. For strong statements on each side of this debate see Corrales, "Hugo Boss" and Wilpert, *Changing Venezuela by Taking Power*, as well as their chapters in this volume.

76. Karl, "Petroleum and Political Pacts." See also Coppedge, *Strong Parties and Lame Ducks*; López-Maya, *Del viernes negro al referendo revocatorio*; Ellner and Hellinger, eds., *Venezuelan Politics in the Chávez Era*; and McCoy and Myers, eds., *The Unraveling of Representative Democracy in Venezuela*.

77. Grindle, *Audacious Reforms*; McCoy et al, *Venezuelan Democracy Under Stress*; McCoy and Myers, eds., *The Unraveling of Representative Democracy in Venezuela*; Hellinger, *Venezuela: Tarnished Democracy*; Corrales, *Presidents Without Parties*; Levine, "The Decline and Fall of Democracy in Venezuela: Ten Theses"; Levine and Crisp, "Venezuela: The Character, Crisis, and Possible Future of Democracy"; Buxton, *The Failure of Political Reform in Venezuela*; Coppedge, "Explaining Democratic Deterioration in Venezuela Through Nested Inference."

78. Indeed, analysts of revolution since Tocqueville have begun by focusing on "state breakdown" that precedes active revolutionary activity. For example, see Goldstone, *Revolution and Rebellion in the Early Modern World* and Goldstone, "Toward a Fourth Generation of Revolutionary Theory," 147–150. Sanderson, *Revolutions*, 2.

79. On crime in contemporary Venezuela see Sanjuán, "La Revolución Bolivariana en Riesgo." The Venezuelan government claims to now be making progress in this connection, since its creation of the Dispositivo Bicentenario de Seguridad Ciudadana in early 2010. Critics of the government are skeptical of official data

suggesting a reduction in crime of 18.2% over the course of three months. Latin American Weekly Report, "Venezuela: Getting a handle on violent crime," June 10, 2010. http://www.latinnews.com/lwr/archive.asp

80. Recent elections in September 2010 will return opposition-aligned politicians to the National Assembly in greater numbers, though it is unclear whether they will have much influence.

81. Latin America Weekly Report, "Tracking Trends: Federal Council," May 20, 2010. http://www.latinnews.com/lwr/archive.asp

82. Petkoff, *El Chavismo Como Problema*, 158–164.

83. For a classic discussion of this possibility see Talmon, *The Origins of Totalitarian Democracy*.

84. Among the most recent works see Gates, *Electing Chávez* and Hawkins, *Venezuela's Chavismo and Populism*. For earlier works see specific references below.

85. As will be clear to readers of the chapters below, there have been multiple stages in the unfolding of social change under the Chávez government, notably several periods of radicalization. Given that in this section I only aim to provide a schematic overview of the origins of the process, I do not discuss these stages here.

86. See works cited above by Alexander, Martz, and Ellner and Tinker Salas.

87. The literature is substantial. See especially Coppedge, *Strong Parties and Lame Ducks*; López-Maya, *Del viernes negro al referendo revocatorio*; McCoy and Myers, eds., *The Unraveling of Representative Democracy in Venezuela*; and Ellner and Hellinger, eds., *Venezuelan Politics in the Chávez Era*. For a brief overview see Sylvia and Danopoulos, "The Chávez Phenomenon: Political Change in Venezuela." See also Adelman, "Unfinished States: Historical Perspectives on the Andes," esp. 49–55.

88. Karl, *Paradox of Plenty*, 184. John Lombardi sees this as part of a longer-run pattern. See Lombardi, "Prologue: Venezuela's Permanent Dilemma."

89. Coronil, *The Magical State*.

90. See, for example, Coppedge, *Strong Parties and Lame Ducks*.

91. Smith and McCoy, "Venezuelan Democracy Under Stress," 2. For more detail on reform efforts see Buxton, *Failure of Political Reform*. See also Navarro, "In Search of the Lost Pact: Consensus Lost in the 1980s and 1990s."

92. Karl, *Paradox of Plenty*, op cit. See also Naím, *Paper Tigers and Minotaurs* and Mommer, "Subversive Oil," 133–134.

93. Kelly and Palma, "The Syndrome of Economic Decline and the Quest for Change." Naím, *Paper Tigers and Minotaurs*, 24–25.

94. Eckstein, ed., *Power and Popular Protest: Latin American Social Movements*.

95. López-Maya, *Del viernes negro al referendo revocatorio*, 22–26. Burgess and Levitsky, "Explaining Populist Party Adaptation in Latin America: Environmental and Organizational Determinants of Party Change in Argentina, Mexico, Peru, and Venezuela," 893, 898.

96. Thus Lusinchi made some small efforts at reform but mostly turned away from the reform process. Carlos Andrés Pérez, as has been noted, campaigned on his

past record but implemented austerity measures that generated tremendous opposition. Velásquez continued the process of political reform/decentralization. Caldera returned and, as Weyland puts it, "ruled during his first 2 years in a populist, autocratic, and erratic fashion," before embracing structural adjustment in the form of the "Agenda Venezuela" program. Weyland, "Economic Voting Reconsidered: Crisis and Charisma in the Election of Hugo Chávez," 827. See also Naim, "The Real Story Behind Venezuela's Woes," 25, and López-Maya, *Del viernes negro al referendo revocatorio*, 22–30. This constant see-saw effect likely had the social-psychological consequence of making the old order seem to be weak and incapable of meeting the needs of the population.

97. Grindle, *Audacious Reforms*, 66–67, 202, 205. See also Álvarez, "State Reform Before and After Chávez's Election," 147–150 and Levine, "The Decline and Fall of Venezuelan Democracy," 257, 258–261.

98. Naím and Piñango, eds., *El Caso Venezuela: una ilusión de armonía*. See also the discussion of these and other critiques in Hillman, "Intellectuals: An Elite Divided," esp. 120–121.

99. Buxton, *The Failure of Political Reform in Venezuela*. On decentralization see also Borgucci, "Representaciones y discurso en los procesos de descentralización administrativa en Venezuela." While many of the arguments for decentralization came from what many would call a "neoliberal" orientation—which the Bolivarian Movement takes as one of its fundamental negative discursive points of reference—this should not prevent us from seeing the important role that it has played in this process. Moreover, as García-Guadilla notes, decentralization initiatives were from the beginning linked to a desire to promote "participatory democracy." See García-Guadilla, "Democracy, Decentralization, and Clientelism: New Relationships and Old Practices."

100. Mangon, Pérez Baralt, and Sonntag, "La batalla por una nueva Constitución para Venezuela," esp. 92–93.

101. Both political actors and scholars hoped, of course, that the reform process would *preserve* the old order. Some scholars, such as Jennifer McCoy, continue to attribute the collapse of the *Punto Fijo* order to insufficient reforms, characterized as "too little, too late." See McCoy, "From Representative to Participatory Democracy?" in *Unraveling of Representative Democracy in Venezuela*, 268.

102. Buxton, *Failure of Political Reform*, 43. See also Penfold-Becerra, "Federalism and Institutional Change in Venezuela," 203–205 and passim; Levine, "The Decline and Fall of Democracy in Venezuela: Ten Theses," 250 and passim; and Levine and Crisp, "Venezuela: The Character, Crisis, and Possible Future of Democracy," 142–143 and passim.

103. Buxton, *Failure of Political Reform*, 43.

104. Grindle, *Audacious Reforms*, 60–64, 76–81.

105. The best sources in English on the *Caracazo* are López-Maya, "The Venezuelan *Caracazo* of 1989: Popular Protest and Institutional Weakness" and Coronil and

Skurski, "Dismembering and Remembering the Nation: the Semantics of Political Violence in Venezuela." The latter work, in particular, provides indispensable analysis of its context.

106. Naím, Coppedge, and especially Hawkins all emphasize the importance of corruption or perceived corruption in producing Venezuela's crisis. Naím, "The Real Story Behind Venezuela's Woes," 21–23; Coppedge, "Explaining Deterioration in Venezuela through Nested Inference," 311–312; Hawkins, *Venezuela's Chavismo and Populism*, 97 and passim.

107. Karl, *Paradox of Plenty*, op cit.

108. Buxton, "Venezuela: Degenerative Democracy," 256–257. Crisp, "Lessons from Economic Reform in the Venezuelan Democracy," 19. Hellinger, "Tercermundismo and Chavismo," 325. Karl, *Paradox of Plenty*, 172–178 and passim.

109. Buxton, *Failure*, 42. See also Williams, "Escaping the Zero-Sum Scenario: Democracy versus Technocracy in Latin America," 126 and passim.

110. Buxton, *Failure*, 44. Penfold-Becerra, "Federalism and Institutional Change," 204–213.

111. Myers, "Perceptions of a Stressed Democracy," esp. 110–111. Regarding the Venezuelan public's high expectations for the future more generally during this period (despite the critical situation Venezuela faced and because of the relative success of Venezuela's modernizing project of the previous decades), see Briceño-León, "La expectativa de futuro del venezolano y la crisis," and "Violencia Urbana en América Latina: Un modelo sociológico de explicación," esp. 557–558. See also Ellner, "Introduction," 18–19, and Marquez, "The Hugo Chávez Phenomenon," 198–201.

112. See especially Corrales, *Presidents without Parties*, the best source on elite political conflict over these reforms. On structural adjustment under Pérez, see also Crisp, "Lessons from Economic Reform in the Venezuelan Democracy," 21–23 and passim.

113. Naim, *Paper Tigers and Minotaurs*, esp. 135–138.

114. Coronil and Skurski, "Dismembering and Remembering the Nation," op cit.; Lopez Maya, "The Venezuelan *Caracazo* of 1989," 128–131.

115. López-Maya, "The Venezuelan *Caracazo* of 1989."

116. López-Maya, Smilde, and Stephany, *Protesta y cultura en Venezuela: los marcos de acción colectiva en 1999* and López-Maya, "La protesta popular venezolano entre 1989 y 1993 (en el umbral del neoliberalismo)" as well as López-Maya, "Venezuela After the *Caracazo*." See also Salamanca, "The Venezuelan Political System: A View from Civil Society"; Levine and Crisp, "Venezuela: The Character, Crisis, and Possible Future of Democracy," 149–154; and Levine, "Civil Society and Political Decay in Venezuela"; as well as Levine, "The Decline and Fall of Venezuelan Democracy," 251–253. Finally, see Rakowski, "Women's Coalitions as a Strategy at the Intersection of Economic and Political Change in Venezuela," 387–405, and García-Guadilla, "Civil Society: Institutionalization, Fragmentation, Autonomy."

117. Kornblith, "Public Sector and Private Sector: New Rules of the Game," esp. 82–83, 91–92. See also Crisp, Levine, and Rey, "The Legitimacy Problem," 144–147. López-Maya, *Del viernes negro al referendo revocatorio*, 31–36 and Canache, "Urban Poor and Political Order."

118. Karl, "The Venezuelan Petro-State and the Crisis of 'Its' Democracy," 49. Indeed, in addition to an increase in poverty, Venezuela by the 1990s saw a decline in educational institutions' ability to foster social mobility. See Romero Salazar, "Al ascensor detenido." On raised and then declining expectations see also Levine, "The Decline and Fall of Democracy in Venezuela," 253.

119. Coronil and Skurski, "Dismembering and Remembering the Nation," op cit. López-Maya, *Del viernes negro al referendo revocatorio*, 41.

120. López-Maya, "La protesta popular," op cit.

121. Buxton, *The Failure of Political Reform in Venezuela*, 45–46.

122. Grindle, *Audacious Reforms*, 73.

123. Petkoff, *Dos Izquierdas* 107–109.

124. Blanco, "Chávez and the Fate of the Left"; Hellinger, "Political Overview," 33–34.

125. Hellinger, "Political Overview: the Breakdown of Puntofijismo and the Rise of Chavismo," 28–29, 42. Marcano and Barrera Tyszka, *Hugo Chávez*, 115–116.

126. Marcano and Barrera Tyszka, *Hugo Chávez*, 12.

127. Trinkunas, *Crafting Civilian Control of the Military in Venezuela*, pp. 180–187.

128. Gates, *Electing Chávez*. See also Ortiz, "Entrepreneurs: Profits without Power?"

129. Some of these elements (military officers, business leaders, "progressive intellectuals" and "small leftist parties" are discussed by Rita Giacalone as elements of "the coalition that supported Chávez in 1998." See Giacalone, "The Impact of Neo-Populist Civilian-Military Coalitions on Regional Integration and Democracy: the Case of Venezuela," 29. On the role of the urban poor, see Canache, "Urban Poor and Political Order."

130. Smilde, *Reason to Believe*, pp. 22–24.

131. On the impact of class polarization in Venezuela's crisis see Ellner, *Rethinking Venezuelan Politics* and Smilde, "The Social Structure of Hugo Chávez."

132. Corrales, *Presidents Without Power*; Naím, *Paper Tigers and Minotaurs*.

133. Penfold-Becerra, "Federalism and Institutional Change," 198. See also Sabatini, "Decentralization and Political Parties," 143. Buxton is quite right to note that "the two-fold reform process, economic and political . . . undermined the fundamental pillars of the *partidocratic* model and the operating norms of the party system." See Buxton, *Failure of Political Reform in Venezuela*, 47. Moreover, she is right to note that much of the opposition to these reforms came from elements of the old regime. Resistance was encountered from both the guardians of the old order *and* from more radical elements that saw neoliberal reforms as a *reactionary* turn. See Buxton, *Failure*, 47–48.

134. López-Maya, *Del viernes negro al referendo revocatorio*, 118. Salamanca, too, notes causal linkages between decentralization and "associational growth." Salamanca, "Civil Society: Late Bloomers," 100.

135. Olson, *The Logic of Collective Action*; Lichbach, *The Rebel's Dilemma*.

136. For a number of analysts of revolution, this feature alone disqualifies events in Venezuela from being a revolution, since violence is often considered a defining feature of revolutions.

137. The Chávez government's relationships with potential opponents in the business community have thus far alternated between aggression and conciliation. While expropriations are growing in number and hostility, as of mid-2010, towards the business sector seems to be increasing, for most of these years many wealthy Venezuelan capitalists have been able to go about their business unimpeded if they refrain from direct confrontation with the government. For example, the government famously achieved reconciliation with Gustavo Cisneros (who had at various times been a supporter and an opponent of Chávez), and only recently has the government begun to seriously interfere with the Polar Company and Lorenzo Mendoza.

138. See discussion in Wilpert, *Changing Venezuela by Taking Power* and Hawkins, *Venezuela's Chavismo and Populism*.

139. On polarization among scholarly analysts of Venezuela see Hawkins, *Venezuela's Chavismo and Populism*, 26–29, 47–48.

140. Some in the opposition are very suspicious of official data, and some supporters of Chavismo feel the same way about much of the alternative data employed by some opposition-aligned analysts. We have not endeavored to editorially police data sources here, and readers should judge for themselves.

141. On this coup d'etat see also Cannon, "Venezuela, April 2002: Coup or Popular Rebellion?" For a journalistic account sympathetic to a version of the story told by some in the opposition, see Nelson, *The Silence and the Scorpion*.

142. Coronil, *The Magical State*.

143. On Venezuela's "pacted democracy" see Karl, *Paradox of Plenty*, 93. On class and polarization see Smilde, "The Social Structure of Hugo Chávez"; Ellner, *Rethinking Venezuelan Politics*; Roberts, "Social Polarization and the Populist Resurgence in Venezuela." Oliver Heath's empirical analysis suggests that while inequalities were clearly present before the rise of Chávez, the increasing salience of class in people's consciousness mostly took place after Chávez's taking power, suggesting leadership/framing as a key component of the explanation for increasing class consciousness. See Heath, "Explaining the Rise of Class Politics in Venezuela."

144. ECLAC projects a return to growth in 2011, but at one of the lowest projected rates in the region (2.5%), and inflation far outpaces regional levels, with little sign of change. Economic Commission for Latin America and the Caribbean (ECLAC), *Economic Survey of Latin America and the Caribbean, 2009–2010: The distributive impact of public policies*, published online at www.eclac.org/de, 7, 22, 49.

145. See also Santeliz Granadillo, "1999–2009, La Economía en Diez Años de Gobierno Revolucionario," 115–117.

146. We do not claim to be the first to have noticed individually these "tensions"—for example, Edgardo Lander, among others, also notes the conflict between local "democratization" and "concentration of power," "Presentación: Diez Años de la Revolución," 51—though we are not aware of anyone else parsing them out in this way.

147. Álvarez, among others, suggests that this "revolution" remains oil dependent and thus susceptible to instability. See Álvarez, "Venezuela 2007: Los motores del socialismo se alimentan con petróleo."

148. Humphreys, Sachs, and Stiglitz, eds., *Escaping the Resource Curse.*

149. See, for example, Penfold-Becerra, "Clientelism and Social Funds" as well as Hawkins and Hansen, "Dependent Civil Society" and García-Guadilla, "Ciudadanía y autonomía en las organizaciones sociales bolivarianas." A number of scholars are now working on these and related questions, and I expect that more of such research is likely to appear in the next couple of years. See, for example, McCarthy, "The Practice of Institutionalizing Ideas" and "Ordering Chavismo from above and below."

150. The populism of the Chávez regime has been much discussed in the literature. See Hawkins, "Populism in Venezuela: The Rise of Chavismo" and *Venezuela's Chavismo and Populism*; Roberts, "Social Polarization and the Populist Resurgence in Venezuela"; Ellner, "The Contrasting Variants of the Populism of Hugo Chávez and Alberto Fujimori"; and French, "Understanding the Politics of Latin America's Plural Lefts (Chávez/Lula)."

151. See, for example, McCoy, "From Representative to Participatory Democracy?," esp. 287–288, and Michael Coppedge, "Venezuela: Popular Sovereignty versus Liberal Democracy." For a sympathetic assessment of the conflict between "top down" and "grassroots" approaches within Chavismo see Ellner, *Rethinking Venezuelan Politics*, 175–194. Perhaps the most persuasive reading of these issues is provided by Levitsky and Way's "competitive authoritarianism" framework. See Levitsky and Way, "The Rise of Competitive Authoritarianism." See also McCoy and Myers, "Introduction," *the Unraveling of Representative Democracy in Venezuela,* 1–2. See also Larry Diamond, *The Spirit of Democracy,* 67–70. Others, such as Paul Drake and Eric Herschberg, worry that the Chávez government, like some other recent Andean governments, approaches being a "democradura." See Drake and Hershberg, "The Crisis of State-Society Relations in the post-1980s Andes," 22–23. See also Legler, "Venezuela 2002–2004: the Chávez Challenge," esp. 221–223. Finally, see Krastev, "Democracy's 'Doubles.'" On the ambiguities of "liberal" and "radical" democracy in Venezuela see Ellner, "Hugo Chávez's First Decade in Office," 79–80, 82–83.

152. Ellner, generally an optimist with regard to the Chávez government, acknowledges this as a potential problem in "Hugo Chávez's First Decade in Office," 84.

153. Selbin, *Latin American Revolutions.*

154. See discussion in Ellner, "A 'Revolutionary Process' Unfolds in the Absence of a Well-defined Plan," 16.

# Part

# I

## STATE/SOCIETY RELATIONS

# 1

# State Reflections: The 2002 Coup against Hugo Chávez[1]

*Fernando Coronil*

This essay is both a historical interpretation of transformations in Venezuela under the presidency of Hugo Chávez and a theoretical reflection on the state. In the first part I examine the coup against Chávez of April 11–14, 2002, focusing on the competing views of the opposition and government supporters with regard to three events: the protest march organized by the opposition on April 11 against the breach of "meritocracy" in the state-run oil industry; the public representation of the April 11 massacre around the Llaguno Bridge centering on the influential Venevision report on it; and the ceremony proclaiming Pedro Carmona as president on April 12. By analyzing contests over history and its representation during these liminal junctures, I explore emerging conceptions of the state and the nation in the Chávez period. Far from offering a comprehensive account of the coup, I use this historical rupture—a time when competing ideals were publicly set against each other and power was up for grabs—to examine transformations in ideological imaginaries and political culture in Venezuela. I conclude this section by exploring the coup's aftermath and presenting an overview of changes in Venezuela after a decade of Chávez's rule. In light of this discussion, in the second part of this chapter I engage some theoretical ideas on the state, focusing on the formation of hegemony and the trinity of state form, state effects, and state fetishism.

## Modernity in Question

The third millennium, still barely begun, already surprises us. At the close of the 20th century, as a result of the fall of the Berlin wall, the dissolution of the Soviet Union, and China's immersion in capitalist markets, the old rivalry between capitalism and socialism seemed to have been finally settled and the free market had emerged as the favored if not exclusive engine of historical progress. Eulogists of capitalism celebrated its victory and Francis Fukuyama even heralded the "end of history"—the beginning of an era of global harmony sustained by capitalist markets and common sense. From a Latin American perspective, however, this promise of a world of universal bliss paved by the unbridled capitalist market clashed against the reality of persisting social fragmentation, economic inequality, and international subordination. These obstinate barriers prompted not so much treading a given path as breaking new ground.

Already at the end of the 20th century, in a region laden with memories of struggles for justice, the disenchantment with capitalism had started to reawaken the old specter of socialism. Socialist ideals were proclaimed by a wide range of social actors, particularly by the radical sectors of new social movements—from the *piqueteros* of Argentina and the landless peasants of Brazil to the *cocaleros* of Bolivia and the Zapatistas of Mexico. In the first decade of the new millennium, socialist ideals have been invoked by several government heads in the region, from Lagos and Bachelet in Chile, Nestor and Cristina Kirchner in Argentina, Lula and Roussef in Brazil, Tabare Vásquez and Mujica in Uruguay, Lugo in Paraguay, Correa in Ecuador, Morales in Bolivia, and Ortega in Nicaragua. But more than anyone else, Hugo Chávez of Venezuela, igniting this process in 1998 with his promise of revolution and crowning it with his endorsement of socialism in 2005, has reawakened this old ideal, generating boundless hope among some, but also intense panic among others.

The 2008 financial crisis at the heart of capitalism exploded the myth of the free market. The meltdown of major financial institutions in the United States and the state's active role in stabilizing the U.S. economy suddenly helped forge as a new common sense the notion that states must regulate unbridled markets. The election of President Obama, made possible by severe collective anxiety about the state of the nation and by his promise of state-led change, was a response to the housing and financial crises and the need to reorganize a capitalist economy that had suffered the violent effects of deregulation.

Despite obvious differences, I see the election of leftist presidents in Latin America as an earlier and more rebellious response to the negative impact of neoliberal policies in the region. It must be remembered that under Augusto Pinochet's harsh "shock treatment," Chile became the experimental ground of a neoliberal recipe for economic growth that was eventually transformed into a hegemonic common sense for the rest of the continent. The Ten Commandments of the "Washington Consensus," as formulated by John Williamson in 1989, expressed the sacralization of neoliberal ideology and its transformation into technical orthodoxy.

Modernizing technocratic dogmas do not last long in Latin America. In this region, the contest over competing blueprints for the future has always been alive because no proposed solution has managed to address effectively its persisting problems. In a context where the formal and informal capitalist economy has been able to offer the possibility of job security and well-being only to a minority, many in Latin America have increasingly sought their fortune through the use or abuse of public power. This perverse use of the state as a source of personal advantage has intensified the duplicity of a discourse of public welfare that often acts as a cover for the pursuit of private gain. "Corruption," a word that condenses multiple meanings related to the self-seeking violation of public norms—from idleness on the job to clientelism and nepotism, from petty theft to blackmail and murder—has become an endemic structural phenomenon widely accepted as an inevitable part of everyday normality. But this economic and moral crisis, far from extinguishing it, has rekindled the hope that someone, or something, will offer a solution to our social fragmentation and establish a sense of collective well-being. The turn to the left has been an expression of this hope.

While this shift towards the left was taking place south of the Rio Grande, north of it George W. Bush initiated the War on Terror in 2001 after the attack against the Twin Towers and the Pentagon. This war, fought mostly in the Global South, has replaced the Cold War, which was more accurately baptized by Subcomandante Marcos as the Third World War, in order to call attention to the fact that it was fought in several nations of the Third World through numerous local "hot" wars at the cost of several millions of lives.[2] Even as Obama has sought to limit the fight against terrorism and to define it as "global counterinsurgency," it continues to appear as an endless war against an elusive and often faceless enemy. As in other imperial confrontations, any opposition to it falls under the rubric of a war against the United States. As President Bush said after the attack of September 11, 2001, whoever is not "with us" in the war on terror is "against us."[3] During the 2004 U.S. presidential electoral campaign, John Kerry was repeatedly portrayed in the media as an ally of the terrorists for having opposed the war in Iraq.

Similarly, because of his anti-imperial stance, but also because of his support of Colombia's FARC and relation with Iran's Mahmoud Ahmadinejad, Chávez has been portrayed in the United States as belonging to the terrorist camp. The more Washington accuses Chávez of allying himself with the terrorists, and the more he accuses the United States of being the world's greatest terrorist, the more terrorism is confirmed as an essential part of our reality, independently of the truth of these allegations. As typically happens in Manichean contests, these polar adversaries end up resembling one another as they reproduce the dichotomous discourse that both separates and unites them.[4]

I believe the sharpened divisions of Venezuelans under Chávez should be seen in the context of the current global crisis of modernity, of its intensified anxieties about the future and polarized discourses. Though capitalism still dominates the political landscape as humanity's only viable destiny, the glowing future it had once forecast has been clouded over by an ongoing imperial war on terror, and projections of persistent marginalization, poverty, and environmental devastation around the world. This global crisis has drawn especially dark clouds over Latin America, the region with the world's deepest social inequalities as well as the longest postcolonial experience and most varied record of modernizing projects. This juxtaposition of hopes, fears, and frustration makes Latin Americans particularly susceptible to unstable political devotions, to volatile dreams, to sudden enchantments, and to no less sudden and intensely painful disillusionments. This darkened landscape offers a fertile ground for movements and leaders promising the light of hope.

## 2002: Venezuela at a Crossroads

By 2002, for those who believed that Chávez's incendiary rhetoric would lead to radical actions, his anti-imperialist populism and his solidarity with Cuba were enough to evoke the specter of socialism in Venezuela. As in a Coney Island cavern of fantastic terrors, there was no need for evidence that socialism actually existed; its spectral evocation was terrifying enough.

Before the 2002 coup, socialism as a program was not part of official discourse in Venezuela. At that early stage of the Chávez regime, efforts to institute a more democratic system at the economic or social levels were still limited; the main changes that Chávez made had taken place basically in the political domain, such as the formulation and approval of the 1999 constitution. But Chávez's announcement of 49 decrees at the end of 2001, formulated under legally granted special powers but without consulting with the private sector in the customary manner, threatened to give the state more control over key sectors of the economy, particularly in three areas involving the production of primary commodities: the subsoil (oil and gas), farmlands (agricultural products), and sea and rivers (fish). While these early policies should not be confused with the socialization of the economy in the form of social ownership of productive and financial capital, farmland, and urban real estate, they signaled growing state control over the economy. They also revealed that the state under Chávez intended to rule independently of the former ruling class; for representatives of this class, some of whom had supported his candidacy and believed he was indebted to them, this was an intolerable affront.

Whether these sectors brought up the prospect of socialism to defend established privileges or in response to a sincere fear, debates about state policies served to place Chávez's ultimate purposes at center stage, but even among those who opposed Chávez there was no consensus about what his confrontational words truly meant. Before the 2002 coup, a key actor famously addressed this question by calling attention to the tension between Chávez's words and his deeds. According to U.S. Ambassador John Maisto, one must "watch what Chávez does, not what he says." Many, however, believed that Maisto did not read Chávez accurately.

While it might not have been clear what he truly meant, it was evident that Chávez would follow his own convictions, even if he had no clarity about their policy implications. In the face of uncertainty about state policies and goals, everyday life in Venezuela evolved as a permanent chore of deciphering public spectacles, reading between the lines, peeking behind the façade, revealing the pretenses of power, and guessing what Chávez would do next.

As seen by leading sectors of the opposition, in 2002 the Chavista government harbored a totalitarian or at least authoritarian project beneath a democratic mask. In spite of the enormous differences between Venezuela and Cuba, the possibility that Venezuela would follow the Cuban model weighed on the opposition like a nightmare, partly due to the close connection between Hugo Chávez and Fidel Castro, the role of Cuban advisors and personnel in the government, and the presence of an influential community of Cuban émigrés in Venezuela who interpreted current events in their adopted country in light of their previous experience in their homeland. This collective fear, whether genuine or fabricated, was a fundamental factor in the events that led to the 2002 coup. Although if the coup had not happened it is likely that the course of events would have been different, a decade later this fear seems to have been at least partially justified, as Chávez has concentrated power in his person and has sought to move the country toward a form of socialism whose closest model, despite claims to novelty, seems to be Cuba.

In a context marked by growing anxieties about modernity at the national and global levels, the coup against Chávez both reflected and intensified these concerns and the polarized terms in which they were expressed. While my discussion of the April coup focuses on the views that divided Venezuelans into two factions, by illuminating a common ground and questioning fixed convictions I hope this account may narrow this divide.[5]

## The Nation's Two Bodies

As a result of democratic struggles against autocratic or partisan governments that used state wealth for private gain, it had become natural in Venezuela to believe that that the duty of the state is to establish a harmonious relationship between citizens and oil, between people and their territory—between what I have called the "nation's two bodies." In their opposition to dictator Juan Vicente Gómez (1908–1935), the emerging twentieth-century leaders of Venezuela came to represent the nation as an entity composed of both a social and a natural body. They conceived the state, typically embodied in the figure of the president, as the agent that protects and unifies the nation's two bodies.[6] Claims to legitimately represent the nation came to depend on the ability to appear to be protectors of the people and of the territory by guaranteeing that the nation's collective wealth—for the oil belongs to all Venezuelans—would be safeguarded and used for the common good. Achieving this goal meant not only increasing the nation's monetary wealth by developing the oil industry, but also protecting it from the crooks who constantly threaten to treat it as their private booty. After 1936, the state took shape as the guardian of the nation by "sowing the oil"—that is, transforming the nation's ephemeral mineral wealth into permanent social value. This goal was to be achieved by using oil money to promote agricultural and industrial production as well as public welfare in the domains of health, education, housing, communications, and other social services.

As other politicians had typically done before him, Chávez campaigned in1998 promising to protect the nation against what he repeatedly presented as a corrupt elite that had mismanaged the nation's wealth and impoverished the *pueblo*. After he was elected with 56 percent of the vote in 1998, Chávez's popularity soared to 80 percent in 2001, but by early 2002 it had fallen to around 30 percent. This massive disenchantment coincided with a polarization of Venezuela's political world into radically opposed camps. In a country accustomed to celebrating our social harmony, however illusory, people split furiously into two factions, each more passionate than the other and convinced that only it possessed the real truth. Chávez's opponents became so disenchanted that by the end of 2001, due in good measure to their control of the media, they managed to create a climate of opinion that questioned the viability of the Chávez regime. Convinced that the country was being led adrift by an incompetent captain, the opposition sought to rid Venezuela of Chávez; while the main public impetus was to find legal ways of ousting Chávez, certain powerful sectors sought to do so backstage, by any means necessary.

At a time marked by intense passions and rather flat public debate, this re-politicization of Venezuela at least had the virtue of drawing into the political arena groups from both sides that had seldom before participated in national politics, particularly women from all classes, but also certain middle class sectors. Abruptly politicized, having little contact with their political adversaries from other social strata, many took their own reality to be reality itself. The centrality of Caracas in national politics and its social geography as an elongated valley with distinct separations between rich and poor, and therefore between the opposition and government supporters, reinforced the isolation and self-sufficiency of each side.

### *The Wounded Natural Body: The April 11 March*

During the first weekend of April, Chávez had used his legal powers to fire and retire a number of executives from the state oil company, PDVSA (Petróleos de Venezuela, S.A.). He added insult to injury by announcing the firing in a dramatically irate fashion on his nationally broadcast television program *Aló Presidente* (Hello President). He replaced them with close supporters who bypassed the promotion ladder normally required to reach such leadership positions. As president he named Gastón Parra Luzardo, an academic with theoretical expertise on petroleum but without managerial experience in the industry itself.

Opposition leaders used this breach of meritocratic procedure as a banner to rally people against the administration. They called for a protest march under the familiar political slogan "Not one step back" (*Ni un paso atrás*), intended to establish a kinship between their movement and other historically significant struggles for democracy, as in Chile's protests against Pinochet's authoritarian rule. From its base in the eastern part of Caracas, the opposition had developed a boundless sense of expectation. Their discontent crystallized in the largest protest march in the country's history up to that point. An ardent crowd gathered in the recently baptized Meritocracy Square in front of PDVSA headquarters, where they had a permit to assemble.[7] While the march was cast as a protest against the breach of the principle of meritocracy in the oil industry, for many, including some who were involved in conspiracies at that time, its goal was to remove Chávez from power.

Moved by their own desires as well as instigated by those who had a preconceived plan, the protesters quickly radicalized their aims: by mid morning they went from requesting the reinstatement of meritocracy to demanding Chávez's resignation. By noon leaders redirected the march toward the Miraflores Palace, the president's office and residence. As it moved from eastern to western Caracas, traversing the seven miles between the Plaza de la Meritocracia and Miraflores, the march expanded, reaching several hundred thousand (estimates range from 300,000 to one million). The extraordinary size of the march encouraged the opposition's perception that the whole country was with them and that history was on their side. On that day, chanting slogans from other historic struggles—"The people, united, will never be defeated"; *El pueblo unido jamás será vencido*—the marchers came to believe that their collective action could wrest control of the state, save the country from misrule, and change the course of history. As the opposition newspaper *El Nacional* put it, in an article commemorating the third anniversary of April 11: "the feeling of power of these masses of humanity was absolute."[8]

### The Wounded Social Body: The Llaguno Massacre

The goal of removing Chávez from power, however premeditated, was publicly presented in the early hours to the people gathered at PDVSA's Plaza de la Meritocracia and embraced by people who had not previously contemplated it. But it was the afternoon's bloody events that made it possible to present the ousting of Chávez not just as a pressing political demand but as an urgent moral necessity. In several areas around the Miraflores Palace and the Llaguno Bridge over Baralt Avenue, nineteen people were shot dead. Soon afterwards, widely watched private television network news programs showed a report that accused the government of responsibility for these deaths.

The video produced by Venevision, a T.V. station owned by Gustavo Cisneros, a major leader of the opposition and influential magnate with deep pockets and international connections, showed images of people wearing red shirts firing from the bridge while a narrative asserted that government officers and sympathizers had fired at "peaceful demonstrators." The repeated showing of this video magnified its significance and sense of truth.

The Llaguno massacre quickly served to transform a civil rejection into an open military rebellion against Chávez.[9] The image of government representatives and supporters firing from Llaguno Bridge together with images of dead or wounded bodies were repeatedly shown to demonstrate, as was constantly stated, the absolute illegitimacy of the government that killed "innocent people."

In the wake of the massacre the media insisted that it was no longer possible to tolerate a government that had "soiled its hands with the blood of the people," as veteran leader Luis Miquilena proclaimed on the evening of April 11, thus breaking definitively with his precocious political disciple. Miquilena had been Chávez's main mentor and supporter since he was jailed as leader of the failed 1992 coup against Carlos Andrés Pérez. Miquilena had also been his main political ally in the government until Chávez refused to respond to his efforts to reform the 49 presidential decrees in December 2001.

But even more decisive than Miquilena's rupture was that of the top commanders of the four branches of the armed forces, who one after another announced their rejection of Chávez on the evening of April 11. The images of the massacre were shown to officers at military bases to legitimize the demand for Chávez's renunciation. They were also circulated by the media in the United States, Europe, and other Latin American countries, where they were used to back up official declarations, such as Bush administration press secretary Ari Fleischer's statement in support of the Carmona administration on April 12, when he remarked that Chávez had provoked his downfall through his own improper actions on April 11.[10]

While the April period remains controversial, the Llaguno massacre is still perhaps its most divisive issue, separating Venezuelans between those who believe that these deaths were caused by the government, whether to discourage any further protests or to prompt an insurrection so as to depurate the Armed Forces, and those who believe the opposition was responsible for them, whether to justify the coup or as a spontaneous response to its confrontation with Chavista forces.

## Manufacturing Legitimacy

Even before April 11, opposition-controlled television and print media branded the Chávez administration as a usurper that had seriously injured the oil industry. The defense of meritocracy was used to shield against the alarming prospect of a state that would use oil money for partisan ends and turn PDVSA, a company with an exceptionally good public image and reputation, into a typically inefficient state-run enterprise. Even though the opposition presented the meritocracy controversy as a technocratic issue, it was implicitly understood that defending PDVSA entailed protecting the nation and attacking Chávez.

From the Chavistas' point of view, however, the meritocracy discourse was just a smoke screen—a "mythocracy," as Chávez frequently called it— meant to hide the opposition's intention of ousting the government and taking over the national oil industry. According to official spokesmen, the new board of directors was composed of known and respected career petroleum experts, each with more than twenty years of involvement in petroleum affairs; they had only skipped over a handful of merit levels to reach the directorship (between four and seven levels out of a total of thirty-six);

similar changes had occurred in the past without arousing any protest. The fundamental problem was one of politics, not management norms.

The Chavista state had been changing Venezuela's oil policies since 1998, for in its view after the nationalization of the oil company in 1976, PDVSA had become a "state within a state." From 1998 up to 2002, the administration's energy policy was to control PDVSA by selecting its presidents and subjecting it to closer control by the Ministry of Mines. Rejecting the policies of the previous administration, Chávez sought to strengthen OPEC, raise oil prices by reducing production in agreement with price targets that OPEC established in 2000 (largely at Venezuela's insistence), limit the opening of the oil industry to foreign capital, and establish laws to increase oil profits and state control over energy sector investments. Chávez's opponents came out not only against the management that the state wanted to impose on PDVSA, but its entire oil policy. Perhaps at the public level the most criticized measure, besides the appointment of a partisan managerial board, was an oil subsidy given to Cuba. But in private circles it was widely known that leaders of the opposition generally endorsed the policies of Luis Giusti, PDVSA's president under the second Caldera administration, which sought to make Venezuela a major oil power by maximizing production rather than increasing prices, and thus distancing it from OPEC and its regulations.

As the administration saw it, the internal opposition was receiving assistance from abroad, especially from the United States, which even before the tragic attack of September 11 was already preparing for war in Iraq and worried about the likely election of Luiz Inácio Lula da Silva as president of Brazil in the forthcoming elections of October. Given the identification of energy with national security in the National Energy Policy Report issued by Vice President Dick Cheney's energy task force in May 2001, it made sense to assume that the United States would support regime change in Venezuela in order to bring it in alliance with its own geopolitical and economic interests.

It is curious that, in the public debate that took place in Venezuela during those tumultuous days, neither the administration nor the opposition based their arguments on the basic points of oil policy or petroleum geopolitics. For example, the speeches delivered by oil executives in the Meritocracy Square on the morning of April 11 did not raise substantive issues, just simplistic slogans meant to motivate the protesters. Likewise, Chávez's speech later that day did not provide a careful explanation of technical problems with meritocracy (which he did not even mention) or the fundamental points of his oil policy. While his speeches build on a tradition of dazzling the audience, this lack of detailed explanation is somewhat surprising, because Chávez also uses them to educate the public on basic matters. Yet at this time everyone was acting as if the issues were clear: the point was not to debate matters but to mobilize people.

The Venezuelan flag that the opposition raised during the march on in order to defend the oil industry was displayed later that afternoon, but now smeared with the blood of the dead bodies of civilians, in order to demand the resignation of Chávez. Videos of dead bodies wrapped in the Venezuelan flag were broadcast over the private television networks as irrefutable evidence that the government had lost all legitimacy. Commentators claimed that these images alone spoke a thousand words. The footage of the Venevision report provided proof to the views of the opposition on this topic (it later won the prestigious King of Spain International press award).

People who had been on the bridge at that time had experienced a very different reality. According to them, the gunmen shown on the Venevision report fired not at the marchers, who were far away, but at armored vehicles of the Metropolitan Police under the command of opposition leader and mayor of Caracas Alfredo Peña. The wounded and the dead were not people on Baralt Avenue, as the journalist reported, but on the bridge itself. The government TV station was taken over by opposition forces and could not present an alternative view. At that critical juncture, opposite ideas were not in dialogue with each other but in a mortal battle; the power of evidence became drowned by the evidence of power. Those who controlled the media managed to define public truths.

These and other competing versions of events and visions of the future remained in tension on the afternoon of April 11. While the opposition felt that Chávez would transform PDVSA into an appendage of his political party, his followers thought that PDVSA would at last serve the people. For the opposition, the people killed on April 11 were innocent victims killed by a government that revealed the true face of an authoritarian state; for Chavistas, their deaths, at the hands of hired snipers, showed the fascist face of oligarchic groups willing to plan a macabre massacre to legitimate a coup and return to power.

The sheer exertion of power tilted this impasse toward the opposition. Massively deploying the media under their control, leaders of the opposition used the deaths of April 11 to legitimize their demand for Chávez to resign. While civilian demands for Chávez's resignation were not loud enough to persuade him, the measured statements of the heads of the four branches of the military produced that afternoon and evening were backed up by the threat of force. If Chávez would not resign, the threat was privately communicated to him that the presidential palace would be attacked. This threat was heard.

Accounts of the events that followed remain particularly controversial and confusing to this day. The official story is that Chávez, seeking to avoid a bloodbath, followed the advice of his domestic and international advisers (mainly Fidel Castro), and agreed to let General Lucas Rincón—his only three-star general, the highest military rank—announce his resignation early on the morning of April 12, so long as certain precautions were taken regarding his departure from the country. Nevertheless, minutes after this announcement, the officers at Fort Tiuna (an army base near downtown Caracas) changed the condition that had been negotiated. They objected to letting Chávez flee to Cuba, demanding instead that he be tried in Venezuela for the killings of the previous day. Chávez then refused to sign the text of his resignation that had been faxed to him. Still, hoping to avoid a bloody confrontation, he agreed to be held under arrest.

The opposition's various versions of the coup share the notion that General Rincón announced Chávez's resignation, either in recognition that the president had lost power (and this is the most widespread belief), or as a trick to gain time and find out who was really against him. In either case, this situation created a de facto power vacuum, even if the constitution establishes legal procedures to determine who would remain in command given the absence of the president. General Rincón's dramatic announcement of Chávez's resignation continues to be held as evidence for the widespread belief that on April 12 there was a power vacuum in Venezuela; many, in fact, still argue that therefore it is improper to speak of these events as a coup.

### State Making: The Self-Proclamation of Pedro Carmona

Early on the morning of April 12, with Chávez in custody, Vice President Diosdado Cabello in hiding, and the National Assembly disbanded, the Chavista state, so centered on the figure of the president, was in effect suddenly decapitated. A group of officers and civilians at Fuerte Tiuna took up the functions of the state, occupying their positions with no more legitimacy than the might of power. Far from public scrutiny, this small group, clearly acting on the basis of predesigned plans and with the apparent aid of high military commanders and other key national and international actors, put the final touches on previously elaborated decrees and on the terms of the transition, and named business leader Pedro Carmona as interim president. In this chaotic environment, rushing between hurried talks and meetings, Carmona, with the support of his followers, went along with a plan that rejected the idea that the interim president should be named by a majority vote of the National Assembly.

In Ayacucho Hall at Miraflores Palace, in the late afternoon of April 12, at a ceremony that aspired to be spectacularly historical, Pedro Carmona proclaimed himself provisional president in the name of the laws of Chávez's constitution. Immediately afterwards he named some members of his cabinet, summarily dismissed the National Assembly, the state governors, and municipal leaders (all of them democratically elected), disbanded the Supreme Court, and fired the Attorney General and the People's Defender. He also annulled the forty-nine laws that Chávez had decreed under special powers in November of 2001. Finally, he changed the country's official name back from the "Bolivarian Republic of Venezuela" to simply "Venezuela," and he suspended the agreement to provide subsidized oil to Cuba.

Carmona's inauguration ceremony included two highly symbolic actions that implicitly evoked, at a historically crucial juncture, the imagery of a wounded nation and its new guardian state. As if to communicate his desire to heal the wounds in the nation's social body, Carmona began his speech by asking for a moment of silence in honor of the fallen from the previous day and offering to help the victims' families.[11] And in a gesture that indicated his intention of safeguarding the nation's natural body, Carmona took special care to name as president of PDVSA General Guaicaipuro Lameda, a competent engineer who had demonstrated that he agreed with the corporate vision of PDVSA and the views of its former president, Luis Giusti, who was at that time a senior adviser at the Center for Strategic and International Studies in Washington and an informal energy consultant to President Bush. To underscore the importance of this move, which was warmly welcomed by state-linked domestic and foreign circles and by United States corporations, suffice it to say that immediately after he was chosen as interim president by the officers at Fort Tiuna, Carmona called General Lameda to his house at half past six in the morning on Friday in order to offer him the directorship of PDVSA. In a way, this was Carmona's first act as president. While he named some members of his cabinet Friday afternoon during his inaugural ceremony, he left others to be named at some point in the future.

Some sectors of the opposition euphorically received Carmona's self-proclamation as the liberation of the country from Chávez's rule. Yet Carmona's self-inauguration caused understandable concern not only among Chávez's supporters. The basic criticism at the public level was that Carmona had violated the law by dissolving other branches of government, especially by dismissing the deputies of the National Assembly and the governors, all of whom were legally elected representatives of the people. More privately, another opposition sector criticized this event for excluding many of the groups that had worked to overthrow Chávez and establishing an elitist and partisan government, largely composed of naval officers, important leaders of the Christian Democratic party COPEI, church officials, and members of Opus Dei. The general impression made by Carmona's team, particularly after Chávez's administration, was that it simply looked "too white." As a prominent member of the Church hierarchy privately insisted to Carmona on the evening of April 12, "Pedro, you have to put a black man in there."[12]

A coup typically results in a state of emergency that breaks the legal order in the name of upholding the law; a coup manufactures its legitimacy. In this case, all sides invoked the law. Yet given the lax attitudes toward observing the legal order since colonial times, as well as an easy acquiescence to its violation during other recent Venezuelan coups (those of 1945, 1948, 1952, and 1958, for example),[13] their inflated legalist discourse makes one wonder whether they worried less about violation of the law and more about who was doing the violating and to what end. Noting the links between the violation of the law and the logic of power, Teodoro Petkoff expressed his indignation in a brave commentary on television that same evening of April 12, in which he asserted that he was as opposed to Carmona's arbitrary self-proclamation and dissolution of legally constituted institutions as he had been to Chávez's arbitrary actions. At this critical juncture, Petkoff gave voice to a collective reproach and fear.

On the stage that was the Miraflores Palace on April 12, the performance of the group claiming to be the new state was unconvincing because of flaws not only in the "script"—their violation of legal norms—but in the "casting"—their exclusion of influential actors. Their ceremony failed to convince both because they represented legality ineptly and because they were not sufficiently representative. When the curtain fell in Ayacucho Hall at the end of Carmona's speech, an exclusive audience enthusiastically clapped its approval of the act that had just drawn to a close, but a much larger television audience viewed the applause as part of the play itself, and the clapping audience as a chorus in a tragedy announcing the true meaning of the action on the main stage. This broader audience viewed this ceremony, including the elite chorus that applauded it, as a gathering of country club people celebrating their return to power while sporting fine, name-brand clothes: Armani suits, Gucci ties, Zegna shirts, and Christian Dior and Hermés scents that, from what I have been told, "you could smell through the TV screen." For this larger public, this chorus announced the birth of an elitist, exclusive autocratic state behind a facade of democracy. On the streets, at the same time, the rather violent persecution of Chavistas intensified fear of the establishment of an authoritarian government, one unfortunately all too familiar in Latin America.

The problem was not only that the new government had broken the law, but that it had concentrated state power in a small group, leaving out those who felt they had the right to be part of the new regime and had enough power to back up such conceit. The *Carmonazo*, as it came to be called, entailed breaking not just the law, but the opposition's alliance and implicit pact; the legal violation mirrored a political transgression. Perhaps if there had been no political transgression, the legal violation would have been accepted—or would never have occurred, or would not have taken the same form. In the historical contingency of that moment, other options seemed possible. Carmona could have gone through the National Assembly to be named interim president, as many advised him to do. Or, even within the political framework that he chose, he could have included a wider swath of society. For example, he could have named General Efraín Vásquez Velasco to be Minister of Defense or someone from the army rather than the navy, as he tried to do on Saturday; he could have placed in the cabinet representatives from different parties (especially Acción Democrática), as well as his major public ally before April 11, trade union leader Carlos Ortega; he even might have named a dark-skinned representative of the workers to be his vice president, as he also belatedly tried to do on Saturday, April 13, when he considered Acción Democrática labor leader Manuel Cova for this position. But if it is difficult to know what actually happened in this convoluted history, it is impossible to know what might have happened if the initial steps taken by Carmona had been more inclusive and skillful.

What certainly did happen, though, was that a wide range of Venezuelan society immediately rejected Carmona's actions. Many felt that instead of changing the country's course and entering into history as the nation's savior, he had derailed the opposition. Commenting on these events in their aftermath, sharp observers such as Carlos Blanco argued that it was the popular mobilization against Chávez that forced him from power on April 11 (the idea that Chávez really did resign plays an important role in this interpretation), whereas the real coup was carried out against the opposition on April 12, when Carmona took power for himself. Other commentators, including reporters from *Newsweek*, presented Carmona's taking office as a "hijacking" of the coup, or as "a coup within a coup," an interpretation I believe is more accurate, for it recognizes not just the coup against the opposition on April 12, but the coup against Chávez on April 11.[14]

The person in command over the military, General Efraín Vásquez Velasco, had grown cold toward Carmona, as he felt that his role as head of the army had entitled him to be named Defense Minister. In response to the general repudiation of Carmona's actions, he and his high ranking officers forced Carmona to set things straight—or at least less crooked. On the afternoon of Saturday, April 13, Carmona called for a session of the National Assembly to select the provisional president. As a solution, it was a perfectly logical proposal: aside from offering a mantle of legality, it signaled that he was willing to include a variety of social groups and to engage in political negotiations; power would be shared, not concentrated. But as a course correction, not only was it too little and too late, it was far too blatant. Carmona convened the National Assembly not only after first dissolving it the day before with the stroke of a pen on Friday, April 12, but at a moment when his power was vanishing, after he had barely slipped away from Miraflores to Fuerte Tiuna late on April 13, when Chavista forces were retaking the presidential palace. Fortunes had already shifted.

Indeed, this gesture of supposed inclusiveness on April 13 by those who on Friday April 12 had proclaimed themselves the exclusive power brokers was generally seen on Saturday as an evident sign of weakness, not as evidence of a change of heart. Regarded by most observers as a desperate effort to remain in the state while no longer controlling power, this act only served to mobilize further virtually all political forces against Carmona. Even those who had once supported him now rushed to make him the scapegoat for a plan that many of them had helped to concoct.

At Miraflores, the Presidential Guard, which surprisingly had not been replaced by the insurgents and had feigned to support and serve Carmona, retook the presidential palace and arrested the members of his cabinet who were there for their swearing-in ceremony planned for Saturday afternoon and had not managed to escape. In an inverted replay of the events of Friday, when insurgent officers threatened Chávez that they would attack Miraflores if he did not resign, the officers supporting Chávez now threatened, through their spokesman General Baduel, commander of the paratroopers stationed in the nearby city of Maracay, to shell the insurgents if they did not support the constitutional order.

The opposition forces quickly folded. The streets that they had occupied so massively and dramatically on April 11 were populated after April 12 only by growing numbers of Chávez's followers. In contrast to the military officers supporting constitutional rule, who had gained the firm loyalty of mid-level officers in direct command of the troops, the high-ranking officers who plotted against Chávez, having no true control over any troops, had little choice but to surrender, flee, or be arrested.

When the National Assembly finally made its appearance on the political scene late on that confused Saturday afternoon, it was not to legitimate Carmona, as he had proposed under the pressure of changing circumstances, but to show that the constitution was still in effect and to return the Chávez administration to power by nominating a new president. After Chavistas regained control of the state television channel, television viewers could watch on the evening of Saturday April 13 another presidential proclamation. This time, however, it was Willian Lara, President of the National Assembly, swearing in Vice President Diosdado Cabello as president of Venezuela. This event was exclusively performed for a television audience in order to keep invisible the stage set that made it believable. In fact, the National Assembly had been unable to convene in a body; the cameras only showed images of the two leaders, Lara, the president of the National Assembly, and Cabello, the newly anointed president of Venezuela. In this new theater of state power, a legitimate constitutional principle was confirmed through a simulated act.

Hours later, at four in the morning on Sunday, April 14, the television broadcast Hugo Chávez's return to the presidential palace in the midst of an emotional crowd, where he was recognized as the president he had legally never ceased to be. During these contested and confusing events, between Saturday night and dawn on Sunday Venezuela seemingly had three presidents: Pedro Carmona, as head of the insurgent government, Diosdado Cabello, representing the state when Chávez was ousted, and Hugo Chávez, who was never formally deposed.

During the April days, in dramatic actions intended to direct the course of history in accordance with conflicting views and interests we can recognize the common and ever-painful paradox that we humans make our own history, but under conditions that form us and often escape our control. As liminal moments, coups make us feel our power as individuals to make history, but also the weight of history as a force that shapes us. Perhaps a deeper understanding of these situations will help us understand how, in 2002, so many people could act with such faith in their ability to make history follow the path of their visions and how, in the end, the unfolding of events led to unexpected results that surprised even those who set them in motion.

## Historical Truth: Facts and Fiction

The events of April 11 to 14 continue to be depicted according to different scripts: as a civil rebellion, when the large anti-Chávez march of April 11 is emphasized; as a coup by Carmona against the massive anti-Chávez movement of April 11, when the exclusive character of that brief regime is emphasized and Chávez is assumed to have resigned; as a civil-military coup, when the emphasis is on the arrest of Chávez and Carmona's self-inauguration as president in disregard of the constitution; as a power vacuum, if one takes

General Lucas Rincón's announcement of Chávez's resignation literally and disregards constitutional rules of presidential succession (this was position that the Supreme Court of Justice took when they decreed on August 14, 2002, that what had happened was not a coup but a "power vacuum"); as a "self-coup" engineered by Chávez in a Machiavellian maneuver pretending to lose power to discover who his enemies were; as several uncoordinated coups, if one assumes that in a country as poorly organized as Venezuela there could be a number of conspiring groups and that none of them could manage to coordinate what happened; as a "hijacked coup" or a "coup within a coup," if one sees Carmona's team as a conservative faction tied to powerful right-wing economic groups (and Opus Dei) that turned their backs on their co-conspirators and tried to take power for themselves; or as an imperialist coup, organized by or with the participation of one or more of the following administrations and their intelligence agencies: United States' Bush (CIA, NSA, and others), Israel's Sharon (Mossad), England's Blair (MI6), and Spain's Aznar (CESID), if one favors the geopolitics of oil and the agency of metropolitan centers, whose interests converged on guaranteeing oil supplies to the United States, weakening OPEC, avoiding an oil embargo against Israel, protecting Spanish investments in Venezuela, and defending the alliance among the United States, Israel, England, and Spain. These versions, or variations thereof, can be complementary. Perhaps because it has been hard to prove what really happened, while all these scripts have believers, some people do not believe in any of them or in the possibility of the truth ever emerging.

Despite new information or evidence, people tend to cling to their original convictions. A telling example concerns the report by Venevision that played such a critical role in turning the tide against Chávez on April 11. As it turned out, the report was inaccurate, but not because of a visual montage. The images were truthful, but the narrative that accompanied them was not. A verbal script made them tell a story that did not correspond to the images themselves. As a documentary directed by Angel Palacios makes evident, the Venevision video was taped at a time when the marchers were four blocs away from the Llaguno Bridge. The people shooting from the bridge fired at armored vehicles belonging to the Metropolitan Police under the command of opposition leader Alfredo Peña, the mayor of Caracas. The wounded and dead bodies shown in the video did not belong to members of the opposition, as the reporter asserted, but were in fact Chavistas. In effect, the Venevision camera that filmed this video had no angle of vision on Baralt Avenue below, only on the bridge itself; it could show people shooting, but it could not show what they were shooting at. The people who were reported dead or wounded as a result of these shootings were actually Chavistas on the bridge. Another video filmed at the same time shows that at least at that time, people on the bridge were not shooting at the march, but at armored vehicles of the Metropolitan Police controlled by opposition leaders and that the march was located at around 400 meters away. Of course, this only proves that the Llaguno gunmen did not fire at the march during the period covered by the Venevision report, leaving open the possibility, as many have asserted, that they could have done so at another time.[15]

Typically, the common reaction to evidence that contradicts one's original convictions is to dismiss it as biased or partial and to appeal to the truth of opposite accounts or experiences. In the case of the Llaguno massacre, many in the opposition dismiss the Palacios documentary because it openly favors the government or because it is inaccurate with respect to lesser matters or, more validly, because it does not account for what happened at other times in the same area. Similarly, the fact that the Llaguno gunmen were tried and considered innocent after Chávez returned to power (they had been arrested under the brief presidency of Carmona) is treated as an expression of a biased judicial system, not as proof of their innocence.

Subsequent reports that suggest that the killings were part of a plot have been subjected to the same fate. For example, a few months after the coup, CNN's Otto Neustaldt reported that the April 11 pronouncement against Chávez, by a set of high-level military who presented the death of six civilians as a major justification for their rebellion, was planned *before* the march had taken place (he was invited to report on it the evening of April 10), and was taped at mid day on April 11 before any deaths had yet taken place. Yet his report did not lead to a careful investigation, but to a battle of convictions supported by alternative facts, stories, rumors, and pressures. According to some accounts, at least two deaths had taken place by the time of these officers' pronouncement and the officers had been told about them; it is claimed that it is Otto Neustaldt who remained uniformed about what had happened elsewhere and what the officers knew. Apparently subjected to pressure, he vanished from the scene and has not given any further interviews. This incident, as so much else about the April events, remains shrouded in mystery.

Even eight years after the coup, contradictory versions of the controversial April events remain in circulation. As expected, new political dramas and scandals have displaced older ones and made it ever harder for a persuasive truth to emerge. Attempts to resolve conflicting versions and to develop a more accurate account are typically interpreted as maneuvers to benefit certain interests or to pursue ulterior goals. While the massacre of

April 11 has not been legally resolved or definitively chronicled, a deafening, shameful silence still hangs over the many more deaths that occurred during the looting and confrontations on April 12 and 13. An expanded Supreme Court, whose legitimacy was in doubt because of the dozen new justices whom Chávez had appointed, rejected the earlier ruling that the events of April did not constitute a coup but a "power vacuum," but this ruling served more to question the independence of the judicial system than to settle competing versions about the April events.

### Nation and State under Chávez

While competing convictions tend to remain in place despite the passage of time or the emergence of new information, basic images of the nation and the state, formed throughout the course of the twentieth century and already modified by the crisis of the 1980s, have been significantly transformed under the Chávez period. Declining economic conditions began to erode the image of the nation as a harmonious community sustained by oil wealth as well as the view of the state as the agent that would bring about modernity. Given the country's social polarization, impoverished middle and working classes, and crushing debt, such a myth was hard to maintain.

The event that crystallized this change was the *Caracazo* of 1989, a huge urban upheaval centering in the capital. At that time, the state forcibly suppressed a massive protest against declining economic conditions and structural adjustment policies imposed by the International Monetary Fund. This repression led to the death of almost four hundred protesters, which came to be justified at the time as a means to restore order and control the widespread looting that took place during several days. In contrast to the nineteen deaths in April 2002, the 399 killed by the state in 1989 were accepted by the media and the sectors that define public opinion as a necessary cost for keeping social order and entering a period of rationality as defined by the capitalist market. According to Chávez, this event also radicalized the Boliviarian movement he had founded in 1982 and prompted it to seek to overthrow Carlos Andrés Pérez in 1992.[16]

The political myth of the Fourth Republic was a modernizing capitalist project led by the state on behalf of the nation as a united community. In contrast, the foundational myth of Chávez's Fifth Republic is a project of social justice on behalf of the majority in the context of an uncertain modernity and a polarized world dominated by imperialism. Earlier presidents promised progress to all in a nation imagined as a united community; Chávez has promised justice and a better life to the majority of a divided nation; to bring into being a new History.

The events of April 2002 expressed but also intensified the nation's fragmentation. As the opposition saw it, the state under Chávez had wounded the nation's economy and population; to his supporters, Chávez had protected the nation from a privileged group that wanted to regain the benefits they had enjoyed under the Fourth Republic.[17] One of the effects of the April coup was to intensify divisions in Venezuela. It encouraged Chávez to concentrate further powers in the presidency. Stimulated in part by winning the referendum on his rule in August 2004 (after regaining popularity through the missions he began to create in 2003), Chávez increased his control of every branch of the state and of society. The fear of his critics seemed to have been validated early in 2005, when Chávez proclaimed that Venezuela would be socialist.

After winning his reelection in 2006, Chávez further intensified efforts to exert state control over society, to turn the armed forces into a defender of the "socialist" fatherland, to integrate the parties that supported him into a unified socialist party, and to promote various forms of popular participation in production and decision-making. However, after the defeat of his constitutional reform in the referendum of December 2007 (his first major electoral setback), he was forced to modify his program of socialist change—not so much to abandon it as to try to implement it through other means. In February 15, 2009, he won a referendum that modifies the constitution so as to allow the indefinite re-election of the president.

Chávez's rule incarnates the archetypical fears and hopes of his supporters and adversaries. For those who believe in him, he embodies public virtue itself, which he has come to identify with socialism; socialism for many of his supporters means not so much a particular doctrine, but whatever Chávez stands for. For those who oppose him, he appears typically disguised, whether as an authoritarian ruler wearing a democratic mask who only cares about power, or as a typical socialist donning the mask of a socialism of the twenty-first century to hide the emergence of a new privileged class, the *boliburguesia*, a newly rich sector of parasitical capitalists dressed in revolutionary costume. Removing his mask has become the task of the opposition. From the perspective of Chavistas, the defense of democracy by the opposition is voiced by leaders who had no qualms about overthrowing democratic institutions and legality in 2002 by violent means; their call for democracy hides their partisan ambitions and oligarchic interests. In a theater of specters, simulation rules.

Masking seeks to render wicked behavior invisible and to disguise private interests as public virtues. A more perverse form of invisibility, one that requires less masking, takes place with respect to the state's entanglement in capitalist relations, as this appears as a natural necessity and therefore requires less simulation. In Venezuela, as in other countries in Latin America, new rulers have come to power criticizing the inequities and irrationality of capitalism, but once in power they have had to govern capitalist societies that depend on financial resources generated by the capitalist economy. Even as they seek to reduce these inequities, to democratize social services, and even to develop at the margins collective forms of ownership, they are constrained to promote national development through various forms of capitalist accumulation.

Ironically, their attempt to maximize national income continues a long colonial tradition of reliance on developing the region's comparative advantages. Now as in the colonial past, these advantages are inexpensive labor and, more importantly, natural resources. Given the emergence of China as the global factory, Latin America has increasingly become the world's global field of natural resources. Despite the pervasive critique of neoliberalism, during this leftward turn the pursuit of comparative advantages continues to define the core national economic policies throughout Latin America. This outcome, an effect of the global division of labor and of nature under capitalism, appears as an inevitable fact of the normal order of things.

Given its nature as an oil producer, this neocolonial syndrome is particularly present in Venezuela; in the last decade Venezuela has become even more dependent on oil. Under Chávez, the oil industry has become ever more entangled in capitalist markets and associations. While massive oil income (over 900 billion dollars in 10 years) managed to bring benefits in health, education, and subsidized food to significant sectors of the population, Venezuela is facing a significant decline in industrial and agricultural production, high inflation rates, alarming insecurity and criminality, and, ironically in a country with abundant energy and rivers, severe shortcomings in the provision of water and electricity. It is particularly damaging that the decline in basic services has taken place at a time when a banking crisis revealed the emergence of a *boliburguesía*. After a decade of rule, the Chávez regime has shown signs of serious fatigue.

The 2002 coup helped to de-legitimate coups as political weapons and to value democratic procedures. The pursuit of political change through democratic elections and popular support has become a deeply rooted ideal shared both by the opposition and the government. It is a hopeful sign that the legitimacy and power of both the Chávez regime and the opposition now depend on their ability to make their proclaimed ideals correspond to effective political practices.

# Reflections on the State[18]

A coup d'état is obviously an extraordinary act. Nevertheless, here I examine the coup in relation to ordinary life, not only because a coup is composed of a series of everyday acts, but because these acts, taken as a whole, form a phase whose exceptional intensity highlights the organizing principles and relationships that underlay quotidian social life. I thus seek to illuminate the state by placing it in society, observing their mutual relations, and dissolving their appearance as separate and independent entities.

In a sense, the rupture of order during a coup resembles the liminal or intermediate phase of rituals discussed by Arnold Van Gennep[19] and Victor Turner.[20] According to them, the liminal period in rituals corresponds to the process of transition between the time one leaves the habitual order and the time one returns to that order after experiencing the changes imposed during the transition, as in healing rituals or rituals that regulate changing social or personal status. In liminal periods, conventional social guidelines are relaxed and cultural representations are intensified; social actors appear without the attributes of their customary roles, as "naked unaccommodated man" in Turner's felicitous phrasing,[21] while acquiring such new attributes as health, adulthood, or chiefdom over the group. During this phase, social norms and values are simultaneously questioned and affirmed, in a sort of metaphysical and sensual carnival that subverts and exaggerates axiomatic principles in order to make them more visible and, in the final analysis, to reinforce the prevailing order.

Similar processes also occur during coups. But while rituals are carefully structured in order to assure the attainment of given outcomes, coups are historical ruptures with in-built uncertainty concerning the achievement of desired ends. In addition, coups carry the burden of having to restructure the social order, not simply of preparing social actors to return to a given order. This obligation to restructure society from the highest levels of the state after a successful coup also differentiates coups from the kind of millenarian movements that crop up in complex societies with the mission of establishing a distinct order at the margins of society, as analyzed by Victor Turner.[22]

In contrast to liminal situations of cyclical rituals, during a coup, the separation from the normal order tends not only to reveal and affirm its axiomatic values but also to redefine or transform them. The liminality of a coup often leads to criminality; it blurs principles and norms, brings about abrupt identity changes, generates shifts in positions and loyalties, spotlights contradictions normally kept under wraps, reveals occult knowledge, and redefines power relations. In cyclical rites, the established order controls liminal disorder; in coups, the disordered liminal period seeks to establish a new order. In a successful coup, liminal disorder imposes a new order; in a failed coup, the established order controls the liminal disorder and reasserts the old order. But even then, its comeback necessarily entails changes; nothing can remain as it was before.

In the liminal phase of a coup, the state appears as it truly is: not merely an embodiment of order, but also its creator. As a self-created entity that pretends to be the creature of sovereign power, the state appears in many places and guises through many agents that claim to represent this sovereign power: its embodiment varies by place, and by the entity that defines it and claims to represents it as well as by the nature of the sovereign power it pretends to represent. The state is the factory that manufactures the state. Its products bear its solemn trademark, but disguise their mundane production.

During a coup, state laws may seem to be arbitrary or legitimate, its agents genuine representatives or imposters, its performances genuine or artificial, its subjects' loyalties solid or fickle; its various reifications change to the beat of the rhythms of power. During a coup, from within the state or from some part of society claiming to represent the state, another state proclaims that it is the legitimate one. If the new state's action is effective, it may manage to displace the old one; if not, then those who aspired to portray it as such become its illegitimate usurpers.

During the coup in Venezuela, Pedro Carmona quickly went from being acclaimed by the media as a great statesman, to being nothing more than "Pedro the Brief," as he was jokingly but scornfully called after his fall even by the same people who praised him when he held power. The contrast was still more extreme in public representations of Chávez during these fluid hours, as he suddenly went from being publicly scorned in the shameful terms normally reserved for private conversations among the most racist and classist sectors of the opposition, to being praised as a president whose extraordinary talents could no longer be spurned: from being a "monkey" (a species of monkey, *mico* is a racist slang term in Venezuela that was often used to refer to Chávez, as in *mico-mandante)* unable to talk, to being a "brilliant orator," an enviable "snake charmer," and a "shrewd politician."

The state, as embodiment of the nation, is objectified through multiple discourses and practices that seek to represent the nation; the "state effect" is achieved through the success of these reifications. The state is thus the set of discrete relations and objectifications that constitute it as the agent of the nation. As a general form, its complex identity is formed by items that reflect and constitute a whole cartography of power: presidential palace, ministers, officials, army bases, bureaucracies, dignitaries, discourses, laws, codes, ceremonies, acts. Any agency, position, or particular individual may represent or redefine the state from wherever they stand, so long as they are able to do it well and have the power to do it, whether they are a crowd in the street, military officers on an army base, political leaders on television, or a businessman in the presidential palace. If, as Benedict Anderson argues, a nation independently of its age appears to be immemorial,[23] the state, as its representative, must express its permanence through timeless forms—through embodiments that fuse time and place and evoke eternity. Its fetish quality grants it a sense of immortality; we know it can vanish, yet it must live forever. The state is a fetish, a set of particular objects that represent a general whole. Its majestic and mystifying form of representing the nation and representing itself through multiple particularities is an essential part of its constitution as the nation's representative. But the liminal moments of a coup reveal that this cartography of state power, drafted by many hands, may sculpt forms as permanent as statues or as ephemeral as lines traced in sand.

From my perspective, the state is not, as Philip Abrams argues, the mask that covers the political system,[24] nor the political system behind the mask, but the union of mask and what is being masked, the visible and the hidden. The state is produced by a process of masking, of creating a visible stage as well as its invisible backstage. Visibility and invisibility are two sides of the state. State secrets are an essential core of its being; the state's greatest secret is its ultimate invisibility in spite of its permanent objectification through multiple entities.

Under capitalism, the state and the commodity come to be formed through a common process and assume related forms. Marx's discussion of the relation between cultural forms and material practices offers an insightful view of this process. He convincingly shows how the "commodity form" unfolds in the domain of circulation through formal relations of equality, equivalence and freedom that conceal and render invisible the relations of inequality, coercion and exploitation that prevail in the "hidden abode of production." While the "commodity form" is realized through ever expanding number of products for sale in markets mediated by money, the state form is achieved through a wide range of entities capable of representing the state in a political field mediated by multiple forms of power. While commodities are measured by their exchange value or price, state embodiments define their self-representational value or "state value" through their effects; their power must be constantly defined in a political field of forces. The value of the state, its legitimacy, achieves currency through public contests.

As a general form, the state is reified through multiple particularities—institutions, discourses, objects, emblems, individuals, buildings. These objectifications are not merely independent entities with their own attributes, nor simply symbols, but the means through which the state is constituted and acquires meaning; the state comes into being through them. As such, the state is formed through reifications that establish a relation of equivalence between the particular and the general; individual entities, such as a policeman or a president, a law or a building, appear as the state without the state ever being reduced to any one of them.

Chávez had managed to appear as the embodiment of the state; the opposition tried to break the link between his person and the state, presenting him as the agent responsible for the massacre of April 11. For the army to be able to force him from Miraflores Palace, they first had to displace him from the majestic place he occupied in the nation's imaginary and break the charm that made him an icon of the nation; he had to be reduced to an everyday person, or worse, a usurper of the true seat of power. The first thing the officers did when he arrived as their prisoner at Fort Tiuna was to take away his military uniform and dress him in a common jumpsuit (*un mono para el mono*, "a jumpsuit for the monkey," as someone commented, punning on the double meaning of *mono* in Spanish).

Carmona's self-inauguration, despite all the efforts to choreograph it as a solemn state ceremony, did not manage to embody the general form of the state, but instead made evident its partiality, offering a glimpse into the private interests that organized this simulacrum of state power. It may be accurate to say, as the brilliant Venezuelan playwright José Ignacio Cabrujas once observed, that the Venezuelan state is constituted through acts of simulation. I would add that every state is constituted by differing, and historically specific, forms of simulation; the secret of the state is to make those simulations invisible. If this is so, the task of critical analysis is to resist the enchantments of power, and to explore its simulations.

Ardent conflicts obviously emerge between opposing groups during coups: the state embodies reasons and passions. Its ability to persuade and dominate political and cultural spaces, to appear as natural and necessary—its hegemony—involves controlling its subjects in their integrity as conscious and sensual beings. The concept of hegemony itself refers to an order that is constantly being constructed and disputed. For this reason I find of little use to identify hegemony with the dominion of the habitual, in contrast to ideology as the terrain of consciousness.[25] The concept of hegemonic ideology shows the intimate and fluid bond between habitual practices and conscious actions and ideas. Moreover, this union between habits and consciousness underscores the fact that hegemony involves the construction and the maintenance of common interests, feelings, and ideas between opposed classes, and that this "common sense," so central to the notion of Gramscian hegemony, is realized by the complex communion of all the senses. This integration of cognitive and emotive factors, of judgment and faith, contributes to the formation of both individual and collective bodily and spiritual positions and dispositions.

Following a long tradition of spectacularly staged dramas in Venezuelan politics, the public events that I have analyzed here were the means for the reproduction of society through the production of the state. Like stages for displaying the presence of the state—while hiding the artifices of its construction—their aim was less to convince people through the force of reason, than to draw them in with the emotional flow of rhetoric and action. During the tumultuous days of the coup, performances such as the "Not One Step Back" march from Meritocracy Square to Miraflores, the televised reports of the "Llaguno Massacre," or Carmona's self-inauguration in Ayacucho Hall at the presidential Miraflores Palace achieved their effects as much by illuminating as by dazzling—reasons and passions were fused. Amidst the drama of the moment, the public scripts that orchestrated these performances created "states of enchantment"—complexes of ideas and feelings that seduced people (or repelled them) through their overall sensory impact, not just through reason, despite the artful display of an ordered set of ideas or reasons. As in cases of ritual possession, conventional formulas were deployed to invoke a vast repertoire of ideas and feelings embodied deep within every person. These performances were accompanied and settled by the force of arms, confirming once again that state making involves not just the force of reasons and passions but the reasons of force.

### Endnotes

1. This chapter is built from an earlier attempt to analyze these events written while I was Professor at the History Department and Cisneros Fellow at the David Rockefeller Latin American Center, Harvard University; my thanks to fellows, colleagues, friends and students who helped me produce it. My thanks to many in Venezuela who shared their ideas and experiences with me. Special thanks to Gustavo Cisneros, Beatriz Rangel, Antonieta Lopez, Victor Ferrer, and other members of the Cisneros Organization for opening the doors of VENEVISION and allowing me to research the VENEVISION report discussed in this essay; my gratitude also to Angel Palacios for sharing his insights concerning the various representations of the Llaguno massacre. The earlier essay was published in Spanish in *Anuario de Estudios Americanos*, Vol. 62, No. 1 (enero-junio, 2005). My thanks to David Frye and Jon Eastwood for their translation of this original article; I have revised and expanded it considerably for this publication.

2. For this reason Marcos calls the Cold War, "World War III" and refers to the current neoliberal period, involving growing disparities and violence, "World War IV" (See Subcomandante Marcos, "La 4e guerre mondiale a commencé." *Le Monde diplomatique* 1 (August 1997): 4–5.

3. Remarks by George W. Bush on 6 November 2001, as cited in the White House press release at http://www.whitehouse.gov/news/releases/2001/11/20011106–4.html.

4. I owe this insight to many conversations with Yolanda Salas (1948–2007), a sharp Venezuelan cultural analyst.

5. The polarization of Venezuela into two factions changed after the opposition's failed recall of President Chávez in the August 15, 2004 referendum and the decision not to participate in the congressional elections of 2005. While its traditional leadership lost support, the opposition became more diverse and widespread, even though it did not manage to develop effective political representation. The defeat of the government-sponsored referendum on the proposed constitutional reform in 2007 has broken the conviction that Chávez could not be defeated and has given the opposition new impetus to gain positions and power through electoral politics.

6. Coronil, *The Magical State*; also Coronil, *El estado mágico*.

7. I develop the concept of the "nation's natural body" in *The Magical State*, based on a broad study of Venezuelan political discourse over the course of the twentieth century that I support theoretically by integrating the Marxist concept of landed rents with Lefebvre's and Massey's ideas on space and time and Kantorowicz's arguments in *The King's Two Bodies*.

8. "El sentimiento de poder de esas masas humanas era total," *El Nacional* (Caracas), April 11, 2005.

9. I discuss this controversial issue in *Crude Matters*, a book I am writing on the April events.

10. "We know that the action encouraged by the Chávez government provoked this crisis. According to the best information available, the Chávez government suppressed peaceful demonstrations. Government supporters, on orders from the Chávez government, fired on unarmed, peaceful protesters, resulting in 10 killed and 100 wounded." Remarks by Ari Fleischer as transcribed in an official press release dated 12 April 2002, on http://www.whitehouse.gov/news/releases/2002/04/20020412-1.html.

11. Without dismissing the value of this gesture, it is worth recalling that in 1989 no business organizations or political parties protested the massacre of hundreds of Venezuelans at the hands of the National Army. COFAVIC, the nongovernmental organization that took it upon itself to help the victims, worked practically alone and against the current.

12. Confidential interview.

13. For a discussion of these coups and the double discourse they occasioned, see Coronil, *The Magical State*.

14. The reference to the coup "being hijacked" by Carmona is cited in Contreras and Isikoff, "Hugo's Close Call," *Newsweek*, April 29, 2002. The "coup within a coup" phrase comes in an analysis by Encarnación, "Venezuela's 'Civil Society Coup,'" 38: "In what can be best described as a coup within a coup, Carmona jettisoned the plan for a broad civilian-military coalition government in favor of an interim government staffed almost exclusively with ultraconservatives."

15. While the documentary *Puente Llaguno, claves de una masacre* (Llaguno Bridge: Clues to a Massacre, 2004), directed by Angel Palacios, offers persuasive evidence that shows that Venevisión's documentary was misleading, many regard it as a biased account that misrepresents what happened; in the polarized Venezuelan context, its open pro-government position renders invalid its fundamental and fundamentally accurate point.

16. For a detailed discussion of these events and their public representation, see Coronil and Skurski, "Dismembering and Remembering the Nation: The Semantics of Political Violence in Venezuela." The figure of 399 refers to the number of dead identified by COFAVIC (Comité de Familiares de las Víctimas, a nongovernmental organization of the families of victims of the *Caracazo*). The official figure is 277. Some journalists have speculated that hundreds more were killed.

17. Venezuela's "Fourth Republic" (IV República) refers to the political system in place before Hugo Chávez's declaration of a "Fifth Republic" after his election as president in 1999, though there is no clear sense as to whether the "Fourth Republic" refers to the period that began with the 1958 return to democratic elections, or a century earlier, with Venezuela's separation from Colombia in 1830.

18. This section elaborates ideas that I have developed in other works, especially *The Magical State*.

19. Van Gennep, *Rites of Passage*.

20. Turner, *The Forest of Symbols*.

21. Ibid., 99.

22. Turner, *The Ritual Process*.

23. Anderson, *Imagined Communities*.

24. Abrams, "Notes on the Difficulty of Studying the State," 32.

25. Comaroff, *Christianity, Colonialism, and Consciousness in South Africa*, Vol. 1 of *Revelation and Revolution*.

# 2

# Why Polarize?
# Advantages and Disadvantages of
# a Rational-Choice Analysis of
# Government-Opposition Relations
# under Hugo Chávez[1]

*Javier Corrales*

This chapter shows how deliberate state policies to promote polarization affected regime type in Venezuela under Hugo Chávez (1999 to the present). Venezuela has always been a favorite case for studying regime change. In the 1970s, the country was considered a paradigmatic case of unexpected democratic consolidation. Then it became a paradigmatic case of democratic unraveling, first under a two-party system (in the 1980s), and then under party fragmentation (in the 1990s).[2] In the 2000s, Venezuela emerged as a paradigmatic case of competitive authoritarianism,[3] in which the government upholds competitive elections and a few other liberties but also introduces a series of policies and laws that systematically disadvantage the opposition and erode checks and balances. I will argue that it is impossible to understand this evolution of regime type, especially the emergence of competitive authoritarianism, without invoking the deliberate pursuit of polarization by the state.

A few months into Chávez's administration, Venezuela came to exhibit the highest degree of political polarization in the country since the late 1940s. To explain this polarization, I propose a (semi) game-strategic argument. Polarization under Chávez, I argue, is not so much the result of entrenched and thus inevitable socioeconomic clash between classes, as a structuralist analysis would contend, but rather, an artifact of state design. Recent work on polarization shows that often it is political elites, rather than the masses, that promote or incite polarization.[4] I build on this insight to show that the Chávez administration discovered early on the political payoffs of polarization and soon became its most important promoter. The onset of state-society confrontation under Chávez might not have been intentionally impelled by the state. But once polarization set in, the state realized that the gains from sustaining it exceeded the gains from abating it.

The burden of any intention-driven argument for polarization such as the one I put forward rests on showing exactly how polarization can reward incumbents. In this chapter, I show how this reward can come about. I illustrate how, given a certain distribution of voters, it is more rewarding for the incumbent to exaggerate rather than reconcile conflicts across the political spectrum. Under certain conditions, extremism can pay electorally.

At the same time, I also want to identify some limitations of a strictly rational-choice explanation for polarization. In looking at the behavior of the state under Chávez, it is clear that its preference for polarizing policies actually intensified even when evidence surfaced of declining electoral rewards, especially after 2007, and of changes in the behavior of the opposition in the direction of greater moderation. This suggests that electoral incentives and counterpart emulation (tit-for-tat)—two key elements in any rational-choice account of polarization—are not the only feeders of radical politics in Venezuela. Other factors play a role, and I conclude with a brief discussion of some of these, namely, increasing homogenization of the ruling party and, more importantly, path dependence, the term used in the social sciences to describe how steps taken in the past lock actors in a hard-to-reverse trajectory.

In short, I seek to show both the advantages and limitations of relying on semi-rational choice tools to explain the origins of one of Latin America's most memorable cases of polarization in decades, and one of the world's most renowned cases of competitive authoritarianism. My focus will be on the electoral reasons that encouraged the state to change the regime from representative democracy toward competitive authoritarianism—not because I think that electoral incentives is the sole explanation for this move. Rather, I offer this explanation because it strikes me as the most understudied factor that contributed to the rise in Venezuela of an odd combination of electoralism with autocracy, and progressivism with reactionary policies.

## Polarization[5]

Polarization could be defined as a situation in which two leading forces compete politically by moving increasingly in opposite directions ideologically, discursively, and policy-wise. Ideologically, the leading poles drift farther apart, with fewer areas of common ground. Discursively, the protagonists adopt increasingly insulting language to refer to each other. And policy-wise, they refuse to engage with each other through institutional means: state holders exclude the opposition from policy deliberations, and the opposition adopts increasingly "disloyal" forms of behavior such as street marches, electoral boycotts, and obstructionism.[6] Two years after Chávez came to office, the political system was fully polarized to a degree seldom seen in Venezuela and rare even for Latin America.

All scholars agree that Venezuela under Chávez became highly polarized, almost from the start. Yet there is no consensus on the causes. For structuralists, polarization in Venezuela stems from the refusal of old winners (mostly white elites, mostly leaders of the traditional parties) to accept newly empowered but previously excluded actors (mostly, the majority of Venezuelans, who happen to be non-white, poor, disconnected from traditional parties and victims of two decades of economic contraction).[7] All scholars agree that Chávez's electoral strategy in 1998 consisted precisely in mobilizing this broad constituency of economically and politically disaffected Venezuelans, advocating a turn to the left. According to the structuralist view, in moving to the left and employing aggressive language toward opponents, the state under Chávez has merely reflected an existing polarized social structure characterized by an irreconcilable conflict of interest between the haves and the have-nots, the politically included versus the excluded.[8] Any state has to choose sides, and the state under Chávez chose to side with the latter group, leading to policies that simply reflected pre-existing societal polarization.

There is no question that by the time Chávez took office, Venezuelan society had been accumulating tensions between economic winners and losers for two decades. However, the argument that the resulting state simply reflected a former, class-based societal polarization faces some empirical and theoretical problems. Empirically, there is evidence that by 2003 and to this day, the opposition to Chávez came to include a multitude of income levels (not just the rich), and ideologies (not just the right, but also groups that had fought alongside Chávez actively against the status quo).[9] The revolution brought disillusionment (to borrow from Carlos Blanco's book title) and this disillusionment bred opposition.[10] Theoretically, the key problem is that this argument fails to consider the idea that extreme positions in politics are often the willing choice of politicians who see political advantages in provoking rather than accommodating their opponents.[11] Many societies are riddled with intense conflicts and cleavages, and yet political parties may decide to interact with others cooperatively rather than combatively regardless of existing cleavages.[12] It is thus useful to consider the idea that the state, or the ruling party, chooses extremist policies as an autonomous act rather than as a response to societal demand.

However, one problem with this second school of thought is that it seldom specifies the conditions under which choosing an extremist strategy breeds rewards. Polarization sometimes engenders electoral majorities for rulers, but at other times it fails to pay off. Here I intend to show the conditions under which polarization might work to the incumbent's advantage. Specifically, I will argue that the expected payoff of polarization for the state depends on the distribution of ideological preferences across the electorate: if these preferences are somewhat (albeit not necessarily significantly) skewed toward one pole of the ideological spectrum, choosing to side with that pole in an extremist fashion can end up rewarding the state electorally.

## Polarization in Eight Steps: Government-Opposition Relations, 1999–2006

Before demonstrating the political payoffs of pursuing polarization, I begin with a quick overview of polarization in Venezuela from 1999 to 2006. The object of this exercise is to generate inductively a conceptual account of how polarization unfolds. In this account, polarization occurs as a result of state-initiated policies to expand the powers of the president, what I hereby call power grabs. From this point forward, Venezuelan politics polarized between incumbent and opposition in a manner that, analyzed using some rational-choice tools, was fairly predictable.

The first step in the rise of polarization in Venezuela was a major *power grab* on the part of state-holders. A power grab consists of an expansion of control over crucial political institutions at the expense of the opposition. All transfers of powers after democratic elections involve some form of power grab by winners, but in Venezuela in 1999–2001, the seizure went far beyond what anyone had expected. The power grab occurred through formal, informal, and in some cases, unconstitutional mechanisms, all in a period of two years. It included:

a) the president's imposition, against the recommendations by an official advisory board, of a rule for electing delegates to a constituent assembly that eliminated the traditional system of proportional representation in favor of a majoritarian system;

b) the speedy enactment of a hyper-statist, hyper-presidentialist, anti-party, pro-military constitution[13] by an assembly in which the opposition had less than five percent of seats;

c) the abrogation of political institutions in which the opposition had a presence (the new constitution permanently abolished the Senate; the constituent assembly decreed the temporary suspension of all public authorities including the Congress but not the president), and the creation of a new legislative body, the Congresillo, consisting of 11 members of the constituent assembly and 10 unelected appointees;

d) the restaffing with loyalists of the national electoral monitoring body (the CNE) and the judicial system (unconstitutional means);

e) the cessation of subsidies to unions, together with attempts to dissolve unions;

f) the effort to increase control over the education system (the 1011 Decree created new state-appointed supervisors for schools) (informal means);

g) the 2001 enabling laws, which gave the Executive full discretion to change legislature without consultations or approval, as was done on 49 different laws;

h) the creation of Círculos Bolivarianos in April 2001, which were groups of citizens, often armed, charged with defending the revolution in local neighborhoods;[14]

i) the proposal to reform education by decree, aiming to increase the discretion of the office of the president to appoint teachers and change the curriculum in both public and private schools (Decree 1011, never implemented).

It is important to highlight that these measures were less radical than some proposals advocated by many Chavistas and sometimes even Chávez.[15] In addition, in the area of economics, the changes were probably less radical than in the realm of politics, which frustrated one of Chávez's main political allies, the PPT (Patria para Todos).[16] Chávez's power grab was mostly at the level of politics and political institutions. More than any previous administration, that of Chávez reduced the power of organized political groups and expanded the powers of the Executive branch dramatically in two years. For the opposition, these measures meant only one thing: "the elimination of horizontal accountability."[17]

Presidential power grabs have a predictable consequence for government-opposition relations. In addition to lessening horizontal accountability, power grabs *increase the insecurity* of the opposition. This new insecurity, in turn, had its own predictable secondary effect: it helped the opposition solve collective action problems and thus encourage *unification*. Consistent with the classic argument made by O'Donnell and Schmitter,[18] and reiterated more recently by rational-choice scholars,[19] power grabs by state-holders increase the stakes of politics and the insecurity of those who do not control the state. Such grabs make those in the opposition feel more precarious than how they felt shortly after losing recent elections. The opponents see that they have been denied resources, institutional doors, and arenas to compete. As realists in international relations theory argue, power concentration and perceptions of threat lead to alliance formation.[20] Hence once ideologically incompatible opposition groups, feeling equally threatened by rising presidential powers, begin to join forces against the state. Heightened fear revives and emboldens the opposition, which begins to consider more radical, extra-institutional means to assert itself.[21] Venezuela thus experienced what Norden deems the surest way to radicalize the opposition: the state became both "combative" and "exclusionary." This explains why Venezuela's fragmented party system suddenly coalesced into a united front (the Coordinadora Democrática). The opposition proved capable of organizing one general strike, 19 massive marches—some of the largest ever in Venezuela—endless *cacerolazos* (collective pot-banging actions) and two massive signature-collection campaigns demanding a recall referendum, all in the space of two years.[22] The resuscitated opposition did not agree on all tactics or even on a common leader, but its ability to act in unison had never been so clear in Venezuela's democratic history.

Power grabs also have a predictable effect on incumbent forces: *soft-liners defect*, causing a significant recomposition of incumbent forces.[23] Defections were seen among close advisers to the president, allied parties, cabinet members, pro-government legislators, the military, and key electoral constituencies. As early as 2000, for instance, three close friends of Chávez and leading participants of the February 1992 coup left the movement; one of them, Francisco Arias Cárdenas, ran against Chávez in the 2000 election.[24] A second one, Luis Miquilena, Chávez's first Minister of the Interior and close campaign adviser, also joined the opposition in early 2002, because he did not want to be linked with a government that is "stained with blood" and which makes laws "in which no one participates."[25] In addition, the ruling coalition suffered the defection of one of its most important party allies, the MAS (Movimiento al Socialismo), several leading legislators (Ernesto Alvarenga, former leader of the MVR parliamentary bloc), and a smaller party, the PPT (Patria Para Todos; Alí Rodríguez's party), which defected in protest of Chávez's numerous military appointments.[26]

Defections occurred among cabinet ministers as well, leading to a very high degree of cabinet instability during Chávez's early years. Table 1 provides the rate at which Venezuelan presidents changed cabinet yearly. It shows that the Chávez cabinet has been the most unstable one since 1958 by far, even exceeding the second Pérez administration, which had been the most embittered of

## Table 1.
## Ministerial Turnover Rates, Venezuela 1959–2006.

| Presidency | Total Annual Changes | Number of Ministers | Rate Change |
|---|---|---|---|
| 1959 | 13 | 13 | 1.00 |
| 1960 | 6 | 13 | 0.46 |
| 1961 | 6 | 13 | 0.46 |
| 1962 | 3 | 13 | 0.23 |
| 1963 | 0 | 13 | 0.00 |
| **Total Rómulo Betancourt** | 28 | 65 | 0.43 |
| 1964 | 17 | 13 | 1.31 |
| 1965 | 1 | 13 | 0.08 |
| 1966 | 3 | 13 | 0.23 |
| 1967 | 6 | 13 | 0.46 |
| 1968 | 5 | 13 | 0.38 |
| **Total Raúl Leoni** | 32 | 65 | 0.49 |
| 1969 | 19 | 13 | 1.46 |
| 1970 | 3 | 13 | 0.23 |
| 1971 | 7 | 13 | 0.54 |
| 1972 | 4 | 13 | 0.31 |
| 1973 | 1 | 13 | 0.08 |
| **Total Rafael Caldera** | 34 | 65 | 0.52 |
| 1974 | 18 | 14 | 1.29 |
| 1975 | 7 | 14 | 0.50 |
| 1976 | 4 | 14 | 0.29 |
| 1977 | 17 | 18 | 0.94 |
| 1978 | 2 | 18 | 0.11 |
| **Total Carlos Andrés Pérez** | 48 | 78 | 0.62 |
| 1979 | 24 | 18 | 1.33 |
| 1980 | 1 | 18 | 0.06 |
| 1981 | 8 | 18 | 0.44 |
| 1982 | 9 | 18 | 0.50 |
| 1983 | 4 | 18 | 0.22 |
| **Total Luis Herrera Campins** | 46 | 90 | 0.51 |
| 1984 | 23 | 17 | 1.35 |
| 1985 | 7 | 17 | 0.41 |
| 1986 | 8 | 17 | 0.47 |
| 1987 | 7 | 17 | 0.41 |
| 1988 | 10 | 17 | 0.59 |
| **Total Jaime Lusinchi** | 55 | 85 | 0.65 |

## Table 1.
### Ministerial Turnover Rates, Venezuela 1959–2006. (continued)

| Presidency | Total Annual Changes | Number of Ministers | Rate Change |
|---|---|---|---|
| 1989 | 33 | 17 | 1.94 |
| 1990 | 9 | 17 | 0.53 |
| 1991 | 6 | 17 | 0.35 |
| 1992 | 18 | 17 | 1.06 |
| 1993 | 24 | 17 | 1.41 |
| **Total Carlos Andrés Pérez** | 90 | 85 | 1.06 |
| 1994 | 36 | 18 | 2.00 |
| 1995 | 6 | 18 | 0.33 |
| 1996 | 12 | 18 | 0.67 |
| 1997 | 8 | 18 | 0.44 |
| 1998 | 12 | 18 | 0.67 |
| **Total Rafael Caldera** | 74 | 90 | 0.82 |
| 1999 | 33 | 14 | 2.36 |
| 2000 | 28 | 16 | 1.75 |
| 2001 | 11 | 18 | 0.61 |
| 2002 | 26 | 19 | 1.37 |
| 2003 | 9 | 20 | 0.45 |
| 2004 | 19 | 25 | 0.76 |
| 2005 | 12 | 27 | 0.44 |
| 2006 | 15 | 27 | 0.56 |
| **Total Hugo R. Chávez Frías** | 153 | 118 | 1.30 |

all. Most of the instability occurred between 2002 and 2004. Even sectors of the military defected.[27] There are many reasons for high turnover rates (firings, policy change, internal struggles, etc.). But a significant factor was also voluntary cabinet departures due to ideological or policy disagreements with the president.

Many members of the National Assembly switched to the opposition as well. By early 2005, the share of seats in the National Assembly controlled by the ruling party coalition was 51 percent, down from 65.5 after the 2000 legislative elections.

Defections occurred not just at the level of political and military leaders, but also among Chávez's two core constituencies: the previously disenchanted voters, and the very poor. The former group consisted of ardent critics of the status quo ante who had supported Chávez's election and then

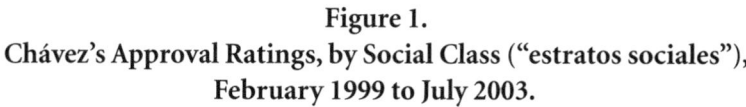

# Figure 1.
## Chávez's Approval Ratings, by Social Class ("estratos sociales"), February 1999 to July 2003.

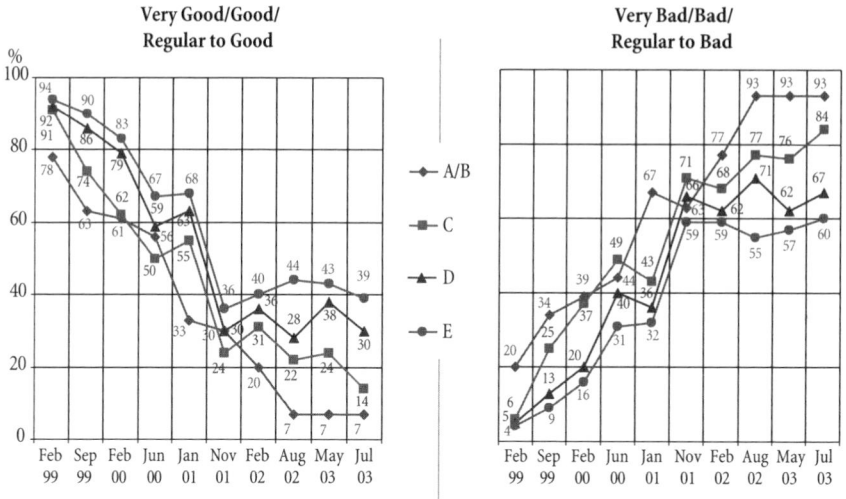

*The difference between 100 percent and totals represent the "don't know/no answer" category.

Note: A/B = Uppermost income levels; E = lowest income levels.

Source: Datanálisis (2003).

became dismayed by the way in which the new majority ended up replicating, rather than mending, the old majorities' proclivity toward exclusion. The latter defecting group was the least expected. The defection of the very poor is clear from a series of public opinion polls in 2000–2003 that identify the social class of respondents (Figure 1): Chávez's approval ratings among the very poor, initially overwhelmingly high, declined precipitously. Indeed, his approval ratings plummeted across all income groups (A/B = uppermost income category; D = lowest income). By 2003, disapproval rates surpassed approval rates in all income categories.

Defections of this magnitude—among leaders, professional peers (military officers), organizations, and voters—were rare in Venezuela. They were last seen, perhaps to a lesser degree, during the second Carlos Andrés Pérez administration (1989–1993), when significant portions of his party and constituents abandoned him, producing a political "black hole" that ended up destabilizing the political system.[28] Such defections are a predictable response to the deliberate pursuit of radical policies.

Defections have a huge feeding effect on polarization: they *change the balance of forces* between the incumbent and the opposition. First, defections allow the opposition to obtain new allies and, more important, new reasons for hope: they feel that they have a good chance to unseat state-holders, and they feel vindicated. This is one more reason that the opposition felt so galvanized in 2001–2004. Second, defections may make the incumbent feel increasingly insecure (as a result of its political shrinkage) and, more important, further inclined toward radicalization (because moderates are leaving, and the power holder's inner circle becomes more homogenous and radical-dominated). In short, extremism on each side becomes *mutually reinforcing*. Once the political system splits between an inflamed and revived opposition and a shrinking and less moderate incumbent force, each side experiences a spiraling sense of political threat. The opposition observes the incumbent taking increasingly hard-core positions; the incumbents observe the opposition adopting increasingly obstructionist positions, for example in this case, the marches and the call for resignation. Observations of reality confirm everyone's suspicions that adversaries are threatening.

Each pole increases its preference for engaging with the other through *extra-institutional* means. The opposition, for instance, prefers an extra-institutional turn because it feels emboldened by a surge in numbers and yet denied institutional opportunities to influence policy. Thus, the Venezuelan opposition organized massive marches (2002–03), supported the coups of April 2002, and collaborated with the oil strike of the winter of 2002–03, while using the media to virulently attack the government. The government in turn observes that existing institutions, such as the organizations of civil society, remain in the hands of opponents and, because it is suffering defections, it worries about elections. Thus, Chávez pursued further power grabs in 2002–2003 to maintain his hold on power: the illegal firing of 20,000 oil strikers, further attempts to politicize electoral institutions and avoid a referendum, and declining inclusion of opposition in policy dialogues.

At some point, polarization results in *some type of showdown*—the state calls in the military to repress its opponents; the opposition decides to take up arms; or both sides work out an institutional solution. In Venezuela, the showdown took the form of an epic fight for a recall referendum between 2003 and 2004.[29] The government made a great effort to prevent this electoral process from taking place. For a government that was claiming to be thoroughly democratic, these delays were a blatant contradiction of its own ideology, to say the least. But the opposition's mobilization together with international pressure finally compelled the state to agree to carry out the referendum. Each side devoted huge resources to win, but the state's spending campaign was simply unprecedented and in the end decisive, reversing the incumbent's approval ratings and allowing the president to prevail electorally.[30]

Beyond this showdown, it is unclear how the opposition will respond; this is where the game-theoretic approach becomes a bit more indeterminate. Analysts have spent a lot of time explaining the government's victory in 2004. But an equally important question is why the opposition did not respond violently, when so many were convinced that the process was unfair and the outcome fraudulent. Instead, the opposition went into a peaceful retreat. Maybe it was exhaustion, demoralization, lack of international support, internal recriminations, the sudden economic boom starting in 2003, or a combination of the above that explains this retreat. Whatever the cause, the sudden deflation of the opposition was indeterminate and cannot be explained deductively with rational-choice arguments.

Equally indeterminate was the state's behavior following this showdown; namely, its decision to carry out further power grabs following the 2004 referendum. Why would a winner in a political struggle, in this case the incumbent, pursue radicalization rather than reconciliation?[31] Prior to 2004, one possible explanation for persistent polarization is that the opposition had also turned hard-line. But after the 2004 referendum, the opposition became increasingly tame, in part demoralized by its stunning defeat. The new president of Fedecámaras, for instance, José Luis Betancourt, announced his willingness to accept the government's economic policy. The opposition agreed to participate in the 2006 presidential elections and was not involved in a single act of violence or disruptive strike. And yet, rather than engage in a process of reconciliation, as some victors do, the incumbent in Venezuela responded to its 2004 electoral victory by escalating extremist political decisions that further scared the opposition. The government drafted a new military doctrine to prepare the country against "an asymmetrical war"; embarked on the creation of two million urban reservists to help in the "maintenance of internal order"; expanded the presence of Cuban technical advisers from 20,000 to 50,000; surprisingly announced—abroad, in Porto Alegre—that the president and his governments were "socialist" (no more emphasis on participatory democracy); reformed the criminal code to ban *cacerolazos* and acts of disrespect against public officials; turned more aggressive in prosecuting citizens of the opposition who participated in the April 2002 march; and targeted more than 800 private properties for expropriation in 2005. Furthermore, between 2005 and 2006, the government activated the largest job and welfare discrimination in the history of Venezuela, using electoral lists (Lista Tascón and Lista Maisanta), which included how people voted in the referendum, for deciding who garnered state employment and benefits.[32] All these acts were highly threatening to opponents, to say the least, and not exactly easy to explain as a tit-for-tat response to the opposition since the opposition was actually in retreat.

## Why Polarize?

If my argument that Venezuela's polarization from 2001 through 2006 was intentionally driven by the state is correct, I must be able to show motive. This can be done by looking at electoral payoffs and determining whether the pursuit of radicalization can ever be electorally rewarding. Electoral payoff from radicalization can be demonstrated by examining the electoral consequences of different strategies—moderation and radicalization—on the political loyalties of voting blocs across the ideological spectrum.

The effect of moderation and radicalization on voters depends on the voters' position in the ideological spectrum. Let us assume that a leftist government decides to pursue moderate policies such as establishing a cooperative relation with the United States and the opposition, as well as promoting pro-business policies, the so-called shift to the center in policy.[33] This would have the following impact: the center left applauds and becomes supportive, but the extreme left becomes disappointed. The extreme right, never happy with a center-left government, remains unimpressed. Complications occur within the center right, which probably splits into three groups: one small portion supports the government (the result of pro-incumbent pull in presidential politics); a second portion becomes ambivalent, not exactly sure how to respond (swing voters, or what in Venezuela are called the *ni/ni,* or neither/nor); and a third group may decide to join the opposition.

If a leftist government instead decides to radicalize, for example, by pursuing a heavy dose of statism, issuing decrees, increasing nationalizations and expropriations, or inviting 20,000-plus Cuban advisors to come in, which in Latin America is a clear marker of radical preferences, the consequences across the political spectrum are different. The extreme left cheers. The extreme right panics and becomes even more extremely disloyal. This in turn has an impact on both the center left and the center right.[34] The center left splits, with the majority moving further to the left (in shock at the rise of a far right) and a minority staying in an ambivalent position, repulsed by the extreme position of each camp. The center right suffers a similar split.

For the sake of the analysis, Table 2 stipulates a series of hypothetical rules based on the previous analysis. In a nutshell, state policies of moderation split the center right three ways (support, ambivalence, and defection), and policies of radicalization split both the center left (two-thirds turns sup-

## Table 2.
## Moderation or Radicalization:
## Hypothetical Consequences across the Ideological Spectrum.

| Leftist Government Policies | Voters | | | |
|---|---|---|---|---|
| | Extreme Left | Center Left | Center Right | Extreme Right |
| Moderation | Defects | Support | Splits: ⅓ support; ⅓ ambivalent; ⅓ defect | Defects |
| Radicalization | Supports | Splits: ⅔ support; ⅓ ambivalent | Splits: ¼ ambivalent; ¾ defects | Defects (Turns Extremist) |

portive; one-third turns ambivalent) and split the center right (one-fourth turns ambivalent; three-fourths turn to the extreme right).

If one applies these hypothetical rules to different political settings, the political payoffs of moderation and radicalization on voters become easy to see. Loyalties to either the government or the opposition will vary the more asymmetrical the ideological distribution of voters. Table 3 provides political settings with various degrees of asymmetry, that is, in terms of proportion of left to right, and proportion of extreme left to center left. The table also provides the number of supporting, ambivalent, and opposing forces that, given each setting, would result from moderation versus radicalization.

The first setting consists of a political spectrum in which moderate voters dominate. This setting reflects the median-voter assumption, namely, that most voters are concentrated in the middle of the spectrum. Table 3 lists two possible cases under this context: extreme forces constitute tiny minorities (Case A), and extreme forces constitute larger minorities (Case B). Applying the rules from Table 2 to Case A shows that a strategy of moderation is unambiguously optimal for the incumbent: it maximizes the number of supporters (relative to a policy of radicalization) and minimizes the number of opponents. For Case B, moderation is less optimal but still appealing: while moderation increases the number of opponents slightly, it significantly increases the number of supporters relative to a policy of radicalization.

## Table 3.
## Impact of Moderation and Radicalization on Voters' Political Loyalties toward Incumbents.

| | Hypothetical Voter Distribution Across Political Spectrum | | | | Outcomes: Political Loyalties | | |
|---|---|---|---|---|---|---|---|
| | EL | CL | CR | ER | Supportive | Ambivalent | Defectors |
| **Center Forces Dominate** | | | | | | | |
| A. Extremists are weak minority | 10 | 40 | 40 | 10 | | | |
| Moderation | | | | | 53.3 | 13.3 | 33.3 |
| Radicalization | | | | | 36.7 | 23.3 | 40.0 |
| B. Extremists are strong minority | 15 | 35 | 30 | 20 | | | |
| Moderation | | | | | 45.0 | 10 | 46.7 |
| Radicalization | | | | | 38.3 | 19.2 | 42.5 |
| **Left Is Stronger than Right (60/40)** | | | | | | | |
| C. CL Stronger than EL | 20 | 40 | 30 | 10 | | | |
| Moderation | | | | | 50.0 | 10 | 43.3 |
| Radicalization | | | | | 46.7 | 20.8 | 32.5 |
| D. EL as Strong as CL | 30 | 30 | 25 | 15 | | | |
| Moderation | | | | | 38.3 | 8.3 | 55.0 |
| Radicalization | | | | | 50.0 | 16.3 | 33.8 |
| **Left Is Dominant (65/35)** | | | | | | | |
| E. CL is stronger | 30 | 35 | 25 | 10 | | | |
| Moderation | | | | | 43.3 | 8.3 | 51.7 |
| Radicalization | | | | | 53.3 | 17.9 | 28.8 |
| F. EL is dominant | 35 | 30 | 25 | 10 | | | |
| Moderation | | | | | 38.3 | 8.3 | 55.0 |
| Radicalization | | | | | 55.0 | 16.3 | 28.8 |

Notes:
EL = Extreme left; CL = Center-left; CR = Center-right; ER = Extreme right.
To determine percentage of supporters, ambivalent groups, and defectors, the rules in Table 2 were applied to the values in the "Hypothetical Voter Distribution" Column.

As the size of the left increases relative to the right, and with it the proportion of the extreme left, the political payoffs reverse completely. Rows C and D show political settings in which the median-voter assumption has been altered by increasing the overall size of the left relative to the right by 20 points. In case C, the moderate left is stronger relative to the extreme left; in case D, the reverse is true. In both cases, a strategy of polarization is more appealing for the incumbent: it always produces more supporters than opponents. Although in case C radicalization reduces the number of supporters relative to moderation, it is still an appealing strategy because it diminishes significantly the number of defectors.

The final set of cases relaxes the median-voter assumption further: the left is far larger than the right (65 to 35). In these circumstances, polarization is even more preferable: the number of supporters relative to defectors increases by a significant degree.

An important observation from Table 3 is that it is not necessary for a majority of the electorate to be extreme left for a leftist government to derive political payoffs from taking an extreme left position. Even in situations where the extreme left represents just 20 percent of the electorate (Case C), a leftist government can profit from radicalization, provided the left in general is slightly larger than the right.

In another work I provide evidence that Venezuela in the early 2000s probably found itself somewhere among cases C, D, E: the left, and in particular the extreme left, were strong relative to the right, albeit not majoritarian.[35] Under these conditions, radicalization can be politically rewarding for a leftist incumbent. Radicalization is thus more supply-side than demand-side driven. It is preferred by the incumbent because of its political advantages, rather than demanded by a majority of the electorate.

### Tangible and Intangible Rewards

Political reward does not mean absence of risk. While the move to radicalization can increase the number of supporters and reduce the number of opponents, which is optimal for incumbents, it yields a new type of risk: the size of ambivalent groups increases. These are voters who are undecided about which pole to support. By definition, ambivalent groups have no fixed loyalties or even desire to vote. As case C in Table 3 shows, choosing radicalization over moderation can lead to a huge increase in these ambivalent groups. Ambivalent voters can be risky for the government. Insofar as their loyalties remain in flux, such independents can at any point turn toward the opposition. The safest strategy for any government is to find a way to court these groups, or at least prevent them from ever siding with the opposition.

Most polls provide evidence that the expectation derived from Table 3 became reality in Venezuela: ambivalent groups increased soon after Chávez began to radicalize. By July 2001, one reputable poll was already beginning to classify some Venezuelan voters as "repentant Chavistas."[36] The size of this group swelled from 8.9 percent in February 2001 to 14.7 percent in July 2001 and 32.8 percent in December 2001.[37] By June 2002, these repentant Chavistas turned into "light Chavistas," "light anti-Chavistas," and "hard anti-Chavistas," confirming the hypothesis that radicalization yields incumbent defections. By mid 2002, the government found itself confronting the largest opposition since coming to office.

The key point is simply that even in situations of polarization, the size of the swing group is nontrivial and likely to grow. These voters are far more important at that time than in situations of moderation. And in cases C and D, ambivalent groups can turn to the other side, thereby imperiling the government. Thus, even radical leftist governments pursuing polarization, and thus maximizing supporters, need to develop strategies to deal with ambivalent groups.

What has the Chávez administration done to address ambivalent groups?[38] This is where the three other pillars of Chavismo in office come into place: clientelism, impunity for those who engage in corruption, and job discrimination. These practices exist in all regimes. But in Venezuela under Chávez, they assumed two key characteristics: First, they became central to the regime.[39] Second, they were specifically targeted toward the *ni/ni* groups.

Clientelism refers to the distribution of material benefits from a strong political actor (in this case, the state) to a less powerful actor (in this case, ordinary citizens and small civil society organizations). In the context of a radical leftist government, clientelism is likely to work mostly among the less ideological sectors of the population: the extreme left does not need such incentives to support a radical leftist government, the extreme right will not be swayed by them either. In the context of polarization, clientelism works mostly to court the less ideology-driven voters.

Another strategy that Chávez has deployed is corruption and impunity for those friends of the government engaged in corruption.[40] In contrast to clientelism, corruption entails passing benefits from strong actors, in this case, the state, to other strong actors, such as the military or business groups. Like clientelism, corruption is a strategy designed for the non-ideologized groups. Because strong actors can act as major veto groups, not just of policy but also of the administration's tenure in office, it is important for governments in unstable political settings to deploy significant resources to deal with these actors.

To explain the explosion of corruption under Chávez, it is perhaps not necessary to invoke the rise of ambivalent groups in need of being co-opted. The oil boom and the lack of accountability that characterized the regime are enough to provide an explanation for rising corruption. What the rise of ambivalent groups helps to explain is the main destination of the corruption under Chávez. In situations of radicalization, the opposition is so galvanized that it is vital for the ruling group to have a mechanism for co-opting other elites (military and business groups) as a shield against possible coups. Chávez began to offer corruption and impunity to the military almost since the first day in office, and he started offering corruption and impunity to cooperative business groups in 2003, when state revenues began to swell.

The final strategy deployed by the Chávez administration to deal with ambivalent groups is job discrimination. The administration has repeatedly stated, in no uncertain terms, that the largest benefits of his administration (government jobs, government contracts, and government subsidies) are earmarked exclusively for supporters, which the government in 2006 called the *rojo, rojitos* (red, very red ones). Matching names in the Maisanta List with household surveys, Rodríguez et al. find that voters who were identified as Chávez opponents experienced a 5 percent drop in earnings and a 1.5 percentage point drop in employment rates after the voter list was released.[41] In addition, the government does all it can to publicize the notion that it knows who signed the recall referendum petition (via the famous Lista Tascón and Lista Maisanta).[42] The Chávez administration thus likes to portray itself as a watchful government that rewards supporters and punishes opponents through exclusion from clientelism, corruption, and government jobs. This image means to convey that there are large gains from staying loyal and large losses from dissenting. Again, this is a strategy that affects mostly the non-ideological, ambivalent groups.

In sum, the Chavista coalition changed enormously by 2005. Back in 1999, the movement offered a progressive ideology that promised to free Venezuela from the stranglehold of the old parties and frequent economic crises. This agenda was pro-change, but not radical. It attracted the vast majorities. Since then, the agenda has turned radical. This attracted the loyalty of the extreme left, but it also created polarization, and with the two poles also a large group of ambivalent voters.[43] To keep this ambivalent group from completely defecting, the administration has relied on clientelism, impunity, and job discrimination. These strategies allowed the government to target ambivalent groups and thus increase the number of supporters beyond that which the extreme left bloc provides.

Consequently, the coalition of leaders and voters who supported Chávez in the 2006 election was different from those who supported him in the beginning. It was revolutionary, but also conservative. Chávez's supporters no longer included the extreme left and the losers in Venezuela, but new and old winners: welfare recipients, actors with ties to the state, and those who profit from corruption. Although these winners came from different income groups (welfare recipients are mostly poor, state employees come from the lower-middle class, and corrupt folks are wealthier), they share the same electoral objective—to preserve their gains. These gains are access to social programs, state jobs and contracts, and impunity. What unites these groups is a fear that the opposition will take their gains away.

We can now understand why the Chávez administration relies on radicalism *and* intense clientelism/impunity/intimidation. The former maximizes the number of supporters relative to defectors, due to the large albeit not majoritarian status of the extreme left, but it also increases the number of ambivalent groups. The latter policies target such groups. Combined, both sets of policies give rise to electoral winning coalitions that, paradoxically, include the odd combination of committed revolutionaries and less ideological, state-dependent actors, many of whom are social elites. In addition, the government seeks to encourage the abstention of opponents (by never entirely offering guarantees that the vote is secret and safe). The aim is to win elections by more than a small minority.

## Power Grabs after 2006: The RCTV Case, the Constitutional Reform, and the 2008 Elections

After 2006, the government pursued its radicalization drive further. The three most important examples were: the May 2007 decision not to renew the operating license of Radio Caracas Televisión (RCTV), the proposal to reform the constitution, and the decision to blacklist opposition candidates for the 2008 elections for governors and mayors. Yet these steps did not provide any substantial electoral payoff.[44] This section discusses each of these policies of radicalization and why there was no electoral payoff this time around.

### The RCTV Case

RCTV was the most widely viewed TV network in the country, covering 90 percent of the territory with 35–40 percent of audience share, consisting mostly of poor and uneducated sectors. Its programming focused mostly on comedy and soap operas. In December 2006, Chávez announced that he would not renew RCTV's license. The government never tried to conceal its political bias: its argument for shutting down RCTV was that the station supported the 2002 coup and since then had been broadcasting critical stories about the government. RCTV responded that the license was not due to expire in 2007 and that these allegations were unfair, unproven, and thus unfounded grounds for shutting down a media company in a democracy.

Venezuela's ambassador to the United States called the suspension a "simple regulatory matter."[45] Yet the suspension of RCTV's license represented one of the most serious attacks against the media, and thus freedom of expression, in the entire Western Hemisphere since the transition to democracy in Latin America began in the early 1980s, arguably as serious as Peru's President Fujimori's decision to take over Channel 12 in 1997. The Chávez government acted without offering any proof of guilt of RCTV authorities, consulting the public through a referendum, or discussing the issue with the National Assembly.

During the five-month period between the date that the decision was announced and the date in which it was finally carried out, almost every major opposition group and renowned international NGOs condemned the government's plan. As the decision date approached, with the government showing no sign of yielding, a series of massive protests by university students enveloped various cities, prompting the government to use tear gas, rubber bullets, and water cannons.

Hinterlaces, a polling firm that accurately predicted Chávez's victory in December 2006, revealed that more than 74 percent of the population disapproved the RCTV decision, which plunged Chávez's approval ratings to 31 percent, the lowest since 2002.[46] Condemnation from abroad was also harsh: The socialist Spanish government, the European Parliament, the French Socialist party, the Brazilian and Chilean senates, the Costa Rican congress, Human Rights Watch, Reporters without Borders and Amnesty International, among other international NGOs, strongly condemned Chávez. Not since 2004 did Chávez face such massive domestic and international condemnation. The president responded by calling his critics "saboteurs" and "lackeys of imperialism,"[47] telling them *"qué se vayan al carajo,"* a more vulgar way of saying that they can go to hell, threatening to unleash "Jacobin revolutionary violence" against them,[48] and traveling to Cuba on June 13.

### The Constitutional Reform Case

The 2007 proposal to reform the constitution constituted an even more serious attempt to enlarge presidential powers than ever took place in Venezuela since 1958. This proposal was brought up through extremely undemocratic channels. The president designated a small, secretive group of advisers to draft the proposed changes, without much input from anyone else in Venezuela, not even close political allies. The resulting proposal—a 44-page single-spaced document—constituted the most radical blank check on presidential powers in the democratic history of Latin America. Here are some highlights:

a) The president's term in office is extended from 6 to 7 years.

b) Indefinite reelection is allowed for the president but not for any other elected office.

c) Presidentially appointed *consejos comunales* receive constitutional ranking as key government units at the local level, thereby bypassing and possibly replacing elected offices at sub-national levels. Chávez spoke of creating 600,000 such *consejos.*[49] No mention was made as to whether members to these *consejos* would be elected democratically.

d) The Missions, the government's famous social programs funded directly by the Executive branch with almost no scrutiny or accountability, obtain constitutional ranking. Because these programs are under the complete jurisdiction of the president, assigning them constitutional ranking would undermine the authority of local and regional offices (elected bodies) to provide social services.

e) Private monopolies are penalized, but state monopolies (on strategic sectors of the economy) are expanded. The state would obtain the right to expropriate private property without prior judicial authorization.

f) The reforms sought to eliminate Article 115, which stipulates that all persons have the "right to . . . enjoy and use freely (*disponer*) their property (*bienes*)," thereby abolishing the right to private property.

g) External funding of political groups would be banned (while simultaneously allowing the state to finance the ruling party).

h) The reforms expanded the number of vice presidents, all of whom would be designated without legislative approval.

i) The new constitution assigned a domestic enemy for the armed forces (the *oligarquías*) as well as an external enemy (imperialism), in violation of the democratic principle against declaring one group of citizens enemies of the state without a trial.

j) The education sector was called to promote a socialist state, thereby undermining the notion of freedom of education.

k) Presidential powers during states of siege would expand (due process would be eliminated; no limits to the duration of states of siege were stipulated; the right to the presumption of innocence would be abolished); thereby violating key rights enshrined in the United Nations Committee for Human Rights and the Inter-American Court for Human Rights.[50]

l) Voters had the right to vote for the reforms, but no mechanism was established to introduce amendments or to vote item by item.

The constitutional reform, together with the RCTV affair, generated the same effects as previous power grabs (unification of the opposition, defections from the government, showdown in the streets). The most important defections were: the departure of one of Chávez's allied parties (Podemos); the open criticism by Chávez's first wife (Marisabel Rodríguez, herself a pro-Chávez member of the 1999 Constituent Assembly); and the virulent criticism of a former Defense Minister (Raúl Isaías Baduel), who openly campaigned against the constitutional reform, calling it a form of coup.

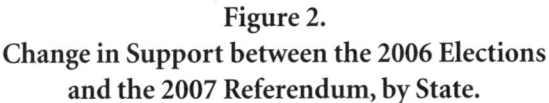

**Figure 2.**
**Change in Support between the 2006 Elections**
**and the 2007 Referendum, by State.**

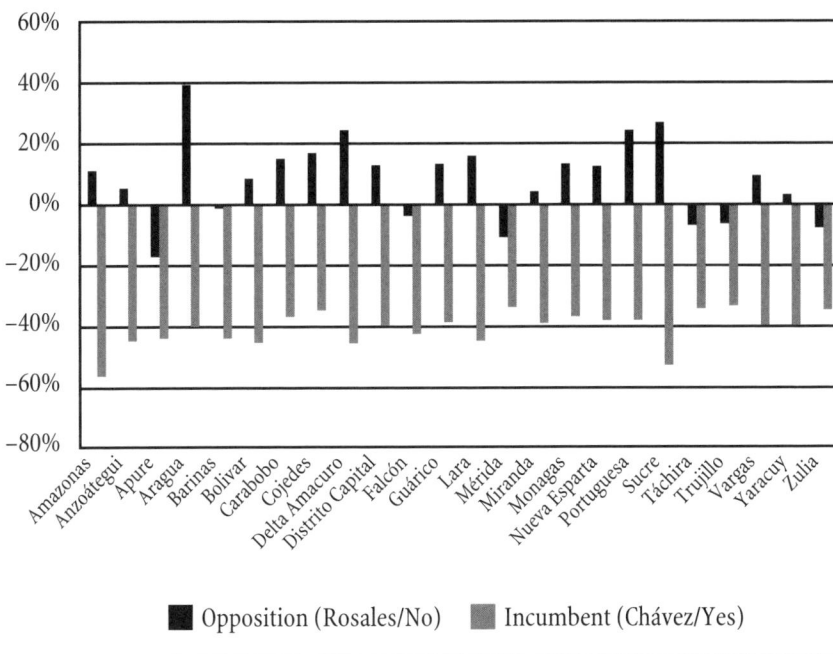

Source: CNE.

Despite these similarities, there was one difference: in 2007, radicalization did not pay off for the government. The government lost the December 2007 referendum to change the constitution. Although the margin of defeat was small (1.4 percent), these results were nonetheless historical because they were the first electoral defeat for the government. More dramatically, the election revealed a worrisome electoral trend for the regime: rising abstentionism among its ranks. The pro-Chavista vote was 3 million short of the one in 2006. Figure 2 compares the results of the 2007 constitutional reform referendum with the 2006 presidential elections state by state. The difference between the pro-Chávez vote in 2006 and the YES vote in 2007 in some cases was as large as 40 percent. In contrast, the opposition gained votes in 17 of 24 states; elsewhere, it lost very little, seldom more than 10 percent. More than de-alignment (switching sides), these figures suggest massive voter abstention (and thus, possible defection) among Chavistas.

### The 2008 Election for Governors and Mayors

The trend in the direction of increasing state radicalism continued after 2007, also with negative consequences for the government. The next contest was the 2008 elections for governors and mayors. The government intensified its bellicose discourse against the opposition, calling them "disgusting traitors," "criminals," "*pitiyankis,*" "*escuálidos,*" and "lackeys of imperialism," but actually went beyond mere name-calling. It also introduced a list of citizens who were disqualified from running for office.

This list was drafted by the comptroller general Clodosbaldo Russián in February of 2008. It included the names of approximately 400 Venezuelan citizens who were declared disqualified to run. Eventually, the list was reduced to 270 people. The reason given by the government was that these people faced accusations of corruption. Without trials, the government nevertheless denied them the right to run for office. Among the names on this list were two of the most prominent opposition candidates, Leopoldo López and Enrique Mendoza.

The opposition did not fall into the trap of repeating the extremist positions of 2001–2004. Instead of declaring an electoral boycott, the opposition reiterated its intention to participate. Instead of demanding that the government step down, the opposition campaigned against the poor public administration, promising solutions to municipal problems like crime, trash collection, and the deterioration of infrastructure. The government wanted the elections to be a referendum on Chávez (who remained popular), but the opposition was able to mold the elections into a referendum on municipal issues. Furthermore, the opposition avoided the problem of fragmentation. Achieving greater unity for a regional election was not a trivial feat. Initially, there were more than 80 official registered parties nationwide. In Caracas alone, 48 parties identified themselves as anti-Chavistas. Yet the opposition produced "unity candidates" (one candidate supported by all of the opposition parties) in 17 of the 22 states.[51]

The opposition's avoidance of extremist and disloyal positions proved fruitful. Almost 45 percent of the Venezuelan electoral population ended up in the ranks of the opposition, including two of the most important mayorships (Caracas, Maracaibo) and three of the most populous and economically diverse states (Maracaibo, Carabobo, and Miranda). The opposition had never before achieved such an important electoral advance.

### Explaining Polarization in 2007–2009

State-led extremism in 2007–2009 had different consequences than it had in the 2001–2004 period: it did not prove as electorally rewarding for the

government. This raises two questions. First, why did extremism stop pay-
ing off electorally? Second, why did the government persevere with extremism despite declining payoffs?

Regarding the first question, the rational-choice analysis offers two possible hypotheses. One is that the ideological distribution of voters in Venezuela
may have changed since 2006, returning perhaps to a more symmetrical distribution (a rise of the center). Another way of stating this point is that after
a certain point of leftward movement by the government, radicalization stops
generating gains if the electorate does not shift ideologically in tandem with
the state. The second reason might be that policies to target the *ni-ni* groups
began to falter. There is evidence on behalf of both explanations.

### Exhausting the Supply of Radicals

The more a state pursues radical politics (while the opposition de-escalates in
its response), the more the size of incumbent support is likely to shrink. This
is possibly what happened in 2006–2009. The government pursued more radical policies, but the opposition shied away from the destabilizing acts of
2002–03 (no more call for military coups, massive protests, recall referenda,
electoral boycotts). In this context of deradicalized opposition/radicalizing
government, the size of government supporters, especially the center-left,
shrinks. Perhaps the most critical mistake made by the government was to
interpret the 2006 presidential election as a mandate for more radicalism. No
doubt, some Chavista voters longed for more radicalism. But the government
may have overestimated the size of this bloc. One possible indicator of the
real size of the radicals by 2007 is the number of Venezuelans still hoping for
Chávez to press ahead with the defeated constitutional reforms. An early 2008
poll revealed that this bloc represents 28 percent of respondents.[52] This is evidence that the number of radicals is diminishing, which is what one would
expect the more the government turns to more extremist positions.

### Exhaustion of Social Policies

The second possible reason for the 2008 defeat is exhaustion of state policies to mobilize supporters and *ni-ni* voters. Despite record levels of economic growth in 2003–2007, serious microeconomic strains surfaced in
2007, followed by serious macroeconomic strains in 2008. This economic
turnaround hurt incumbent support. Most of it was the result of the state's
ill-advised policies.[53]

The government's position of discouraging private-sector investment
yielded persistent unemployment. Chávez has implemented the most anti-
business policies in Latin America. Venezuela ranks at number 172 of 178

**Figure 3.**
**Misery Index (Inflation and Unemployment Rates):**
**Venezuela and LAC (Latin America and the Caribbean).**

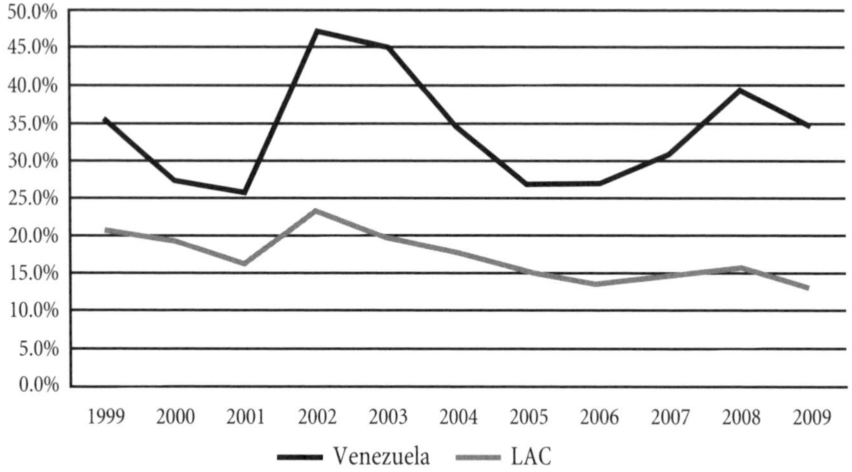

countries worldwide in terms of "ease of doing business," a World Bank ranking of degrees to which countries are pro-business; no other Latin American country scores lower.[54] In 2007, Venezuela actually experienced capital flight, which is rare for a country in the midst of a growth boom but predictable for a country with such an anti-business climate. By discouraging private investment, the government fuels unemployment. It then tries to fight unemployment with only one engine—the public sector. Thus, despite the dramatic expansion in public-sector jobs (almost 60 percent expansion since 2003), which actually helped to reduce in half the unemployment rate since 1999, private-sector job creation is lagging seriously, with a mere 13 percent growth, leaving the economy with a serious shortfall in employment of approximately 8.7 percent.[55]

Another mistaken policy is that of fiscal profligacy, which yields inflation. Government spending jumped from approximately 19 percent of GNP in 1999 to almost 30 percent in 2007. The result of this spending spree is that Venezuela, despite implementing one of the broadest systems of price controls in the Americas, began to experience the highest inflation rates in the world, which, combined with stubborn unemployment, is a recipe for poverty expansion (see Figure 3).

Venezuela is also suffering from consumer good shortages, the explanation for which would be quite easy to understand for any Economics 101 student. Price controls, especially in the context of inflation, produce supply constraints that lead to shortages. Stated simply, producers are unwilling to produce if the costs of production exceed profit projections. Inflation pushes costs up; price controls push revenues down. The result is production shortfalls. A study of 60 grocery stores in October 2007 revealed that three basic products (powdered milk, sugar, and beef) were unavailable in more in than 40 percent of the stores ("grave" scarcity); five products (black beans, chicken, white cheese, sardines, oatmeal) were missing in 21 to 40 percent of stores.[56] Even though some ministers are aware of this problem of *desabastecimiento* (lack of supply), Chávez refuses to lift price controls, arguing that lifting controls is "too capitalist" a solution.

Chávez's Missions, which were a crucial state policy to court independent voters, began to show signs of inefficacy by 2007. One of the most serious studies of the Missions' impact reveal that poverty reduction is considerably smaller than what is expected given the level of spending; education and health achievements are no more impressive than those expected from Venezuela's historical trend since the 1960s; and income inequality has actually expanded.[57] Furthermore, there is plenty of corruption and politically directed spending.[58] In 2007, with diminishing returns and dearth of new initiatives,[59] together with inattention to crime—currently, the top-priority issue for most Venezuelans[60]—as well as housing shortages, collapsing hospitals, decaying schools, and decrepit infrastructure, the government's image as champion of the poor might have eroded.

In short, the explanation for Chávez's 2007–08 electoral setback involves poorer microeconomic conditions than in 2004–2006, which depressed the Chavista vote; the president's tenure was not in question, which encouraged abstention and defections among Chavistas; few new social initiatives were launched; and there were fewer signs that the government was aggressively tackling corruption, crime, and other social problems. This became a period therefore of additional power grabs with fewer new "carrots" to co-opt ambivalent groups. It was also a period in which the opposition became less rather than more radical, in direct contrast with the state's behavior, which turned more rather than less radical. This meant that Venezuela's electorate came closer to approximating the prediction for case D in Table 3 (a pro-incumbent vote of approximately 49 percent).

### Limits of Rational Choice

The trickier question is: why did the government persist on a radicalization course despite signs of decreasing electoral returns after 2007? Here we reach the limits of the rational-choice argument laid out thus far.

One hypothesis that can be ruled out is that persistent radicalism was a response to opposition behavior. The most notable change in Venezuelan politics between 2001–2005 and 2006–2009 was that the opposition actually moderated its behavior.

A better explanation is that not enough time elapsed between 2007 and 2008 (or not enough concluding evidence surfaced) to persuade the government that the electoral payoff of radicalism had peaked. After all, the government's losses in 2008 were still not that costly and did not affect the 2009 referendum to extend term limits for all elected officers.

An even more persuasive explanation is path dependence. After so many years on a radical course, by 2008 the government had acquired plenty of institutional reasons and means to stay the course. One such reason was greater homogenization of the ruling coalition. By 2007, the moderate members of the ruling party were mostly gone, either as a result of defections or political defeats. Thus, internal pressures against radicalization had eased. Moreover, the state had already invested so much effort in defending radical positions that announcing an abrupt change of policy toward moderation would have been too inconsistent a policy switch. Yet a third possible reason was institutional capacity. By 2008, the government had acquired enough institutional capacity to continue to push for radical policies (state interventions and expropriations, excluding detractors and silencing the press) even if electoral support for these policies was waning. In other words, the utility of electoral rewards declined as the institutional capacity of the government to move forward with radical policies increased.

These last points are consistent with a path-dependence argument. The idea is that the chosen course (radicalization) generated feedback mechanisms that by 2007 were encouraging continuity. Path dependence thus trumped the potential power of political learning (acknowledging the declining electoral returns of radicalism) and strategic interaction (strict imitation of the opposition's behavior) in determining the behavior of the government after 2007.

Though I have no way of demonstrating it, my sense is that among the possible hypotheses for Chávez's continued radicalization beyond 2007, the least powerful is probably ideological conviction—the notion that Chávez has a strong ideological taste for radicalism. To me, this is a less powerful explanatory variable, not because it weighs little, but because it does not vary enough to explain the intensification of radicalism over the years. The argument could be made that Chávez had an affinity for radical, polarizing politics since he entered the political scene. In the 1990s, there is plenty of evidence suggesting that Chávez had such a preference (coup participation, aggressive discourse against politicians, close ties with Cuba starting the moment he was released from jail in 1994). The issue is why did Chávez contain those preferences, or kept them unrevealed, between 1998 and 2001, and began to exhibit them increasingly more openly thereafter. My argument suggests that Chávez needed first to discover the electoral payoffs of radicalism and polarization (circa 2001) and acquire the policy tools to deal with the risks of radicalism (social policies for the *ni-nis*, circa 2003).

In short, the persistence of radicalism after 2007 no doubt depends on ideological conviction (probably always present). But more fundamentally, it reflects the policy's acquired momentum (path dependence), which made this preference sustainable (at least until clearer signs of disaster surface). By 2009, there were signs of declining electoral payoffs, but the decline was still not severe enough to induce a major corrective action.

## Conclusion

This chapter provided an explanation for two salient aspects of revolutionary politics under Chávez. First, why did the regime become a leftist competitive-authoritarian regime, that is, why did the state increase radical and confrontational policies while still maintaining elections? I argued that radicalization under Chávez became the state's preferred strategy given its potential electoral payoffs. Polarization is not always electorally beneficial, but when one of the ideological blocs (left or right) in the electorate is somewhat large, polarization can be electorally rewarding, even if those in the extreme factions within the electorate are minoritarian. In these contexts, radicalism in office can produce more supporters than detractors, which is the reason for its appeal for incumbents. It is also the reason that Chávez has preserved and conducted so many electoral contests.

Radicalism in Venezuela no doubt has other sources. Scholars, for instance, have identified myriad explanations, ranging from ideological and formational factors (Hugo Chávez's own values); socioeconomic factors (the persistence of poverty and the need for strong distributionist policies); the status of domestic institutions (the collapse of parties and other institutions capable of posing checks on the Executive branch); international political economy (Venezuela's dependence on a commodity experiencing a price boom, which freed the state from the need to heed market forces); and international politics in general (the foreign policy of the United States under George W. Bush, which gave Chávez reasons or excuses to turn radical). My point has been to emphasize an alternative explanation that is less frequently acknowledged: the idea that polarization can be electorally rewarding and therefore seductive for the state. Even in the absence of all the other sources of radicalism stressed by the literature, politicians may discover that radicalization can help them win elections. Even more worrisome, it does not take much for polarization to be this rewarding. All that is necessary is that the distribution of voters be *slightly* skewed in the direction of one of the poles. Societies need not be all that divided or already polarized for the state to benefit electorally from policies that accentuate polarization.

A second aspect of Venezuela's revolution that I sought to explain was the combination of radical policies with non-revolutionary, almost reactionary policies: clientelism, impunity, and intimidation. I argued that these policies were aimed at preventing ambivalent groups from defecting. Polarization, even in contexts where it can prove electorally beneficial, also carries a huge risk: the opposition may overcome barriers to collective action and turn potent. Furthermore, the size of ambivalent groups increases, repulsed by the extremism of each side. These ambivalent groups can determine elections, so deploying alternative policies to co-opt these groups is indispensable for incumbents.

A third objective of this chapter was to show some of the limitations of a strictly game-theoretic approach to the study of polarization. There is no question that the dynamics of polarization in Venezuela at first followed a predictable path that can be traced through a simple rational-choice analysis. However, the next iterations of this trend were less predictable. A rational-choice informed explanation sufficiently construed the rise of the opposition, the defection of soft-liners, and the escalation of extremism following major power grabs, but it did not easily clarify why the incumbent opts for power grabs when it enjoys sufficient powers and the opposition calms down. Understanding the 2007–2009 power grabs requires supplementing the analysis with an understanding of path dependence (internal homogenization, sunk costs, acquired institutional capacity, etc.).

Obviously, polarization is not always state-driven. For instance, polarization in Venezuela in the 1990s was also the result of declining oil income, which split the political actors on the question of who should absorb the costs of austerity. During the 1990s, then, polarization was less the result of a deliberate strategy on the part of the state (to achieve political gains) but rather the result of a power struggle between state and society over declining resources: the state wanted to save; economic agents wanted to retain and expand rents. In such contexts the state does not benefit politically from polarization; quite the contrary, it is hurt by it. That is why most major efforts at reform were abandoned—they generated so much state-society conflict that the state (under all administrations since Lusinchi) sooner or later ceased to insist on making economic adjustments.

Studying polarization thus requires a broad approach that combines a) structuralism, which is well qualified to explain the distribution of resources, b) historic institutionalism, which is well qualified to explain the availability of opportunities and allies available to state and societal actors, c) some constructivism, which is well qualified to explain ideologies, and d) some rational choice, which is well qualified to explain the incentives to adopt or drop behaviors. Singly, none of these approaches can explain the totality of polarization, even if for different periods and contexts one of these variables might be more powerful than the others.

## Endnotes

1. I am grateful to Manuel Hidalgo, Merilee Grindle, Chappell Lawson, Miriam Kornblith, Steve Levitsky, Patricia Márquez, Francisco Monaldi, Michael Penfold, Francisco Rodríguez, Kurt Weyland, several anonymous reviewers, and the editors for their comments. Thanks also to Daniel Mogollón for his research assistance.
2. Coppedge, *Strong Parties and Lame Ducks*. Corrales, *Presidents without Parties*. Monaldi et al., *Political Institutions, Policymaking Process, and Policy Outcomes in Venezuela*. McCoy and Myers, eds., *The Unraveling of Representative Democracy in Venezuela*. Dietz and Myers, "From Thaw to Deluge."
3. Levitsky and Way, "The Rise of Competitive Authoritarianism." Levitsky and Way, *Competitive Authoritarianism: Hybrid Regimes after the Cold War*. Corrales, "Hugo Boss." Corrales and Penfold, *Dragon in the Tropics: Hugo Chávez and the Political Economy of Revolution in Venezuela*.
4. See Cohen, *Radicals, Reformers, and Reactionaries*, and Bermeo, *Ordinary People in Extraordinary Times*.
5. This section draws from Corrales, "In Search of a Theory of Polarization."
6. For polarization in general, see Alford and Hibbing, "The Origins of Politics: An Evolutionary Theory of Political Behavior." For polarization in Latin America, see Norden, "Party Relations and Democracy in Latin America."
7. Gott, *In the Shadow of the Liberator*. See also Roberts, "Social Polarization and the Populist Resurgence in Venezuela." López-Maya and Lander, "The Struggle for Hegemony in Venezuela." This perspective is less apparent in the López-Maya and Lander chapter in this volume. See also Ellner, "Introduction: The Search for Explanations" and Wilpert, *Changing Venezuela by Taking Power*.
8. For a non-Marxist version of this argument, see Easterly, *The Elusive Quest for Growth*.
9. Lupu, "Who Votes for *Chavismo*? Class Voting in Hugo Chávez's Venezuela," 7–32.
10. Blanco, *Revolución y desilusión. La Venezuela de Hugo Chávez*.
11. See Cohen, *Radicals, Reformers, and Reactionaries*; Weyland, "Clarifying a Contested Concept"; and Bermeo, *Ordinary People in Extraordinary Times*.

12. Lijphart, *Democracy in Plural Societies: A Comparative Exploration*. Sartori, *Parties and Party Systems: A Framework for Analysis*.

13. The 1999 constitution is pro-military because it grants the military new rights (the right to vote) and lessens legislative control of promotions.

14. Hawkins, "Populism in Venezuela." See also Hawkins and Hansen, "Dependent Civil Society."

15. Ellner, "The Radical Potential of Chavismo."

16. Ibid., and Hawkins, "Populism in Venezuela."

17. Coppedge, "Venezuela: Popular Sovereignty versus Liberal Democracy," 177.

18. O'Donnell and Schmitter, *Transitions from Authoritarian Rule*.

19. Weingast, "Constructing Self-Enforcing Democracy in Spain."

20. Walt, *The Origins of Alliances*.

21. See Norden, "Party Relations and Democracy in Latin America."

22. González de Pacheco, "Encuestas, cacerolazos, y marchas."

23. For a discussion of the divisions within Chavismo between soft- and hard-liners, see Ellner, *Rethinking Venezuelan Politics: Class, Conflict and the Chávez Phenomenon*.

24. Ellner, "The Radical Potential of Chavismo," 13.

25. *El Nacional*, April 12, 2002. By 2005, Arias Cárdenas returned to the Chavismo camp whereas Miquilena became increasingly critical of Chávez.

26. Kozloff, *Hugo Chávez*, 85–86.

27. Weyland, "Will Chávez Lose His Luster?"

28. Corrales, *Presidents without Parties*.

29. Kornblith, "Elections versus Democracy."

30. Corrales and Penfold, "Venezuela: Crowding Out the Opposition."

31. I thank Chappell Lawson for raising this question.

32. Jatar, *Apartheid del siglo XXI*.

33. For examples of these moderate leftist policies, see Weyland, Madrid, and Hunter, eds., *Leftist Governments in Latin America: Successes and Shortcomings*.

34. See Cohen, *Radicals, Reformers, and Reactionaries*.

35. Corrales, "Explaining Chavismo."

36. Gil Yepes, "Public Opinion, Political Socialization, and Regime Stabilization."

37. Ibid.

38. This section draws from Corrales and Penfold, "Venezuela: Crowding out the Opposition."

39. See Corrales and Penfold, *Dragon in the Tropics*.

40. Coronel, "Corruption, Mismanagement, and Abuse of Power in Hugo Chávez's Venezuela." On the most serious corruption scandal ever to surface, see "Fall of the Boligarchs: Banking in Venezuela," *The Economist*, December 10, 2009.

41. Rodríguez, Chang-Tai Hsieh, Miguel, and Ortega, "The Price of Political Opposition: Evidence from Venezuela's Maisanta" (mimeo 2009).

42. Kornblith, "Venezuela: de la democracia representativa al socialismo del siglo XXI."

43. See Corrales and Penfold, *Dragon in the Tropics*.
44. See Corrales, "Venezuela: A Setback for Chávez," *Journal of Democracy*, January 2011.
45. Alvarez, "Letter to The Honorable Nancy Pelosi, Speaker of the House, U.S. House of Representatives, Washington, D.C., May 30, 2007."
46. *Latinnews*, June 15, 2007.
47. Latin American Regional Report, Andean Group, June 2007.
48. De Córdoba, "A Bid to Ease Chávez's Power Grip," *Wall Street Journal*, June 8, 2007.
49. Carlson, "What Is Venezuela's Constitutional Reform Really About?"
50. Human Rights Watch, "Venezuela: Proposed Amendments Threaten Basic Rights." Retrieved November 29 and December 13, 2007, from http://hrw.org /doc/?t=americas&c=venezu.
51. For more on the oppositions's change of strategy, see Corrales, "Polarización y oposición en Venezuela: ¿Existe evidencia de aprendizaje político?"
52. Varianzas de opinión, "Resultados Estudio de Opinión."
53. For more, see chapter 3 in Corrales and Penfold, *Dragon in the Tropics*.
54. World Bank, "Doing Business 2008," accessed from www.doingbusiness.org.
55. Veneconomía, "Daily Report."
56. Datanálisis, "Monitoreo exploratorio del mercado de productos con precios regulados por el Estado."
57. Rodríguez, "An Empty Revolution: The Unfulfilled Promises of Hugo Chávez."
58. Coronel, *Corruption, Mismanagement, and Abuse of Power in Hugo Chávez's Venezuela*; and Penfold-Becerra, "Clientelism and Social Funds: Empirical Evidence from Chávez's Misiones Programs."
59. España, "Programas Sociales y Condiciones de Vida en Venezuela 1999–2007."
60. Keller y Asociados, "Estudio de la opinión pública nacional: 1er trimestre 2008."

# 3

# Venezuela's Experiment in Participatory Democracy

*Gregory Wilpert*

*The participation of the people in the formation, execution, and control of public administration is the necessary means for achieving the involvement that ensures their full development, both individual and collective. It is the obligation of the State and the duty of society to facilitate the generation of the most favorable conditions for putting this into practice.*

—Article 62, Constitution of the Bolivarian Republic of Venezuela

Supporters of Venezuela's Bolivarian project refer to Venezuela's new political system, the Fifth Republic, as a "participatory and protagonistic democracy,"[1] which they consider to be superior to liberal representative democracy. Venezuelan critics of the Chávez government, though, generally question the seriousness of the concept, arguing instead that it is, at best, a sham and, at worst, a cover for eliminating representative democracy and replacing it with a clientelistic dictatorship, much like the ones that existed in the Soviet Union, Eastern Europe, or currently in Cuba.

Interestingly, though, both international critics and even many supporters of Chávez appear to be largely unaware of the participatory democratic element of the Bolivarian movement. International observers tend to single out the Chávez government's foreign policy and its social programs, completely leaving aside the political changes the country has been undergoing during his presidency. Yet there is good reason to believe that Chávez's popularity and his long string of electoral victories have as much to do with these political changes as they do with the government's social programs, on which most observers tend to focus.[2] A more careful analysis of participatory democracy in Venezuela is thus long overdue, precisely because these changes in Venezuela's democracy have had an important impact on increasing citizen participation and inclusion in the democratic process, despite the resurgence of old clientelistic processes and structures within the new institutions. As will be discussed in greater detail below, prior to Chávez's election many analysts considered the Venezuelan regime to be a sham or rigged democracy,[3] while it also was one of Latin America's oldest and most stable democracies. After Chávez's election in 1998, the new constitution of 1999, the introduction of communal councils in 2006 along with the populace's general politicization, and other new forms of citizen participation broke with the old model of Venezuelan politics as being only for a class of professional politicians, and significantly opened up the political system to the general population. The consolidation of the Chávez government after eleven years in office, though, threatens to recreate some of the previous clientelistic structures as the government tries to find ways to maintain its hold on power.

While the participatory democratic aspect of the Chávez government's project is visible in both the economic and the political spheres, this chapter will be limited to the political dimension of participatory democracy. First I will examine the concept's theoretical background and justification. Next, I present the various ways in which participatory democracy is said to be practiced in Venezuela. Finally, I look at some of the main criticisms that have been leveled against the concept and its application and discuss their validity in accordance with existing research and observations on democratic practice in Venezuela.

## Participatory Democratic Theory

To understand why supporters of the Bolivarian project place so much emphasis on the participatory aspect of the Chávez government's reform of the political system, one needs to understand how they conceive representative democracy and why they reject it. For Chávez and the Bolivarian movement, representative democracy was the kind that predominated during the Fourth Republic, before the 1999 constitution that came into effect under Chávez. For them, this type of democracy meant a system run by and for the country's elites, which excluded ordinary citizens from the country's political affairs. Citizens could vote for president once every five years, and other than that, they were not expected to be involved in politics, unless they served as foot soldiers of one of the two dominant parties or their affiliated organizations, such as those in the unions or student movements. The consequence was that politicians were free to do as they pleased, since there was no one looking over their shoulders. This then made corruption and the abuse of power almost a necessary consequence of representative democracy.

The key event that crystallized the rejection of liberal representative democracy for Venezuela's poor majority and for progressives was the 1989 economic reform package and consequent riots and accompanying massacre known as the *Caracazo*. That is, in late 1988 ex-president Carlos Andrés Pérez (known as CAP) ran for president on an anti-neoliberal platform, promising to bring back the country's glory days of the last time he was president in 1974–1979. After ten years of steady economic decline, his campaign held tremendous appeal for Venezuelans, who saw poverty and corruption increase dramatically in those years. CAP thus won the election by a nearly unprecedented majority of 56 percent of the vote. However, less than a month after taking office, on February 27, 1989, CAP completely reversed his campaign promise and instituted a Structural Adjustment Program (required by the International Monetary Fund, IMF) that dramatically increased prices on bus fares, bread, and numerous other basic goods.

The reaction to the economic reform package was immediate and spontaneous. At first people from the country's poor neighborhoods, the *barrios*, protested and blockaded streets. As the anger of the population increased, riots and large-scale looting broke out. Even though the protests and riots died down after two days, CAP imposed a curfew and ordered the police and the military to repress anyone disobeying the curfew or the order to disperse. State security forces ended up killing *barrio* inhabitants indiscriminately, even firing into homes at random. Many believed that the repression was an act of retaliation, an effort to permanently squash any resistance against the president. In the end hundreds, maybe even thousands of people were killed, many in their homes, and many were later found in mass graves.[4]

It is this incident that became paradigmatic for a representative democracy gone amok. Venezuelans had elected a president on the basis of the memory of Venezuela's glory days during the oil boom and his promise to pursue similar policies to the ones operative then, but, once in office, he turned around and not only launched an opposite agenda, but also violently repressed all resistance to his action.

Also, the political system itself appeared to be unfairly rigged against fundamental change due to a pact that the country's main political parties had signed in 1958, after the overthrow of Venezuela's last dictator, Marcos Pérez Jiménez. This pact, known as the *Punto Fijo* (named after the building in which it was signed), was signed by the social democratic Acción Democrática party, the Christian democratic party COPEI, and the left of center party Unión Republicana Democrática (URD), the country's three mainstream parties. It established a system of sharing the spoils of government among them even when the other parties were out of power. In addition, the pact tried to keep all challengers, particularly from the extreme left or right, out of political power by funneling campaign funds only to pact members and sometimes even by rigging elections.

Thus, the criminality and impunity of the *Caracazo,* combined with the perceived injustice of the *Punto Fijo* Pact, provided the context against which Chávez and civilian progressive forces in Venezuela developed a fundamental distrust of representative democracy. The constitution's "Elucidation of Reasons" for establishing a participatory democracy expresses this negative evaluation of representative democracy and explains the improvement as follows:

> This regulation [in favor of participatory democracy] responds to a felt aspiration of organized civil society that strives to change the political culture, which so many decades of state paternalism and the dominance of party heads generated and that hindered the development of democratic values. In this sense, participation is not limited to electoral processes, since the need for the intervention of the people is recognized in the processes of formation, formulation, and execution of public policy, which would result in the overcoming of the governability deficits that have affected our political system due to the lack of harmony between state and society.
>
> To conceive public administration as a process in which a fluid communication between governed and the people is established, implies a modification of the orientation of state-society relations, so as to return to the latter its legitimate protagonism.[5]

In other words, for opponents of Venezuela's Fourth Republic, representative democracy was synonymous with "partyarchy" (*partidocracia*), in which the dominant parties divided up the spoils of Venezuela's political and economic system amongst themselves and used their power to exclude all challengers. According to the Bolivarian interpretation of Venezuelan representative democracy, the only way to overcome this system is to bring the people back into politics, by including them as participants and active protagonists. More than that, the constitution also places limits on political parties to prevent their "vertical organization" that in the past have "obstructed the deepening" of democratic values.[6]

The Bolivarian critique of representative democracy is certainly not new. Already Max Weber pointed out the problems of representative democracy, referring to the U.S. electoral system of the 1920s as one in which parties "are purely organizations of job hunters drafting their changing platforms according to the chances of vote-grabbing."[7] Also, according to Weber, as parties become more bureaucratized, "The member of parliament thereby ceases to be in a position of authority over the electors and becomes merely an agent of the leaders of the party organization."[8] In other words, the problem of elected representatives who become increasingly removed from the electorate, and who opportunistically issue campaign promises but then follow the dictates of their party or of other powerful special interests, has long been recognized as a weakness of representative democracy.

More recent political theorists, such as John Rawls and Jürgen Habermas, have emphasized the importance of political deliberation in the formulation of laws and policies and have suggested that the existing liberal democracies need to be modified to improve the opportunities for political deliberation.[9] Representative democracy, especially its bureaucratized political parties and the influence of lobbies and mass media on political will formation, has made citizen deliberation irrelevant, if not impossible. According to theorists of participatory democracy such as Carole Pateman and Steven Schalom, greater grassroots citizen participation in politics could, in theory, address this problem.[10] Participatory democracy, if it ensures citizen involvement on a regular and effective basis, would not only enable real deliberation but also make policies more accountable to the citizenry. Moreover, studies have shown that real citizen participation in politics reverses apathy and cynicism toward politics and has a positive effect on personal development.[11] The institution of participatory democracy in Venezuela thus connects not only with the public's negative experiences with representative democracy, but also resonates with some recent strands of political theory on the shortcomings of existing representative democracy and how these might be overcome.

## Institutionalization of Participatory Democracy in Venezuela

Exactly what participatory democracy might look like is still up for debate, both within Venezuela and in political theory. While many innovative forms of governance have been developed that are supposed to bring about a participatory democracy there, one should keep in mind that the country is also still governed by representative democratic principles, in that regular periodic elections are held for city council members, mayors, governors, National Assembly representatives, and the president. According to some political theorists of participatory democracy, this is in fact the way it should be:

> Many of the central institutions of liberal democracy—competitive parties, political representatives, periodic elections—will be unavoidable elements of a participatory society. Direct participation and

control over immediate locales, complemented by party and interest-group competition in governmental affairs, can most realistically advance the principles of participatory democracy.[12]

The elements of participatory democracy in Venezuela are developed in a wide variety of its laws and in its constitution. The perhaps six most important areas are: referenda, local democratic planning, social oversight (*contraloría social*), citizen assemblies, cooperatives, and civil society involvement in state institutions and programs. Following a review of these, we will examine how they function in conjunction with the more traditional representative democratic structures.

### Referenda

Referenda are in some ways both the center of Venezuela's participatory democracy and its most superficial aspect. That is, they are at the center in the sense that they represent the most visible and dramatic difference from the previous constitution and are potentially the most powerful means by which "partyarchy" and ossified representative democracy are subverted. Citizens can directly petition for four different types of referenda and, if they meet the necessary requirements, can impose their will between regular elections and against the will of the political parties and of elected representatives. However, it is also a relatively superficial aspect of participatory democracy because it is difficult to make use of.

The four different types of referenda are: consultative, recall, approbatory, and abrogatory. The consultative referendum can be convoked if the president, the National Assembly, or 10 percent of registered voters request it. The purpose of such referenda is to ask the population a question of "special transcendent national interest." Such referenda can also be convoked on a municipal or state level.

Recall referenda may be convoked for any elected office, once half of the official's term in office has passed. To convoke it, at least 20 percent of registered voters have to petition for it. For the official to be turned out of office, at least as many have to vote for his or her recall as originally voted for that individual. In August 2004 the opposition organized a recall referendum against President Chávez, which failed with a vote of 58 percent in favor and 42 percent against the president.

The main controversy this process caused was that the names of the petition signers were made public on a website by a pro-Chávez member of the National Assembly. The list (known as the "Tascón list" after the assembly member who posted it, Luis Tascón) was later often used by both Chavistas and anti-Chavistas to determine who their supporters were and then to deny jobs or services in the sectors that they each control. This meant that many Chavistas were excluded from jobs that opposition supporters controlled, mostly in the private sector, and many opposition supporters were denied jobs in sectors that Chavistas control, mostly in the public sector.[13] In February 2007, though, the National Electoral Council (CNE) changed the procedures for organizing petitions, so that the signers' names would be protected.[14]

Approbatory referenda may be convoked for the approval of laws when two-thirds of the National Assembly supports such a move. Also, international treaties may be submitted to referenda if the president, the National Assembly, or 15 percent of registered voters request it. Changes in the constitution also need to be approved in this way.

Finally, abrogatory referenda are convoked to rescind laws when the president or 10 percent of registered voters request it. For so-called law decrees, which are laws passed by decree when the National Assembly allows the president to pass such laws under an "enabling law," the number of citizens requesting such a referendum drops to 5 percent of registered voters, which makes it fairly easy for such a referendum to be convoked for laws that were not passed via the normal legislative process.

The main obstacle for the organization of referenda is the process by which signatures can be collected. In the polarized political climate of the 2004 recall referendum there was much distrust on all sides about whether petition signatures would be collected without fraud, and so the Electoral Council imposed fairly strict rules on how to collect such signatures. The rules specified that signatures could only be collected under the close supervision of the CNE and only on four designated signature collection days. Also, signers had to provide their fingerprints for additional verification. This is quite different from the procedure in other places where referenda are allowed, such as California, which places practically no restrictions on how the signatures are collected. Also, the fact that the names were used afterwards for political purposes will have a chilling effect for future signature collection efforts, even though the CNE has promised to maintain the confidentiality of signers in future petition drives.

Given these limitations on referenda, it seems that they will not be used as frequently as they are used in California. As a result, though, referenda in Venezuela will probably play a less important role in establishing participatory democracy than the other five applications mentioned here.

## Local Public Planning Councils

The Local Public Planning Councils (CLPP—Consejos Locales de Planifi-cación Pública) and the Communal Councils (CC—Consejos Comunales) potentially represent the most far-reaching transformation of Venezuelan political life on the day-to-day level. The CLPPs are modeled to a large extent after the participatory local budgeting process first pioneered in Porto Ale-gre, Brazil, during the 1990s.[15] While the CLPPs took most of their inspira-tion from Porto Alegre, they also bear some similarity to planning boards that exist in many communities in the United States. The key difference, however, is that while in Venezuela the constitution and a national law guar-antee their existence, in the United States they are formed by community charters and local laws and thus are not part of citizens' basic rights.[16]

In Venezuela, CLPPs were first called into existence via Article 182 of the new 1999 constitution. Then, in June 2002, the National Assembly passed the CLPP law, which regulates their functioning. According to the law, the CLPPs are formed by municipalities and are constituted by the mayor, the municipal council, the presidents of the district (known as parishes) coun-cils, representatives of neighborhood groups, and representatives of other civil society organizations, coming from sectors such as healthcare, educa-tion, sports, culture, ecology, security, formal and informal businesses, women, transportation, land committees, the elderly, and people with dis-abilities. The elected officials (mayor, district council presidents, and city council representatives) are supposed to outnumber the representatives of neighborhood groups and other organizations by one vote. Participation in the councils is on a volunteer basis.

The central purpose of the councils is to gather and evaluate proposals for community projects, to work on the municipal development plan, to develop a map of the community's needs, to elaborate the municipality's investment budget, and to coordinate with other municipalities and with state authori-ties, among others.[17] The key difference between the CLPP's areas of respon-sibility and those of the mayor is that the mayor's task is to execute the plans, whereas the CLPP plans and oversees the mayor's execution.

The implementation of the CLPPs ran into numerous serious problems, however, due to larger political events, poor formulation of the law, and resistance from elected officials. The interfering events included the April 2002 coup attempt, which occurred just before the law was passed, then the December 2002 oil industry shutdown, and, finally, the mayoral elections of October 2004. Nonetheless, many communities managed to get the CLPPs off the ground despite these interferences, but most have, as of this writing, yet to do so. The practical implementation of the councils, though, has left much to be desired for several other reasons. Long-time community organizer and former Vice-Minister of Local Planning, Roland Denis, outlines three serious obstacles to the functioning of CLPPs.[18]

First, basing the CLPPs on the municipal level makes them far too large in some cases. At its worst extreme, the main municipality of the heart of Caracas, Libertador, has at least two million inhabitants, which is larger than many states in Venezuela. To apply local planning in a participatory manner on such a large scale is impossible and defeats the entire purpose of the CLPPs. Members of the Libertador CLPP are every bit as removed from the communities they represent as the governors of some states, if one goes by the number of people they represent.

Second, the financial resources allocated to each district within a municipality are not based on population size. Large districts (parishes) receive more or less the same financial resources as very small ones. Considering that the size difference between districts can be enormous, activists consider this to be extremely unfair. For example, the Caracas municipality of Sucre, with its 1.2 million inhabitants, has three districts, while the Caracas municipality of Libertador, with its 2 million inhabitants, has 22 districts. If each district receives more or less the same amount of funding, then the three Sucre districts receive about one quarter of what the Libertador districts receive. Similarly, a rich neighborhood, such as Chacao—also in Caracas—with only 75,000[19] inhabitants, receives, per capita, five times the amount Sucre inhabitants receive. As such, the CLPPs will be much more effective in small upper-class districts like Chacao than in the densely populated and poor districts of Sucre. This was surely not the original intention behind the law.

Partly to address this problem, Chávez announced on January 10, 2007, during his swearing-in ceremony for his second full term in office, that he plans to reorganize Venezuela's municipalities in order to address the funding disparities and to reconfigure the territorial "geometry of power" in Venezuela.[20]

The third problem with the CLPPs is that the law that governs them does not give them sufficient power. That is, decisions of the CLPPs can still be overruled by the mayors or district councils. Overruling CLPP decisions, though, can act as a deathblow, since the volunteers who participate in them are hardly going to feel motivated to put much hard work into any project that then ends up being overruled. "The Councils create a lot of hope," says Roland Denis, "but when they try to apply this law they are going to realize that it is flawed, I would even say that it is criminally flawed because now that the Councils are appearing it is becoming apparent that they don't have power or legitimacy."[21]

A fourth problem with the CLPPs is that they presuppose citizen education, interest, skills, and dedication that is often not available. Unless citizens are well informed about the functioning of CLPPs and have the skills to participate in them and the motivation to put in countless hours of volunteer work, they will fall apart.[22] Unfortunately, for many districts and municipalities in Venezuela, there often is a lack of qualified citizens for this work. The CLPP law ought to take this into consideration, so that training and some sort of compensation is available for those who work in these organizations.

Finally, there is a fifth problem which has nothing to do with the CLPP law, but with the fact that mayors and city councils often feel threatened by the planning councils. Rather than seeing the councils as a welcome help in guiding their decisions, they see them as challengers and usurpers. As a result, mayors often create obstacles for the organization of CLPPs or try to manipulate them by getting their friends to control them. When this happens, of course, community activists rapidly lose interest in working on the planning councils at all.

The National Assembly conducted a study in 2006 to examine the various problems and to harmonize the CLPPs with the newly formed communal councils. The result of the research was a list of 13 problem areas, ranging from the law being unclear about how to constitute CLPPs, to lack of sanctions for violating the law, to insufficient training and preparation of CLPP members, to fraud in the process of choosing CLPP members, among other issues. As a result, in December 2006 the National Assembly approved a reform to the law that was supposed to substantially improve the functioning of the CLPPs and their participatory budgeting process. Whether this reform actually managed to fix the problems is doubtful, since central government priority has now moved towards promoting communal councils and communes, which fulfill many of the same functions as the CLPPs.

### Citizen Assemblies

The inspiration for citizen assemblies comes from a movement that emerged following the 1989 Caracazo, when citizens in the *barrios* got together for "*barrio* assemblies." Following the riots, these assemblies attempted to articulate the grievances of the people living in the slums, such as inadequate utilities in their neighborhoods, lack of protection against crime, and a general lack of attention from governmental authorities. The citizen assemblies of the Fifth Republic address the frustration of the *barrio* assemblies by giving citizens a forum in which such assemblies would be more effective than the *barrio* assemblies ever were.

Citizen assemblies are briefly mentioned in Article 70 of the 1999 constitution, which states that citizens have the right to convoke citizen assemblies that have a binding character. The details of how these assemblies are to be convoked and exactly what this "binding character" means were left to a separate law on citizen assemblies, which, eleven years into Chávez's presidency, still has not been passed. Other laws, though, such as the communal council law and the Organic Law on Participation and Popular Power (OLPPP, which is slated to pass in 2010) do make reference to citizen assemblies and regulate some of their functioning. Despite the lack of a law dedicated to citizen assemblies, however, Venezuelans have long been gathering in such groups, particularly in order to form communal councils.

The citizen assemblies' areas of competence include the election of delegates to the communal councils, the evaluation of government and community programs, and approval of community norms and of a community development plan. In effect, citizen assemblies are a forum for direct democracy and represent the basic building block for the creation of communal councils.

### Communal Councils

Since early 2005, the Chávez government has been implementing another form of participatory democracy, the communal councils, which operate on a far smaller scale than the CLPPs. The Ministry for the Commune is in charge of directing this project, which aims to create communal councils in all of Venezuela's 335 municipalities. By the end of 2009, Venezuelans launched over 23,000 communal councils, out of a total of about 50,000 needed to cover the entire country.

According to the communal council law (first passed in April of 2006 and then substantially reformed in 2009), communal councils are constituted via a citizen assembly of 150 to 400 families that share a common history and geography.[23] The citizen assembly identifies work committees for the council and elects delegates from each committee to make up the council's executive unit. Also, it elects an administration and finance unit and an independent comptroller unit. These three units together constitute the actual communal council. Finally, there is also an independent electoral unit, which organizes the elections for communal council spokespersons (and their recall elections, if called upon to do so).

Perhaps the most interesting innovation of the communal councils is that they are designed to integrate the wide variety of committees that have formed in communities over the course of the Chávez presidency. For example, various social programs have, in the name of citizen participation, required communities to form committees that would help implement social programs, such as the missions. Consequently, most *barrio* communities now have urban housing committees for the urban land reform, health committees for the community health program, water and electricity committees for the planning of connections to these utilities, defense committees for the formation of the Bolivarian militia, alternative media committees, recreation and sports committees, etc. Each of these committees would now become a work committee of the community council. Each work committee then sends one spokesperson to the executive unit, which oversees the decisions of the citizens' assembly, which is the highest decision-making body of the community (Article 20, Law on Communal Councils).

When the new communal council law was passed, communities began to organize them rather quickly, and by the first half of 2006 Chávez handed out grants to 653 community improvement projects drawn up by the initial group of communal councils. Over the course of the year, a total of approximately $1.5 billion was turned over to these councils for their projects. Additional funds would come from local and state governments, donations, and other fundraising activities of the councils. Chávez announced in early 2007 that the funds for community councils would be increased to $5 billion that year.[24] This represents a significant redirection of state funds, away from governors and mayors and towards the communal councils. Currently about 30 percent of the funds for local and regional governments go to communal councils, but Chávez supporters in the National Assembly are proposing to increase this amount to 50 percent.[25]

If successful, these communal councils could transform the nature of the Venezuelan state in the long run, because of the way their decisions are binding for the next higher level. That is, according to Chávez[26] and the proposed citizen participation law, community council associations will be created that would bring together councils on a parish, municipal, state, and national level to coordinate large-scale projects for all of the member councils. As such, this council system would become a governing structure parallel to the existing representative democratic structures, but based on the more direct democratic councils. In January 2007, Chávez referred to the implementation of this idea as one of the "five motors" for the next phase of the Bolivarian Revolution, the creation of 21st century socialism. The goal is to eventually create a "communal state."[27] He also proposed, for the short term, the creation of experimental "socialist communal cities," where the entire city government is based entirely on the communal council structure. With the passage of the Organic Law on Participation and Popular Power in 2010, communal cities would become a regular feature in the Venezuelan system of governance. Whether the long-term goal is to replace representative democracy altogether is not clear. However, with the failure of the December 2007 constitutional reform, any such replacement is unlikely in the foreseeable future because such a change would require a major modification of the constitution.

Chávez emphasized that the communal councils run the danger of becoming mere budgeting organs if they do not take on other tasks. These might include the formation of citizen consciousness, self-defense, cooperation with state institutions, and the development of self-reliance when central government funds are unavailable. Also, when and if several communal councils in an area federate in entities known as "communes," these federations could develop participatory planning processes on a wider level and in coordination with cooperatives and socialist production enterprises (EPS).[28] None of this has happened yet, as these proposals are still in the planning phase for developing 21st century socialism in Venezuela. However, if fully realized, the communal councils would become the most radical and important means of creating participatory democracy in Venezuela.

### Social Audit/Comptrol (Contraloría Social)
One of the key tasks of the local public planning councils and of the communal councils is to conduct audits of the work of the public administration. The principles and legal base for the so-called "social" audit, though, apply not just to CLPPs and communal councils, but are a right that any Venezuelan citizen may exercise. What is meant by social audit is that citizens have the right to request an accounting (financial and non-financial) of all activities of any public administration. That is, if someone has reason to believe that a public office is not being administered properly, a citizen may place a request with the attorney general's office to have the office audited. The individual or group making the request may then fully participate in the audit.

The principle of social auditing is a key element in Venezuela's concept of participatory democracy because it forms the basis of direct citizen involvement in and oversight of the public administration. That is, it is not enough for citizens to be able to propose and perhaps implement projects and programs, but, via social audits, they also can make sure that those projects and programs are being run properly.

Venezuela's public administration law describes social audits as follows:

> The national public administration . . . must establish systems that will supply to the population the broadest, most timely, and accurate information about its activities, so that social auditing may be exercised over the public administration. Anyone may solicit from the organisms and bodies of the public administration the information that they desire about their activity, in conformity with the law.[29]

The entire legal framework for social auditing is covered by a wide variety of laws,[30] which is perhaps why it rarely gets mentioned as an important aspect of Venezuela's participatory democracy. However, more and more organizations and individuals have taken advantage of this right. For example, the Vargas Hospital in Caracas underwent a social audit because neighborhood groups suspected that many of the hospital's resources were being diverted by corrupt officials. In another example, in 2003, Venezuela's National Council on the Rights of Children and Adolescents was socially audited for similar reasons. A new law that gathers and deepens all of the existing regulations around social audits is still in the works.

### Civil Society Involvement in State Institutions and Programs
Organizations of civil society in Venezuela have the right to become involved in a wide variety of governmental operations, ranging from public institutions such as the Councils on the Rights of Children or the Directorate for Social Responsibility in Television and Radio, to nominations of Supreme Court judges and of members to the National Electoral Council. For example, half of the members of the Councils on the Rights of Children and Adolescents (regional bodies that are supposed to protect children's rights in Venezuela) are appointed by representatives from civil society organizations that are involved with children's issues. Similarly, for the nominations of Supreme Court judges, a nominations commission is set up with five members from the National Assembly and six from civil society organizations concerned with legal matters. Other entities of public administration that are set up similarly include the National Electoral Council and components of the citizen branch of government (Attorney General, Human Rights Ombudsperson, and Comptroller General).

In addition to these examples of citizen and civil society involvement on the highest levels of government, citizen participation is also sought out on various other levels on a regular basis. For example, for the redistribution of rural and urban land as part of the land reform programs, citizens are encouraged to form committees that help governmental institutions in many of their tasks of measuring the land that is to be redistributed and in deciding who gets which plots of land.[31] Similarly, the capital's water company, Hidrocapital, has encouraged communities to set up "technical water committees" that help the water company determine where there is a need to improve service and how to best organize this service for the community. As a result of this community consultation process, it has been possible for the water company to significantly expand its service from 60 percent of the population to over 90 percent in six years.[32] Other examples of community involvement in public services have been the health committees, which have helped shape the Misión Barrio Adentro program of community doctors and clinics in the country's poorest neighborhoods.

Similarly, many other missions, such as the Misión Robinson, which provides literacy training to the country's illiterate, and Misión Ribas, which provides adult education to those who did not finish their primary schooling, also involve extensive citizen participation in the execution of these programs. This participation ranges from actual decision-making, to volunteering with the teaching programs, to providing one's home for the necessary courses.

This enormous variety of committees in the communities that work with government programs are now in the process of being bundled via the communal councils. That is, instead of being independent committees working with the different government agencies, these are now becoming committees of the communal councils in the areas of health, education, land titles, water supply, electricity supply, community media, culture, and so forth.

### Cooperatives

Finally, the last major area in which the Chávez government has promoted participatory democracy is in supporting the creation of cooperatives. With the help of technical advice, small business loans, and the creation of a legal framework, over 100,000 cooperatives operate in Venezuela[33] since Chávez became president, in all areas of business, with over one million members. Cooperatives, due to their governance system in which the members are able to elect the managers and have a constant say over the decision-making within the organization, represent an important instance of participatory democracy. While cooperatives are not governmental institutions and thus do not contribute to the participatory democratic governance of the state, they do promote a political culture of participatory democracy and lay the foundation for a participatory and democratic economy.

A 2006 proposal that would further strengthen workplace democracy in Venezuela sought to draft a law creating workers' councils in all public and private workplaces. These councils would allow workers "processes of control over production, planning, and the efficient use of resources," according to Oscar Figueroa of the Communist Party of Venezuela, who is working on drafting the law.[34] It remains to be seen, though, if Chávez and more moderate factions of Chavismo will support such a project. The failed constitutional reform did include mention of workers' councils, but did not specify their functions, as these were to be left to a separate law.

## Relationship between Participatory and Representative Democracy

The relationship between participatory and representative democracy is still being negotiated in Venezuela. Many aspects of the new participatory paradigm are undetermined and untested. For example, of the most important participatory elements, only the communal councils and the local public planning councils (CLPP) have their own laws that regulate their functioning. The Organic Law on Participation and Popular Power, which will regulate citizen assemblies, the associations of communal councils (parish, municipal, state, and national), and the integration of communal councils and representative structures on a national level, still waits to be passed.[35] Also in the works are a law governing social comptrol and one governing referenda.

However, judging on the basis of the law projects, it is possible to identify the general contours of the relationship between the two structures that are gradually evolving. Essentially, Venezuela is developing a dual democracy where both representative and participatory processes stand on more or less equal footing. On the participatory side are communal councils and their parish, municipal, state, and national associations. The higher levels are participatory in the sense that communal councils send delegates—not representatives—to these organizations; these individuals can be recalled at any time, serve for relatively short terms of two years, and must fulfill the mandates of their councils. On the representative side are all the traditional structures of representative democracy, such as the executive and legislative branches on municipal, state, and national levels.

Exactly how these two forms of governance would interact is, as of this writing, still unclear. One proposal, as expressed in the proposed participation law (OLPPP), would ensure coordination via planning councils on the municipal, state, and national levels, according to Venezuela's 1999 constitution. These councils bring together different levels of government, as well as members from the representative and the participatory structures. That is, the local public planning council brings together elected representatives from the parish and municipal levels, as well as delegates from the communal councils and from civil society groups. The state planning and coordinating council brings together elected representatives from both the municipalities and the respective state, as well as civil society representatives,[36] to identify and coordinate projects on a state level.[37] The federal governing council would bring together mayors, governors, ministers, the president, and civil society representatives to identify and coordinate projects on a national level.[38] However, so far only the laws governing local planning ouncils and the federal governing council have been passed, so that the exact functioning of all the higher coordinating bodies has not yet been determined (see Figure 1).

## Participatory Democratic Practice and Problems

Without a doubt, the Venezuelan government has made a tremendous effort toward empowering ordinary citizens, from recall referenda to land, water, and health committees, to civil society participation in nomination processes, to legally binding citizen assemblies, to the creation of communal councils and public planning. The opportunities for Venezuelans to become involved in politics have expanded as never before. During the Fourth Republic, under the *Punto Fijo* political system, Venezuelans were expected to be spectators of the political game, not participants. Now, as a result of the political transformation that has occurred since Chávez's election, Venezuelans have become more involved in the political life of their country than ever before. In Caracas, this involvement extends from the poor *barrios* of the mountainsides, such as Petare, Catia, and La Vega, to the relatively wealthy upper middle-class neighborhoods of Altamira, Prados del Este, and Cafetal. In all socioeconomic classes, but especially among the poor, Venezuelans are organizing themselves.

Critics have identified at least four problems with the newly developing participatory democracy, however. These problems involve the supposed lack of pluralism, the emergence of new patronage/clientelism structures, meeting overload, and conflict of participatory democracy with the presidentialism of Venezuelan government. Let us briefly examine each of these.

### Lack of Pluralism

The criticism is that the communal councils cannot assure minority participation on the higher levels, such as the municipal, state, and national. That is, since each lower level communal council sends only one delegate (and

## Figure 1.
## Venezuela's System of Participatory and Representative Democracy.

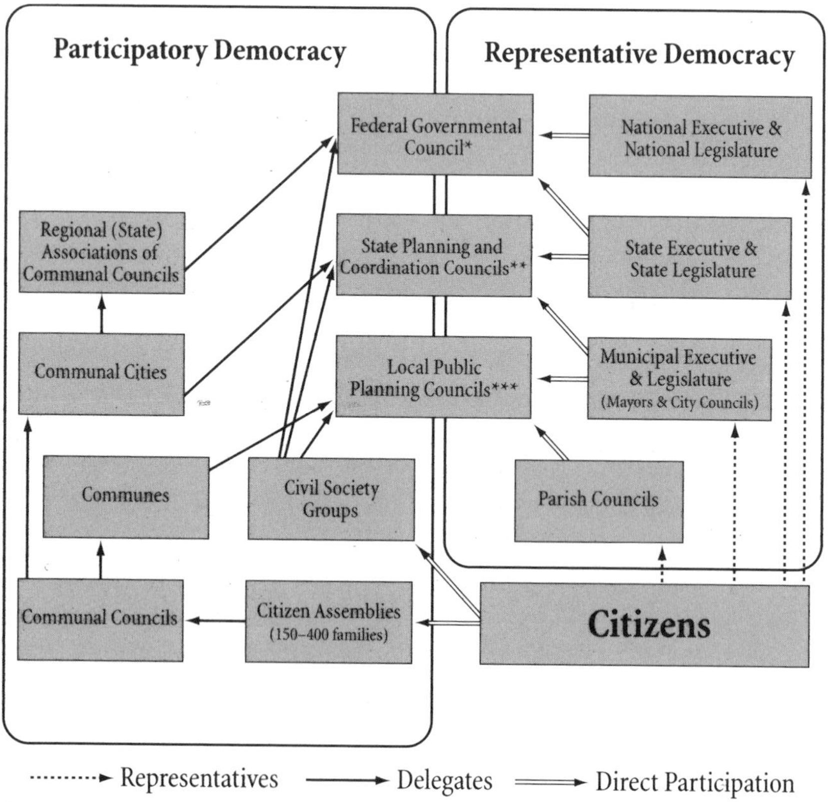

Notes:
*President, vice-president, ministers, all governors, one mayor per state, and civil society reps.
**Governor, all mayors, state reps. of ministries, state reps in National Assembly, state legislative council, municipal council members, indigenous reps., and civil society.
***Mayor, council members, presidents of parish councils, and delegates from civil society and from communal councils.

one substitute) to the next higher level, only the majority view on any given issue is represented.[39] Minority views would only be represented in cases where a majority of a community council held the minority view of the larger communal council association. In other words, the representation of different views, as is possible in an elected legislature with proportional representation, is not possible in a community council system in the participatory democracy.

There are, though, at least three responses to this type of criticism. First, so far, no effort has been made to completely abolish the proportional rep-·resentation system that exists in the representative structures. Rather, the communal councils complement the representative structures. Second, it is not a given that pluralism would indeed be reduced, even if the communal council system were to eclipse the representative system. After all, direct participation assures pluralism in a political system in that it gives everyone an equal voice in politics. What protects pluralism and avoids the tyranny of the majority is not proportional representation, but a strong legal framework in place that protects the rights of the minority. After all, neither the United States nor the British political systems allow for proportional representation, but these are generally considered to be pluralist by most political scientists. Third, in Venezuela minority views tend to be geographically bundled in upper-class neighborhoods, for example, so that these would still be represented at the higher levels of the communal council system. There is nothing in the existing legal framework that would allow only members of a certain party or political tendency to participate in the communal councils—unlike what happened in past state socialist societies.

McCoy's criticism of Venezuelan participatory democracy goes further, though, arguing that pluralism and representative democracy have been undermined by Chávez's supposed centralization and politicization of state institutions.[40] While it is no doubt true that Chávez and his supporters dominate all branches of government, this is much more a result of electoral contests and thus of electoral will than of willful undermining of the constitutional separation of powers. Moreover, this critic reduces Venezuelan participatory democracy to its "plebiscitarian forms of mass participation,"[41] completely ignoring all of the other forms of participation mentioned here.

The focus on referenda as the main form of mass participation allows McCoy to argue that the intermediaries of political parties and interest groups have become weakened. This weakening of intermediaries who would hold the president accountable, combined with the erosion of the separation of powers, means that Venezuela is now a "hybrid regime" just as it was under the Punto Fijo system, although for different reasons. The country is in a "grey zone," "neither liberal democracy nor outright dictatorship," a situation that was brought about, says McCoy, "by asserting governing party control over courts, electoral authority, attorney general, ombudsman, and comptroller general."[42]

What this critic fails to describe, though, is how this supposed control was asserted. This omission makes a large difference, because if control was asserted by an undemocratic subversion of the constitution, it would mean that Venezuelan democracy has indeed been significantly weakened. However, if this governing party control over state institutions was gained by democratic means, through repeated electoral victories, then this result is nothing less than democracy itself. As long as minority rights are protected, there is no reason to say that the Venezuelan political system is less of a democracy than any other country where a governing party manages to control all branches of government by winning elections. In addition, the Chávez government's introduction of two new and independent branches of government, the electoral and the prosecutorial, strengthens checks and balances in the long run, even if their loyalties currently lie with the governing coalition and are, as a result, not as effective as they might be. Also, the other forms of participatory democracy mentioned here, which go far beyond the merely plebiscitarian forms mentioned by McCoy, provide additional checks and balances even when the governing party controls all branches of government.

A counterargument to the claim that the different forms of participatory democracy represent checks and balances and that minority rights are protected is that in practice these have not worked so far. Critics of the Chávez government argue that the government has politicized key institutions, such as the judiciary and the national electoral council; that it has undermined opposition-leaning mayors and governors; and that it has persecuted the opposition by preventing its members from getting hired for positions in public administration (the previously mentioned Tascón List). Unfortunately, as is generally the case in politically polarized situations, nothing is simple or straightforward, and if one examines these claims in detail one can find that they tend to be a mix of valid points, exaggerations, and at times outright falsehoods. Distinguishing which claim fits into which category can easily become a time- and space-consuming enterprise and can thus be dealt with only in a very superficial manner here.[43]

In evaluating these claims, the bottom line is that the judiciary is indeed politicized, but that the opposition bears a substantial portion of responsibility for this politicization, because judges who sympathized with the opposition's 2002 coup attempt ruled that had been no coup, even though there is a general consensus within and outside Venezuela that it was a coup. To be sure, the 2004 "packing" of the Supreme Court, when 12 additional judges were appointed to the court in order to shift its political balance, represents an instance of politicization, but this act was preceded by the court's earlier political stance in support of the coup. A similar situation pertains to the nomination of the members to the National Electoral Council (CNE), which the National Assembly (AN) was supposed carry out in 2004. Because of the country's extreme polarization, the AN could not reach the two-thirds majority required to nominate CNE members, and so the Supreme Court stepped in and ruled that the constitutional vacuum required the justices to nominate the electoral council members. This too resulted in an institution that was more pro-government than would otherwise have been the case. Again, this consequence was a result of political polarization and not of a government decision to politicize state institutions.[44]

## Patronage/Clientelism

It is too early to determine whether or to what extent patronage is a problem in the participatory democratic system of Venezuela, but it is a common opposition criticism, based on the practice of previous governments and on anecdotal evidence. Hawkins and Hansen conducted the main study of this problem with regard to the Bolivarian Circles, the small groupings of 7–12 Chávez supporters that the president launched in 2001.[45] The purpose of these circles was to both mobilize in support of Chávez and to work on community improvement projects. According to Hawkins and Hansen, this is indeed what took place. However, due to members' preferential access to government officials, they also served as conduits for government favors, thereby becoming a patronage system. Following the 2004 recall referendum, though, the Bolivarian Circles declined in importance and, with the creation of the communal councils in 2006, practically disappeared.

Given this precedent, and the fact that the existing communal council system is also quite susceptible to establishing a patronage system, it is possible that such a system will gradually develop if no measures are taken to prevent it. That is, currently the funding for communal councils has to be approved by a presidential commission, which evaluates all projects the councils propose.[46] As long as there are no safeguards to assure that this presidential commission does not favor projects presented by communities that are known to support the president, the criticism that this system is susceptible to patronage will be valid, no matter whether this is actually happening or not. It is indeed possible, and likely, that for the time being funds are being disbursed regardless of the councils' political views, but no political system can rely only on the goodwill of the people in power.

According to two designers of the communal council system,[47] a potential patronage problem exists, but will largely be avoided by requiring that the decisions about whether communities receive funding fit specific technical and transparent criteria. Also, while the funding volume for projects can vary slightly, the average amount is well established and basically guaranteed for every communal council.

## Meeting Overload

That participatory democracy requires too many meetings and too much motivation is perhaps one of the most common criticisms of such a system (or of any system that introduces greater democracy than representative democracy does). Lerner (2007), in his observation of numerous communal councils in operation, sees this as one of their problems.[48] He points out, though, that the government is aware of this problem and is trying to overcome it by allowing people to take time off from work to participate in the councils. The Vice-Minister for popular participation, which at one point was the ministry responsible for promoting the councils, explained to Lerner, "We need to arrange that employers will let employees off from work for a couple hours a week if they participate in a communal council. This could be coordinated by the state, like a form of community service."[49] However, as long as such measures depend on the employers' goodwill, it is unlikely to have much effect. Rather, the communal council law or the labor law needs to be amended so as to make time off for communal council work a citizen's right, much as jury duty is in many countries.

## Conflict with Presidentialism, Personalism, and State Bureaucracy

The fourth problem with participatory democracy in Venezuela has to do with the context in which participatory democratic structures or procedures are embedded, which tends to be presidentialist and personalistic, and at times features an overbearing state bureaucracy. That is, there is a contradiction between the participatory policies the government is developing and the rather top-down management style[50] of Venezuelan political culture and its focus on individual personalities[51] rather than on programmatic ideas.

Chávez, presumably as a result of his military background, tends to have an authoritarian management style that demands absolute loyalty and requires all subordinates to execute his commands faithfully and unquestioningly. As a result, it is rather difficult for those near him to question or criticize policy decisions. This management culture appears to affect not only the formulation of policies at the presidential level, but to permeate the entire public administration and the organized national Bolivarian movement, including Chávez's own party, first the MVR (Movement for a Fifth Republic) and now the PSUV (United Socialist Party of Venezuela).[52] This type of political party and this type of public administration then inevitably end up clashing with the demands that come from below, increasingly via the participatory democratic structures. In the party these clashes became particularly apparent in the April 2003 internal party elections and in the August 2005 local elections; on both occasions party leaders tried to impose candidates against the will of the party membership. In public administration these clashes are felt, for example, in conflicts between the more participatory local public planning councils, the communal councils, and the elected local government representatives.[53]

The top-down management style is further compounded by the personalistic Venezuelan political culture, which tends to value personal charismatic leadership qualities over programmatic ideas. This culture is reflected in the countless political parties that have cropped up in Venezuela recently, formed when a political leader leaves a party and forms a new one with his[54] followers. The most obvious case of personalism in Venezuelan politics today is, of course, the adoration Chávez's followers show him. The problem with such personalism is that it can overshadow debates about policy ideas. If someone questions a proposal Chávez has made, the point can too easily be dismissed as coming from someone who does not support the president, since that is more important than the merits of the question itself. With reference to the Bolivarian Circles, Hawkins refers to this devotion as a "charismatic mode of linkage" that exists between Chávez and his followers and that creates "an internal contradiction or tension" between the goal of autonomy/internal democracy and serving Chávez.[55]

This personalistic political culture in Venezuela is precisely the cause of Chávez's success as politician and as president. His charisma and appeal to poor Venezuelans are legendary and are what has enabled him to bring about radical change in Venezuela, against tremendous resistance from the country's old elite. While Chávez's charisma has enabled this transformation in the short and medium term, it is his movement's total dependence on him that threatens the project's long-term viability. It seems, though, that Chávez and his supporters have recognized this and are therefore now engaging in a year-long process of re-founding his movement by building a truly grassroots democratic political party for "21st century socialism" in Venezuela. Ideally, such a party would enable and channel political debate and the development of new political leaders, so that the Bolivarian movement becomes less dependent on Chávez. Whether this will actually happen is, as of this writing, too early to tell. However, even if it happens, the contradiction between top-down management and bottom-up participatory democracy is bound to continue to cause friction unless Chávez's management style changes.

## Participatory Democracy versus Liberal Democracy?

Venezuela's experiment in participatory democracy is one of the very few instances in the world today where a conscious effort is under way to try out new forms of governance that deepen democracy. Its introduction of referenda, of communal councils, of social oversight, of cooperatives, and of direct civil society involvement in the state represents a departure from conventional liberal representative democracy. As will be shown below, the measures have already significantly improved Venezuelans' perception of their democracy and could, in the long run, create a government that is more responsive to the needs of ordinary citizens, less under the sway of powerful private interests, and has a more informed and engaged citizenry.

The short-term success of these measures is becoming increasingly evident, despite the dire warnings from Chávez's opponents that Venezuela is "refashioning dictatorship for a democratic age."[56] That is, Chávez's recent reelection, the 2004 recall referendum, and the numerous elections his supporters have won since 2004 are not just owing to the favorable effect his social programs have had, but also to these measures that deepen Venezuela's democracy. Evidence for this claim can be found in the annual Latinobarómetro surveys of 2005 to 2009, which clearly demonstrate that Venezuelans' approval of their democracy and its functioning are at an all-time high since these surveys were first taken in 1995.

According to the 2006 Latinobarómetro survey, Venezuelans give their own democracy a score of 7.0, on a scale of 1 to 10, where 1 means a country that is not democratic and 10 is a country that is completely democratic. The Latin American average was 5.8, with Uruguay having the highest score, of 7.2, and Paraguay the lowest, at 3.9.[57]

In the same survey, Venezuelans say more often than the citizens of all other countries except Uruguay that they are satisfied with their democracy, with 57 percent of Venezuelans saying they are happy with their democracy, compared to 66 percent of Uruguayans expressing satisfaction. The average for all countries surveyed was 38 percent. These figures changed a bit between 2006 and 2009, with Venezuelans' satisfaction with their democracy dropping to 47 percent (same as Brazilians' satisfaction) and the Latin American average rising to 44 percent in 2009. However, when asked whether they agree with the statement, "democracy allows the solving of the problems we have," 72 percent of Venezuelans (the highest in the region) support this statement, compared to 51 percent for the Latin American average. Similarly, when asked if the government governs for the good of all the people, Venezuelans responded in the affirmative 42 percent of the time in 2009, which is 9 points higher than the Latin American average of 33 percent. No results were reported on these questions in earlier Latinobarometro reports.[58]

One might attribute these results to a presumed appreciation Venezuelans always had for their democracy. However, this appreciation increased in Venezuela during Chávez's first six years as president more than in any other Latin American country between 1998 and 2006, going from 32 percent to 57 percent.

Political participation has also increased significantly, with Venezuelans indicating that they are more politically active than the citizens of any other surveyed country. Venezuelans have the highest percentage of citizens who say they discuss politics regularly (47 percent, Latin American average is 26 percent), who say that they try to convince others on political matters (32 percent, average is 16 percent), who participate in demonstrations (26 percent, average is 12 percent), and who say they are active in a political party (25 percent, average is 9 percent).[59]

These results are surprisingly positive, especially if one considers all of the problems that still exist with the implementation of participatory democracy in Venezuela. In addition to the problems discussed above, of patronage, presidentialism, and motivation issues, there are also smaller problems, such as citizens' lack of political experience, resistance from elected officials who stand to lose power, and the lack of a completed legal framework for the new participatory democracy. One can only surmise how much more positive the Latinobarómetro results would be if Venezuela were to overcome these problems.

Another issue these initiatives for participatory democracy face is that mainstream observers of Venezuela generally do not accept them as genuine. Often they are regarded with intense suspicion because every departure from representative democracy is interpreted as anti-democracy, since some observers consider representative democracy to be the only viable form of government for a civilized country. Thus, when Chávez refused to sign the 2001 Summit of the Americas closing statement because its signers praised representative democracy and refused to include participatory democracy as another democratic option, he was generally condemned for having refused to sign a statement in support of democracy, with the implication that he actually opposes democracy per se.

Venezuelans who support the increased opportunities for political participation, though, are generally unfazed by these negative outside interpretations. We hope, however, that they are not oblivious to the more serious criticisms mentioned here. They need to take these criticisms seriously, so that Venezuela might eventually serve as a worldwide model for how countries can overcome the hollowing out of democracy that has been taking place in practically all representative democracies, as a result of the power of economic interest groups and the representatives' removal from citizens' concerns.

## Conclusion

Ultimately, Hugo Chávez's promise to bring about a Bolivarian Revolution, which in 2005 morphed into a promise to bring about 21st Century Socialism, has its roots in Venezuelans' profound disappointment with the ways in which both representative democracy and capitalism were practiced in Venezuela. The 20-year economic decline, from 1979 to 1999, which led to an unprecedented increase in poverty,[60] gave most Venezuelans the impression that their political and economic systems were hopelessly flawed. After all, with all of its oil wealth and other natural resources, Venezuela was supposed to be a rich country. Chávez rode this wave of popular discontent into the presidency in 1999 and set about to fulfill his promise to fundamentally overhaul the Venezuelan polity and economy. While most analysts of Venezuela tend to agree that this discontent swept Chávez into office, analysts' opinions start to diverge sharply as to what happened next.

In this chapter I argue that Chávez did indeed launch a fundamental overhaul of Venezuela's political system, but that this overhaul met with massive resistance that resulted in political polarization. That is, the new democratically ratified constitution and Chávez's consecutive electoral victories swept Venezuela's old political class almost completely out of power. Its reaction to this defeat was vehement and ultimately led to the 2002 coup attempt and the shutdown of Venezuela's vital oil industry. Some analysts (such as Human Rights Watch) would argue that Chávez's reaction to these efforts to oust him were excessive and that he used these incidents as an excuse to impose an increasingly authoritarian system by packing the Supreme Court, not renewing a TV broadcast license, and purging opposition supporters from posts in public administration. More sympathetic analyses, such as the one presented here, argue that the government had to do something about a court that essentially legalized a coup and TV stations that went beyond criticism and actively participated in destabilization. These moves, in turn, did politicize and reduce pluralism within state institutions (most importantly the judiciary), but these flaws were a consequence of polarization and illegal opposition activity, not its cause. In effect, the government's effort to introduce participatory democracy and to transform the economy had the unintended consequence of politicizing state institutions because of the opposition's vehement reactions to these moves.

However, while the introduction of participatory democracy in Venezuela has been a slow process, it has involved millions of Venezuelans and has demonstrably increased their satisfaction with their democracy. Millions of Venezuelans who were previously excluded from the political system now feel that they are a part of it. This too must be taken into consideration in any balanced accounting of the transformation that Venezuela has been going through. As pointed out here, serious obstacles (such as clientelism, personalism, and state bureaucracy) need to be overcome if the participatory democratic dimension of Venezuelan politics is to remain viable in the long run. Given that Venezuela is a vibrant democracy, it is up to the citizens themselves to decide, in future elections, for example, whether to continue this experiment.

**Endnotes**

1. The term "protagonistic" (*protagónica*) does not translate well, but it means to say that citizens are not only supposed to participate in the democratic process, but that they also take an actively involved (a protagonist's) role.
2. Evidence for the claim that Chávez's support draws just as much on the political changes as on the increased social programs can be found in the studies of Latinobarómetro (www.latinobarometro.org), which show that support for the president and appreciation of Venezuelan democracy have increased in tandem during the Chávez presidency and have done so to a far larger extent than in any other country in Latin America. For an analysis that examines this development in detail, see Gregory Wilpert, "Poll: Venezuelans Have Highest Regard for Their Democracy" and Serrano, "Venezuelans See Economy and Democracy More Positively Than Other Latin Americans." Also, unpublished informal interviews of this author with Venezuelans living in the barrios support this hypothesis.
3. The literature on the limited democracy that the *Punto Fijo* pact created in Venezuela is quite extensive and includes Myers, "The Normalization of Punto Fijo Democracy," Derham, "Undemocratic Democracy: Venezuela and the Distorting of History," and Coppedge, *Strong Parties and Lame Ducks*.
4. See Coronil and Skurski, "Dismembering and Remembering the Nation," for a fuller discussion of the consequences of the *Caracazo*.
5. Chapter 4, section 1 ("on political rights"), paragraphs 3 and 4, of the Exposition of Motives of the Constitution of the Bolivarian Republic of Venezuela (CBRV).
6. Terms used in chapter 4, section 1, paragraph 11 of the CBRV.
7. Weber, "Politics as Vocation," 99.
8. Weber, *The Theory of Social and Economic Organization,* 421.
9. Rawls, *A Theory of Justice;* Habermas, *Between Facts and Norms.*
10. Pateman, *Participation and Democratic Theory;* Schalom, "ParPolity: Political Vision for a Good Society." Another strand of political theory that would also

tend to support participatory democracy is communitarianism, as developed by Charles Taylor, for example.

11. For a summary of these effects of participation, applied to the workplace, see Bernhard Wilpert, "A View from Psychology."

12. Held, *Models of Democracy*, 269.

13. Evidence for this practice, though, has been mostly anecdotal on both sides of the political divide. Until now it has been almost impossible to know which side made greater use of the list.

14. See "Venezuela's Electoral Council Rules Referendum Petition Signatures to be Kept Secret," *Venezuelanalysis.com*, February 8, 2007 (http://www.venezuel-analysis.com/news.php?newsno=2213).

15. See de Sousa Santos, "Participatory Budgeting in Porto Alegre"; Avritzer, "Civil Society, Public Space and Local Power"; Bruce, *The Porto Alegre Alternative;* and Baiocchi, *Militants and Citizens.*

16. See Purcell, "Urban Democracy and the Local Trap" for a critique of U.S. planning boards.

17. The full list of functions in the CLPP law names 22 functions altogether.

18. Wagner, "Problems and Opportunities for Citizen Power in Venezuela."

19. National Institute of Statistics (INE: http://www.ine.gob.ve/sintesisestadis-tica/estados/miranda/index.htm).

20. The proposal to reorganize Venezuela's municipalities was presented to the country as part of the president's constitutional reform proposal, which would have allowed the president and the National Assembly to determine municipal boundaries instead of the states. The constitutional reform proposal was narrowly defeated, though, on December 2, 2007, so that this plan has since been put on hold. For more on the constitutional reform and its failure, see Gregory Wilpert, "Chávez Announces Nationalizations, Constitutional Reform for Socialism in Venezuela," and Gregory Wilpert, "Making Sense of Venezuela's Constitutional Reform."

21. Wagner, "Problems and Opportunities for Citizen Power in Venezuela."

22. Alexis de Tocqueville's analysis of democratic mores in U.S. society is particularly insightful in this regard. De Tocqueville, *Democracy in America.*

23. Rural community councils may be constituted with as few as 20 families and indigenous community councils with as few as 10 families, according to Article 4 of the community council law.

24. "Venezuelan Government Announces $5 Billion for Communal Councils in 2007," Venezuelanalysis.com, January 10, 2007 (http://www.venezuelanalysis.com/news.php?newsno=2188)

25. "Más fondos para consejos comunales," *El Universal*, January 12, 2007 (http://buscador.eluniversal.com/2007/01/12/eco_art_138895.shtml). Fifty percent of the amount for states and municipalities would be equal to 10% of the national budget. For the failed constitutional reform, though, Chávez proposed to give constitutional rank to community council funding and to set its

minimum at 5% of the national budget, or 25% of the amount reserved for states and municipalities (Article 167 of the reform).

26. Gregory Wilpert, "Chávez Announces Nationalizations, Constitutional Reform for Socialism in Venezuela."

27. Ibid.

28. Social production enterprises (EPS) are enterprises that operate on principles of solidarity and are certified as such by the government. To qualify, companies must ensure that they are organized cooperatively, rotate tasks, have a minimum amount of hierarchy within the company, contribute 10% of their revenues to the community, and work with the community in which they operate.

29. Ley Orgánica de la Administración Pública, Article 138.

30. Asamblea Nacional Constituyente, *Constitución de la República Bolivariana de Venezuela*, Caracas, *Gaceta Oficial* Nº 36.860, December 30, 1999, articles 51, 62, 178, 184; Ley Orgánica de la Administración Pública, articles 1, 135, 138; Ley Orgánica de Planificación Pública, articles 14, 58, 59; Ley Orgánica de la Contraloría General de la República y del Sistema Nacional de Control Fiscal, articles 1, 6, 14 sec. 9, 24 sec. 4, 25 sec. 7, 75, 76; Ley de los Consejos Locales De Planificación Pública, articles 5 sec. 21, 8, 24.

31. For more information on the urban land committees, see Gregory Wilpert, "Venezuela's Quiet Housing Revolution."

32. Kuiper, Jeroen, and Gregory Wilpert (2005) "Interview with Jacqueline Faría, Minister for the Environment: The Many Tasks of Environmental Protection in Venezuela."

33. See Piñero Harnecker, "The New Cooperative Movement In Venezuela's Bolivarian Process." The official figure is at about 200,000, but it is well known in Venezuela that many of these cooperatives do not function as cooperatives or have gone bankrupt since they were first counted.

34. "Proyecto de ley establece 'control obrero' en empresas," *El Universal*, January 13, 2007 (http://buscador.eluniversal.com/2007/01/13/pol_art_140072.shtml).

35. This law may have been passed by the time this book is published.

36. Presumably they will also integrate delegates from the communal councils, but since the law has not even been drafted yet, it is not known exactly who will be in the state and national coordinating councils.

37. Article 166 of the CBRV. Asamblea Nacional Constituyente. *Constitución de la República Bolivariana de Venezuela*. Caracas, Gaceta Oficial Nº 36.860, December 30, 1999.

38. Article 185 of the CBRV. The National Assembly passed the law for this council on February 10, 2010.

39. The contemporary Venezuelan historian Margarita Lopez Maya (2007) is the most prominent person to have leveled this criticism against the council structure. More indirectly, Jennifer McCoy makes this argument. See McCoy, "From Representative to Participatory Democracy?"

40. Ibid., 287.

41. Ibid., 288.

42. Ibid., 295.

43. For very detailed examination of all of these claims and many more, readers should see Gregory Wilpert, "Smoke and Mirrors: An Analysis of Human Rights Watch's Report on Venezuela," about the 2008 Human Rights Watch Report on Venezuela entitled "A Decade Under Chávez: Political Intolerance and Lost Opportunities for Advancing Human Rights in Venezuela." The report and my response discuss practically all of the accusations of erosion of separation of powers and politicization that have been leveled against the government.

44. One place where this dynamic of polarization and subsequent politicization has been less at work and where the government is indeed vulnerable to accusations of undermining democratic processes is when it appointed a mayor for Caracas and took away the elected opposition mayor's competencies (Tamara Pearson, "Venezuelan President Designates New Caracas Head and Communications Minister"). Legislators defended this move by pointing out that the 1999 constitution and administrative efficiency justify it. A similar case took place with regard to the central government's takeover of all the country's seaports and airports, which, according to the constitution are supposed to be co-managed between state and national governments (James Suggett "Venezuela Transfers Administration of Ports and Airports to National Government"). In this case the government justified the move by arguing that state governments were being ineffective in the fight against drug trafficking and other forms of smuggling. In both cases the government's reasons and methods can be considered suspect. However, they seem to pale in comparison with the numerous means the government has introduced that enable citizen participation in politics, whether via referenda, communal councils, or civil society participation in state institutions.

45. Hawkins and Hansen, "Dependent Civil Society."

46. Article 30 of the *Ley de los Consejos Comunales*.

47. Haiman El Troudi and Marta Harnecker, in separate personal interviews, February and March 2007.

48. Lerner, "Communal Councils in Venezuela."

49. Ibid.

50. Ellner, "Las estrategias 'desde arriba' y 'desde abajo' del movimiento de Hugo Chávez."

51. Hawkins and Hansen, "Dependent Civil Society."

52. It is possible that the formation of the new United Socialist Party of Venezuela (PSUV) will change this because its goal is to create a far more democratic party than the MVR ever was. Strong internal party democracy would mean that the leader's ability to direct the party would be significantly weakened.

53. Numerous accounts of such conflicts can be found in two excellent recent studies of Venezuela's social movements and communities. See Martinez, Fox, and Farrell, *Venezuela Speaks! Voices from the Grassroots*, and Bruce, *The Real Venezuela: Making Socialism in the 21st Century*.

54. To my knowledge, this has never happened with female politicians.
55. Hawkins and Hansen, "Dependent Civil Society," 119.
56. Corrales, "Hugo Boss."
57. While this figure held steady in the 2009 Latinobarómetro report, the Latin American average rose to 6.7. These reports may be downloaded at: http://www.latinobarometro.org/latino/LATContenidos.jsp (accessed May 25, 2010).
58. Ibid.
59. Latinobarómetro has been conducting an annual poll in Latin American countries for the past 14 years. The polls are financed by a variety of multilateral agencies, such as the European Union, the Inter-American Development Bank, and the World Bank. The 2006 poll was conducted in 18 countries in the month of October 2006 and involved interviews with over 20,000 people. Its margin of error is about 3% (varies from country to country). Source: http://www.latinobarometro.org/fileadmin/intranet/Informe_Latinobarometro_2006.pdf.
60. Poverty increased from 17% to 65%, according to research conducted at the Universidad Católica Andrés Bello, as part of its Proyecto Pobreza (Poverty Project).

# 4

# Venezuela's Presidential Elections of 2006: Toward 21st Century Socialism?

*Margarita López-Maya and Luis E. Lander\**

On December 3, 2006, President Hugo Chávez Frías was put to the test of popular scrutiny for the third time, and if one thinks of the recall referendum of August 2004 as the functional equivalent of a presidential election, this was the *fourth* time that Chávez faced elections. In contrast to the previous cases, on this occasion the electoral process proceeded in a climate more consistent with the norms of formal democracy, where distinct political actors agreed on consensual rules of the game and accepted the official results as announced by the National Electoral Council (CNE). Nevertheless, important institutional weaknesses persisted, and the level of political polarization that has characterized the Venezuelan political process since 1998 remained high, expressed as much in the results as in the course taken by the electoral campaign.

Our aim here is to contextualize and interpret the campaign and results of those 2006 presidential elections, taking them to have been a strong re-legitimation of the Bolivarian project and the leadership of President Chávez. As a result of the decisive electoral victory—which was the largest in both absolute and relative terms since (and including) Chávez's first electoral victory—the Venezuelan political process led by the president took a more radical path, moving from a "participatory and protagonistic democracy" to "21st century socialism." We have organized the chapter in four sections. In the first section we analyze the socioeconomic and political context in which the elections took place. In the second we explain the basic characteristics of the Venezuelan electoral system. In the third we lay out the major themes and episodes of the campaign itself. The fourth part is dedicated to the analysis of the electoral results, comparing them with those of earlier elections in order to evaluate the advances of Chávez's base. We close by assessing the implications of the results for subsequent Venezuelan political life.

## The Socioeconomic and Political Contexts

Since August of 2004, when the recall referendum produced favorable results for the president, Venezuela observed a strengthening of the perceived legitimacy of the Bolivarian political project of the government and the forces that supported it. This legitimacy was further reinforced by the beneficial international market for petroleum during this period. As a result, the government was able to make use of abundant fiscal resources, which had a positive effect on the economy (for further discussion see Chapter 6). Thanks to these developments and to the deployment of a new series of public policies, between 2004 and 2008 socioeconomic indicators showed a consistent improvement in the conditions of life of the population, especially among the poor. For this reason the president had important advantages in the 2006 election.

Beyond these indicators, other policy areas, such as those that are strictly political, international, or concerning crime and the personal security of citizens, reveal a more complex picture, with results less clearly positive for the government. On the one hand, the weakness of political actors opposed to the government had become very evident, a factor favoring presidential re-election, since the opposition had failed to convince the broader public that they were a sufficiently trustworthy alternative. On the other hand, in the first months of 2006, discontent over corruption, inefficiencies in the state bureaucracy, crime and personal insecurity, and Chávez's personalism were more plainly in view and had a negative impact on the president's campaign. Moreover, Venezuelan foreign policy, very active in these years, had been quite polemical and produced mixed results. Initiatives like Petrocaribe, for example, had strengthened ties between Venezuela and many Caribbean and Central American countries, giving Venezuela greater political influence in the region (see more detailed discussion of these issues in chapters 6 and 8). But on the other hand, the government's close relationships with countries like Cuba and Iran repeatedly produced tensions with the United States, Venezuela's principal client for oil exports. The government's strategy of both domestic and international political polarization produced some defeats, both before the 2006 election, such as the case of Peru, where it contributed to the candidacy of Alan García, or after, as in Honduras, where it proved impossible to restore President Zelaya to office after the coup d'état.

### The Petroleum Bonanza and Socioeconomic Improvements

After the economic contraction caused by the political turbulence between 2001 and 2004, an important economic recovery took place. An international

### Table 1.
### Some Macroeconomic Indicators, 2003–2006.

| Year | Price of the Venezuelan barrel basket (US$) | International reserves (in millions of U.S. dollars) | Inflation (% of variation in consumer price index) | Variation in Gross Domestic Product | Exchange rate (Bs. × $) |
|------|------|------|------|------|------|
| 2003 | 25.8 | 21.366  | 27.1   | −7.7  | 1600 |
| 2004 | 33.4 | 24.208  | 19.2   | 17.9  | 1920 |
| 2005 | 45.5 | 30.368  | 14.4   | 9.3   | 2150 |
| 2006 | 55.9 | 31.917* | 13.4** | 9.6** | 2150 |

Notes:
*First semester.
**Accumulated through the month of October.
Source: Central Bank of Venezuela (2006) and Ministry of Energy and Petroleum (2006).

market yielding a highly favorable export price for hydrocarbons contributed to the improvement. The average price for Venezuela's "exportation basket" rose from $25.80 in 2003 to $55.90 in 2006. In addition, petroleum industry reforms implemented by the Chávez administration increased the national treasury's share of gross petroleum receipts. This bonanza made possible an increase in social spending, provided resources to develop planned policies, and gave impulse to economic resurgence.

As can be seen in Table 1, between 2003 and the election in 2006 the Venezuelan economy enjoyed robust growth, at the same time showing a decline in inflation (see Chapter 6 for more details). Venezuelan macroeconomic performance in this period yielded improvements in the quality of life for the most vulnerable sectors of the population. Table 2 describes, for the same years, a sustained decrease in the rate of unemployment, as well as of the percentage of households living in conditions of poverty and of extreme poverty. Other measures—for example, a rising Human Development Index (HDI)—also suggest an improvement in living conditions in this period. While HDI has shown a sustained increase in Venezuela starting in the early 1990s, when it was first calculated, since the beginning of the Chávez government HDI has risen more rapidly, with the exception of the years 2002 and 2003, when it fell due to the profound political polarization and turbulence in the society. Venezuela, according to the criteria of the United Nations Development Program, is now among the countries with a high level of human development (between 0.8 and 1).

## Table 2.
### Some Socioeconomic Indicators, 2003–2006.

| Year | Unemployment Rate (%) | Homes in Poverty (%) | Homes in Extreme Poverty (%) | Human Development Index |
|------|------------------------|----------------------|-------------------------------|--------------------------|
| 2003 | 16.8 | 55.1 | 25.0 | 0.76 |
| 2004 | 13.9 | 47.0 | 18.5 | 0.80 |
| 2005 | 13.0 | 37.9 | 15.3 | 0.81 |
| 2006 | 9.9* | 33.9** | 10.6** | – |

Notes:
*Third trimester.
** First semester.
Source: National Institute for Statistics (INE 2006).

In addition to the demonstrated indicators, which show a general improvement in the socioeconomic situation of the population, other factors are both relevant and in themselves contribute to the improvements in quality of life for the citizens. Particularly relevant is the array of social policies, including the so-called missions, that the national government has developed since the end of the petroleum strike of early 2003.

Mercal Mission, for example, has since 2003 built a vast network for the distribution of food and other basic consumption goods. Compared with the private, commercial food chains, Mercal offers consumers savings of 40 percent. According to official figures, this Mission serves close to half of the country's population, yet its subsidized prices are not included in the formula used to establish the value of the basic food basket used by the INE to calculate poverty and extreme poverty lines. This indicates a possible further improvement for certain popular sectors.[1]

The increase in educational expenditures since the beginning of the Chávez government has also contributed to improvement in the quality of life and the expectation of a better future for the poor. One of the key areas of government activity has been the Bolivarian schools, which return children to a full school day, while giving them two meals and two snacks, free uniforms, and books for their classes. These schools also guarantee free matriculation, reversing the tendency of the 1990s of both declining enrollments and increasing school dropout rates. According to official statistics, from 1999 to 2005, 5,654 Bolivarian schools were built, serving a student population of more than 1 million. Spending on education increased to above 8 percent of the Gross Domestic Product, surpassing the recommendations of UNESCO.

Barrio Adentro Mission is another policy that had an important political impact. It is fundamentally focused on offering free health services in the poor urban *barrios*, which include primary medical attention, provision of medications, house calls, and 24-hour medical services.[2] This mission began in April of 2003, soon after the end of the strike in the petroleum industry, offering services to the residents of the municipal zones of Libertador and Sucre in the Metropolitan area of Caracas, and from there the network was expanded to include all of the states and municipalities of the country. Official data indicated by 2006 that 33,321 persons (Cubans and Venezuelans) were working in Barrio Adentro I, having made some 210 million consultations. After June 2005, a new stage was opened to complement the first mission: Barrio Adentro II, consisting of Centers of Integral Diagnosis, Centers of High Technology, and the Facilities of Integral Rehabilitation. This new level of expertise allows the program to give more sophisticated medical attention to the sick and injured.[3]

These initiatives, along with others, like the Missions Robinson I and II, oriented towards ending illiteracy and offering the opportunity to complete primary studies to adults who could not previously do so; or Decree 1,666, which began the process of regularization of urban land rights in the popular barrios, continued to raise hopes in popular sectors of tangible improvements in their quality of life in the immediate or short-range future. Decree 1,666 started a vigorous dynamic of community organizing through the Urban Land Committees (CTU), facilitating other processes of organization for popular self-expression. The Water Community Boards (Mesas Técnicas de Agua), another participatory innovation launched by the state's water companies to manage, with the communities, water problems affecting them, and the Communal Councils, created throughout the country by law in 2006, are other popular organizations that contributed support for Chávez's re-election in 2006.[4]

### The Political Context: The Weakness of the Opposition and Presidential Leadership

In spite of the importance of these economic and political facts, the element that played the most important role in reinforcing the re-election of Chávez for the next constitutional period was, without doubt, the political loss suffered by opposition groups in the insurrectional confrontations that they brought against the government between 2001 and 2004.[5] The march and coup d'état of April 11, 2002, the general strike, with the lockout of the petroleum industry, between December 2002 and February 2003, the multiple mass demonstrations taking place before the presidential recall referendum in August of 2004, some of them violent, like those in the street actions of Operation *guarimba*,[6] and, indeed, the result of the referendum itself, not only failed to produce the fall or exit of the president and his government, but created problems among the groups in the opposition that became difficult to repair in the following two years.

It is revealing that a little after the recall referendum, in the midst of tensions and conflicting accusations, the Democratic Coordinator (CD), an umbrella organization of various opposition groups, crumbled. This made visible the heterogeneity of the opposition, and the range of preferences and positions that had co-inhabited this political bloc. Business organizations and the private media, leaders up to this point, lowered their tone and de-emphasized their role. The hierarchy of the Catholic Church also lowered its profile. The opposition-aligned management of PDVSA was replaced, hence lost its position as a political force. The political parties of the opposition, after they had been displaced by "civil society," were timidly reprising their role of mediation and representation, although with internal fragility and without the confidence of the population. A differentiation between two groups within the opposition became clearer. One group considered it necessary to embrace the rules of democracy and to construct a renovated opposition within them. Another insisted on continuing to seek extra-institutional shortcuts. Until December of 2005, when parliamentary elections were held, the less democratic forces tended to prevail.

In August of 2004, for example, the Democratic Coordinator denounced alleged electronic fraud in the results of the referendum, rejecting the endorsement of the results given by international observers such as the OAS and the Carter Center. However, they never provided proof that backed up their allegations. With this immediate antecedent, they went to the regional elections in October of that year in a politically weak position, since their supporters did not trust the electoral process. As a result, they only won in two of the 23 federal entities in dispute and gained several mayoral positions.[7] In the parliamentary elections of 2005, alleging again that they did not trust either the National Electoral Council or the conditions of the electoral process, the opposition forces withdrew from participation just a few days before the electoral vote. A few days earlier, they had promised to international observers, such as the OAS and the European Union, to remain in the contest if certain minimal conditions were guaranteed. These conditions were agreed to, but they withdrew nonetheless, leaving themselves entirely out of the National Assembly for the period 2006–2010. At the beginning of 2006, the outlook for the rebuilding of opposition political forces gave little reason for optimism.

As mentioned above, another political element influencing the electoral climate of 2006 was the government's developing approach to international relations. Since 2005, it had been advancing a very active international agenda. The first months of that year saw constant verbal confrontation with high officials of the U.S. government over Venezuela's purchases of military equipment from Spain and Russia. Another source of friction with the United States was the influence that Venezuela exercised in Latin America over political processes of other countries, for example in Bolivia. With few interruptions, these tensions continued throughout 2006, becoming one of the thematic axes that polarized Venezuelans in the electoral campaign.

Conditioned by these tensions and the regime's desire to develop a multipolar international system, these years have been characterized by constant efforts of the Venezuelan government to amplify and strengthen new alliances. It has done so without being inhibited by the consequences that some of its actions could provoke in its increasingly difficult relationship with the United States, which remains, in any case, its principal commercial partner. Caracas has been developing policies to bring Venezuela closer to countries in Latin America and the Caribbean, using as its central tool its petroleum, and developing an alternative proposal to the Free Trade Area of the Americas (FTAA), the Bolivarian Alliance for the Peoples of Our America (ALBA). The energy agreements with island countries of the Caribbean, with Argentina, Colombia, and Brazil, among others, and also its attempt to incorporate as a member of Mercosur are some examples. In the years since 2005, the president made frequent trips to South American countries where he had prominent status. The government also increased its presence in Africa and strengthened its relationships with China, Iran, and Russia, projecting a growing international image.

A third political theme present in the national debate since 2005 refers to 21st century socialism, proclaimed by President Chávez as the new orientation of the Bolivarian project. This proclamation generated enthusiasm, skepticism, and frank rejection in diverse sectors of society. It is, in any case, an open formulation and has been subject to tension and polemics ever since. To the climate of uncertainty that this new presidential proposal provoked were superimposed episodes of land invasion, expropriation, and announcements of confiscations. These were seen by some as welcome indicators of the advance of socialism, while for others, as unacceptable threats to private property and moves toward an approximation of the Cuban model. This theme too was incorporated forcefully in the electoral campaign.

Finally, it is necessary to mention other diverse political elements present in the 2006 campaign, such as the growing tendency of the president to exercise power in a personalist way. This semi-dictatorial tendency, as his critics have insisted, broke the necessary independence of public powers in a democratic system. But personalism has also limited the possibility that inside the Chavistas' own forces a genuinely democratic debate could develop over the direction of the country, including, for example, over what is understood by 21st century socialism, or what the confirmation of legitimate and recognized collective leadership would entail.

## The Electoral System

The Venezuelan electoral system has been changing to adjust to the new orientation of the political regime, marked by participatory democracy. Among the most evident novelties incorporated in the constitution of the Bolivarian Republic of Venezuela, sanctioned through a popular referendum in December 1999, was the extension of the presidential term to six years and the possibility of immediate re-election for a single additional period (Article 230). Through a constitutional amendment approved by referendum in February of 2009, this and other articles were modified to permit the indefinite re-election of those holding any elected public office. The 1999 constitution assures the rights of "associations with political ends" through democratic methods of organization, functioning, and direction (Article 67). However, the constitution changed the term for political parties to "organizations with political ends," now obligated to hold internal elections, both for their directing agencies and for choosing their candidates for popular elections. The constitution also recognized the authority of the state to regulate the private contributions that organizations with political ends receive and eliminated any public funding for them.

The constitutional text also, as in the past, conceives of public power on three levels: the national, regional and municipal. The national public power is now organized in five powers that are formally independent of each other. In addition to the three traditional ones in representative democracies—the legislative, the executive, and the judicial—two additional ones are incorporated—citizen power and electoral power—that are meant to increase the autonomy and independence of the traditional branches and are responsible for controlling the rest of the powers and administering the electoral process.

The electoral power office is in charge of all that is related to organizations with political ends and electoral processes at all levels. It is conceived as an autonomous power that forms and executes its own budget. It is presided over by the National Electoral Council, composed of five principal directors and ten substitutes. The constitution requires that all of the directors and their substitutes be independent: three of them proposed by civil society, one by the faculties of juridical and political science in the national universities, and the other by the citizen power branch of government. They remain in their offices for seven years and can be re-elected. They are chosen at two separate moments: the three by civil society are put forward first, and three and a half years later the other two ones are chosen. They are finally ratified by the National Assembly with a vote of two thirds of the members, from a list prepared and presented by a nomination committee composed by eleven NA deputies and ten representatives of other social organizations. The five directors in turn elect the president of the National Electoral Council (articles 295 & 296).

According to the law, presidential campaigns should not last longer than four months. Seven months in advance of the date fixed by the National Electoral Council for elections, the political parties, groups of electors, and candidates should develop their internal campaigns and other preparatory acts (Organic Law of Suffrage and Political Participation, Articles 196 & 199).

Finally, it is a legal mandate (ibid., Article 153) that the Venezuelan electoral system be automated, from the act of voting itself, with electoral machines that register the votes and store them electronically, to the process of scrutiny over the initial act, the transmission of these data to the collection centers, and the national totaling of the results. This law was replaced in August 2009, with the approval of the Organic Law of Electoral Processes; the new law will be applied for the first time in the September 2010 legislative elections.

## The Electoral Campaign

By the close of the period during which presidential candidacies were presented to the National Electoral Council, the number of candidates had swelled to 25. Nevertheless, it was clear that only two had a chance: President Hugo Chávez and the Governor of Zulia, Manuel Rosales. The electoral campaign officially began on August 1, 2006, though campaign activities by both the government and the opposition began months earlier. Here we concentrate on two aspects of this campaign: the themes presented for debate, and the strategies developed by the respective campaigns.

### Themes and Platforms of the Candidates

The electoral process, in terms both of the proposals and the interchange of ideas, had an essentially conventional character. It privileged the use of media resources, investing substantially in advertising. For this reason it was poor at the level of content.

As early as April, the would-be themes of the campaign began to appear. With the launching of the pre-candidature of Teodoro Petkoff,[8] the opposition showed a less antagonistic public position than this sector had made us accustomed to. Petkoff presented himself as a candidate open to negotiation and tolerance, placing himself at the center of the ideological spectrum. He insisted on the necessity of redoubling efforts to eradicate poverty, recovering the ability of Venezuelans to live together, and establishing a government that respects the law. In advancing this proposal he made a call to construct a "Venezuela without fear."[9] This agenda, which was initially only one of the opposition's options, ended up becoming the thematic axis articulated in the campaign of Manuel Rosales under the motto "Atrévete" (Dare!).

During June and July there was an intense debate among the opposition groups to put forward a single candidate and a common platform. Multiple surveys indicated the characteristics of the ideal figure: "a candidate different from those of the past, who comes from below, who has suffered, who has been successful in his life and knows how to listen."[10] Among the three principal candidates of the opposition—Petkoff, Rosales, and Julio Borges of the Primero Justicia Party—it was Rosales who best fit this image. The surveys also revealed the enormous public acceptance of the social policies of the government, especially the *misiones*. For this reason the message of the opposition candidate could no longer be, as it had been in the past, the total rejection of these policies.

The search for a proposal that could compete with the missions of the government materialized in early September with the "Mi Negra" card, a kind of debit card that, according to the opposition, would allow for fair distribution of petroleum rents. The card would offer a direct subsidy to middle-income and poor families—without further intervention of the state—of a monthly amount that would vary between 600,000 and 1,000,000 bolívares (between $280 and $465), depending on the production and price of crude petroleum. It was a proposal that, while making concessions to Chavismo, conceptually was consistent with the approach of the liberal market that the opposition supports. It would also be distributed to the unemployed, and could accumulate like a savings account.[11] This card was a reformulation of the proposal that Petkoff had made in April, with his "cesta ticket petrolero."[12]

In the middle of October, reaffirming that the choice of him over Chávez did not aim toward "annihilating" his electoral adversary, Rosales discarded the possibility that an eventual government of his would bring about a constitutional reform. His campaign chief affirmed that the 1999 document included sufficient constitutional mechanisms to guarantee democratic governability in a transition.[13] With this proclamation, the central slogan of the campaign ("Atrévete") acquired a less pugnacious or confrontational tone.

While the general ideas of the Rosales campaign gave evidence of the opposition's movement toward the political center, the ambiguity of the way in which it was handled in the discourse permitted the sectors located more toward the right of the political spectrum to live with them. As the general tone of the campaign did not surpass the polarization of the earlier years, sectors more to the political right, such as business sectors or the owners of the large private media conglomerates, prioritized unity in the confrontation with Chávez over differences within the opposition that they recognized as less significant. But this dynamic contributed to weaken the credibility of these proposals to voters whom the surveys identified as "ni-ni."[14]

For his part, incumbent candidate Chávez announced in May a constitutional reform for the year 2007, although he did not yet provide the content of this planned reform. In August he did not yet touch on the theme in his rally to celebrate his inscription as a candidate before the National Electoral Council.[15] But at the end of that month the head of his campaign team, Francisco Ameliach, in an announcement of an offensive that they would be preparing in case the opposition candidates withdrew from the electoral race, provided some of the details of the planned reform: the indefinite re-election of the president and the elimination of the principle of proportional representation in the election to deliberative bodies.[16]

In a rally held on September 1, the incumbent president reiterated the proposal for his indefinite re-election, which would be sanctioned, he said, by a popular referendum. In this speech Chávez presented the themes and strategies of the electoral campaign that would follow. He announced that December 3 would mark the beginning of a new phase of the process leading toward "a socialist and revolutionary participatory-democratic model." The discourse had a strong tone, pugnacious and polarized. He reiterated that in the contest there were only two candidates, himself and President Bush of the United States, whom he baptized as Señor Diablo (Mister Devil). He called it shameful that the counter-revolutionary opposition "doesn't have a real candidate, who can present an idea." He advised Mister Devil that "what we have here are *puro bates partidos,*"[17] and on December 3, if they (the opposition forces) come, "we are going to pulverize them, not even their dust will be seen." Once more he reaffirmed that if the twenty two *frijolitos*[18] "come out with a trick, the shot is going to come out the butt end of the rifle."[19]

Another theme of the Chávez campaign was the role of private property in the socialist model announced for the next period. It was abruptly introduced in the debate a few days before the rally mentioned above, in the Teresa Carreño Auditorium, where the Metropolitan Mayor of Caracas, Juan Barreto, announced planned expropriation measures, which days later were brought against the main golf courses of the city.[20] The national executive, through the vice president, officially expressed its disagreement with these decrees of expropriation and called for a resolution of the conflict through judicial channels.[21] Without an explicit pronouncement from Chávez, the issue was left floating in the air.

In the televised program *La Hojilla*, the program most emblematic of the political polarization on the Chavista side, the president introduced another polemical theme: that of the single party of the revolution; this generated discontent and even malaise within the columns of Chavismo. The day he registered as a candidate, the president was backed formally by twenty-five political organizations from among the multitude of political and social organizations that identified with him. Some came to believe that what was being proposed was a single-party political system like the Cuban one. This was repeatedly denied by various mouthpieces of the government, who declared that the president's proposal referred exclusively to the unification of the parties and organizations that backed him. Nevertheless, this proposal brought discomfort among Chavistas, some alleging that the unification should be the result of a democratic debate among and within the parties themselves.

### Campaign Strategies

The electoral campaign—as expected—stirred up the intensely polarized political climate that Venezuela has lived with since 1998. Taking account of this reality, the campaign managers defined their strategies. They had in common an abundant use of the media resources and a great deal of money, along with an unwillingness to conduct a substantive debate of ideas. Equally, both sets of antagonists returned to the expedient of using state resources in their electoral activities. Obviously, the magnitude of the resources that the president controls is much greater than that of a governor, but both made illegal use of government publicity. The open participation of government officials in proselytizing activities was likewise notorious.[22]

From the beginning the president's campaign was clearly designed to emphasize polarization, believing that it would again favor him, as occurred during the recall referendum. The campaign identified the "enemy to defeat" in the figure of the devil personified by the president of the United States. All opposition candidates were nothing more than representatives of this maleficent pole. Since it was not clear to the government and its strategists that the opposition candidates would not withdraw before the end of the electoral contest, they aimed to gain 10 million votes. The purpose was to motivate the participation of supporters and lower abstentions, thereby guaranteeing the legitimacy of the electoral result, since 10 million votes would represent 62.5% of the registered electorate.

The Miranda Command—the president's campaign team—selected men and women in the confidence of the president, many coming from the military world. The Command included also representatives of diverse social organizations, while the representatives of political parties, except for the MVR (The Fifth Republic Movement), were invited to participate only as advisers.

The strategy of accentuating polarization was maintained until early October, when surveys consistently showed that if the candidate maintained this stance he would not appeal to undecided voters. Further, polls such as those carried out by Hinterlaces indicated that there was a very high level of undecided voters.[23] A message centered on "love" was then introduced, reducing the bellicose discourse that preceded this shift. The press viewed this change as a product of foreign advice. The campaign likewise decided to reduce its use of the color red and to combine it with other colors, especially blue.[24]

This change produced friction and discontent among sectors of Chavismo. It could have been as a result of this discontent that at the beginning of November Rafael Ramírez, president of PDVSA and Minister of Energy and Petroleum, speaking at a company event attended by high-level managers and employees, emphasized the commitment of all of the workers and employees of PDVSA to the Bolivarian revolutionary project. He said that the company should be "*roja, rojita.*" When the recording of this meeting was made public, President Chávez supported the Minister, going on to say that "the petroleum workers, like the members of the National Armed Forces, are in this process . . . and if they don't like it they can go to Miami."[25] Raúl Isaías Baduel, the Defense Minister, later declared that the National Armed Forces are "institutional" and not politically aligned.

At the same time, the confrontational and polarized discourse coexisted with one that was more tempered and focused on achievements. The public learned about the inauguration of public works such as new branches of the Caracas Metro subway system, the first stage of the metro of Valencia, the train to the Valleys of the River Tuy, and the second bridge over the Orinoco River. In addition, the state television and radio stations continued to show images of Chávez granting subsidies, scholarships, and financing community projects.

The opposition groups, in contrast, entered the campaign on August 1 without being able to establish a common strategy. They had several candidates as well as a number of supporters of abstention from the electoral process. The possibility of settling on a single candidate did not seem certain. However, an intense process of negotiation among the three principal aspirants culminated in the selection of Manuel Rosales, made public on August 9, a week into the electoral campaign. On this day, in a gesture of unity that would become one of the lines of the Rosales campaign, five candidates withdrew, including Julio Borges of the Primero Justicia Party. Teodoro Petkoff had done so a week earlier. This left, nevertheless, two more candidates of some relevance: the comedian Benjamín Rausseo—Er Conde del Guácharo (The Count of Guácharo)—and the ex-Minister Roberto Smith, who would both end up withdrawing.

The negotiation within the opposition expressed a return to formal political competition, and produced, among other things, the reduction in the leadership of organizations and social actors who had played leading roles in the recent past. The most notorious was the case of Súmate, an organization "without political aims" that, however, had been dictating standards of conduct for the opposition and was trying to take upon itself the function of organizing primary elections to select the opposition unity candidate.

This return to formal political competition, for Rosales, meant that it was a priority for him to convince his base that, in this instance, it was worth voting, contradicting one of the recurrent themes used by the opposition in the preceding years. The *captahuellas* machines, for example, part of the technological platform to automate the electoral process, were stigmatized when some parliamentarians during the 2005 parliamentary elections alleged that they violated the secrecy of the vote. Though they were brought under an exhaustive external audit that probed those allegations and judged them to be without basis, it was an important part of the 2006 opposition strategy that its potential voters get over the fears that these allegations had incited.

In contrast to the strategy of the Miranda Command, the Rosales team looked to present its candidate with a more moderate tone. Rosales, being a man of few words, centered his campaign on gestures and activities rather than speeches. His travels over all of the territory were very intense, something that opposition leaders had not done in recent years. Most important, he went into the popular *barrios* in several cities. On various occasions he was confronted, to the point of being assaulted with rocks and bottles, by radical elements of Chavismo.[26]

The president's polarizing slogan, "to stuff your mouth with 10 million votes" ("10 millones por el buche"), met its response on the Rosales side with the slogan "for the 26 million Venezuelans." His campaign centered on problems considered relevant to the majority and that indicated failure of governmental action, such as unemployment, poverty, and the increase of insecurity and crime. It also criticized international cooperative programs developed by the government and, helped by surveys indicating voter concerns about these issues, represented them simply as "gifts of free money."[27]

In September the battle of surveys began, with results that formed part of the publicity campaigns of both candidates. Nevertheless, in November the majority of surveys indicated clearly that Chávez would obtain victory. Datanálisis reported on November 15 that Chávez would obtain 52% of the votes while Rosales would obtain 26%, which would amount to a difference of 26 points. IVAD signaled on November 23 that the advantage of Chávez over Rosales would be 27%. International survey firms, such as Associated Press-IPSOS and the Universidad Complutense de Madrid, also granted to Chávez an advantage of more than 20%. Nevertheless, some survey results declared a "technical tie" and augured that on December 3 Rosales would win. The most quoted were from Keller and Associates and Observatorio Hannah Arendt, both politically tied to the opposition.

## Analysis of the Results

On December 3 after 10:00 P.M., thanks to the almost complete automation of the electoral process, the National Electoral Council released its first official bulletin with results that showed a definite tendency. The following day, with 95.2% of the votes counted and totaled, the results were as follows: for Chávez 7,161,637 votes, which represented 62.9% of the valid votes and for Rosales 4,196,637, or 36.9%. The polarization between these two candidates was the most acute registered in the history of Venezuelan voting, in that they shared 99.8% of the valid votes. The third place candidate did not achieve 5,000 votes. The abstention rate fell to 25.1% and the null votes represented 1.4% of the counted votes.

Comparing these results with results of previous presidential elections, we observe that both Chávez and the opposition candidate increased the absolute number of votes. In 1998 Chávez won with 3,673,665 votes and his opponent, Henrique Salas Römer, obtained 2,613,161. In the elections of 2000, Chávez went up to 3,757,773 votes, while his then-opponent, Francisco Arias Cárdenas, dropped slightly to 2,359,459 votes. In the 2004 recall referendum, the NO choice of the Chávez side captured 5,800,629 votes, while the opposition's SI received 3,989,008. As can be seen, since 1998 the votes for Chávez consistently increased in absolute terms, while the votes of the opposition suffered a slight decrease in the 2000 elections, even

### Table 3.
### Presidential Elections
### 1998, 2000, 2004, and 2006, by State (percentages).

|  | Elections 1998 | | Elections 2000 | | Referendum 2004 | | Elections 2006 | |
|---|---|---|---|---|---|---|---|---|
|  | Chávez | Salas | Chávez | Áreas Cárdenas | NO | SI | Chávez | Rosales |
| **National** | 56.2 | 40.0 | 59.8 | 37.5 | 59.1 | 40.6 | 62.9 | 36.9 |
| Amazonas | 44.0 | 54.3 | 62.4 | 36.8 | 70.3 | 28.9 | 77.8 | 22.0 |
| Anzoátegui | 62.0 | 35.1 | 61.4 | 36.9 | 54.1 | 45.6 | 61.2 | 38.5 |
| Apure | 38.6 | 59.9 | 54.4 | 44.9 | 67.6 | 32.1 | 69.8 | 30.0 |
| Aragua | 69.1 | 26.3 | 73.9 | 23.1 | 68.0 | 31.9 | 71.8 | 27.9 |
| Barinas | 64.8 | 33.7 | 62,6 | 36.2 | 69.2 | 30.4 | 68.9 | 30.9 |
| Bolívar | 59.0 | 37.6 | 69.0 | 29.1 | 66.4 | 33.3 | 68.6 | 31.1 |
| Carabobo | 43.9 | 52.7 | 61.4 | 35.5 | 56.8 | 43.1 | 61.7 | 38.1 |
| Cojedes | 54.8 | 43.3 | 58.7 | 39.6 | 67.0 | 32.6 | 73.3 | 26.4 |
| Delta Amacuro | 46.0 | 52.2 | 65.6 | 35.5 | 70.4 | 28.6 | 78.1 | 21.7 |
| Distrito Capital | 62.5 | 31.5 | 61.4 | 33.9 | 56.0 | 44.0 | 62.6 | 37.1 |
| Falcón | 47.6 | 48.4 | 56.8 | 40.9 | 57.2 | 42.2 | 62.2 | 37.5 |
| Guárico | 56.5 | 41.4 | 59.7 | 38.8 | 71.0 | 28.8 | 71.9 | 27.9 |
| Lara | 58.5 | 38.1 | 63.0 | 34.6 | 64.8 | 35.0 | 66.5 | 33.2 |
| Mérida | 51.5 | 45.3 | 57.5 | 40.5 | 53.8 | 45.8 | 53.8 | 46.0 |
| Miranda | 51.5 | 43.0 | 51.9 | 44.6 | 50.9 | 49.0 | 56.4 | 433 |
| Monagas | 56.5 | 40.9 | 58.8 | 39.8 | 61.0 | 38.8 | 70.9 | 28.9 |
| Nueva Esparta | 44.8 | 51.1 | 57.9 | 39.1 | 50.0 | 50.0 | 58.6 | 41.2 |
| Portuguesa | 63.3 | 33.7 | 72.3 | 26.1 | 72.9 | 26.4 | 77.0 | 22.7 |
| Sucre | 51.4 | 46.3 | 63.5 | 34.8 | 66.9 | 32.6 | 73.6 | 26.2 |
| Táchira | 47.9 | 49.0 | 54.8 | 43.7 | 50.6 | 49.1 | 51.1 | 48.6 |
| Trujillo | 47.9 | 44.1 | 65.2 | 33.9 | 66.3 | 33.2 | 69.4 | 30.4 |
| Vargas | 62.7 | 33.0 | 70.0 | 27.0 | 64.2 | 35.6 | 69.3 | 30.4 |
| Yaracuy | 50.0 | 46.7 | 58.1 | 38.5 | 60.2 | 39.4 | 65.1 | 34.5 |
| Zulia | 55.3 | 40.8 | 47.2 | 48.7 | 53.1 | 46.6 | 51.4 | 48.5 |

Source: CNE www.cne.gov.ve

adding the votes obtained by the candidate who came in third place, Claudio Fermín, who obtained 171,346. Expressed in relative terms, the matter changes slightly. In Table 3, the results of presidential elections since 1998 can be seen in percentages of valid votes, with data shown at both the national and state levels.

In the 1998 elections, Salas Römer obtained the majority of the votes in seven states. In 2000, Arias Cárdenas won only the state of Zulia. In the recall referendum of 2004, the YES response, the option of the opposition, triumphed only in Nueva Esparta, and by only 113 votes. In 2006, Chávez won in all of the states of the country.

What does not seem to have changed much is the political polarization. As in previous contests, the middle and upper social sectors tended to vote

## Table 4.
### Referendum 2004 and Elections 2006: Examples of Electoral Polarization, Rich and Poor Parishes (percentages).

| | Referendum 2004 | | Elections 2006 | |
|---|---|---|---|---|
| | NO | YES | Chávez | Rosales |
| **National** | 58.9 | 40.6 | 62.9 | 36.9 |
| **Metropolitan Caracas** | 48.7 | 51.3 | 54.8 | 44.9 |
| Municipio Libertador | 56.0 | 44.0 | 62.6 | 37.1 |
| Parroquia Antímano | 76.7 | 23.3 | 81.9 | 17.8 |
| Parroquia San Pedro | 28.0 | 72.0 | 32.3 | 67.5 |
| Municipio Baruta | 20.6 | 79.4 | 24.2 | 75.6 |
| Parroquia El Cafetal | 9.3 | 90.7 | 10.9 | 88.9 |
| Municipio Chacao | 20.0 | 80.0 | 23.3 | 76.5 |
| Municipio El Hatillo | 17.9 | 82.1 | 20.3 | 79.6 |
| Centro Club La Lagunita | 5.7 | 94.3 | 7.8 | 92.1 |
| Municipio Sucre | 47.1 | 52.9 | 53.1 | 46.6 |
| Parroquia La Dolorita | 73.1 | 26.9 | 78.4 | 21.3 |
| Parroquia Leoncio Martínez | 21.8 | 78.2 | 26.4 | 73.3 |
| **Zulia State** | 53.1 | 46.6 | 51.4 | 48.5 |
| Municipio Maracaibo (Maracaibo) | 47.9 | 52.1 | 46.9 | 52.9 |
| Parroquia Ildefonzo Vasquez | 67.4 | 32.6 | 57.8 | 42.0 |
| Parroquia Olegario Villalobos | 2.3 | 73.7 | 26.9 | 73.0 |
| **Carabobo State** | 56.8 | 43.1 | 61.7 | 38.1 |
| Municipio Valencia (Valencia) | 47.6 | 52.4 | 54.4 | 45.4 |
| Parroquia Santa Rosa | 62.0 | 38.0 | 65.5 | 34.1 |
| Parroquia San José | 14.1 | 85.9 | 17.6 | 82.3 |
| **Lara State** | 64.8 | 35.0 | 66.5 | 33.2 |
| Municipio Iribarren (Barquisimeto) | 60.9 | 39.1 | 64.8 | 34.9 |
| Parroquia Unión | 72.5 | 27.5 | 74.7 | 24.9 |
| Parroquia Santa Rosa | 40.5 | 59.5 | 45.4 | 54.4 |

Note: municipio = municipality subdivision; parroquia = parish, subdivision of municipio.

Source: CNE www.cne.gov.ve

mainly for whatever option was opposed to Chávez, while the more popular sectors voted for him. One can also discern a polarization between the countryside and the city. While Venezuela is a highly urbanized society, the vote of the small cities, towns, and villages tended to lean more in Chávez's favor, while in the large cities the tendency is not so pronounced. In Table 4 some examples of these tendencies are illustrated, comparing the results of the recall referendum of 2004 with the 2006 elections.

The table shows a selection of the behavior of voters in distinct cities and at different socioeconomic levels. In the city of Caracas, the three small municipal zones with the highest income levels—Baruta, Chacao, and El Hatillo—consistently vote against Chávez, while the large municipal zones of Libertador and Sucre, which contain the largest *barrios* in the Caracas area, consistently favor Chávez with their vote. For the metropolitan Caracas region, the table presents data that are still more discriminating. Among the various municipal zones it shows parishes with distinct social compositions, demonstrating with clarity the mentioned tendency of voting preferences to align with socioeconomic status. For example, the Antímano Parish of the Libertador Municipal Area is one of the poorest of the city and votes solidly for Chávez. In contrast, that of San Pedro, largely of the middle class, votes for the candidate of the opposition. An extreme example is the Club La Lagunita center, a residential center for middle and upper-class sectors, where the opposition captures more than 90% of the votes.

The table also shows data corresponding to three states of the country that are seats to three of the most important and populated of the country's cities. There the vote in favor of Chávez in the entire state is proportionally superior to that obtained in the state's capital. This confirms that in rural and outlying zones Chávez has a stronger electoral support. Also, for each of the cities, the table compares the electoral votes in the richest and in the poorest parishes. Consistently Chávez loses in the rich ones and wins in the poor ones.

After the 2006 presidential elections, three additional national elections have been held as of the time of this writing. In December of 2007, a referendum was held to decide on the presidential proposal for constitutional reform. This proposal was narrowly rejected, with 50.7% voting against it and 49.3% voting for it. This is the only national election as of this writing that the president or the position he supports has lost. In November of 2008, elections for state governors and mayors were held. The president's candidates received 52.7% of the votes, and those of the opposition 40.2%, with the remaining votes being cast for local candidates or dissidents from Chavismo. In February of 2009, a new referendum was held to modify the articles of the constitution that placed limits on re-election of public office holders. This too was a proposal of the president and it was approved, with 54.6% of the vote versus 45.1% who voted against it.

## From Participatory Democracy to 21st Century Socialism

As the presidential rhetoric of December 2006 forecast, 2007 proved to be another year of intense polarization and political confrontation. The constitutional reform, with "five motors" to drive the society towards socialism, was announced by the president at the close of 2006, sharpening tensions, especially after August, when the specific contents of the proposal to change the constitution were known. The presidential proposal was amplified with other articles elaborated by the National Assembly and brought to a popular referendum in December, and ended up being rejected by the voters. After 9 years in government, and 12 electoral processes, Chávez and his political alliance tasted the bitterness of defeat for the first time.

Despite the asymmetry of resources in favor of the government, the reform did not pass. In the calculations of the National Electoral Council, the president saw the support he received in the presidential elections of 2006 reduced by more than three million votes. And the 25% abstention rate in the 2006 election increased to 44%. In other words, part of the Chavista voters abstained from voting.

Many diverse factors explain this reversal, including errors of the president himself. Chávez began this new process of change by proposing his own indefinite re-election, a bad start in a country with a long tradition of *caudillos* and dictators who had changed the constitution to maintain themselves in power. When he spoke of the Unified Party's need to achieve the advance towards his socialism, he created discontent among his allies. In August, he presented the reform proposal as a work "in his own handwriting." Should a constitution, or its reform, be someone's personal work? The debate that followed was scarce, superficial, and of short duration, causing still more confusion about what Chávez understands by 21st century socialism. The contents of some of the articles were deep and substantial—they were not a reform—and should have been considered through a constitutional assembly, since they substantially modified the constitution of 1999. Among the reforms that contributed to making this proposal unpopular were a return to state centralization, the opening to a territorial reorganization of the country, and the creation of a Popular Power; in addition to indefinite re-election, increasing the power of the president to name authorities in all of the new territories, to control the Central Bank, and personally approve all military promotions.

However, following the defeat suffered in the 2007 referendum, Chavista candidates achieved important victories in the mayoral and gubernatorial elections of 2008. Strengthened by these new favorable results, the president again took up some of his previously defeated proposals. Two and a half months after the regional elections, the new referendum of February 2009 was held, with the proposal to eliminate limits to re-election emerging victorious. Various other aspects of the defeated constitutional reform have since been introduced through laws passed by the National Assembly, where the president controls an obedient majority. Thus the narrow defeat suffered in the 2007 referendum seems to have amounted to nothing more than a simple slip on the path to 21st century socialism.

## Conclusions

The electoral triumph of President Chávez in December of 2006 emphasized the positive impact that the implementation of a variety of social policies, especially the missions, had on virtually all social sectors. The government, during a period of three years, was able to finance them with abundant resources provided by oil rents. The elections also occurred after three years of economic expansion that contributed to the improvement of all macroeconomic and social indicators.

While sectors of the opposition were indeed able to unify in order to present a single candidate, they obviously could not overcome the consequences of the torpid policies of their immediate past. Candidate Rosales not only had to confront an opponent of vast strategies and resources, but had to overcome obstacles that the opposition itself had placed before him. For example, the lack of confidence in the electoral system, product of denunciations of fraud that were never demonstrated, made ample sectors of the opposition at least initially inclined toward abstention.

The victory of Chávez on December 3 has proved decisive. He augmented his electoral gains both in absolute and relative terms, for the first time getting over 60% of the votes. Paradoxically, it was not easy to interpret the mandate that he obtained. During the campaign, the incumbent candidate produced two parallel discourses, occasionally contradicting one another. On the one hand, he made use of a confrontational discourse that in moments of crisis produced success. On the other hand, he talked of peace and love, with more tolerance toward those that did not share his projects. The co-existence of both discourses initially generated uncertainty over the direction the new presidential period would follow. At the same time, the two postures elicited support in different sectors of Chavismo.

The theme that raised the most interest and concern was that of 21st century socialism. Apart from some few proposals to modify the political system, such as the indefinite re-election of the president, the creation of a new "popular power" based on the "parliament of the street,"[28] and the elimination of the principle of proportional representation in the election of the deliberative bodies, little else was said during the campaign about the contents of this model of society.

However, a little before finalizing his campaign—and later empowered by the electoral triumph—President Chávez announced his intention to form a commission to evaluate, formulate, and open a debate about the details of the proposed constitutional reform, which he announced would strengthen the socialist project, qualified by him as "native, indigenous, Christian, and Bolivarian."[29]

During the first months of the new period, his approach began to clarify. The radicalization of the process prevailed as a predominant tendency. With the presidential initiative to bring together the factions supporting him into one political party, the United Socialist Party of Venezuela (PSUV), and the proposal to turn on what he called the "five engines"[30] to drive society towards socialism—one of which was the constitutional reform itself—the confrontational language once again took center stage and this time was not limited to opponents, but also targeted dissident voices within Chavismo itself. The electoral results also created a new situation of a game open to multiple interactions of the sociopolitical forces in society. The interaction of these forces and political actors within each pole and the relationships established among blocs within them, together with the strong legitimacy of President Chávez, explain some of the events of recent years.

**Endnotes**

\* Translation by Jon Eastwood.

1. See Encartado de *Últimas Noticias,* "Los 10 grandes logros de la revolución bolivariana en Distrito Capital." Caracas: November 2006.

2. Retrieved from: www.barrioadentro.gov.ve, accessed on December 4, 2003.

3. See Encartado *Últimas Noticias,* November 2006.

4. López-Maya and Lander, "El gobierno de Chávez: democracia participativa y políticas sociales."

5. López-Maya, "Insurrecciones de 2002 en Venezuela: causas e implicaciones."

6. This is the name given to a series of street closings that were realized in the main cities of the country, some of them violent.

7. Lander and López-Maya, "Referendo revocatorio y elecciones regionales en Venezuela."

8. Petkoff is a very well-known figure in Venezuelan politics. He was a guerilla leader in the 1960s and later founder of the political party Movimiento al Socialismo (MAS). He was Minister of Coordination and Planning in the second government of Rafael Caldera and currently is director of the daily *Tal Cual.*

9. *El Nacional,* April 21, 2006.

10. Oscar Shemel of Hinterlaces, quoted in *El Nacional,* November 9, 2006.

11. *Últimas Noticias,* September 7, 2006.

12. In Quirós, *El Nacional,* April 30, 2006.

13. *El Nacional,* October 25, 2006.

14. This designation, "ni-ni," is a common expression in Venezuela used to identify those who do not identify with either of two poles in any context.

15. *El Nacional,* August 13, 2006.

16. *El Nacional*, August 27, 2006.
17. This is a baseball term referring to an especially poor hitter.
18. "Frijolito" was the name of the horse of a candidate whom Chávez opposed in the 1998 elections. Chávez began calling that candidate by the name of his horse, and has periodically used the term in a more general sense to refer to opposition candidates.
19. *Últimas Noticias*, September 2006.
20. *El Nacional*, August 23, 2006.
21. Retrieved on August 20, 2006, from: www.aporrea.org.
22. See, among other sources, *Ojo Electoral*, 2006, 2007, and the report of the European Union's Mission, 2007.
23. *El Nacional*, September 20, 2006.
24. *Últimas Noticias*, October 17, 2006.
25. www.aporrea.org, downloaded in November 2006.
26. Muñoz, "Rosales disputa la política territorial."
27. According to the survey firm Hinterlaces, in the month of September 87% of respondents expressed disagreement with the "giving away of money" to other countries; 79% rejected the Cuban influence in Venezuelan politics; and 76% considered the diplomatic conflict with the government of the United States to be negative (*El Nacional*, September 19, 2006).
28. The "parliament of the street" is a new modality of consulting the population about laws that are being discussed in the National Assembly, to be held in public plazas on weekends.
29. *Últimas Noticias*, December 4, 2006.
30. The others being an enabling law (una ley habilitante) so the National Executive could assume legislative faculties, an educational strategy called "moral y luces" to develop socialist values in the society, a new "power geometry" that would relocate political, economic and social powers in Venezuela's territory in order to serve a socialist society, and the creation of a "Popular Power" that would transform the nature of the Venezuelan state to make it socialist.

# PART

# II

## THE BOLIVARIAN PROJECT

# 5

# Advancing Women's Rights from Inside and Outside the Bolivarian Revolution, 1998–2010

*Cathy A. Rakowski and Gioconda Espina*

## Introduction

Confusion prevails, both in Venezuela and among outside observers, regarding women's legal advances since Hugo Chávez Frías was first elected president in 1998. Some facts are widely agreed upon—Venezuela has a "non-sexist" constitution, a National Institute for Women (INAMUJER), a Women's Development Bank (Banmujer), a law defending a woman's right to freedom from violence, and a Ministry of Popular Power for Women and Gender Equality (MinMujer). Other information is less clear. Do housewives receive social security pensions, a right established in the constitution and two separate laws? Will the government decriminalize abortion? Are there guarantees of parity, 50 percent representation of women among elected officials and government appointees? Does the constitution guarantee equality to gays, lesbians, bisexual, and transgender/transsexual persons?[1] Is advancing women's rights a key policy objective of President Chávez for his Bolivarian Revolution? Is this, as former Minister of Women María León and President Chávez have proposed, a revolution that not only has a "gender perspective" but can even be called "feminist"?[2]

Part of the problem is that the answers to these questions are not always simple or straightforward. For example, there is a difference between passage of a law and its implementation. There is also some misunderstanding of the origin of rights initiatives, particularly the role of actors inside the revolution relative to those outside.[3] Much of the confusion is spread by websites, the press, and radio or television interviews that treat plans, rumors, and political rhetoric as if they were facts or that deliberately exaggerate or misrepresent facts to support a political agenda.

In this chapter we will resolve some of this confusion by highlighting the chronology and genealogy of selected rights advances and unsuccessful efforts to advance sexual rights as part of the revolutionary process (*El Proceso*).[4] We attempt to clarify the relative importance to specific rights initiatives of state actors (elected, appointed), feminist academics, lawyers, and middle-class and "popular" women's non-governmental organizations (NGOs).[5] We also outline the contributions of two state institutions whose objectives include women's rights and empowerment—INAMUJER and Banmujer.

We argue that a) civil society feminists and women's organizations active since the 1940s but especially in the 1980s and 1990s set the stage for many of the women's rights advances that Chávez implemented following his election; b) on paper, advances have accelerated since 1998 but many have not been implemented; c) collaborations among women of different political affiliations and classes were strongest in the beginning, but over time those who do not support Chávez or criticize *El Proceso* have been progressively marginalized; and d) even some strong supporters of Chávez and the revolution have been silenced because they promote reforms that are not at the center of the socialist project, including such controversial issues as abortion rights or equal rights for GLBT persons. We provide possible explanations for why certain rights initiatives passed and others failed.

The discussion here builds on many years of research by both authors on women's organizing in Venezuela and on direct involvement by the second author in civil society organizing, in multiple campaigns for legal reforms, and as formal or informal advisor to diverse legal projects, elected and appointed officials, and national women's committees and INAMUJER.

## Background and Contemporary Context

Between 1978 and 1990, most legislative reforms that advanced women's rights in Venezuela were civil society initiatives. Leadership for those initiatives involved women lawyers and judges, journalists, academic feminists, labor union activists, and women's NGOs.[6] Civil society groups sought collaboration with women in diverse political parties and government offices. There are many documented instances of politicians and high-ranking femocrats[7] also recruiting women of diverse backgrounds and political affiliations to participate in presidential and ministerial advisory committees.[8] In the 1990s, leadership shifted from civil society groups to women in Congress[9] and to a new National Women's Council (CONAMU), charged in 1993 with working closely with women's NGOs to advance women's rights, policies, and programs.[10]

This shift led to the growing institutionalization of women's rights in the 1990s, a big change from the first experience of broad-based collaboration among women from different social and political sectors during the campaign to reform the Civil Code (1978–1982).[11] The reform became law in July 1982.

Coalitions between civil society groups, labor unions, and members of Congress also supported a successful reform of the Organic Labor Law in 1990. One unsuccessful coalition-based attempt took place in 1992, when lawyers of the FEVA (Federación Venezolana de Abogadas) and members of the CFP (Círculos Femeninos Populares), the national network of women's groups in working-class and low-income neighborhoods, submitted a proposal to women in Congress with over 30,000 signatures calling for a law against domestic violence. Collaborations involved women from political parties, women in labor unions, housewives' groups, professional associations, feminists, and others. Some feminists involved have referred to collaborations as "unity in diversity."

As leadership for legal reforms shifted to women in Congress in the 1990s, many civil society women's groups supported politicians' initiatives. These included a reform of the Suffrage Law (1997) mandating quotas of 30 percent for party-supported electoral candidates, and passage of two new laws—the Law of Equal Opportunities (1993) which mandated creation of the National Council for Women (CONAMU),[12] and a Law against Violence against Women and the Family (1998), which addressed diverse forms of violence and established punishment for perpetrators and services for abused women.

When Hugo Chávez won his first presidential election in 1998 and announced his intention to reform the constitution, a broad spectrum of civil society groups, contemporary and former femocrats, and politicians were galvanized both by new political opportunities to advance rights and by perceived threats to rights already won. The result was widespread mobilization and a very public year-long campaign that took advantage of the process of public consultations for the new constitution. Since 1998, there have been other instances of collaboration for women's rights among civil society groups that support the Bolivarian Revolution and those that do not.

Three issues stimulated the new wave of activism and collaboration immediately following the 1998 election. One was the announcement of a 50 percent cut to the CONAMU budget, and the second was sparked by a rumor that Chávez planned to name the wife of a military officer as its president. The third was the absence of women on his first cabinet and other high level posts and almost none on his list of approved candidates for the National Constituent Assembly (NCA) that would draft the new constitution. Former ministers, members of NGOs, labor unionists, academics, autonomous feminists, lawyers, and women from diverse social and political sectors mobilized successfully to defend the CONAMU and to propose María León—long-time feminist, community activist, and member of the Communist party—as its president. They were joined by women from the MVR (Chávez's 5th Republic Movement, Movimiento V República)[13] and other political parties and groups that supported Chávez. Feminist supporters with access to President Chávez also worked to educate him on the political importance of women as an interest group and to raise his consciousness regarding the need to avoid sexist language during public addresses (early speeches were riddled with sexist jokes and paternalistic comments on women's sacrifices and suffering as mothers).

Results of this activist collaboration include heightened policy and programmatic attention to poverty and racism as "women's issues" and establishment of INAMUJER by presidential decree in 1999 to replace CONAMU (as an institute, INAMUJER has had more authority and a larger budget). However, the best known result of women's intensive and extensive mobilizing to defend rights already won and to guarantee new rights is what femocrats, feminists, and women across a broad spectrum of political and class affiliations proudly call the world's first "non-sexist constitution"—a constitution "with a gender perspective."[14]

> [W]omen's groups . . . organized intensive campaigns to guarantee that gender equity would be consecrated in the new Constitution. They swore that there would be not one step back on rights. They took advantage of the fact that members of the constitutional assembly were obliged to consult with all sectors of civil society . . . Several coalitions of women . . . [and] CONAMU organized strategy-building meetings across the country . . . dozens of workshops and conferences were held.[15]

The result, ratified through a nation-wide referendum in 1999, was a new constitution characterized for the first time by:

> non-sexist language; principles of equality and equity; recognition of women's rights as human rights that are universal, indivisible, inalienable, inviolate and protected by the State; non-discrimination based on gender, age, sex, . . . creed, or social condition; the right to a life without violence; the right to [women's] eligibility and exercise of power and decision making; . . . [certain] reproductive rights; recognition of the economic value of housework . . . equal pay for work of equal value . . .[16]

This constitution is heralded widely in Venezuela and abroad as President Chávez's achievement, the basis for the Bolivarian Revolution, a "first step" in the long process of transition to what Chávez calls his Socialism of the 21st Century project, and, more recently, as evidence that the president is a "feminist." Nonetheless, it is well known that this is the product of an almost nine-month-long process of consultation by members of the National Constituent Assembly with all sectors of society to consider proposals and ideas for the content of the new Constitution. What is not well known or acknowledged by Chávez or supporters of the revolution is that most legal initiatives that focus on women that made it into the new constitution had origins in the pre-1998 period. The 1999 constitution includes almost all demands sought by Venezuelan women activists since 1936, including the recognition of housework as an economic and productive activity.

Lack of clear information about the genealogy of women's rights and of the non-sexist language in the constitution is one source of confusion regarding the origin of women's rights advances. Another factor has to do with the difference between passage of legislation—laws on paper—versus implementation.

## Passing a Law versus Implementing a Law

The passage of new laws, approval of legal projects, and the consecration of certain rights in the constitution do not guarantee their implementation. Many of the groundbreaking legal projects introduced in the National Assembly (AN)[17] and many laws already passed—whether pre- or post-1998—have never been implemented. There are several possible explanations.

Legal reforms or proposals for new laws should go through several steps. The process begins with introduction of a project for discussion in the AN; legal projects may go through two or more discussions and many revisions before a final decision is made. The law must be formally "sanctioned" (passed) by the full chamber of deputies of the AN and approved by presidential decree. The entire process can take years, although some laws appear to have been passed quickly, with little formal discussion (see Table 1). Such is the case of the Organic Law to Protect Families, Maternity and Paternity in 2007 and the breastfeeding law.

Even after a law has been passed, other factors can interfere with implementation. Laws require *reglamentos*—the explicit rules governing implementation and that assign responsibilities for funding and implementing the law. In some cases, members of the AN can simply fail to develop and approve *reglamentos*, making implementation impossible. The president can also give the order to implement by presidential decree, as part of his

# Table 1.
# Advances, Reversals and Attempted Advances in Women's Legal Rights, 1998–2009 (updated as of Dec. 17, 2010).

| Year | Advance |
| --- | --- |
| 1998 | CONAMU preserved by coalition of women in politics, government, & civil society. |
| 1999 | New Constitution approved; non-sexist language. |
| | Reform of 1993 Law of Equal Opportunities and order to implement by presidential decree through the Ley Habilitante. |
| | INAMUJER & Women's Defender Office created by Presidential Decree 428 in October; published in *Gaceta Oficial* 5398. |
| 2000 | National Electoral Council (CNE) declares Article 144 of the Law of Suffrage and Political Participation is unconstitutional. Eliminates 30% quota for inclusion of women on party candidate lists. |
| | CEDAW international agreement outlawing discrimination against women is ratified by the National Assembly. By law, principles should be incorporated in subsequent related legislation. |
| 2001 | Banmujer created by Presidential Decree 1243 in March; published in *Gaceta Oficial* 37154. |
| | International Convention against Trafficking in Persons ratified by the National Assembly. Principles to be incorporated in subsequent related legislation. |
| | Project to reform Penal Code submitted to National Assembly (AN) by Committee on Family, Women and Youth (CFWY) of the AN with support from INAMUJER and widespread support from diverse civil society groups and feminists. Focuses on making all forms of violence against women a crime against the person, decriminalizing adultery and abortion, among others. No action taken; see 2005 and 2010. |
| | Law on Land and Agricultural Development is passed by the AN. Includes articles that qualify women as household heads eligible to lead agricultural projects and with preferential property rights. No information on implementation. |
| 2002 | Organic Law of Social Security approved by AN. Submitted by Committee on Social Security of the National Assembly in response to a 2001 proposal from the CFWY with widespread support from civil society groups. No action taken on pensions for homemakers. |
| | Project for Special Regulation (*reglamentos*) of Social Security Law's article on pensions for housewives submitted to AN. Developed by a coalition of women in the National Assembly, INAMUJER, legal advisors, and civil society groups. Tabled and never discussed by the AN. |
| | Project for Law on Responsible Paternity. Submitted to AN by CFWY in the name of a "women's movement." Tabled for several years. |
| 2003 | Legal petition submitted to Supreme Court against Attorney General's request that precautionary measures in the Law against Violence against Women and the Family (1998) be suspended. Introduced by INAMUJER and Office of Women's Defender. Second petition introduced by civil society groups (academics, lawyers, women's NGOs). Supreme Court delays decision until 2006 when it approves suspension of precautionary measures as unconstitutional. |
| | Coalition of civil society women's groups and INAMUJER protest failure by the CNE to implement Article 144 of the Organic Law on Suffrage and Political Participation (1997) which established quotas of 30%; denounce dearth of women on candidate lists for December elections. CNE reaffirms that quotas are unconstitutional; 50-50 campaign (for women to be half of all candidates and among those elected) initiated by INAMUJER with support from diverse civil society groups inside and outside the revolution. |

## Table 1, continued.

| | |
|---|---|
| 2003 | Project on Organic Law for Women's Rights to Gender Equity and Equality introduced by the CFWY. Would replace the Law of Equal Opportunities reformed in 1999. See 2008. |
| | Proposed Organic Law to Protect the Family, Maternity and Paternity introduced by CFWY. Discussion delayed until 2007. |
| | INAMUJER, in consultation with advisors and women's groups inside and outside the revolution, produces the first five-year National Plan for Equal Opportunity. |
| 2004 | Two documents are introduced by a coalition of civil society women's organizations (inside and outside the revolution) to AN Committee working on Penal Code reform proposing decriminalization of abortion and redefinition of legal concepts of rape and domestic violence. No action taken on reform of Penal Code, but proposals for reforming the legal conceptualization of rape, domestic violence and other forms of violence as crimes against the person (and not against morals) were included in the 2006 Organic Law for a Life Free from Violence. |
| 2005 | AN approves Law of Social Services. Article 41 affirms stipend for impoverished housewives. Chávez mandated implementation of Article 41 through the Misión Madres del Barrio. But population targeted was 100,000 "young mothers in need"—that is, those without husbands or employment—not women age 55 and over as stated by the law. |
| | Coalition of women inside and outside the revolution proposes a reform of Suffrage Law to include 50-50% representation by gender and "alternability" of candidates for all elections. Introduced to the AN by CFWY with support of INAMUJER. AN has not discussed. |
| | In November, 28 civil society women's organizations representing diverse political and non-political groups (known as MAM, Movimiento Ampliado de las Mujeres) submit to the NA's Committee on Women's Rights and Gender Equality an "Agenda for Parliamentary and Legislative Work," calling for implementation of existing laws, elimination of discrimination in all laws, and support for women's political and economic participation. |
| | Chávez signs a Punto de Cuenta in May (No. 273) authorizing a gender perspective in public budgets in response to an agreement made with UNIFEM. *Action followed slowly*: María León sends letter to Chávez in April 2008 asking him to order the Ministry of Finance to create a mechanism to enforce. Since 2007, INAMUJER has trained small groups of community activists, produced a booklet on the "ABCs of Gender Sensitive Budgets," and conducted training workshops for government agencies in an effort to support implementation. |
| | Despite calls for reform that predate 1998 and two reform projects submitted in 2004, the AN ratifies only a minimal reform of the existing Penal Code. This move reinstates several articles previously stricken down as unconstitutional or discriminatory and creates a legal crisis for implementation of other legislation including the honor killing defense, adultery by women as a cause for divorce, rapists' legal forgiveness if they marry victims, among others. Critics believe main objective of the AN was to ratify abortion as a crime. |
| 2006 | First National Encounter on Violence against Women held in Maracaibo (March 17–19). Attended by members of MAM/Women's Assembly, Women's Rights Defender, supportive members of AN, and NGOs to discuss strategies for advancing women's legal rights. |
| | Law of Communal Councils decreed on April 10 and published in *Gaceta Oficial* 5806. Mandates a gender perspective in the design of local-level public policies and participation of women on councils. INAMUJER charged with guaranteeing implementation. Done so through training of women organized into their national network of *Puntos de Encuentro* (estimated by INAMUJER at 25,000 member groups). Implementation has been slow and uneven due to resistance at the local level and limited resources for implementation. |

# Table 1, continued.

| | |
|---|---|
| 2006 | AN approves Organic Law for a Woman's Right to a Life Free from Violence; replaces 1998 anti-violence law. Published in *Gaceta Oficial* 36668 in April 2007 following order to implement by presidential decree in March 2007. Partial implementation began in 2008 and is supported by international funding. As of April 2009, 29 courts for violence against women functioning with plans to open 20 more tribunals. Law defines rape and domestic violence as crimes. |
| | Reform of Organic Law to Protect Girls, Boys and Adolescents passed. Substitutes 1998 law. No information available on implementation. |
| 2007 | Organic Law to Protect Families, Maternity and Paternity approved September 20, 2007, published in *Gaceta Oficial* No. 38773. Provides generous terms of maternity and paternity leaves with full pay (contradicting provision of Labor Law). No evidence of application for such leaves to any firm or government agency. |
| | Organic Law to Promote and Protect Breastfeeding passed. Implementation appears to be voluntary and limited to isolated cases, for example in the Ministry of Culture and by the Colegio de Odontólogos (national association of dentists). |
| | November. First National Encounter of INAMUJER's *Puntos de Encuentro* groups held in Caracas to discuss policy and program needs. |
| | A new coalition of feminists and *sexodivers@s*, including *El Grupo Ese*, met with high level government officials to discuss including constitutional reforms to decriminalize abortion and to guarantee rights for non-heterosexuals. Their demands were not included in the proposed reform, which was voted down through an electoral referendum in late November. |
| 2008 | The National Electoral Council (CNE) publicly approves and recommends reform of Suffrage and Political Participation Law to include 50-50% parity and alternation by gender among party-sponsored candidates. The measure is again supported by INAMUJER, a group of women in the National Assembly, and diverse civil society groups. A new Law of Electoral Processes is passed to replace the Suffrage and Political Participation Law and makes no mention of gender parity or quotas. In the meantime, the CNE has left it up to political parties to voluntarily implement and most claim they do not have enough women willing to be candidates. |
| | Project on Organic Law for Women's Rights to Gender Equity and Equality approved in first discussion. Included in the draft were promotion of sexual and reproductive rights, application of the principle of 50-50% parity with alternation of men/women in all elections and public employment, protection for mothers, ratification of principle of a right to a life free from violence, outlaw use of non-sexist language by mass media, prohibition of sexual exploitation in marketing, protection for housewives. Also proposed new responsibilities for national, state and municipal level agencies for women. The principle of gender parity and alternability was removed prior to submission for the second discussion in 2009. |
| | Chávez creates the Ministry of State for Women's Affairs through presidential decree 5919. It functioned as an extension of INAMUJER's work, with María León as minister; replaced in 2009. |
| | National Congresillo de Mujeres held in April with hundreds of women attending. Preliminary report indicates that among the policies and programs requested by women were gender training for men, legalization of abortion, social security for women, implementation of all laws that include women's rights, reform of discriminatory legislation, rights for women in non-legalized relationships, and more political training. |

**Table 1, continued.**

| | |
|---|---|
| 2009 | President Chávez announces the creation of a new Ministry of Popular Power for Women and Gender Equality on March 8, Presidential decree 6,663. María León, president of INAMUJER, is named the first Minister. This move grants greater authority and funding to implement women's programs and legislative reform. Five new vice minister positions are created. INAMUJER, Banmujer and the Fundación Madres del Barrio Josefa Joaquina Sánchez (aka Misión Madres del Barrio) are assigned to the new ministry. |
| | U.N. Conference on Gender Violence is held in Caracas in April. Such conferences can be politically strategic for legal reforms and program funding. |
| | I Latin American Camp for Women in Popular Movements is held in Vargas State, November 25–29. Some 350 women attend from 7 countries, including 14 women's groups in Venezuela. A declaration was released by Alba TV on November 30 with a list of demands for change in Venezuela: implementation of 50-50 with alternation principle in the 2010 elections, an end to clientelistic practices in the Missions (denounced as a mechanism to garner votes), legalization of a woman's right to interrupt pregnancy (defined here as a class issue), and education on feminism and sexual diversity for popular women. |
| 2010 | In June, María León steps down as minister and is replaced by Nancy Pérez Sierra, a physician. |
| | Women from inside (Frente Bicentenario de Mujeres) and outside the revolutionary process (acting as MAP) collaborate once again to demand implementation of all articles of the 2006 law against violence in response to a highly publicized murder of a woman by her husband. Specific demands include training of police and judges and creation of special violence courts throughout the country. |
| | Members of the AN work on a new, "modern" Penal Code. There is strong speculation that it will include decriminalization of abortion. |

special powers designated under the Ley Habilitante.[18] If there are no approved *reglamentos* and the president fails to order implementation by decree, then the law remains unimplemented. Good examples of this outcome include the three laws that establish the right of social security pensions for housewives who fit certain prerequisites. None has been implemented as approved.[19] The president also sends laws he drafts to the AN for their discussion and approval.

Critics of several hastily passed laws point to other problems. Some laws are so general and poorly written as to be un-implementable without significant reform. In other cases, one law may contradict another or be in conflict with the constitution. For example, laws passed in 2007 on protection of maternity and paternity and on breastfeeding contradict regulations already implemented that are based on the 1990 reform of Organic Labor Law.

Other issues can delay passage of *reglamentos* or implementation of a law. The first is the cost involved in the implementation of certain rights, such as pensions for housewives, and the second is the lack of political will to implement such rights—a lack that is usually explained within the context of whether or not a law is relevant and useful for garnering votes (is

## Table 2.
## Articles in the Constitution That Support or Establish Women's Rights.

| Article | Content |
| --- | --- |
| 21 | Everyone is equal before the law. Discrimination based on race, sex, creed, social condition and other features is abolished. All people have the same rights and liberties. |
| 75 | Protection for families. Family relations based on equality of rights and obligations, solidarity, joint efforts, mutual understanding and respect. |
| 76 | Maternity and paternity are fully protected, regardless of marital status of mother or father. State guarantees maternity protection, in general and from the moment of conception…guarantees access to family planning … couples have right to decide freely the number of children they want and have right to information and means to exercise right. |
| 77 | Marriage between a man and a woman is protected. It must be founded on free consent and absolute equality of rights and obligations. Stable unions between a man and a woman that comply with legal requirements will be treated the same as a marriage. |
| 78 | Boys, girls and adolescents are subjects with rights and will be protected by the law. |
| 80 | The state will guarantee elderly men and women the full exercise of their rights … including right to work if they desire. |
| 81 | The state guarantees equality for people with disabilities … right to human dignity … and employment … according to their conditions and the law … right to use sign language. |
| 82 | Everyone has the right to secure … housing with basic services … that humanize family relations. |
| 83 | Health is a fundamental social right, an obligation of the state that will guarantee it as part of the right to life. |
| 84 | The state will create a national public health system … everyone has a right to health protection and the obligation to promote and defend this right. |
| 86 | All persons have a right to social security … that guarantees … protection for maternity, paternity. |
| 87 | All persons have the right and obligation of work. ..and a productive occupation that dignifies their existence. |
| 88 | The state will guarantee equality and equity among men and women in the exercise of their right to work. The state will recognize domestic work as an economic activity that creates added value and produces wealth and well-being. Housewives have the right to social security in conformity with the law. |
| 92 | All workers, male and female, have the right to worker benefits that reward long-term employment and support them in the event of a layoff. |

there strong public support?). A third factor is what some deputies who supported passage of women's rights legislation and some academic feminists have complained about: the "androcentric culture" that is alive and well among Chávez supporters, members of diverse political parties, and most members of the AN.[20] A fourth factor is the conflict between one law and another, or the charge that some aspect of a law is "un-constitutional." This strategy was used to strike down the "precautionary measures" in the

1998 Law against Violence and was used to overturn gender quotas established in the 1997 Suffrage and Political Participation Law.

## Examples of Legislative and Institutional Supports for Women's Rights

Table 1 presents a chronology of women's rights proposals and their status since 1998. Table 2 presents key articles relevant to women's rights in the constitution. Following discussion of features of specific legislative initiatives, we comment on INAMUJER and Banmujer.[21] Until the creation of the Ministry of Popular Power for Women and Gender Equality (MinMujer) in 2009, these were the most visible institutions charged with promoting women's involvement in the revolutionary process.

For Table 1, we compiled data from the legislative agenda on the National Assembly's website and supplemented these with relevant discussions from agency reports, INAMUJER's website, articles and commentaries from major news sources, critiques of laws and legal projects that have been circulated through the Internet for discussion and feedback or included in scholarly publications, and insights provided through personal communication with contacts in the National Assembly and INAMUJER. For Table 2, we used the official version of the 1999 constitution.

### 1999 Constitution

The 1999 constitution uses feminine and masculine versions of all nouns and includes explicit references to women's contributions and rights throughout. The constitution is groundbreaking, a fact made more remarkable as it was the product of a National Constituent Assembly (NCA) whose members included few women.[22] Groups and individuals involved in the writing of texts for specific articles related to women's rights acknowledge readily that these were the result of widespread collaborations between members of the NCA's Committee on Family and Women (CFW), CONAMU staff, academic feminists, and coalitions of women and women's groups that organized for this purpose.[23]

Members of the CFW held meetings with women from all walks of life and political affiliations. The committee welcomed proposals submitted by women's groups. They particularly sought out women's affairs ministers and femocrats from previous administrations as well as women who had worked on earlier legal rights campaigns, gender advisors from international agencies and local NGOs, women's groups from all classes, feminist academics and lawyers, labor union and small business leaders, members of the Popular Women's Circles (CFP), etc. The CFW lobbied members of the assembly to get proposed text included in the final draft of the constitution. Two academic feminists edited the final version of the proposed constitution to eliminate sexist language.[24] Although the constitution of 1999 includes almost all rights sought since 1936, it does not include the right to a safe abortion and does not explicitly guarantee equal rights of gay, lesbian, or transgendered persons.

Key provisions that guarantee women's rights are found in Articles 75, 76, 77, 80, 81, 82, 83, 84, 86, 87, 88 and 92. Academic feminists wrote Articles 76, 86 and 88. Where an explicit statement of rights was impossible (that is, abortion), advisors helped phrase texts in such a way as to leave open possibilities for broad interpretation. For example, some insiders have argued that the constitution guarantees the rights of GLBT persons—if a very broad interpretation of sexual and reproductive rights is applied. Such an interpretation has not held up in court; in 2008 the Supreme Court (Tribunal Supremo de Justicia) stated that neither rights of same sex partners nor those of cohabiting but unmarried heterosexuals are covered in the constitution—nor are they denied.[25]

The constitution guarantees a woman's right to work and to health services, and the right to social security and pensions. Perhaps the best known is Article 88:

> The state will guarantee equality and equity among men and women in the exercise of their right to work. The state will recognize domestic work as an economic activity that creates added value and produces wealth and well-being. Housewives have the right to social security in conformity with the law.[26]

Following approval of the constitution in 1999 and elections for the new National Assembly in 2000, a new Committee on Family, Women and Youth (CFWY) of the National Assembly has made several attempts to support implementation of Article 88 through other legislation but without success.

### Laws Including Pensions for Housewives

Passed in December 2002, the Organic Social Security Law's Article 17 calls for special protections and "integral social security" to persons who are disabled, indigenous, or who have any other condition that may merit such protection. One such group is housewives who "lack personal, family or social economic protection." Advisors to the CFWY, including academic feminists, have proposed the following criteria for housewives to be eligible for social security: a housewife must be 55 or older, have been a homemaker for 25 consecutive years, not receive social security or a pension from any other source either as the recipient or his/her dependent, and register as an eligible housewife. The principle of a pension for housewives is also mentioned in Article 4 of the Law of Equal Opportunities (1993 and 1999 versions) and in Articles 32 (housewives in economic distress or *estado de necesidad*) and 41 of the Social Service Law (housewives' pensions should be 60–80% of the minimum wage). The Social Service Law was approved in September 2005, but it lacks *reglamentos* for implementation (as of this writing in December 2010).

Feminist academics and legal scholars again worked together with members of the CFWY to develop a proposal for developing *reglamentos* so that the assignment of responsibilities and sources of funding needed to implement a law for social security pensions for housewives would be made explicit legally. Submitted to the AN in 2002, the draft *reglamentos* were tabled and never given serious discussion. The main reasons given at the time were the enormous costs that would be involved and the administrative incapacity of the social security administration. The state would have to assume 100 percent of the costs (since there would be no employer contributions). New taxes might be needed to generate revenues, a move that would be greatly unpopular and cost votes in upcoming elections.

In 2006, Chávez announced his approval for a type of pension for some 100,000 poor young mothers through the Misión Madres del Barrio, but not for older women as was the intent of Article 88 of the constitution. During several *Aló Presidente* radio programs, Chávez also mentioned the need for pensions for the elderly (program no. 245, January 29, 2006). In May 2006, President Chávez authorized the Ministry of Labor to enroll 50,000 housewives over 65 (not the age of 55 stated in the constitution and social security legislation) in the pension system on a trial basis (presidential decree 5370). Women's groups both inside and outside the revolution requested in 2007 that the National Assembly make provisions for "retired" housewives; however no action was taken.[27]

The issue of social security payments for housewives has continued to be a consistent demand of women's groups and organizations across classes and among those inside and outside the revolution. For example, in each of the reports following national or regional level meetings of women sponsored by Banmujer and INAMUJER from 2006–2009, there is a call for pensions to be implemented. One report also demanded removal of the funding for the Misión Madres del Barrio because of clientelism and use of funds for vote buying.[28] Nonetheless, written demands like these have not been backed up by marches or demonstrations by women; this makes it easier for legislators and the president to ignore them.

## Organic Law for a Life Free from Violence

Following the 2000 elections, the 1998 Law against Violence against Women and the Family was partially implemented by INAMUJER with the help of international advising and funding.[29] Still, implementation was constrained by response capacity relative to level of demand. As some weaknesses (vague wording) in the text of the law became clear during attempted implementation, work began to reform it. Replacement by a new law became the focus when the constitutionality of certain provisions was raised by critics.

A major catalyst for a new law was the Supreme Court's decision to overturn (in 2006) the so-called precautionary measures that allowed police to remove an abuser from the home he shares with the victim. The constitutionality of these measures had been under review since 2003. INAMUJER, women in the AN, and a broad spectrum of civil society women and groups (across all political factions) joined together in 2004 and 2005 to fight the pending decision. Their statements were covered widely in the media. There were many strategy meetings and several protests in front of the Supreme Court building.[30]

In addition to the need to keep the precautionary measures about to be stricken from the 1998 law, a second reason for a new law was femocrats' and feminists' growing awareness that their proposals for a new Penal Code or a partial reform of the existing code were unlikely to pass in the near future. The Penal Code contains many articles that validate men's violence against women, including a stipulation that a rapist can avoid prosecution by marrying the victim and a definition of rape as a crime against society and good morals, not a crime against the person.[31] The Penal Code also defines abortion as a crime. Given resistance in the AN to two proposals for reform submitted by the CFWY, feminists and femocrats concluded that a proposed new 2006 anti-violence law would have to include a redefinition of rape as a crime against the person and expand the range of strategies for dealing with domestic violence, including mandatory training for criminal justice authorities, establishment of domestic violence tribunals (special courts) to deal with crimes of violence against women, legally mandated punishment for perpetrators, and funding for services for victims.

The urgency perceived by many activists led to renewed collaboration and coalition networks. One network, known variously as MAM (Movimiento Amplio de Mujeres) and as the Women's Assembly, focused on developing effective policy strategies and welcomed all women to participate in discussions, regardless of political affiliation. Women from the MAM, the Women's Rights Defender, a representative of INAMUJER, and diverse NGOs participated in the First National Encounter on Violence against Women in March

2007, where they discussed strategies for advancing women's legal rights. Many of their proposals were included in the final draft of the new Organic Law for a Woman's Right to a Life Free from Violence.

The new law was approved by the AN on November 25, 2006, at a meeting organized by INAMUJER on International Violence against Women Day and attended by hundreds of cheering women. It went into effect on March 19, 2007, and was published twice in the *Gaceta Oficial*, first on April 23, 2007, and again on September 17 of that year (to correct certain "clerical errors").[32] Both the 1998 and the 2006 laws reflected the principles in international accords to which Venezuela had subscribed prior to the election of Chávez. These include the Convention on the Elimination of Discrimination against Women (CEDAW), which was re-affirmed in 2000, and the 1994 Belem do Pará Accord against violence, re-affirmed in 2004. At the time that the law was under development, there were transnational advocacy campaigns taking place in support of anti-violence laws and a woman's right to a life free from violence (sponsored by the United Nations and Inter-American Development Bank) throughout Latin America.

In sum, while the 1998 law was an initiative of women in Congress (led by a Christian Democrat) that was supported by some activist NGOs,[33] the 2006 law was the result of widespread collaboration between civil society groups, women of diverse political affiliations, and the National Assembly's Committee on Family, Women and Youth (CFWY).[34] Many versions of the proposed text circulated by e-mail (reaching some 3,000 activists and academics), generating much discussion and feedback that improved the proposed text.

President Chávez gave orders to implement the law during his radio program on March 18, 2007, stating that "Venezuela is a *machista* society and we must all be equal."[35] INAMUJER was charged with overseeing implementation either directly or through other government agencies and subcontracted NGOs. Implementation has been slow for diverse reasons. For one, the law has been described as "very expensive"; it calls for the creation of new courts throughout the country to deal with violence against women, especially domestic violence. The Supreme Court had announced in 2007 that it would create 92 courts (tribunals) specializing in processing sexual violence cases, but the target was reduced to 7 specialized courts.[36] Nonetheless, by 2010 the number of special courts reached 29, and an evaluation of the volume of cases brought before the courts led INAMUJER to announce plans to create at least 20 more in the short term.[37] (We could not find data on whether this has been implemented.)

Other stumbling blocks described by Fundamujer (Fundación para la Prevención de la Violencia Doméstica hacia la Mujer), one of the feminist

NGOs contracted to implement anti domestic violence programs, are the "great lack of information" about programs and structures, lack of a comprehensive plan on how the law would be put into operation, and "the incompetence and ineffectiveness of the authorities receiving complaints." Providing training to judges, judicial personnel, police, public prosecutors, and health personnel is costly and budget levels remained a problem for INAMUJER, charged with such training, as of April 2008.[38]

The creation of MinMujer in April 2009, which replaced the shortlived Office of the Minister of State for Women's Affairs, may help to overcome these limitations if, in fact, it is allocated a much larger budget than INAMUJER of the Minister of State had been.

### Law of Equal Opportunities

On INAMUJER's website and in the many speeches and interviews given by María León (as president of CONAMU, INAMUJER and head of both ministerial offices[39]) President Chávez is credited with the creation of INAMUJER and the Office of the Defender of Women in 1999. Technically, this is correct although both institutions were contemplated in the 1993 version of the Law of Equal Opportunities (LEO) that was never fully implemented. This erasure of the history of women's achievements drove a wedge between León and feminists and women's groups outside the revolution and reduced collaborations.[40]

A major change introduced in the 1999 version of the LEO also contributed to conflicts between femocrats like León and feminists and women's groups that remained independent. The 1993 version stipulated that INAMUJER's executive board—like that of CONAMU before it—must include representatives from women's NGOs and that INAMUJER should defend the interests of women from *all* sectors and political affiliations. The 1999 version eliminated the participation of women's NGOs and the mandate to serve the needs of *all* women. Instead, it established INAMUJER as "an authority of the state," leading León to describe it as the institution that connects women to the president. As such, INAMUJER consistently promotes Hugo Chávez's leadership and authority over women. Reinforcing this shift in INAMUJER's mandate, Chávez placed León in charge of organizing women of the popular classes into political groups (beginning with the Bolivarian Women's Circles, then INAMUJER's Puntos de Encuentro—meeting points—groups and more recently MinMujer's Frente Bicentenario de Mujeres[41]) and of promoting revolutionary ideology.[42] The overall goal of organizing women has been to provide electoral support for the president and service to their communities and to government programs like the Missions, and to facilitate organizational and political-ideological training targeting women specifically.[43] For feminists and women of civil society who are not supporters of Chávez or the revolution, this change in INAMUJER's legal mandate and mission was a betrayal of their support for a national women's agency.

### Suffrage and Political Participation Law

In 1993, women in Congress, with support from women's NGOs, successfully sponsored a partial reform of the Organic Suffrage and Political Participation Law to include 30 percent of women among electoral candidates nominated by political parties (Article 144).[44] This provision was overturned in 2000 by the National Electoral Council (CNE), which decided that quotas conflicted with the 1999 constitution's guarantee of gender equality. Women activists inside and outside the revolution protested and tried unsuccessfully to get the decision overturned.

INAMUJER, women politicians and some women's groups have pressed for a new form of quota since 2005; the idea has some supporters in the AN and the support of the CNE (which has publicly recommended a new reform of the Suffrage and Political Participation Law). The proposal is for 50-50 gender parity with "alternability" (alternating men and women) on all candidate lists registered by political parties with the CNE. Alternability would assure that women will be not only 50 percent of candidates, but also 50 percent of those who hold elected office, since they will be half of the candidates at all levels of the list.

The 50 percent principle has long been promoted through transnational campaigns. It was also included in Chávez's failed proposals to reform the constitution in 2007. In 2008, the president authorized INAMUJER to expand the concept in its work with government agencies. That is, INAMUJER can promote gender parity in public employment and in the Consejos Comunales, urban land committees, and other community-level citizen organizations. INAMUJER (and its successor MinMujer) should also provide training to personnel in government agencies and to women's groups on the importance of increasing women's representation and on guaranteeing gender-aware budgets. Women in diverse political parties complain about the resistance of men to the 50-50 principle, and the CNE has reported that parties protest that they do not have enough women candidates to be able to comply with this policy. INAMUJER's training for agencies on employment and gender-aware budgets has been lagging as well, again due to its own budget limitations and the fact that it has been the sole agency responsible for implementing these policies.

Numerous indications show a lack of political will among legislators to implement gender parity—that is, to mandate it through law. Even Chávez, who has publicly spoken in support of parity, has not taken steps to support it in practice. For example, after the 30 percent quota for women candidates was stricken from the 2000 Organic Law of Suffrage and Political Participation, women in politics and civil society have repeatedly called for its reinstatement or a reform of the law to introduce the principles of parity and alternability. INAMUJER's María León and her staff also have been very vocal on the issue. Yet, when a new Law of Electoral Processes that replaced the Law of Suffrage and Political Participation was passed by the AN in 2009, there was no mention of quotas, of women candidates, or of gender parity.

### Laws on Maternity/Paternity and Breastfeeding

Some tensions between women activists inside and outside the revolution are related to hasty and poorly conceptualized new legislation that overlooks already existing protections and interferes with implementation of the provisions in other laws. In 2007, two such legislative initiatives divided women. They were introduced for discussion by the CFWY with strong support from INAMUJER. Both were approved quickly by the AN. The first was the Organic Law to Protect Families, Maternity and Paternity, and the second was the Organic Law to Promote and Protect Breastfeeding. Both have been widely criticized by legal scholars and academic feminists as virtually unimplementable.

On the one hand, both contradict already existing rights in labor law governing maternity and paternity leave, women and men's right to child care at the place of employment, and to a place and time to breastfeed infants. Critics also claim that the new provisions will discourage employers from hiring young workers (those most likely to have children), particularly young women, and that the language of the breastfeeding law practically makes breastfeeding an obligation. They say that this contradicts a woman's constitutional right to work and creates new problems for single and already poor mothers. Compliance with the laws appears to be voluntary. We could find no reported cases of men asking for paternity leave and only anecdotal evidence of a few cases where the new breastfeeding recommendations have been used by individuals in a few workplace settings.

### Organic Law for Gender Equity and Equality

Two issues are under debate in 2010 regarding a project for a proposed new law for gender equity and equality.[45] One has to do with its overall content: the law would not introduce much that is new. Rather, it primarily gathers in one place the principles already included in other legislation. For example, the new law would ratify Articles 21 and 62 of the constitution regarding the principle of non-discrimination for any reason and the right to participate in politics. Its proposed objectives include the development of an egalitarian democratic culture based on constitutional principles, including the principles of gender equality; the "transversalization"[46] of a gender perspective in all public policies and budgets; promotion of rights to health and education; ratification of the principle of women and girls' right to a life free from violence; education promoting equality between women and men in the family and society; social security for older housewives; support for all international agreements signed by Venezuela that are relevant to women's rights; and prohibition of sexual exploitation and sexist language in the media (Articles 18 and 19). To the chagrin of many feminists, including the feminist academic who advised the CFWY on the text, the principle of 50-50 parity with alternability was not included in the final formulation submitted for second discussion, although it was in the draft approved during first discussion by the AN.

Another problem is the vague language of statements such as "equity, equality and non-discrimination in sexual and reproductive life" (Article 7) and "sexual and reproductive rights under conditions of equality without discrimination" (Article 8). These formulations still fail to address decriminalization of abortion or explicit rights for non-heterosexuals or unmarried couples. However, the proposed law may lay out the responsibilities of the state (federal, state, and local) and INAMUJER in the implementation of mentioned rights and principles; it would replace the 1999 Law of Equal Opportunities for Women.

In 2009, the proposed law was the focal point for demands for sexual rights that have not found any other feasible outlet. Activist groups advocated that the right to abortion and the rights of GLBT persons be included.[47] Proponents argued that inclusion of these could lead to other reforms to guarantee, for example, equal rights for sexually diverse persons not explicitly guaranteed in the constitution and could support the decriminalization of abortion (a crime under the existing Penal Code). But, again, the lack of political will stood in the way.[48]

## Institutions for Women: INAMUJER and Banmujer

Two government agencies charged with organizing women, especially poor women, have been at the forefront of "gender mainstreaming" in the Bolivarian Revolution. For information on their work we have relied heavily on official sources, including press releases, internal reports, and websites.[49] We supplement official information with insight provided by contacts who are insiders (employees or advisors to one or both organizations). Since we have discussed some aspects of INAMUJER's work above, this section focuses on its very important role in the Bolivarian Revolution.[50]

INAMUJER, the National Institute for Women, and Banmujer, the Women's Development Bank, have provided extremely important links between popular women, Hugo Chávez, and the Bolivarian Revolution. INAMUJER's officially recognized goals and objectives, identified on its webpage,[51] have evolved over time. In general, since 2000 and until it was assigned to the new MinMujer, INAMUJER has endeavored to identify, develop and evaluate policies on women's issues, and it was charged with planning, coordinating, and executing these policies. These are policies that could affect women's health, education, training, employment, income, and enrollment in social security. INAMUJER was also expected to guarantee women's access to needed services—whether legal, socioeconomic, socio-cultural, political, or domestic—as contemplated in laws. INAMUJER signed international agreements on behalf of Venezuela, received funding from international organizations, and subcontracted programs and projects such as women's shelters, research, and gender training to women's NGOs and gender consultants. In June 2010, these responsibilities passed to MinMujer which continues to designate some to INAMUJER, now part of the ministry's organizational structure.[52]

INAMUJER's status as a government agency became more explicit around 2002. The website described it as "the highest state authority for policies on women," whose objectives "are to achieve equality by gender, ethnicity, and class in all areas of development and the creation of new spaces for women's full incorporation in the exercise of power." INAMUJER's mission statement in that year included some academic concepts such as women's "practical and strategic needs" and emphasized that INAMUJER should

> make visible women's roles as actors in the development of the country; guarantee gender equity through the design, formulation, oversight and control of public policies that interpret the practical and strategic interests of women and those that lead to cultural change and new values [because] this is the way to achieve a society where women and men are equally different and that is just, socially productive, equitable and characterized by solidarity.[53]

When consulted on 3/13/2003, INAMUJER's website showed that its mission had been streamlined:

To exercise as state authority the functions of defining, implementing, directing, coordinating, supervising and evaluating public policies directed at women; guarantee equality of opportunities; promote women's participation as actors/subjects in all areas—political, economic and social . . . [and] to guarantee legal and real equality of women.[54]

In 2006, the Law of Consejos Comunales included as a priority the promotion of women's participation and leadership. The task of promoting women's participation and training women to guarantee gender-aware budgets in the *consejos* became yet another task assigned to INAMUJER staff.

When consulted on 4/25/2007, the webpage defined INAMUJER more clearly in function of its relation to the president, a trend that increased over time: INAMUJER "is the permanent agency that defines, supervises and evaluates policies and affairs related to the condition and situation of women" and whose existence is attributed to "the decisive action of the President of the Bolivarian Republic of Venezuela, Hugo Chávez Frías, for whom achieving women's full rights is of great importance."[55]

INAMUJER's range of activities was broad. But major responsibilities included to oversee implementation of legislation and programs against violence against women, organize women's grassroots groups (the Puntos de Encuentro groups and the former Círculos Bolivarianos de Mujeres), promote women's active involvement in the Bolivarian Revolution,[56] hold regional and national conferences for women of the popular classes, promote a gender perspective in the work of government agencies and public budgets, and obtain funding for women's programs from international sources. Although policy development always had been part of its legal mandate, INAMUJER was only marginally involved in legislative initiatives, most of which originated with women in the CFWY and/or with the feminist academics and lawyers who advise them.[57]

The importance of María León and INAMUJER's work in organizing low-income women and its visibility as THE agency charged with "transversalizing" gender in policy, budgets and employment seem to have been rewarded by President Chávez in 2008 and 2009, when he created two consecutive ministerial offices of high rank under her direction. In 2008, Chávez announced the creation of the office of the Minister of State for Women's Affairs with María León to serve both as minister and president of INAMUJER. Creation of a ministry had been requested since 2006 by women supporters who attended national meetings organized by INAMUJER. But a "minister of state" has no separate budget or permanent staff. Nonetheless, INAMUJER staff turned to a broad spectrum of civil society women activists inside and outside the revolution for advice on what might be the mandate and organizational structure of the office of the new minister. A major criticism was that the "of state" designation meant little power or budget to implement policies and programs. Women activists inside the revolution, particularly those involved in groups and networks organized by INAMUJER and Banmujer, shared this concern. They began to advocate for a ministry with full rights at their meetings, in written pronouncements, and by shouting when attending Chávez's speeches and radio programs. In March 2009, the president announced the creation of the new Ministry of Popular Power for Women and Gender Equality or MinMujer (Ministerio del Poder Popular para la Mujer y la Igualdad de Género)—with full ministerial rank and privileges. María León was named the new minister and continued as president of INAMUJER until June 2010. Chávez also created five new ministerial positions:Vice-minister for Women's Affairs;Vice-minister for the Transversalization of Gender (in politics); Vice-minister for Socio-economic Strategies with a Perspective based on Gender, Ethnicity and Class; Vice-minister for Protagonistic Participation and Socialist-feminist Formation; Vice-minister for Social Strategies to Achieve Gender Equality.[58]

The Women's Development Bank, Banmujer, was created on March 8, 2001, and, according to Nora Castañeda,[59] its president since its inception, was the result of a proposal made by INAMUJER to President Chávez to "develop public policies with a gender perspective to make visible women's poverty and seek solutions."[60] Banmujer is widely recognized in Venezuela and abroad as one of the most successful programs of the Bolivarian Revolution, not only because of its work combating women's poverty through small loans and support for cooperatives, but also for the coverage of its educational, organizational (including "users' networks," the Red de Usuarias), and consciousness-raising work.[61] Banmujer also works with other institutions to "democratize capital" so that it reaches social sectors traditionally excluded from financial services.

From the beginning the bank has offered two types of services: small loans at relatively low interest rates (12%), and technical assistance. Annual reports indicate that users have grown rapidly in number as have its loan portfolio and funding. In 2006 its newsletter announced that a total of 61,086 loans had been approved for a total of Bs. 151.5 billion (a figure confirmed by Finance Ministry data). A press release marking Banmujer's impending tenth anniversary states that 103,000 loans were approved between 2001 and 2009 for a total of Bs.324.1 billion.[62] These figures suggest Banmujer's effectiveness in processing loan applications and distributing funds; they conceal extremely high default rates, however. Some critics claim for political reasons there is no attempt to recover the "loans." What is important, apparently, is the disbursement of funds to people who are poor.[63] Since at least 2005, Banmujer has expanded technical assistance to include non-financial services such as ideological and skill training to women in its user networks, activities that have received increasing attention among bank staff.

At the celebration of the first five years of Banmujer's work, President Chávez awarded the Orden del Libertador en Primera Clase to Nora Castañeda and called Banmujer "an efficient instrument against exclusion, discrimination and women's poverty."[64] He promised to provide an additional Bs. 100 billion to support new programs, but we could find no subsequent reports or news items confirming disbursement.[65] In sum, Banmujer is an organization whose objective is to combat poverty, extend benefits to marginalized social groups, and involve poor women in the political project of the Bolivarian Revolution. As of December 2010, Castañeda continues to head Banmujer, now subsumed under MinMujer.[66]

Given the number of laws that address women's issues that have passed since Chávez took office in 1998, the non-sexist constitution, the creation of agencies such as INAMUJER, Banmujer and the new MinMujer, and given the fact that women are a majority of those who participate in and benefit from the social programs known as Missions have led María León and other high ranking femocrats to claim that the Bolivarian Revolution is a feminist revolution. Beginning in 2008, President Chávez also has declared himself a feminist and has argued publicly that socialism must be feminist to be successful.

## A Feminist Revolution?

A discourse of a "feminist revolution" was heard of infrequently pre-2007 and only from a few femocrats, particularly María León. This claim gained steam in 2009 and early 2010 primarily through statements made by both President Chávez and María León in public venues and more recently replicated by Minister Nancy Pérez Sierra of MinMujer but with some important changes.[67] At the World Social Forum held in Brazil in January 2010, Chávez stated that "true socialism is feminist" and "I affirm here that I am a feminist. In fact, I believe that one cannot be a good socialist if one is not a feminist."[68] He made similar statements in speeches he gave at meetings in Europe in 2010 and on the occasion of International Women's Day on March 8, 2010. For example:

Bolivar was very feminist, I am feminist . . . and I believe that every true revolutionary must be feminist, because women's liberation from cultural machismo is part of the liberating revolution. It's not always easy to understand. It is difficult for me even though I am feminist and defend fully equality between women and men.[69]

Creating a "popular feminist" movement had long been a goal of María León's. Such a movement would emphasize both the class and gender issues of poor women as the basis for women's struggle within the revolution. But in a 2005 interview León expressed frustration with popular women's resistance to the importance of gender issues. She acknowledged that these women respond more readily to race and class issues and to requests to support President Chávez and the Bolivarian project. But, she said, they lag in their understanding of the importance of women's rights. She proposed a type of "gender literacy" training for low-income women and their communities, and workshops on gender, women's rights, and violence against women have been conducted with both INAMUJER and Banmujer group members and with women in the Misión Madres del Barrio. To reinforce the idea that gender is important in the struggle against capitalism and imperialism, INAMUJER has linked themes of "class consciousness, country consciousness, and gender consciousness" in women's training and addresses at women's meetings.[70]

Since 2006, estimates of the number of women organized in support of the revolution have varied from 98,000 to over 200,000. But, other than agency press releases or interviews with agency representatives, we have found very little evidence to verify how many popular women may have been organizing specifically around women's rights and against "patriarchy" and "machismo." We found a few examples of gender activism such as women in INAMUJER's Puntos de Encuentro who attended national meetings, some women who received gender training from MOMUMAS (the Movimiento Manuelita Saenz)[71] and possibly a few activists in some of the five Homemakers' Unions that are registered with the Ministry of Labor.[72] For example, abortion was discussed as a "class issue" in a video of interviews with MOMUMAS' members and staff that was posted to Youtube in 2008. Women in the film stated that only the lives of women who are poor are sacrificed since wealthy women are able to afford safe abortions.[73] Another example can be found in the report from a national meeting of popular women (attendance estimated in the hundreds) organized by INAMUJER in 2009 (El Congresillo); according to the report, women support the right to "interrupt" a pregnancy, 50-50 representation in politics and employment, implementation of pensions for older women. Venezuelan women's declaration from the I Campamento meeting held in November 2009 (fewer than 300) also includes, in a long list of demands, a request for explicit legal rights for women in "consensual" unions (cohabiting but not legally married)[74] and to learn more about sexual diversity and the human rights of the sexually diverse. We cannot conclude, however, that these positions represent those of the majority of the low-income or working-class women who support the Bolivarian Revolution. Nor have we found any evidence to indicate that the demands on paper have ever been raised in decision-making meetings of the PSUV (Partido Socialista Unido de Venezuela)—not even by the feminists who support them on paper (i.e., who have signed petitions) or at women's rallies.

The increasing use of a new rhetoric that links socialism and feminism dates to about 2008, when Jesús Silva, speaker at a meeting of women organized by INAMUJER on the occasion of International Women's Day, declared that "the dictatorship of patriarchy is the daughter of the dictatorship of capitalism . . . We can't transform the world or men without the action of women."[75] Similar references began to appear about the same time in speeches to women by President Chávez: "It is impossible to construct a new social order without gender equity."[76] Since then, this discourse has intensified and in 2010 both President Chávez and Minister Nancy Pérez Sierra emphasized at public events, on MinMujer's radio program, and in interviews that "capitalism created machista culture" and that only through socialist revolution can women be free from oppression and achieve equality. A similar rhetoric even was used by military officers in the recruitment of women associated with MinMujer to new women's militias. One Major General called women the "point of the lance," the "vanguard" of the revolutionary process, needed to help MinMujer "defeat the machista culture inherited from capitalism."[77] Even the president has stated that revolutionary mothers are giving birth to a new Venezuela and that "the revolution has the face of a woman."[78] And Minister Pérez Sierra announced on the occasion of International Violence against Women Day that violence against women is a consequence of a capitalist model.[79]

Over time, the argument has shifted from "in order to defeat capitalism, patriarchy and women's oppression also need to be defeated" to one of "to defeat women's oppression, capitalism must be defeated." Members of the CFWY and INAMUJER staff have used both logics to bolster recent demands for legislative reform, but most men inside the revolution have not been so eager to embrace these ideas. Evidence of their resistance shows up at all levels, from the AN to communal councils, from specific legal reforms (i.e., decriminalization of abortion, rights for GLBT persons) to specific practices (i.e., pensions for older housewives, implementation of the 50-50 principle, gender aware budgets).

The rhetoric of feminist socialism and a feminist Bolivarian Revolution that was employed by President Chávez and María León has been directed primarily at women. Chávez's recent proclamations that he is feminist and that defeating capitalism and machismo must go hand in hand seem to indicate that he also may be trying to reach Bolivarian men in order to overcome continuing resistance to sharing power with women. Even so, have actions matched the words? The legislative history of the revolution suggests that the answer would have to be no.

The passage of certain laws that advance women's rights, the 1999 constitution, and the establishment of institutions like INAMUJER and Banmujer and, more recently, the new Ministry of Popular Power for Women and Gender Equality may seem to provide support for the claim of a feminist revolution. But many factors chip away at this claim. First, the content of the constitution and almost all of the women's rights legislation can be traced to collaborations that involve feminists, women's rights activists, and politicians inside *and* outside the revolution. Second, even when long-term demands are included in legislation, many of the specific demands that focus on expanding women's rights such as social security for housewives have not been implemented.[80] For example, there has been and continues to be little support in the male-dominated AN for the 50-50 principle that would mandate sharing leadership and decision-making power or for decriminalization of abortion, despite long-term support among medical professionals and growing support across class levels.[81] Third, despite the claim that the Bolivarian Revolution defends equality and non-discrimination for all, proposals to make explicit the rights of GLBT persons have consistently been shot down in the AN.[82] Furthermore, Chávez has not taken a stand on these issues, nor has he exercised his power to approve the proposed reforms directly through presidential decree.[83]

Recently, some feminists inside the revolution seemed to be gearing up for a new fight. In 2009, at the III National Encounter on Violence against Women, María León publicly declared her support for the legalization of abortion through the derogation of Articles 432, 433 and 434 of the Penal Code. She declared them to be unconstitutional because "Article 76 of the Constitution gives parents the right to decide the number of children they want to bring into the world."[84] In 2009, AN deputy Romelia Matute tried to convince members of the CFWY to include non-discrimination and explicit rights for the sexually diverse in the proposed law of equity and gender equality; she was pressured by members of the committee and the broader AN to withdraw her proposal. In March 2010, Marelis Pérez Marcano of the CFWY announced that the committee would push the AN to decriminalize abortion and eliminate discrimination against prostitutes in 2010.[85] So far there has been no word from President Chávez on these issues; his silence is interpreted widely as indicating his opposition. These measures are unlikely to pass unless widespread public pressure can be mobilized and sustained and that seems unlikely in the climate of economic, ecological and social crises that will continue into 2011.

Some critics of the idea that the Bolivarian Revolution is feminist point to the contradiction between the empowerment of women and their exaltation of Chávez as their inevitable leader. In the words of María León, for example:

> If the president decides that women's movements should unite, be dignified, and converge in a single organization, it is because he is the one who can convoke women . . . uniting women is a task of President Hugo Chávez . . . I am convinced that above our President in this country there is no one, only God, and God is with Chávez.[86]

The idea that Chávez is women's principal leader merits discussion. One problem is the distortion of the historical record regarding women's advances. Another is the fundamental contradiction between the concepts of feminism and women's empowerment, the nature of socialism, and the origin of patriarchy. A third is the polarization among women inside and outside the revolution that Chávez has caused. All three challenge the idea of a feminist revolution.

Various feminists who support the revolution have opposed the distortion of the historical record regarding women's rights advances, specifically an "official story" that exalts Chávez and the revolution as the origin of women's rights and that ignores the role of women outside the revolution, including women active in political administrations pre-1998. They correctly critique this distortion as divisive and counterproductive.[87] They also fault the failure to acknowledge that there is no single conceptualization of Marxism or socialism or feminism and that there is a fundamental debate among socialists regarding whether the concept of "gender" can be considered a type of "social class" and, therefore, a basis for revolution. The question then arises, whose definition will prevail and whose interests will be served?[88]

A young scholar, Jessie Blanco, a self-proclaimed socialist, feminist, and very active advocate for women's and GLBT rights, has been writing about these issues. She points out that "radical and socialist feminists agree that patriarchy precedes capitalism, while Marxists believe that patriarchy was born out of capitalism." The latter, of course, is the position currently taken by Chávez and leaders of the Bolivarian Revolution, who argue that the struggle against capitalism and imperialism is the key to women's liberation. Blanco disagrees, as do many other feminists who support Chávez. In fact, despite the official position taken by the PSUV, María León, and the president that socialism will liberate women, both León and the president also have argued that women's liberation must go hand-in-hand with the transition to socialism because socialism will not be achieved until capitalist patriarchy is defeated. The inconsistent rhetoric has further confused supporters of the revolution and complicated efforts to pass and implement women's rights legislation.

Some young feminists have tried to confront this important dilemma through venues such as scholarly and Internet publications: "For leftist anti-capitalist feminists the fundamental contradiction is in relation to whether or not to support the president or the process and the proposed revolution that he embodies and leads." Blanco argues

> [We] need to differentiate ourselves ... from patriarchal practices and the logic of domination that [Chávez and the process] imply ... These [practices and logic] gain strength in the exercise of power centered on a single person, a masculine figure, who represents the androcentric and heteronormative world against which we struggle.[89]

To position Chávez, as León has done, as the supreme leader of women, denies women autonomy and their own agency. Autonomy, argues Blanco, is both strategic and fundamental for all popular movements, including women's, if participants are to become empowered. Even more problematic to feminists inside the revolution is the fact that Venezuelan women's struggle against patriarchy continues to be solitary. The comrades who accompany women in the struggle to construct an anti-capitalist and anti-imperialist society tend to disappear, she says, when it comes to constructing an anti-patriarchal one. (A situation evidenced by the failure to pass gender parity among electoral candidates, decriminalization of abortion, and the failure to implement social security for housewives.) The fact that the president has mandated participation in a single political party—the United Socialist Party of Venezuela—is particularly problematic for Blanco. It means that women will continue to do "their" (men's) politics, will be at "their" service and will postpone women's own struggle. As a result, she argues that "feminist agendas have become trapped in the figure and undeniable leadership of President Chávez."[90]

A good example that illustrates this concern was the massive march of women that took place on March 8, 2006 (International Women's Day), an event widely criticized by many feminists outside the revolution in Venezuela.[91] The march was not in support of interests agreed upon by women themselves or even women's rights issues; it was organized in response to Chávez's call for women to rise up against imperialism and march against the U.S. embassy.

A final point that contradicts the idea that the Bolivarian Revolution is a feminist revolution relates to the polarization that it has created among feminists and other women's rights activists.[92] INAMUJER has two mandates—to serve the revolution and to promote women's rights. But the two mandates shifted in importance when Chávez assigned León the task of organizing women in support of the revolution; this task has become a priority for INAMUJER. This places the staff and the institution in the awkward position of having to set aside and postpone women's rights demands that are not explicit priorities for Chávez or the National Assembly or the PSUV—even when they agree with the urgency and rightness of those demands. "It isn't women's agenda where divisions are to be found; it is a division brought on among women by their differing positions surrounding 'the Leader.'"[93]

In sum, the idea of a feminist revolution that has been suggested in revolutionary rhetoric has not been substantiated by actions. The idea of a feminist revolution, the polarization of women over President Chávez, and the practice of attributing gains to the president by feminist insiders have made difficult any significant new collaboration between rights activists inside and outside the revolution.[94]

## Conclusion

In this chapter we have highlighted several issues regarding women's rights advances (achieved and failed) and the roles of actors inside and outside the Bolivarian Revolution in proposing and supporting these rights. Our main goal has been to explain the sources of change and dispel some of the widespread confusion regarding exactly what has changed and what has not and what all of this means in reality.

We argue that much of the confusion regarding legislative advances can be explained by one factor: lack of understanding of the difference between passage of a law and its implementation. An examination of specific legislation such as social security pensions for housewives provided insight into this difference. With respect to the failure to implement legislation, we discussed several reasons. These included failure to assign responsibility and funding through the development and approval of *reglamentos*; the costs of implementation (funding social security for housewives, setting up anti-violence tribunals); a lack of political will in the AN or on the part of the president; contradictions between stipulations of one law and those of others (requiring further legislative reform); laws whose vague and generalized language makes them difficult to implement; fear of losing votes among certain constituents (i.e., over abortion, rights of the sexually diverse); ineffective authorities (that fail to implement protections for battered women); and the androcentric nature of political culture in the National Assembly, the MVR, and the PSUV.

We discussed the origins of specific rights initiatives to determine to whom rights advances can be attributed. These discussions revealed examples of rights initiatives formulated through collaboration between women's rights supporters inside the revolution and outside, and instances of the marginalization of outsiders. Divisions were highlighted not as the outcome of any disagreements over the rights agenda (there is great agreement), but as part of a process of polarization among women's rights advocates over the attribution of rights advances and women's liberation to a single, male figure—the president. The exaltation of the president as women's liberator has led to criticism not only by rights advocates outside the revolution but also among some feminists who support the revolution.

Also discussed were the failed attempts to pass legislation decriminalizing abortion and to guarantee rights to GLBT persons despite repeated organizing for this purpose by feminists and *sexodivers@s* and some evidence of strong support among women inside the revolution, including in the AN.

We outlined some contributions to women's advances that can be attributed to two institutions—INAMUJER and Banmujer—and also explained some of their limitations as institutions mandated to represent the revolution and the president. Because of INAMUJER's dual mandate to advance women's rights and incorporate women into the revolution (a mandate that applies equally to Banmujer and to the new MinMujer), tensions have grown between these institutions and women's rights advocates outside the revolution. One result is the decline in collaborations between insiders and outsiders, now limited to specific events and/or sporadic planning for legal projects that happens less frequently than before.

We concluded that the Bolivarian Revolution cannot be considered a feminist revolution from any feminist perspective. Nonetheless, we see the rhetoric as a strategic move directed not only to women supporters but also potentially to men who support the revolution but who have resisted supporting some women's rights initiatives, particularly those that would lead to sharing power with more women. That is, by calling the revolution and himself "feminist," the president may, without verbalizing his support for specific legislative demands, encourage more serious attention to gender equality issues among men in the revolution or, alternatively, exacerbate the problem of patriarchy in the revolution. But we conclude in general that the use of the rhetoric to mobilize women to provide services and comprise the base of the revolution in their communities and its use to reinforce dependence on the president's leadership operates against women's autonomy, their ability to engage in critical thinking both inside and outside a socialist ideology, and their individual and collective empowerment.

### Endnotes

1. Among political activists, those engaged in GLBT activism for sexual rights are often referred to in written materials as *sexodivers@s*. GLBT and sexodivers@s are used interchangeably in this chapter.

2. Our search of speeches and of transcripts of television and radio programs revealed that prior to 2009 President Chávez almost never used the term "feminist" or the term "machista" in public talks and then only when addressing women's groups. For example, in a search of the president's speeches, we found the following phrases: "Socialism of the 21st Century is anti-machista" (speech by President Chávez on first anniversary of the Misión Madres del Barrio, March 2007); "there can be no revolution or any social process without women" (speech to celebrate the 7th anniversary of INAMUJER, October 25, 2007). Beginning in 2009, not only does he use both terms but he associates feminism with socialism; for example, "true socialism is feminist" (in speech at the World Social Forum in Belem, Brazil, 27 January–1 February, 2009). And, when announcing the Presidential Decree establishing MinMujer, he stated that "gender and feminism go hand in hand"; this statement also appears in the Presidential Decree of March 8, 2009. Quotes translated by the authors from the original Spanish.

3. "Insiders" include actors in state agencies, political parties, and citizen organizations that actively support President Chávez and his political agenda. "Outsiders" include individuals and groups that identify as independents and some who are supporters of opposition parties.

4. "El Proceso" is the term most commonly used by insiders to refer to the Bolivarian Revolution and/or transitioning to Socialism of the 21st Century.

5. "Popular" women are primarily women of the working classes and those who are poor. Popular women sustain the Bolivarian Revolution through their community leadership and volunteer roles, including their participation in over

thirty Mission programs that range from literacy training to job training, food distribution and community kitchens, cash payments to alleviate poverty, conservation initiatives, health care, and others.

6. Prominent civil society organizations have included FEVA (Federation of Venezuelan Women Lawyers), CFP (Popular Women's Circles, community groups organized into a national network), the Women and Communication Group (journalists), feminist academics and women's studies centers (especially the Central University's Center for Women's Studies); AVESA (Association for an Alternative Sex Education); CISFEM (Center for Research, Training and Studies on Women); PLAFAM (Civil Association for Family Planning), among many others.

7. "Femocrats" is a term used to signify feminists who hold bureaucratic positions in national and international agencies.

8. See, for example, Friedman, *Unfinished Transitions.*

9. The Bicameral Committee on Women's Rights was established in 1992.

10. Rakowski and Espina, "Institucionalización de la lucha feminista/femenina en Venezuela." Espina, "Entre sacudones, golpes y amenazas." Espina and Rakowski, "¿Movimiento de mujeres o mujeres en movimiento?" Friedman, *Unfinished Transitions.*

11. The pre-reform Code classified married women as legal minors under the tutelage of husbands, gave husbands control of community property, differentiated children's rights according to circumstances of birth (legitimate, recognized, illegitimate, adulterous), and established men's authority as family heads.

12. Many civil society women's groups wanted a government agency to advance rights. Both CONAMU and INAMUJER, the National Institute for Women, also contemplated in the law, were mandated to include representatives from women's NGOs on their board of directors and to work with civil society women for the purpose of programming and policy-making.

13. Later replaced by the PSUV, Partido Socialista Unido de Venezuela.

14. The phrase "gender perspective" is associated with national and international efforts to "mainstream" gender in policy and legislation.

15. Rakowski and Espina, "Institucionalización de la lucha feminista/femenina en Venezuela," 319–320; translated from the original Spanish.

16. García and Jiménez, "Proceso constituyente, identidad femenina y ciudadanía," 106–107; trans. See also Guerra, "Ley sobre los Derechos de la Mujer a la altura de la Constitución Bolivariana de Venezuela." Saiz, *Bolivarianas.* Jiménez, ed., *Mujeres Protagonistas y Proceso Constituyente en Venezuela.* Espina and Rakowski. "¿Movimiento de mujeres o mujeres en movimiento?"

17. The single chamber National Assembly replaced the two-chamber Congress in the 1999 constitution.

18. A Ley Habilitante gives the president extraordinary powers for a specified period of time in matters that are financial, tributary, political, having to do with national territory, defense and other state matters. Importantly, under a

Ley Habilitante a presidential decree can become law without passing through discussion and approval by the National Assembly.

19. Actually, this serves an important political function. Members of the AN may approve a legal project because the president seems to support it. Both the AN and the president benefit from the political capital (such as women's support) attached to passing the law. But they can subsequently fail to develop reglamentos because they do not actually support some part or all of the law.

20. Among deputies of the National Assembly women held 13% for the period 2000–2006 and 17% for the period 2006–2010. García and Valdivieso, "Las mujeres venezolanas y el proceso bolivariano." Some sources give lower estimates. For example, journalist Sarah Wagner calculated 11% of AN deputies were women in 2005. Wagner, "Coloring Venezuela's Gender Debate."

21. We follow the style preferred by each organization—acronym all in capital letters for INAMUJER, upper and lower case for Banmujer and for MinMujer.

22. In fact, women were fewer than 5% of those elected to the NCA. But replacements of some elected members (men) by others (women) increased the percentage to about 12–13%.

23. García and Jiménez, "Proceso constituyente, identidad femenina y ciudadanía." Guerra, "Ley sobre los Derechos de la Mujer a la altura de la Constitución Bolivariana de Venezuela." Saiz, *Bolivarianas.* Jiménez, ed., *Mujeres Protagonistas y Proceso Constituyente en Venezuela.*

24. These collaborations were facilitated by long-term friendships and work relationships among feminists, some dating from the 1970s or even earlier.

25. "Discutir un Tema Tabú." Article published in *Tal Cual* (Caracas), March 31, 2009 and reprinted at www.guia.com.ve.

26. "In conformity with the law" is critical; laws must be developed that stipulate the conditions under which housewives may have a right to social security.

27. Espina, "Las mujeres del presidente y la pension del ama de casa." Some researchers have attempted to verify the enrollment of the 50,000 housewives. Specifically, they seek to document the number of beneficiaries and how they are selected. They have not been able to find evidence of any recipients other than women who receive pensions because of their history of employment.

28. Examples of such requests to María León or President Chávez include the "Declaración Final del Campamento de Mujeres," issued publicly on November 30, 2009; "Informe del Primer Encuentro Nacional de los Puntos de Encuentro," held in November 2007; and a letter prepared by María León to President Chávez on behalf of the recommendations and suggestions made by women who attended *El Congresillo*: "What Women Propose to the Minister of State for Women's Affairs" (her title at that time), held in April 2008.

29. Especially important has been funding from the Inter-American Development Bank and the United Nations Population Fund.

30. Protesters included staff of INAMUJER, academic feminists, anti-violence activists, and women from diverse political parties.

31. To the consternation of women in the AN, INAMUJER, and civil society groups, members of the National Assembly voted to ratify the old Penal Code with minor changes in 2005, including many articles that had been stricken down by other laws over the years. In 2004, two reform projects for the Penal Code had been submitted by the CFWY (written with the assistance of feminist advisors) to the AN for discussion; both had been tabled. Feminist colleagues have speculated that this move was a response to calls made by diverse women's groups and organizations to decriminalize abortion through the proposed reform. Most members of the AN oppose abortion for personal and religious reasons. Chávez himself has never come out in support of decriminalization. Decriminalization would likely cost votes among Catholics and evangelical Christians. A report on the problem created by the AN's ratification of most articles in the old Penal Code was produced by the Fundación CEPS. "Venezuela. La discriminación de la mujer en el actual Código Penal," January 8, 2010. Available on line at www.larevolucionvive.org.ve-spip.php?article1203&lang=es.

32. Immigration and Refugee Board of Canada, "Venezuela: Implementation and Effectiveness of the 2007 Organic Law."

33. Including PLAFAM, Fundamujer, AVESA, Casa de la Mujer de Maracay and other NGOs that work with victims of violence.

34. León, "Informe sobre observaciones del Movimiento Amplio de Mujeres al proyecto de reforma de la Ley Sobre la Violencia contra la Mujer y la Familia propuesto por la Asamblea Nacional."

35. *Aló Presidente*, no. 276.

36. Gil, "Mujeres bajo la violencia."

37. Pearson, "Venezuela Expands Outlets for Denunciations." Feminists and femocrats organized and brought pressure to bear on the courts and public opinion to achieve these changes.

38. Magally Huggins Castañeda, "Comentarios en relación con la Ley Orgánica sobre el derecho de las mujeres a una vida libre de violencia Venezuela," June 14, 2007. Report cited in Immigration and Refugee Board of Canada, "Venezuela: Implementation and effectiveness of the 2007 Organic Law."

39. She held the positions of Minister of State for Women's Affairs in 2008 to early 2009 and then was the first Minister of Women and Gender Equality from 2009 to mid 2010.

40. There have been no collaborations between feminists and groups outside the Bolivarian Revolution and the new minister, Nancy Pérez Sierra. Future collaborations are highly unlikely since Pérez Sierra has stated clearly that she will not cooperate with anyone "from the right" even if they come "disfrazada con rostro de mujer" (loosely, "dressed up in a woman's face"). Taken from MinMujer press release issued on November 23, 2010 and posted on MinMujer's web page at www.minmujer.gob.ve. Consulted on December 12, 2010.

41. The Frente Bicentenario de Mujeres replaces the Puntos de Encuentro and incorporates women from Banmujer's user networks, women who participate

in the Misión Madres del Barrio, women active in community-level groups, and the new "Mothers Committees" promoted by MinMujer. A press release from June 7, 2010, estimates membership to be about 200,000 women.

42. León had proposed to incorporate all women's groups—inside or outside the revolution—into one national association under INAMUJER's coordination similar to Cuba's national federation of women. This never took place, given strong resistance by autonomous and opposition women's groups.

43. Two centers are charged with providing training on socialism, feminism and gender to employees of INAMUJER and Banmujer, MinMujer, and members of the Misión Madres del Barrio among others The centers are EFOSIG (Escuela de Formación Socialista para la Igualdad de Género) and la Escuela Eumelia Hernández.

44. Although only partly implemented, the quota system was associated with increased representation of women in Congress and state legislatures in the 1990s.

45. Tovar, "Ley Orgánica para la Equidad e Igualdad de Género." See also "Informe para la Segunda Discusión. Proyecto de Ley Orgánica para la Equidad e Igualdad de Género."

46. Transversalization, translated from the Spanish *transversalización*, is understood to mean that gender crosscuts or intersects with all issues. Sometimes the term "mainstreaming" is used interchangeably with transversalization in United Nations documents.

47. In March of 2009, AN deputy Romelia Matute tried to include a range of rights for GLBT persons, including marriage, in the second discussion of the proposed law. Her proposal was denied because, according to Marelis Pérez Marcano of the CFWY, rights to marry would require a change in the constitution and cannot be included in the proposed law. Other proposals were submitted by Mujeres independientes, movimientos sociales y organizaciónes de mujeres. "Ciudadana María León, Ministra del Poder Popular para la Mujer y la Igualdad de Género." Colectiva Alejandra Kollontai. "A propósito de la exclusión de las peticiones feministas y la sexodiversidad." Revolucionarias a favor del Socialismo Feminista. "¿Somos o no somos?"

48. Its principal proponent, Marelis Pérez Marcano, was not re-elected to the AN in September 2010 which does not bode well for the future of the proposed law.

49. These information sources include some "intentions" that are presented as if already achieved. Where we have been unable to verify information, we have omitted it or identified it as an idea or proposal rather than a *fait accompli*.

50. Not only has INAMUJER been subsumed under the new Ministry of Popular Power for Women and Gender Equality, so have Banmujer and the Misión Madres del Barrio. The latter has become the major mechanism for organizing women in low income communities in support of the Bolivarian Revolution through community service and in support of President Chávez.

51. After the establishment of MinMujer, INAMUJER's and Banmujer's webpages disappeared from the Internet.

52. The exact organization structure of MinMujer and the agencies that it has absorbed remain unclear and "under construction" as of December 17, 2010.

53. INAMUJER web site, consulted 5/21/2002, translated, http://www.INAMU-JER.gob.ve/.

54. All quotes from INAMUJER webpage are translations.

55. "Lolita" interview: "María León: 'El Socialismo del Siglo XXI es el Comunismo.'"

56. All women in Puntos de Encuentro or in Círculos were part of a national network and received leadership and ideological training. This is the case for the Mothers' Committees and the Frente Bicentenario de Mujeres that have replaced them.

57. Olivo de Celli and Heredia de Salvatierra (writing as "Foro por la Equidad de Género"), *Informe a la 34ª Sesión CEDAW*. García Prince, "Impacto de las leyes de igualdad en América Latina."

58. We have been able to find very little concrete information on the actual responsibilities of the Vice-ministers, the Ministry, or the current work of INAMUJER and Banmujer.

59. An economist, feminist, and former faculty member in the Center for Women's Studies at the Central University of Venezuela.

60. Banmujer web page: http://www.Banmujer.gob.ve/, consulted 7/21/2004; trans.

61. López and James, *Creando una Economía Solidaria*.

62. Agencia Bolivariana de Noticias-ABN. "Banmujer ha entregado más de 100 mil crédito en más de ocho años." October 31, 2009. Published at http://genero-conclase.blogspot.com/. Accessed on February 21, 2010. YKVE Mundial, "Banmujer entregará 567 créditos a cooperativas y microempresas del pais," September 17, 2007. Published at http://www.radiomundial.com.ve/yvke/noticia.php?32487. Both accessed on February 21, 2010. Texts trans.

63. In fact, Banmujer staff have often stated in interviews and the Banmujer newsletter that recovering loans is not as important as raising women out of extreme poverty. That is, the social function of Banmujer is more important than its economic function.

64. Banmujer news release, 2/2/2007, on web site; trans.

65. Ibid., 11/30/2006, on web site; trans.

66. María León was elected to the AN in September 2010 and INAMUJER has had at least two consecutive directors since June 2010.

67. Pérez Sierra reaffirms the notion of feminist socialism, but her emphasis in speeches and through press releases on the MinMujer webpage emphasize that women need to promote socialism and defeat capitalism through political activism and community work. We could find no pronouncements on women's liberation or women's rights *per se*. She is a physician and militant member of the PSUV.

68. These statements appear in many news outlets. Two accessed by us on February 17, 2010 are *Conciencia Feminista* at http://concienciafeminista.wordpress.com/ and *La Jiribilla*-revista de cultural cubana at www.lajiribilla.cubaweb.cu/noticias/.

69. From *Aló Presidente*, no. 356, April 25, 2010. Trans.
70. "Lolita" interview: "María León: 'El Socialismo del Siglo XXI es el Comunismo,'" trans.
71. MOMUMAS was originally affiliated with the PPT—Partido para Todos (Everyone's Party), that supported Chávez. Since the PPT split from Chávez, MOMUMAS affiliated with the PSUV, United Socialist Party of Venezuela—Chávez's party.
72. Prada and Suggett. "Venezuela's Homemakers Union."
73. The film was produced by a filmmaker who goes by the name Sariazoe. Accessed on February 5, 2010. Available at http://www.youtube.com/watch?v=OqGFey 7WU78 since June 4, 2008.
74. The 1982 reform of the Civil Code established rights for women in consensual unions. This was not included in the 1999 constitution.
75. Silva R., "Hablar de equidad de género."
76. Quote trans. Accessed on INAMUJER website on July 27, 2008. See also Linares, "Gobierno apuesta por abolir discriminación femenina."
77. Press release by MinMujer on April 22, 2010 and posted on the MinMujer webpage. Consulted December 14, 2010.
78. The former comment was repeated in two speeches given by the president on the occasion of International Women's Day in 2002 and 2003 and appeared on INAMUJER's webpage. The latter is attributed to the president by Minister Pérez Sierra and appeared on MinMujer's webpage.
79. MinMujer press release, November 23, 2010.
80. Speaking of the feminists in the revolution who have promoted many laws that have never been implemented, Espina wrote "those who think that leaving a cemetery of unimplementable laws is a bonus on their personal *curriculum vitae* or a political merit that should be recognized as part of their service as legislators are acting in bad faith . . . or suffer from an astonishing naivete." Espina, "El inconsciente saboteador."
81. A press release from the publicity arm of the National Assembly indicates plans in 2010 by members of the Commission on Interior Policies, Justice, Human Rights and Constitutional Guarantees to advance the development of a new "modern" penal code (not a mere reform of a code that is over 100 years old) with the intention of completing the new law by August 15, 2011. Consulted at http://www.asambleanacional.gob.ve/index.php?option=com_content&view= article&id=21511&lang=es on December 17, 2010. There is speculation that a new law will include decriminalization of abortion.
82. GLBT groups who are supporters of Chávez and participants in the revolutionary process strategically link GLBT/*sexodiversidad* issues to the struggle against patriarchy, thereby validating the legitimacy of GLBT issues as part of a "feminist socialism."
83. Coalitions formed around the time that Chávez was drafting his (ultimately unsuccessful) proposals for constitutional reform in 2006. Members of a coalition of feminists and "*sexodivers@s*" (both inside and outside the revolution) met

with the People's Defender and other high ranking officials to advocate for key issues they wanted included in the president's proposed reforms. The coalition was known as "el grupo ese" or "Grupo S." El grupo ese's proposals included many supported by INAMUJER, the CFWY, and diverse women's groups, such as the decriminalization of abortion, elimination of discrimination against prostitutes, and constitutional recognition of the rights of homosexuals and transgendered persons. They also promoted the right to some type of marriage or legally-recognized stable union. But their proposals were not included in the final draft of the reforms. See Espina. "Ley Habilitante y reforma constitucional previa: Propuestas de feministas y sexodivers@s reunid@s hace varias semanas con este propósito." Espina. "Más allá de la polarización"; "El inconsciente saboteador."

84. News item posted at *Palabra de Mujer* at http://palabrademujer.wordpress.com /2009/10/03/ministra-de-la-mujer-de-venezuela-pide-despenalizar-el-aborto/ on October 3, 2009.
85. "Propondrán despenalizar la interrupción del embarazo producto de una violación." *El Nacional* (Caracas), January 22, 2010.
86. This quote, translated, comes from the "Lolita" interview: "María León: 'El Socialismo del Siglo XXI es el Comunismo.'"
87. Blanco, "Nuestro socialismo ¿feminista?" Carosio, "Feminismo en el socialismo del siglo XXI." Ironically, in the Lolita interview, María León also argued for recognition of achievements made by or in collaboration with feminists who preceded or are outside the revolution.
88. Revolucionarias a favor del Socialismo Feminista, "¿Somos o no somos?" Colectiva Alejandra Kollontai, "A propósito de la exclusión de las peticiones."
89. Quote transl. Blanco, "Al debate feminismo revolucionario y socialismo" (2007 and 2009 versions); Blanco, "Nuestro socialismo ¿feminista?"
90. Blanco, "Al debate feminismo revolucionario y socialismo" (2009 version). Quotes transl.
91. Ibid.
92. Espina, "Más allá de la polarización."
93. Quote transl. Blanco, "Al debate feminismo revolucionario y socialismo."
94. The last instance of collaboration among women inside and outside the revolution occurred in April and May of 2010 following the murder of Jennifer Viera by her husband, the boxer Edwin Valero. Activists from sixty-six independent NGOs, calling themselves the Frente Amplio de Mujeres, joined with over thirty women representing XXIst Century Socialism and the Frente Bicentenario de Mujeres in front of the building of the Tribunal Supremo de Justicia to demand justice for Jennifer and other abused women. They demanded an end to impunity, training for police and judges in the interior of the country, and establishment of special violence courts as mandated by the 2006 Organic Law guaranteeing women's right to a life free from violence. Representatives of INAMUJER were present also. López. "Lucha contra la violencia de género venció la polarización." López. "Movimiento de mujeres reclamará ante el TSJ."

# 6

# Venezuela in the Chávez Years: Its Economy and Influence on the Region

*Mark Weisbrot*

## Introduction

Since 2003, Venezuela has greatly increased its influence in Latin America, while the influence of the United States over the region has fallen precipitously. Here in Washington, both trends have become a source of great concern. The conventional wisdom throughout this period has been that the Venezuelan government's success, both domestically and regionally, rested on an oil boom that would inevitably "go bust" in the near future, either through a collapse in oil prices or due to mismanagement of the economy. The loss of U.S. influence in the region is similarly seen as temporary, mainly a result of Washington's preoccupation with its wars in the Middle East.

Here I argue that the conventional wisdom is wrong on both counts. While the Venezuelan economy fared poorly in the early Chávez years, when the country was racked by political instability, it has done remarkably well since stability returned to the country in the first quarter of 2003 and the government got control of its oil industry. To be sure, there are intermediate-run challenges, especially with regard to the exchange rate and inflation, and the long-run challenge of diversifying away from oil. Oil prices did collapse at the end of 2008, and the Venezuelan economy contracted in 2009 (by 3.3%), as was the case for most countries in the hemisphere. But it appears, according to the most recent data at this writing, that its recovery began in 2010. In fact, this chapter will argue that the downturn in 2009 could have been avoided with sufficient counter-cyclical policies, as some other countries (e.g., Bolivia) were able to establish during the world recession.[1]

In the second part of this chapter I look briefly at the regional context and some of the profound changes that have taken place in Latin America and U.S.-Latin American relations in recent years, of which Venezuela is one important part. These changes are now deeply rooted and not likely to be reversed. Among the causes are the collapse of the IMF (International Monetary Fund) and allied institutions' control over credit—once the most important avenue of Washington's influence in the region—and the unprecedented long-term economic growth failure in the region over the last three decades, which has led to revolts at the ballot box and governments' search for new economic policies that would promote economic and social progress.

Thus, despite Washington's numerous efforts to isolate Venezuela in the region, Chávez has maintained a strong alliance with the presidents of Brazil and Argentina (both the late Nestor Kirchner and Cristina Fernández), as well as with the more leftist presidents of Bolivia and Ecuador. All of these governments, plus Uruguay and Paraguay, have recently participated in efforts to forge a more unified and independent South America. This includes an increasingly important role for UNASUR (the Union of South American Nations), which, for example, gave crucial political support to the Bolivian government against a separatist opposition that enjoyed at least tacit support from Washington[2] and launched the Bank of the South as a first attempt to create an alternative to the Washington-dominated IMF, World Bank, and Inter-American Development Bank.

When Venezuela's political changes and regional role are seen as part of the broader trends in Latin America—and not merely as the actions of a "radical anti-American government" using its oil money to buy influence in the region—it is clear that these broader trends are likely to continue. They include increasing economic and political independence from Washington, diversification of trade and finance, some regional integration, and more effective macroeconomic policies. Venezuela has played a significant role in this process and will probably continue to do so in the foreseeable future.

## The Economy in the Chávez Years

Like almost everything surrounding Venezuela, discussion of Venezuela's economy is typically polarized, with almost all information that reaches an international audience focusing on the negative. For example, for almost two years, major U.S. media outlets, as well as more specialized publications,[3] stated that poverty had increased under the administration of President Hugo Chávez. This was false, but the media did not correct its reporting until the Center for Economic and Policy Research published a paper on the subject.[4]

Most accounts of the Venezuelan economy today dismiss the country's very rapid 2003–2008 economic expansion as an "oil boom" that must end in a disastrous bust, similar to what happened in the 1970s and early 1980s.[5]

It is therefore worth taking a closer look at the Venezuelan economy to see if there is any basis for this commonly held view.

Latin America as a region has suffered a sharp slowdown in economic growth since 1980, from which it has yet to recover. It has been the worst long-term growth performance for more than a hundred years, even taking into account the significant improvement from 2004–2008. Venezuela was no exception to this trend, although its decline from peak gross domestic product (GDP) in 1977 was sharper than that of most of the region and lasted longer. Real GDP per capita declined by 26 percent from 1978 to 1986. It hit bottom in 2003, 38 percent below its 1978 peak. From the first quarter of 2003 to the fourth quarter of 2008, the real economy grew by a remarkable 95 percent.[6]

It is also worth noting that the recent economic expansion of 95 percent is far greater than the 1973–1977 upturn, when oil prices were also rapidly rising; during the earlier expansion, real GDP grew by 31 percent. This is despite the fact that oil prices actually rose even more, and to a higher level in real terms, from 1973 to 1980 than in their climb from 1998 to 2008. Although part of the most recent expansion is clearly a rebound from the 2002–2003 oil strike/recession, the vast majority of it is not. Thus the recent economic expansion has seen rapid growth even for an "oil boom," and even given its recovery from the oil strike and recession. It seems likely that the government's expansionary fiscal and monetary policies contributed to this rapid growth.

Figure 1 shows Venezuela's real quarterly GDP from 1998–2010 (third quarter), seasonally adjusted. As can be seen from the graph, the trajectory of the economy appears to be very heavily influenced by external shocks, especially political instability and strikes. Chávez's first year (1999), which began with the price of Venezuelan oil at its lowest point in 22 years, was marked by negative growth. But the economy began to grow in the first quarter of 2000 and continued through the third quarter of 2001. The next few months were a period of the most extreme political instability: in December of 2001 the Venezuelan Chamber of Commerce (Fedecámaras) organized a general business strike against the government. This political instability, combined with much capital flight, continued through April 2002, when the elected government was overthrown in a military coup. Constitutional government was restored within 48 hours, but stability did not return, as most of the opposition continued to seek to topple the government by extra-legal means.[7] Growth remained negative through the summer and fall of 2002, and then the economy was hit with the opposition-led oil strike of December 2002–February 2003. This plunged the economy into a severe recession,

**Figure 1.**
**Venezuela: Real GDP (seasonally-adjusted).**

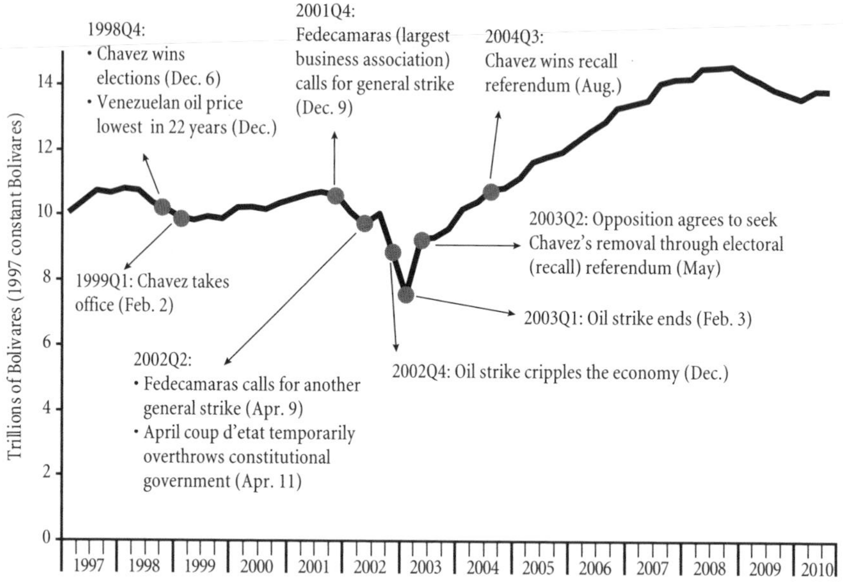
Trillions of Bolivares (1997 constant Bolivares)
1998Q4:
• Chavez wins elections (Dec. 6)
• Venezuelan oil price lowest in 22 years (Dec.)
2001Q4:
Fedecamaras (largest business association) calls for general strike (Dec. 9)
2004Q3:
Chavez wins recall referendum (Aug.)
2003Q2: Opposition agrees to seek Chavez's removal through electoral (recall) referendum (May)
1999Q1: Chavez takes office (Feb. 2)
2003Q1: Oil strike ends (Feb. 3)
2002Q2:
• Fedecamaras calls for another general strike (Apr. 9)
• April coup d'etat temporarily overthrows constitutional government (Apr. 11)
2002Q4: Oil strike cripples the economy (Dec.)
0
2
4
6
8
10
12
14
1997
1998
1999
2000
2001
2002
2003
2004
2005
2006
2007
2008
2009
2010

Source: Banco Central de Venezuela (BCV) and author's analysis.

during which Venezuela lost 24 percent of its GDP. The economy began to recover in the second quarter of 2003 and grew very rapidly until the fourth quarter of 2008.

It is clear that not only the price of oil but political instability played a very large role in Venezuela's business cycles over the past eight years. After the failure of the oil strike in February 2003, the opposition—especially after an agreement reached with the government in May 2003—began to focus primarily on electoral means of dislodging the government. This culminated in a presidential recall referendum in August of 2004. Thus, the political situation stabilized considerably in mid-2003 and continued to stabilize throughout the economic expansion.

There are various ways to evaluate the growth performance of the Venezuelan economy during the Chávez years. One is to simply look at real GDP growth from the time Chávez became president in the first quarter of 1999 to the third quarter of 2010 (last available data at the time of this writing), using seasonally adjusted data. On that basis, the economy has grown 39.8 percent, or 3.0 percent annually over 11.5 years. On a per capita basis, this is about 14.1 percent, or 1.2 percent annually. Although this is a vast

**Table 1.**
**Venezuela: GDP over Three Periods.**

| | GDP | | | | Years Elapsed | Growth | | | |
|---|---|---|---|---|---|---|---|---|---|
| | Overall[a] | | Per Capita[b] | | | Overall | | Per Capita | |
| | Start | End | Start | End | | Period | Annualized | Period | Annualized |
| 1st Q 1999–3rd Q 2010 | 9.9 | 13.8 | 419.9 | 479.1 | 11.5 | 39.8% | 3.0% | 14.1% | 1.2% |
| 1st Q 2003–3rd Q 2010 | 7.5 | 13.8 | 294.2 | 479.1 | 7.5 | 84.5% | 8.5% | 62.8% | 6.7% |
| 3rd Q 2004–3rd Q 2010 | 10.6 | 13.8 | 406.4 | 479.1 | 6.0 | 30.6% | 4.5% | 17.9% | 2.8% |

Notes:
a. Overall GDP is measured in trillions of real 1997 *bolívares fuertes*.
b. Per capita GDP is measured in real 1997 *bolívares fuertes* per person.

Sources: BCV (n.d.), "Agregados Macroeconómicos," and INE (n.d.), "Demografía: Proyecciones de Población."

improvement over the two decades of economic decline that preceded Chávez, it is modest growth, and below the regional average for the decade.[8]

However, looking at the entire decade is misleading, because the Chávez government did not control the state-owned oil company until the first quarter of 2003. For the first four years, the state-owned oil company (PDVSA), which at the time accounted for more than half of government revenue and 80 percent of export earnings, was controlled by people who were hostile to the government. Furthermore, the managers of the company actually used their control over these vital resources to destabilize and even topple (temporarily) the government. Under these circumstances there was not much that the government could do to promote economic growth.

As an analogy, since the United States has no comparable sector of such importance to the economy or government revenue, imagine that the U.S. Federal Reserve were controlled by a board of governors that was determined to use its control over monetary policy and interest rates to destabilize the economy and government. Such a board could wreak havoc on the economy simply by raising the Federal Funds Rate to the level where it would induce a recession. In such a situation, it would not necessarily be fair to hold the executive branch or Congress responsible for the resultant economic destruction.

We could therefore measure growth from the time that the government got control over PDVSA, in the first quarter of 2003. This has the disadvantage that part of the growth since that time is a rebound from a deep recession. Nonetheless it is a better measure to evaluate the performance of the Chávez administration than is the whole ten-year period. Also, it could be argued that this measure is relevant because even the early part of the recovery was a difficult achievement for the government. This was not a normal business cycle but a deep economic recession that involved considerable sabotage in the oil industry. When the strike ended, analysts quoted in the business press predicted a slow and painful recovery, with much difficulty restoring oil production.

Looking at growth from the first quarter of 2003, real GDP grew by 84.5 percent over 7.5 years, or 8.5 percent annually. On a per capita basis, it was 62.8 percent, or 6.7 percent annually. This is rapid growth by any historical or international comparison.

Finally, another way to measure growth that cancels out the effect of the rebound from the 2002–2003 oil strike is to start from the point where GDP reached its pre-recession peak. This would be the third quarter of 2004. On this basis, GDP grew 30.6 percent over six years, or 4.5 percent annually. On a per capita basis, this is 17.9 percent, or 2.8 percent annually. This is still reasonably good growth, although the recession of 2009 reduces the cumulative growth significantly.

The growth during this expansion was concentrated in the non-oil sector of the economy, with the oil sector shrinking in real terms for 2005–2007 (see Table 2). As can be seen in Table 2, the private sector grew faster than the public sector during the expansion.

There is another technical point that must be addressed when looking at the real growth of an oil-exporting economy. By looking at real (inflation-adjusted) growth, we do not capture the other effects of the increase in oil prices during the expansion.[9] In other words, if Venezuela produces the same amount of oil but oil prices rise six-fold, this increase in revenue does not directly change real GDP, since oil production is at the same level in real terms. However, the price increase does benefit the economy and living standards in various ways. First, if the government uses the increased revenue to pursue an expansionary fiscal policy, this will increase real GDP growth. It is important to recognize that this does not happen automatically. Second, there are direct benefits to the population if the increased revenues are used to increase social spending: for example, education and health care. Third, the country can benefit from using the additional revenues to reduce public debt (and foreign debt) relative to GDP, as well as to accumulate reserves. All of these things happened in Venezuela during the expansion, as will be shown below.

## Table 2.
## Venezuela: Real Sector (1998–2009) (real percent change).

| | 1998 | 1999 | 2000 | 2001 | 2002 | 2003 | 2004 | 2005 | 2006 | 2007 | 2008 | 2009 | 2010[a] |
|---|---|---|---|---|---|---|---|---|---|---|---|---|---|
| Real GDP, total | 0.3% | -6% | 3.7% | 3.4% | -8.9% | -7.8% | 18.3% | 10.3% | 9.9% | 8.2% | 4.8% | -3.3% | -2.4% |
| Public | -2.1 | -5.2 | 3.0 | -0.6 | -11.1 | -1.3 | 12.5 | 2.8 | 2.7 | 7.4 | 16.3 | 0.9 | -1.4 |
| Private | 1.1 | -6.9 | 4.2 | 4.9 | -5.8 | -8.9 | 17.2 | 12.9 | 11.3 | 7.5 | -0.1 | -4.5 | -2.8 |
| *By Economic Activity* | | | | | | | | | | | | | |
| Oil Sector | 0.3 | -3.8 | 2.3 | -0.9 | -14.2 | -1.9 | 13.7 | -1.5 | -2.0 | -4.2 | 2.5 | -7.2 | -3.0 |
| Non-Oil Sector | -0.1 | -6.9 | 4.2 | 4.0 | -6.0 | -7.4 | 16.1 | 12.2 | 10.9 | 9.6 | 5.1 | -2.0 | -2.2 |
| Mining | -7.5 | -12.1 | 15.3 | 2.8 | 4.3 | -4.4 | 14.2 | 3.0 | 7.2 | 1.5 | -4.2 | -11.2 | -12.8 |
| Manufacturing | -1.4 | -10.1 | 5.1 | 3.7 | -13.1 | -6.8 | 21.4 | 11.1 | 8.3 | 7.4 | 1.4 | -6.4 | -4.5 |
| Electricity and Water Supply | 0.5 | -2.2 | 4.7 | 4.8 | 2.1 | -0.5 | 8.5 | 11.2 | 4.9 | -1.5 | 5.7 | 4.2 | -6.5 |
| Construction | 1.4 | -17.4 | 4.0 | 13.5 | -8.4 | -39.5 | 25.1 | 20.0 | 30.6 | 15.5 | 3.7 | 0.2 | -6.7 |
| Trade and Repair Services | -1.5 | -5.4 | 5.7 | 4.6 | -13.6 | -9.6 | 28.6 | 21.0 | 15.7 | 16.7 | 4.6 | -8.3 | -7.4 |
| Transport and Storage | -5.2 | -15.3 | 12.5 | -1.3 | -10.4 | -8.0 | 24.6 | 14.7 | 14.3 | 13.3 | 3.8 | -8.5 | -4.3 |
| Communications | 8.2 | 3.6 | 2.1 | 8.1 | 2.5 | -5.0 | 12.9 | 22.4 | 23.5 | 19.8 | 18.2 | 9.8 | 8.2 |
| Financial and Insurance | 0.2 | -15.2 | -0.7 | 2.8 | -14.5 | 11.9 | 37.9 | 36.4 | 47.2 | 16.4 | -4.6 | -2.4 | -7.8 |
| Real Estate | 0.7 | -4.7 | 0.8 | 3.5 | -0.7 | -6.0 | 11.1 | 7.9 | 8.6 | 5.8 | 2.7 | -2.0 | -1.8 |
| Community and Personal Services and Non-Profit | 0.3 | -1.7 | 0.9 | 2.1 | 0.1 | -0.3 | 9.4 | 8.2 | 16.5 | 10.9 | 9.5 | 3.1 | 0.7 |
| General Government Services | -0.6 | -4.8 | 2.8 | 2.5 | -0.4 | 4.9 | 11.1 | 8.0 | 3.0 | 5.7 | 5.3 | 2.4 | 2.1 |
| Other[b] | 3.0 | 0.5 | 5.2 | 1.8 | -1.0 | -2.9 | 7.2 | 12.6 | 3.7 | 5.0 | 5.6 | -0.3 | -1.0 |
| *Expenditure-Based* | | | | | | | | | | | | | |
| Government Final Consumption | -3.1 | -7.5 | 4.2 | 6.9 | -2.5 | 5.7 | 14.2 | 10.7 | 9.6 | 6.1 | 6.7 | 2.3 | 2.3 |
| Private Final Consumption | 1.8 | -1.7 | 4.7 | 6.0 | -7.1 | -4.3 | 15.4 | 15.7 | 15.5 | 18.7 | 7.1 | -3.2 | -3.3 |
| Gross Fixed Capital Formation | 5.5 | -15.6 | 2.6 | 13.8 | -18.3 | -37.0 | 49.7 | 38.4 | 29.3 | 25.3 | -3.3 | -8.2 | -6.5 |
| Exports of Goods and Services | 3.5 | -11.0 | 5.8 | -3.5 | -4.0 | -10.4 | 13.7 | 3.8 | -3.0 | -7.0 | -2.7 | -12.9 | -14.6 |
| Imports of Goods and Services | 11.3 | -9.3 | 12.4 | 14.1 | -25.2 | -20.9 | 57.7 | 35.2 | 34.8 | 29.9 | 3.8 | -19.6 | -12.5 |

Notes:

a. Growth in the first three quarters of 2010 compared to the same quarter in 2009.

b. Includes private agriculture, restaurants and private hotels and various public sector activities.

Source: Banco Central de Venezuela (BCV)

Table 2 also shows the sectoral growth of Venezuela's economy. Since the beginning of the expansion (the first quarter of 2003) through the recession (third quarter of 2010), the fastest growing sector has been finance and insurance, which grew 226 percent during this period. Other fast-growing sectors have included construction (195%) communications (168%), trade and repair services (133%), and transport and storage (129%). Manufacturing grew more quickly than the overall economy, with 99 percent growth, but not nearly enough to contribute to a process of diversification away from its dependence on oil.

In the fourth quarter of 2008, world oil prices dropped suddenly by 50 percent (from $118 to $58 per barrel), and then by another 21 percent in the first quarter of 2009. As Figure 1 indicates, real GDP, which had been increasing steadily since the end of the oil strike, began to decline in the same quarter as oil prices declined. For the year from Q3 2008 to Q3 2009, it declined by 4.5 percent.

As we see in Table 2, the rate of growth of private spending collapsed from 2008 to 2009. Private sector GDP fell by 4.5 percent of GDP 2009. On the expenditure side, it can be seen that private sector consumption growth fell from 7.1 percent in 2008 to negative 3.2 percent in 2009, and negative 3.3 percent in 2010.[10] Capital formation, which includes public and private investment, fell by 3.3, 8.2, and 6.5 percent for the three years 2008–2010. In the face of this collapse of public spending, the economy needed a large fiscal stimulus to avoid recession. However, this did not happen. As can be seen in Table 6, central government spending was flat from 2007 to 2008; it rose by 0.9 percent in 2009, when the economy was in recession. This does not tell us everything about government spending, since there is a sizeable amount of spending that takes place directly from PDVSA, without going through the central government budget. However, given the collapse of oil revenue that began in the fourth quarter of 2008, it is virtually certain that PDVSA's spending was also cut. The fall-off in public sector real GDP, shown in Table 2, which also continued into 2010, is a further indication that the government did not adopt the necessary counter-cyclical policies, and that policy may even have been procyclical.

The recession might very well have been avoided altogether with the proper economic stimulus. Of course, the government could not have known that world oil prices would rebound from their low of $39.95 a barrel in December 2008 to $73.75 per barrel in February of 2010. Nonetheless, given Venezuela's relatively low level of public debt, and especially foreign public debt, a healthy level of reserves, and the ability of an oil-exporting country like Venezuela to borrow on international markets, the government had plenty of room to increase spending, even without knowing when oil prices would recover.[11]

## Social Spending, Poverty, and Employment

An evaluation of the economic and social progress under the current Venezuelan government requires two comparisons. One is the obvious comparison with the situation prior to the Chávez administration, at the end of 1998 or the beginning of 1999. The other is with the period beginning with the first quarter of 2003, since that is when the Chávez government secured its authority over PDVSA.

Compared to the previous administrations, the Chávez government has greatly increased social spending, including spending on health care, subsidized food, and education.

The most pronounced difference has been in the area of publicly provided health care (discussed in more detail in Chapter 7 in this volume). In 1998 there were 1,628 primary care physicians in the public health care system for a population of 23.4 million. By 2007, there were 19,571 for a population of 27 million. In 1998 there were 417 emergency rooms, 74 rehabilitation centers, and 1,628 primary care centers compared to 721 emergency rooms, 445 rehab centers, and 8,621 primary care centers (including the 6,500 "check-up points," usually in poor neighborhoods). In 1999, there were 335 HIV patients receiving antiretroviral treatment from the government, compared to 18,538 in 2006 (SISOV).

The Venezuelan government has also provided widespread access to subsidized food. By the end of 2008, there were 16,626 stores throughout the country that offered mainly food items at subsidized prices (with average savings ranging from 27 percent below market prices in 2005 to 50 percent below market prices in 2008).[12] These, plus expanded special programs for the extremely poor, such as soup kitchens and food distribution, benefited 50 percent of the population in 2008 (Ministerio de Alimentación, SISOV). These percentages do not include the 4 million children that were beneficiaries of a school food program in 2008, compared with 252,000 children in 1999 (Ministerio de Educación).

Access to education has also increased substantially. The number of public schools in the country has increased by over 55 percent, from 17,122 in the 1999/2000 school year to 26,561 in the 2006/2007 school year. By comparison, in the period between the 1994/1995 and 1998/1999 school years, the number of public schools increased by 915 (5.6%).[13] School enrollment has also increased at all educational levels. For example, in the period between the 1999/2000 and 2008/2009 school years, net enrollment rates

## Table 3.
## Venezuela: Public and Social Spending as % of GDP (1998–2008)[a]

| | 1998 | 1999 | 2000 | 2001 | 2002 | 2003 | 2004 | 2005 | 2006 | 2007 | 2008 |
|---|---|---|---|---|---|---|---|---|---|---|---|
| **Total Public Spending** | 23.7% | 24.5% | 29.6% | 31.6% | 29.4% | 31.3% | 29.5% | 30.6% | 39.6% | 34.9% | 32.6% |
| **Total Social Spending** | 11.3 | 12.8 | 14.9 | 16.7 | 16.3 | 16.7 | 18.1 | 17.6 | 21.7 | 21.2 | 18.6 |
| Education | 4.2 | 4.9 | 5.4 | 5.7 | 5.7 | 5.7 | 6.0 | 5.8 | 6.3 | 5.8 | 6.1 |
| Health | 1.9 | 2.5 | 2.6 | 3.0 | 3.4 | 2.5 | 3.2 | 2.6 | 3.6 | 4.4 | 2.9 |
| Housing | 1.9 | 1.6 | 2.6 | 2.4 | 2.4 | 2.1 | 2.5 | 3.0 | 3.8 | 2.9 | 2.3 |
| **Subtotal: Education, Health and Housing** | 8.1 | 9.0 | 10.7 | 11.0 | 11.5 | 10.3 | 11.7 | 11.4 | 13.8 | 13.1 | 11.3 |
| Social Security | 1.7 | 2.3 | 2.7 | 3.8 | 3.2 | 4.2 | 4 | 3.8 | 4.9 | 4.9 | 4.5 |
| Social Development and Participation | 1.1 | 1.1 | 1.1 | 1.2 | 1.1 | 1.7 | 1.8 | 1.8 | 2.5 | 2.5 | 2.1 |
| Culture and Social Communication | 0.3 | 0.2 | 0.3 | 0.2 | 0.2 | 0.4 | 0.3 | 0.4 | 0.4 | 0.4 | 0.4 |
| Science and Technology | 0.1 | 0.1 | 0.2 | 0.4 | 0.3 | 0.1 | 0.3 | 0.3 | 0.2 | 0.3 | 0.3 |

Note:

a. Includes spending by central, state, and local governments, as well as PDVSA Social Investment and FONDEN.

Source: Sistema de Indicadores Sociales de Venezuela (SISOV).

have increased by 60.8 percent for preschool, by 70.7 percent for primary education, and by 60.3 percent for secondary education.[14] According to the government, approximately 1.5 million people also participated in adult literacy programs (Ministerio de Relaciones Exteriores).

The government has also increased its collection of non-oil taxes on businesses,[15] which had been avoiding their taxes, as is common in most of Latin America.[16]

Table 3 shows the central government's social spending from 1998 to 2008. There has been a huge increase, from 11.3 percent of GDP in 1998 to 18.6 percent for 2008. In real (inflation-adjusted) terms, social spending per person[17] has nearly tripled, increasing by 191 percent over the period 1998–2008.

The poverty rate has decreased sharply from its peak of 55.1 percent of households in 2003 to 23.8 percent for the second half of 2009. This would be expected in the face of the very rapid economic growth through 2008, although the data show a continued decrease even during the recession year of 2009. Table 4 shows the poverty rate since 1997, by household and population. If we compare the pre-Chávez poverty rate (43.9 percent in the second half of 1998) with the one for the first half of 2009 (23.8%) this is a 46 percent drop in the rate of poverty, which is quite substantial. The decline in extreme poverty is even more steep, a 65 percent drop from 17.1 percent in 1998 to 5.9 percent in 2009. Moreover, this poverty rate measures only cash income—it does not take into account the increased access to health care or education that poor people have experienced. As we have shown previously, taking the most conservative estimate of just the value of the health care benefits—what the poor would have spent on health care in the absence of these new programs—would lower the measured poverty rate by about 2 percentage points.[18] Of course, this is a very conservative estimate of the value of just the increased health care benefits to the poor, since in the absence of these benefits, most poor people would simply have gone without health care, and therefore suffer from worse health, lower income, and lower life expectancy. So the value of these health care services is much greater than the amount that they would have spent out-of-pocket in the absence of the government programs.[19] The situation of the poor has therefore improved significantly beyond even the substantial poverty reduction that is visible in the official poverty rate, which measures only cash income.

Unemployment also dropped sharply during the economic expansion. As can be seen in Table 5, the unemployment rate fell from 19.2 percent in the first half of 2003 to 7.6 percent in the first half of 2009, its lowest level in more than a decade. At the beginning of the Chávez administration,

### Table 4.
### Venezuela: Poverty Rates (1997–2009).

| Year / | Time Period | Households (% of total ) | | Population (% of total) | |
|--------|-------------|------|----------------|------|----------------|
|        |             | Poor | Extremely Poor | Poor | Extremely Poor |
| 1997 | 1st Half | 55.6% | 25.5% | 60.9% | 29.5% |
|      | 2nd Half | 48.1 | 19.3 | 54.5 | 23.4 |
| 1998 | 1st Half | 49.0 | 21.0 | 55.4 | 24.7 |
|      | 2nd Half | 43.9 | 17.1 | 50.4 | 20.3 |
| 1999 | 1st Half | 42.8 | 16.6 | 50.0 | 19.9 |
|      | 2nd Half | 42.0 | 16.9 | 48.7 | 20.1 |
| 2000 | 1st Half | 41.6 | 16.7 | 48.3 | 19.5 |
|      | 2nd Half | 40.4 | 14.9 | 46.3 | 18.0 |
| 2001 | 1st Half | 39.1 | 14.2 | 45.5 | 17.4 |
|      | 2nd Half | 39.0 | 14.0 | 45.4 | 16.9 |
| 2002 | 1st Half | 41.5 | 16.6 | 48.1 | 20.1 |
|      | 2nd Half | 48.6 | 21.0 | 55.4 | 25.0 |
| 2003 | 1st Half | 54.0 | 25.1 | 61.0 | 30.2 |
|      | 2nd Half | 55.1 | 25.0 | 62.1 | 29.8 |
| 2004 | 1st Half | 53.1 | 23.5 | 60.2 | 28.1 |
|      | 2nd Half | 47.0 | 18.6 | 53.9 | 22.5 |
| 2005 | 1st Half | 42.4 | 17.0 | 48.8 | 20.3 |
|      | 2nd Half | 37.9 | 15.3 | 43.7 | 17.8 |
| 2006 | 1st Half | 33.9 | 10.6 | 39.7 | 12.9 |
|      | 2nd Half | 30.6 | 9.1 | 36.3 | 11.1 |
| 2007 | 1st Half | 27.5 | 7.6 | 33.1 | 9.4 |
|      | 2nd Half | 28.5 | 7.9 | 33.6 | 9.6 |
| 2008 | 1st Half | 27.7 | 7.5 | 33.1 | 9.2 |
|      | 2nd Half | 27.5 | 7.6 | 32.6 | 9.2 |
| 2009 | 1st Half | 26.4 | 7.3 | 31.6 | 8.7 |
|      | 2st Half | 23.8 | 5.9 | 28.5 | 7.2 |

Source: INE (n.d.), "Social: Pobreza."

## Table 5.
## Venezuela: Labor Force Indicators (1998-2010)[a]

| | 1998 | 1999 | 2000 | 2001 | 2002 | 2003 | 2004 | 2005 | 2006 | 2007 | 2008 | 2009 | 2010 |
|---|---|---|---|---|---|---|---|---|---|---|---|---|---|
| | | | | | *(in thousands)* | | | | | | | | |
| Labor Force | 9,699.3 | 10,259.2 | 10,163.9 | 10,576.0 | 11,369.0 | 11,793.5 | 12,036.3 | 11,936.5 | 12,056.5 | 12,217.7 | 12,442.8 | 12,805.3 | 12,967.9 |
| Total Employed | 8,605.1 | 8,691.4 | 8,682.7 | 9,123.5 | 9,611.7 | 9,524.8 | 10,035.7 | 10,344.1 | 10,783.2 | 11,079.7 | 11,458.4 | 11,829.3 | 11,826.7 |
| Public Sector | 1,402.6 | 1,348.2 | 1,354.5 | 1,377.7 | 1,364.9 | 1,371.6 | 1,495.3 | 1,634.4 | 1,800.0 | 1,928.2 | 1,996.2 | 2,283.6 | 2,282.6 |
| Private Sector | 7,202.5 | 7,344.3 | 7,328.2 | 7,745.9 | 8,246.8 | 8,153.2 | 8,540.4 | 8,709.8 | 8,978.5 | 9,153.3 | 9,476.1 | 9,548.5 | 9,544.2 |
| Formal Sector | 4,457.5 | 4,258.8 | 4,115.6 | 4,497.9 | 4,757.8 | 4,533.8 | 4,927.5 | 5,420.3 | 5,852.7 | 6,172.4 | 6,436.0 | 6,697.0 | 6,611.2 |
| Informal Sector | 4,147.7 | 4,432.6 | 4,567.1 | 4,625.6 | 4,853.9 | 4,991.0 | 5,108.2 | 4,923.8 | 4,925.8 | 4,909.1 | 5,036.3 | 5,135.1 | 5,215.6 |
| | | | | | *(% of total labor force)* | | | | | | | | |
| Labor Force | 100.0 | 100.0 | 100.0 | 100.0 | 100.0 | 100.0 | 100.0 | 100.0 | 100.0 | 100.0 | 100.0 | 100.0 | 100.0 |
| Total Employed | 88.7 | 84.7 | 85.4 | 86.3 | 84.5 | 80.8 | 83.4 | 86.7 | 89.4 | 90.7 | 92.2 | 92.4 | 91.2 |
| Public Sector | 14.5 | 13.1 | 13.3 | 13.0 | 12.0 | 11.6 | 12.4 | 13.7 | 14.9 | 15.8 | 16.0 | 17.8 | 17.6 |
| Private Sector | 74.3 | 71.6 | 72.1 | 73.2 | 72.5 | 69.1 | 71.0 | 73.0 | 74.5 | 74.9 | 76.2 | 74.6 | 73.6 |
| Formal Sector | 46.0 | 41.5 | 40.5 | 42.5 | 41.8 | 38.4 | 40.9 | 45.4 | 48.5 | 50.5 | 51.7 | 52.3 | 51.0 |
| Informal Sector | 42.8 | 43.2 | 44.9 | 43.7 | 42.7 | 42.3 | 42.4 | 41.3 | 40.9 | 40.2 | 40.5 | 40.1 | 40.2 |
| Unemployment Rate | 11.3 | 15.3 | 14.6 | 13.7 | 15.5 | 19.2 | 16.6 | 13.3 | 10.6 | 9.3 | 7.8 | 7.6 | 8.8 |

Note:
a. Data correspond to the first half of every year (from the INE's biannual Household Survey).
Source: Instituto Nacional de Estadística (INE), Sistema de Indicadores Sociales de Venezuela (SISOV), República Bolivariana de Venezuela.

unemployment stood at 15.3 percent in the first half of 1999. It rose to 8.8 percent in the first half of 2010, as a result of the recession. By any comparison, the official unemployment rate has dropped sharply. Of course, an unemployment rate of 7.6 percent in Venezuela, as in developing economies generally, is not comparable to the same rate in the United States or Europe. Many of the people counted as employed are very much underemployed. But the measure is consistent over time, and therefore shows a considerable improvement in the labor market. This is evident in other labor market indicators. For example, employment in the formal sector has increased to 6.61 million (first half of 2010), from 4.40 million in the first half of 1998 and 4.53 million in the first half of 2003. As a percentage of the labor force, formal employment has increased significantly since 1998, from 45.4 to 51.0 percent.

Since the first half of 1999, the private sector shows an increase of about 2.2 million jobs, and the public sector gained 900 thousand jobs (see Table 5). Employment as a percentage of the labor force has increased by 6.5 percentage points since then. Private sector employment was a slightly larger percentage of the labor force (73.6%) in the first half of 2010 as compared to the first half of 1999 (71.6%).

### Fiscal and Monetary Policy, Exchange Rates, Balance of Payments, and the Sustainability of the Current Economic Expansion

As Tables 6 and 7 show, the Venezuelan government took advantage of the economic expansion and increased oil revenues to reduce its public debt, and especially foreign public debt, as a percent of GDP.[20] Total public debt had increased quite substantially through the crisis of 2002–2003, reaching a peak of 47.6 percent of GDP in 2003 (see Table 7), with the foreign part of that at 29.7 percent. But by 2008 public debt had been reduced to just 14.2 percent of GDP, with the foreign public debt at only 9.6 percent. This rose in the recession to 18.4 and 10.8 percent, respectively. If we were to include the foreign debt of PDVSA and other state-owned enterprises, the total debt would rise to 26 percent.[21] This is a very low level of public and foreign public debt. Furthermore, Venezuela ran a huge current account surplus of 12.6 percent for 2008, although this collapsed to 2.6 percent for 2009. If we look at the quarterly data (not shown here), what happened was obvious: the current account went into deficit for just the fourth quarter of 2008 and the first quarter of 2009—when oil prices crashed. It rebounded quickly into surplus in the next two quarters as oil prices recovered.

As we saw in Table 2, private spending—which had begun to slow at the end of 2007, when the U.S. recession began—collapsed in 2008. There was therefore a need for the government to increase its spending in order to avoid or mitigate a recession. However, as explained above, the government did not adopt a counter-cyclical fiscal policy. We have also seen in Table 3 that public spending dropped from 39.6 percent of GDP in 2006 to 34.9 percent in 2007 to 32.6 percent in 2008. This probably also contributed to the economic slowdown that began in 2008.

Table 7 also shows that the government dipped into reserves, as would be expected, as it ran current account deficits in the final quarter of 2008 and the first quarter of 2009: official reserves during this period at the central bank fell from $43.1 billion to $35.8 billion. This is still a high level of reserves, however: approximately three-fourths of imports for 2008 and an even higher percentage for the reduced imports of 2009. (The most widely used benchmark is that international reserves should be sufficient to cover three months of imports.[22]) Furthermore, it appears that the government had billions of additional dollars in reserves on hand in other accounts at the end of 2008, although it is difficult to say exactly how much.[23] But even if these numbers are not completely accurate it would not change the basic story, because the government had the ability to borrow internationally as much as it needed to maintain an adequate level of reserves, in order to adopt the necessary stimulus program.

These details on government spending, the current account, and reserves are important to any assessment of the government's macroeconomic policy during the world recession. The main difference between a government such as that of Venezuela during an economic downturn and that of the United States, or to a lesser extent of other governments having hard currencies (the euro area and Japan), has to do with the balance of payments. As we have seen, the United States has been able to run large deficits, even monetizing a significant part of its increase in deficit spending, in order to counteract the recession. Middle-income countries can do the same thing—with the constraint that they do not, as their economies grow and imports therefore also grow, run short of foreign exchange to pay for imports. As can be seen from the above discussion, Venezuela was not in danger of running low on foreign exchange. If oil prices had stayed low for a longer period, the government could have borrowed internationally, given their low foreign public debt. The recession of 2008–2009 was therefore avoidable, despite the collapse of oil prices. It seems then that the Venezuelan economy was, and still is, not as vulnerable to oil price declines as many people had hoped. Furthermore, world oil prices are currently at more than $85 per barrel and projected to rise to $98 per barrel over the next decade, although there is a lot of uncertainty in long-range projections of oil prices (EIA). So there is no obstacle in the form of oil prices to another sustained and high-growth economic expansion.

## Table 6.
### Venezuela: Central Government Finances (1998–2009) (in percentage of GDP).

| | 1998 | 1999 | 2000 | 2001 | 2002 | 2003 | 2004 | 2005 | 2006 | 2007 | 2008 | 2009[a] |
|---|---|---|---|---|---|---|---|---|---|---|---|---|
| **TOTAL REVENUE** | 17.4% | 18.0% | 20.2% | 20.8% | 22.2% | 23.4% | 24.0% | 27.5% | 29.6% | 28.9% | 24.7% | 21.6% |
| Tax Revenue | 12.2 | 13.0 | 12.9 | 11.4 | 10.6 | 11.3 | 12.7 | 15.3 | 15.6 | 16.1 | 13.5 | 13.5 |
| Oil | 1.3 | 2.2 | 4.2 | 2.5 | 0.9 | 1.5 | 1.8 | 3.7 | 4.0 | 4.1 | 2.6 | 1.8 |
| Non-Oil | 10.9 | 10.8 | 8.6 | 8.9 | 9.7 | 9.8 | 10.9 | 11.6 | 11.6 | 12.0 | 10.8 | 11.6 |
| Non-Tax Revenue | 5.2 | 5.0 | 7.3 | 9.4 | 11.5 | 12.1 | 11.3 | 12.3 | 14.0 | 12.7 | 11.2 | 8.2 |
| Oil | 4.5 | 4.4 | 5.8 | 6.9 | 9.6 | 10.1 | 9.4 | 9.7 | 11.9 | 10.5 | 9.6 | 5.8 |
| Non-Oil | 0.8 | 0.6 | 1.5 | 2.5 | 2.0 | 2.0 | 1.9 | 2.6 | 2.2 | 2.2 | 1.6 | 2.4 |
| **TOTAL EXPENDITURE & NET LENDING** | 21.4% | 19.8% | 21.8% | 25.1% | 26.1% | 27.8% | 25.9% | 25.9% | 29.6% | 25.8% | 25.8%[b] | 26.7% |
| Current Expenditure | 16.7 | 16.4 | 17.5 | 19.3 | 19.1 | 20.8 | 19.6 | 19.0 | 21.9 | 19.6 | 19.6 | 20.5 |
| Capital Expenditure | 4.0 | 3.0 | 3.3 | 4.4 | 5.1 | 5.5 | 5.0 | 5.8 | 6.7 | 5.8 | 5.8 | 5.5 |
| Off-Budget Expenditure and Net Lending[c] | 0.7 | 0.4 | 1.0 | 1.5 | 2.0 | 1.5 | 1.3 | 1.1 | 1.1 | 0.4 | 0.4 | 0.7 |
| **Primary Balance** | -1.4 | 1.0 | 0.9 | -1.5 | 0.6 | 0.3 | 1.8 | 4.6 | 2.0 | 4.5 | 0.1 | -3.7 |
| **Overall Balance** | -4.0 | -1.7 | -1.7 | -4.4 | -4.0 | -4.4 | -1.9 | 1.6 | 0.0 | 3.0 | -1.2 | -5.1 |
| **Financing** | 4.0 | 1.7 | 1.7 | 4.4 | 4.0 | 4.4 | 1.9 | -1.6 | 0.0 | -3.0 | 1.2 | 5.1 |
| Domestic | 2.8 | 2.8 | 4.0 | 4.0 | 3.1 | 3.3 | -0.7 | -2.5 | -1.3 | -1.4 | -0.3 | 3.7 |
| Foreign | 1.2 | -1.1 | -2.3 | 0.3 | 0.9 | 1.1 | 2.6 | 0.9 | 1.3 | -1.6 | 1.5 | 1.4 |

Notes:

a.  Latest data available. Subject to revision.

b.  Finance Ministry data shows identical amounts for these expenditure categories in 2007 and 2008. We expect some revisions as such an outcome would be highly unlikely.

c.  These central government expenditures do not include most off-budget expenditures or state and local spending – see Table 2.

Source: Ministerio del Poder Popular para las Finanzas (MF), República Bolivariana de Venezuela.

Another common feature of the "oil boom to be followed by bust" analysis of Venezuela's economy is that government spending fuels rapidly rising inflation, which will spin out of control. According to this theory, which is not well specified, either the inflation itself would cause a crisis—for example become hyperinflation—or the government would be forced to put the economy into a sharp contraction in order to avoid or reduce dangerous levels of inflation.

Figure 2 shows Venezuela's monthly year-over-year inflation rate since 1991. We see that inflation peaked at 115 percent in September 1996 and then declined steadily to 30 percent when Chávez was inaugurated as president in February of 1999. It continued to decline during Chávez's first two years, reaching 12.1 percent in April 2001. It then rose rapidly as political instability accelerated in 2002. This period of instability included the military coup of April 2002 and most importantly, the oil strike of December 2002 to February 2003, which generated major supply shortages and pushed inflation back up to a 39 percent annual rate by February 2003.[24] After the strike ended, inflation declined steadily again for the next three and a half years, despite very rapid growth during recovery that began in the fourth quarter of 2003. From June 2006 there was another upswing, pushing the year-over-year inflation rate from 10.4 percent to a peak of 36.0 percent in September 2008. It then declined to 27.4 percent by December 2010.

How serious a problem is inflation in Venezuela, and could it lead to an economic crisis? First, it should be kept in mind that there is no consensus in the macroeconomic research as to how high inflation can go before it even has a negative impact on growth, with some studies finding a threshold of 20 percent or more.[25] Second, it should be emphasized that double-digit inflation rates in a developing country such as Venezuela are not comparable to the same phenomenon occurring in the United States or Europe. Inflation in Venezuela was much higher in the pre-Chávez years, running at 35.8 percent for 1998 and 99.9 percent for 1996 (IMF). Although much of the public worldwide does not understand this, it is real (after-inflation) growth in incomes—and employment—that affects people's living standards, not the rate of inflation *per se*. This is true so long as inflation does not spiral to the point where it actually reduces real growth. So far, it does not appear that inflation in Venezuela is getting out of control, or that there is a risk of hyperinflation. It is higher than it should be, and is in the range of where much of the macroeconomic literature suggests that it could begin to affect growth negatively; but it is unlikely to cause serious economic problems if the government does not try to reduce it too quickly through demand-side measures, or allow it to spiral out of control.

**Figure 2.**
**Venezuela: Monthly Year-Over-Year Inflation Rate, Consumer Prices**
**(January 1991–December 2010).**

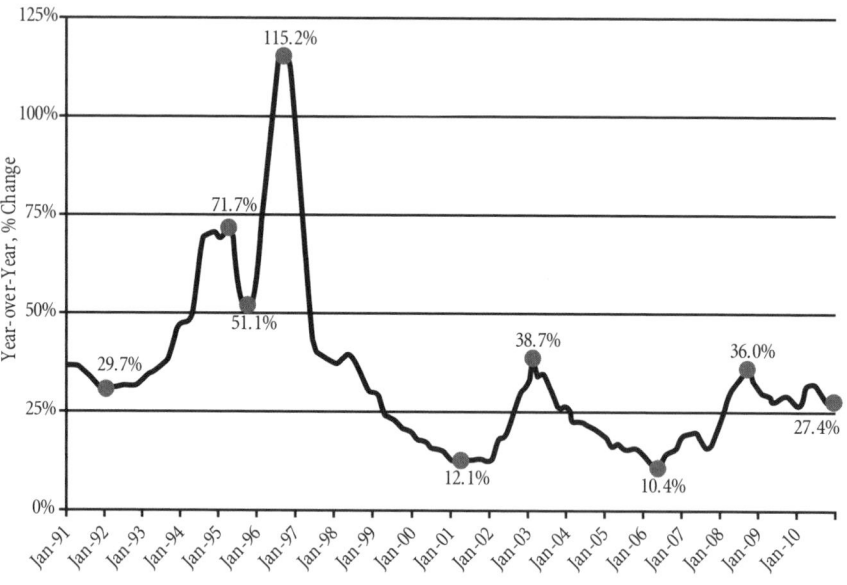

Source: Banco Central de Venezuela (BCV).

The more serious economic imbalance has been the exchange rate. The bolívar was pegged at 1,600 to the dollar in February 2003, when the government implemented foreign exchange controls, then increased in two steps to 2,150 per dollar, or 2.15 *bolívares fuertes* (the currency was re-denominated), by March 2005, where it remained until January 2010. If we assume that the currency was neither overvalued nor undervalued when the exchange controls were implemented—more likely it was already overvalued—we would have expected a depreciation to about 5.46 *bolívares fuertes* by January 2010, as a result of Venezuela's inflation.[26] Thus, by the time of the devaluation in January 2010, the Venezuelan currency was about 154 percent overvalued relative to the dollar—again assuming that it was neither overvalued nor undervalued when originally pegged.

This is the principal way in which inflation negatively affects the Venezuelan economy, and it is not the inflation itself, but the inflation in the context of a fixed, overvalued exchange rate. With the nominal exchange rate fixed, each year that Venezuela's inflation exceeds that of its trading partners, the *real* exchange rate becomes more overvalued. Given the high levels of inflation in Venezuela relative to its trading partners, the real exchange rate appreciated rapidly since 2003, as we have seen. An overvalued currency discourages the development of non-oil sectors, especially manufacturing. It makes imports artificially cheap and the country's non-oil exports more expensive on world markets, thus putting the country's tradable goods at a serious disadvantage in both international and domestic markets. This is a serious long-term development problem. As we saw in Table 3, manufacturing growth lagged behind such non-tradable sectors as construction as well as finance and insurance, before collapsing with the recession. Part of this reduced share of manufacturing in total output is probably due to the increasing real overvaluation of the currency. There are also distortions and inefficiencies associated with the system of exchange controls and the parallel market.

In January of 2010, the government devalued the bolívar to 4.3 to the dollar for most imports, bringing it much closer to a competitive level. At the same time, a rate of 2.6 per dollar was established for sectors deemed essential, which include food, education, science and technology, health, machinery and equipment, family remittances, and transfers to students living abroad.

The overvalued fixed exchange rate, combined with present levels of inflation, also presents a significant intermediate-term problem. Even if inflation is stabilized and begins to be reduced, so long as it remains at or near current levels and the nominal exchange rate remains fixed, Venezuela's currency will become increasingly overvalued. This will increasingly squeeze domestic production outside of oil and non-tradables and would eventually become unsustainable.

Venezuela's overvalued exchange rate is often framed as a case of "Dutch disease," which is a generic description for the negative impact of an overvalued currency on the manufacturing/tradable goods sector, when the domestic currency becomes overvalued as a result of revenues from natural resource (such as oil) revenues. However, this does not describe Venezuela's situation, where the currency has been overvalued because it has been set at a fixed nominal rate, and, as described above, where inflation has been much higher than that of its trading partners. If the currency were allowed to float within some band at a more competitive level, for example, there is no reason to assume that Venezuela would automatically move toward an overvalued exchange rate. Instead, the government could—as Argentina has done throughout most of its 2002–2008 economic expansion—maintain a stable and competitive real exchange rate.[27]

Real interest rates have been negative throughout the recovery as measured by the 90-day deposit rate, or for most of the recovery as measured by the lending rate.[28] This is shown in Figure 3. These low interest rates, combined with the government's expansionary fiscal policy, no doubt contributed to the economy's rapid growth during the 2003–2008 period. It is worth noting that the government's currency controls, originally enacted in February 2003 as a means of limiting capital flight from the country, have helped it to pursue expansionary fiscal and monetary policies while maintaining a fixed exchange rate. Thus the overall combination of macroeconomic policy was successful for nearly six years in promoting rapid growth, although with an increasingly overvalued real exchange rate.

Table 7 also shows gross fixed capital formation since 2001. Not surprisingly, it collapsed by 37 percent in 2003 due to the oil strike/recession. However, it grew enormously during the economic expansion of 2003–2008. It is worth noting that private capital formation also rebounded strongly from the 2003 recession, and continued growing until the economy began to slow in 2008. This is important because it shows that, despite the unpopularity with private investors of many of the government's actions, they are willing to invest quite heavily in Venezuela when the economy is growing and they see private demand growing. Although private capital formation, as a percent of GDP, remained at lower levels than in the late 1990s, the government can compensate for this with increased public capital formation— and has done so in recent years.

Public sector investment had been badly neglected for decades, and there is much potential there to improve the productivity of the economy— neglect that was demonstrated by the collapse in 2006 of the Viaduct 1 bridge that was a vital part of the route from the La Guaira airport to Caracas. More recently, the need for stepped-up public investment has been vividly illustrated by electricity shortages. So if private investment lags behind public investment in the near future, this does not necessarily have to hamper Venezuela's growth and development.

In 2007, the government accelerated its drive toward its announced goal of "21st century socialism," nationalizing the telecommunications giant CANTV and some of the country's electricity generation (which was already more than 80 percent in the hands of the government). It also took a majority stake in its joint ventures with foreign oil companies in the Orinoco basin. These moves have generally been portrayed as very negative for Venezuela's investment climate and for its economic future.

However, it is important to keep some perspective on these changes. The telecommunications sector had been nationally owned and then privatized

**Figure 3.**
**Venezuela: Real Monthly Interest Rates (Annualized).**

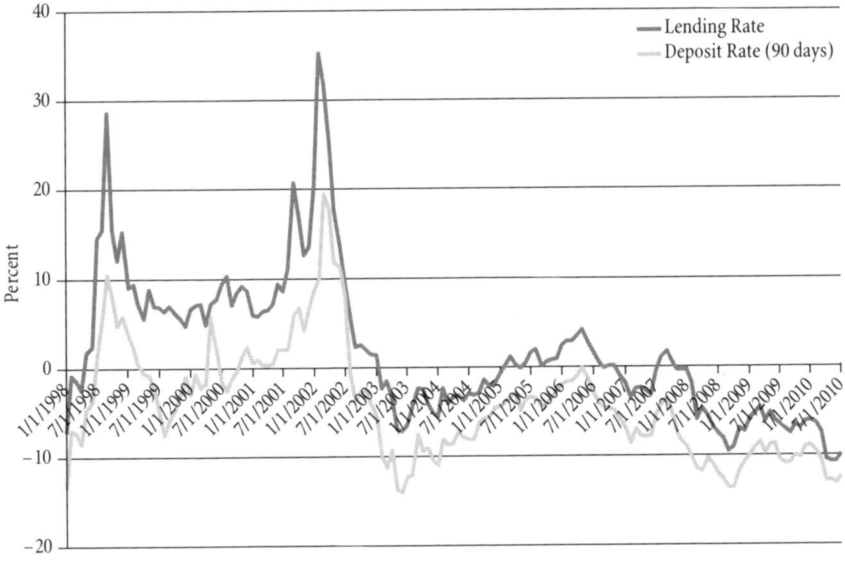

Source: Banco Central de Venezuela (BCV) and author's calculations.

in the 1990s. These nationalized companies have been compensated fully for their assets: "I think this deal is a fair one," AES Corporation's chief executive Paul Hanrahan said at a news conference in Caracas, adding that negotiations had "respected the rights of investors" (Mufson). CANTV had a near-monopoly on land phones and Internet service, and had been slow to expand access—Venezuela's Internet access remains below average for the region, with 20.8 users per 100 people, as compared to 26.6 for Latin America (World Bank). This is particularly low because Venezuela is near the top of the region in its income per capita.

In the oil sector, the first round of negotiations was settled for 31 of 33 contracts, with only Total and ENI choosing to leave. In 2007, most of the remaining joint ventures were also renegotiated, but Exxon-Mobil and ConocoPhillips pulled out, with the dispute going to arbitration at the World Bank's International Center for the Settlement of Investment Disputes. Venezuela is one of the only major oil-producing states in the developing world that allows foreign investment in oil production—even U.S. allies such as Mexico and Saudi Arabia, for example, do not. Venezuela's reserves of heavy crude in the Orinoco region are currently estimated to be

## Table 7.
## Venezuela: Selected Economic Indicators (1998–2009).

| | 1998 | 1999 | 2000 | 2001 | 2002 | 2003 | 2004 | 2005 | 2006 | 2007 | 2008 | 2009 |
|---|---|---|---|---|---|---|---|---|---|---|---|---|
| | *(Percent of GDP)* | | | | | | | | | | | |
| **CURRENT ACCOUNT** | -4.9% | 2.2% | 10.1% | 1.6% | 8.2% | 14.1% | 13.8% | 17.7% | 14.8% | 8.8% | 12.6% | 2.6% |
| **Trade balance in goods** | 1.0 | 6.6 | 14.2 | 6.1 | 14.4 | 20.1 | 20.1 | 22.0 | 17.9 | 10.5 | 14.6 | 5.9 |
| Exports, fob | 19.4 | 21.4 | 28.6 | 21.7 | 28.8 | 32.6 | 35.2 | 38.7 | 35.6 | 30.6 | 30.1 | 17.7 |
| Oil | 13.3 | 17.1 | 23.8 | 17.7 | 23.2 | 26.4 | 29.1 | 33.4 | 31.9 | 27.7 | 28.1 | 16.6 |
| Non-Oil | 6.1 | 4.3 | 4.8 | 4.0 | 5.7 | 6.2 | 6.0 | 5.3 | 3.7 | 2.9 | 2.0 | 1.0 |
| Imports, fob | -18.3 | -14.8 | -14.4 | -15.6 | -14.4 | -12.6 | -15.1 | -16.7 | -17.7 | -20.1 | -15.5 | -11.8 |
| Oil | -1.6 | -1.5 | -1.5 | -1.4 | -1.4 | -1.6 | -1.6 | -1.7 | -1.5 | -1.9 | -1.4 | -1.2 |
| Non-Oil | -16.7 | -13.3 | -12.9 | -14.2 | -13.0 | -11.0 | -13.5 | -15.0 | -16.2 | -18.2 | -14.1 | -10.6 |
| **Trade balance in services** | -2.9 | -2.9 | -2.8 | -2.7 | -3.1 | -3.2 | -3.0 | -2.8 | -2.4 | -2.6 | -2.1 | -2.3 |
| | *(Percent of GDP)* | | | | | | | | | | | |
| **GROSS PUBLIC DEBT** | | | | | | | | | | | | |
| **Total** | 30.4% | 29.0% | 27.3% | 30.0% | 36.6% | 47.6% | 38.0% | 32.4% | 24.1% | 19.5% | 14.2% | 18.4% |
| Foreign | 25.5 | 23.1 | 18.5 | 18.3 | 24.2 | 29.7 | 24.4 | 21.6 | 14.9 | 12.1 | 9.6 | 10.8 |
| Domestic | 5.1 | 6.5 | 9.1 | 12.4 | 150.2 | 17.9 | 14.0 | 11.1 | 9.2 | 7.4 | 4.6 | 7.6 |
| | *(Percent of GDP)* | | | | | | | | | | | |
| **GROSS FIXED CAPITAL FORMATION** | | | | | | | | | | | | |
| **Total** | 28.6% | 23.7% | 21.0% | 24.0% | 21.9% | 15.5% | 18.3% | 20.3% | 22.3% | 24.5% | 20.4% | 22.1% |
| Public | 11.1 | 7.7 | 6.8 | 7.0 | 9.7 | 7.5 | 8.1 | 8.2 | 11.3 | 13.7 | 12.5 | 12.5 |
| Private | 17.5 | 16.0 | 14.2 | 17.0 | 12.3 | 8.0 | 10.2 | 12.1 | 11.0 | 10.8 | 8.0 | 9.6 |
| | *(Real % Change)* | | | | | | | | | | | |
| **Total** | 5.5% | -15.5% | 2.6% | 13.8% | -18.3% | -37.0% | 49.7% | 38.1% | 29.5% | 25.4% | -3.3% | -8.2% |
| Public | 2.4 | -29.0 | 3.8 | 3.6 | 25.1 | -32.1 | 37.6 | 25.5 | 65.0 | 38.1 | 8.4 | -10.7 |
| Private | 7.7 | -6.4 | 2.0 | 19.1 | -38.1 | -41.5 | 62.7 | 49.6 | 2.6 | 9.7 | -21.2 | -2.9 |
| **OTHER** | | | | | | | | | | | | |
| Nominal GDP (US$ millions) | 91,339 | 97,978 | 117,153 | 122,910 | 92,889 | 83,442 | 112,800 | 144,128 | 183,222 | 226,221 | 310,696 | 325,678 |
| Gross Int'l Reserves (US$ millions) | 14,849 | 15,379 | 20,471 | 18,523 | 14,860 | 21,366 | 24,208 | 30,368 | 37,440 | 34,286 | 43,127 | 35,830 |
| Average exchange rate (VEB per USD) | 550 | 609 | 682 | 726 | 1,191 | 1,621 | 1,893 | 2,112 | 2,150 | 2,150 | 2,150 | 2,150 |
| Avg. inflation rate, consumer prices (%) | 35.8 | 23.6 | 16.2 | 12.0 | 31.3 | 27.0 | 19.1 | 14.4 | 17.0 | 22.4 | 31.9 | 26.9 |

Sources: Banco Central de Venezuela (BCV); Ministerio del Poder Popular para las Finanzas (MF), República Bolivariana de Venezuela.

among the largest in the world, with the U.S. Geological Survey estimating Venezuela to have 500 billion barrels (USGS). Venezuela is currently taking less than one billion barrels per year out of the ground. Foreign private companies therefore have strong incentives to stay involved. They also face increasing competition from state-run companies from countries such as China, Brazil, India, Russia, and elsewhere.

The Venezuelan government's moves toward increased state involvement in the economy have not involved nationalizations of large sectors of the economy or anything approaching a planned economy. As noted above, the government has not even increased the public sector's share of the economy. Public spending, at 32.6 percent of GDP in 2008, is far below such European capitalist countries as France (49%) or Sweden (52%). There is still plenty of room for both private and public investment.

In sum, the story of an oil boom followed by an inevitable bust is a gross oversimplification of Venezuela's economy in the Chávez years. Rather, it appears that the economy was hit hard for the first few years by political instability, followed by rapid growth after the political situation stabilized and the government gained control over the oil industry in the first quarter of 2003. It then lapsed into recession when oil prices collapsed, although this could have been prevented with counter-cyclical macroeconomic policy, instead of the pro-cyclical fiscal policy that the government implemented. Looking forward, the Venezuelan economy is much more likely to recover from its recession and embark on a prolonged expansion than it is to suffer a period of crisis or prolonged economic stagnation. Of course, this assumes that the government will abandon its recent pro-cyclical policies and adopt a stimulus package. If the government does not provide a sufficient stimulus, then it could face a prolonged recession and/or stagnation. Containing and reducing inflation, as well as realigning the domestic currency to establish a competitive real exchange rate, appear to be the most important challenges other than growth in the intermediate run; in the long run, diversifying the economy away from its dependence on oil is also a major challenge.

## Venezuela and the Region's Leftward Shift

As analyzed above, Venezuela's economy does not appear to be headed for collapse, so its influence on the region is likely to continue. This influence has expanded enormously since 2003, while Washington's influence has similarly declined. To understand why this has happened, it is necessary to look at some important developments that have not had the attention that they deserve in media and policy circles.

The most significant of these changes is the collapse of the IMF's influence over middle-income countries. This is the most important change in the international financial system since the breakdown of the Bretton Woods system of fixed exchange rates in 1973. The IMF's entire loan portfolio fell from over $100 billion in 2003 to under $20 billion in 2007, with half of that owed by Turkey. In Latin America and the Caribbean, the IMF's lending fell from $49 billion to just $701 million during these four years. Since the world recession began in 2008, the IMF has gained access to more than $500 billion of new funds—vastly more resources that it has ever had. But Latin America mostly avoided borrowing from the IMF during the recession; the IMF's outstanding loans there increased, but only to $1.31 billion.

But it is not the IMF's actual lending, which is much less than that of the World Bank, that made it—until recently—the most important avenue of U.S. influence in Latin America and in developing countries generally. Rather, it is the IMF's position as the leader of a creditors' cartel that includes the World Bank, the Inter-American Development Bank (IDB), the United States and other rich country governments, the Paris Club of official creditors, and other lenders. As part of an informal arrangement that has only recently broken down, a government that did not meet IMF conditions would not be eligible for most loans from these other official lenders, and sometimes even from the private sector. This monopoly over credit is a very powerful force that many governments have found themselves unable to resist. Since the U.S. Treasury Department exercises a formal veto over IMF decisions, and is in fact the overwhelmingly dominant influence within the Fund, this creditors' cartel was the main instrument of U.S. foreign economic policy for as long as it was in force. Many of the neoliberal reforms, as they are known in Latin America, were adopted over the last 25–30 years under pressure from the IMF and its allied institutions and governments.

The system began to break down after the East Asian financial crisis of 1997–1999. The middle-income countries that were hard hit by the crisis— Indonesia, Thailand, Malaysia, South Korea, and the Philippines—had a terrible experience with the IMF, which attached damaging and unwanted policies to its crisis lending.[29] Partly as a result of this experience, these countries and others began to "self-insure" against possible future economic shocks by accumulating large amounts of foreign exchange reserves, so that they would never have to return to the Fund again.

The Fund's power and influence took another blow in the Argentine crisis of 1998–2002. The Fund's policies were widely seen as responsible for a deep recession that pushed the majority of the country—once one of the richest in the region—into poverty. Furthermore, when the crisis peaked in 2002 and the economy was in a state of near-collapse, the IMF offered no help but rather continued to push for a number of unwanted macroeconomic policies and for the government to offer a better settlement to its defaulted foreign creditors. Argentina refused to accept IMF conditions, and the Fund, together with the IDB and World Bank, took a net $4 billion (4 percent of GDP) out of the economy during the worst crisis year of 2002. But to the surprise of most observers, the Argentine economy began to recover just three months after its record debt default, and grew an enormous 63 percent over the next six years, pulling more than 11 million people (in a country of 39 million) out of poverty in the process (IMF).[30] Argentina's remarkable recovery showed that a flat-broke debtor country could stand up to the Fund in a way that no one had tried before, and succeed.

Venezuela delivered the final blow to the creditors' cartel in Latin America by offering an alternative source of credit, with no policy strings attached. Argentina has borrowed more than $6 billion from Venezuela, partly to pay off the IMF entirely in 2005 so as to remove its influence altogether. Venezuela has also committed hundreds of millions of dollars in loans and grants to Bolivia, Ecuador, Nicaragua, and other countries—for example, by providing discounted financing for oil to Caribbean countries through its PetroCaribe program.

The importance of this alternative source of financing to Latin America is enormous. For example, until 2006 Bolivia had been under IMF agreements almost continuously for 20 years. Under these agreements it had undertaken a vast array of reforms including those that privatized much of its energy production and even its social security system. Its per capita income as of 2005 was less than it had been 27 years earlier. Despite this terrible economic failure, Bolivia would normally have been seen as having no choice but to continue operating under IMF agreements and conditions. Its loans and grants from other multilateral institutions, as well as governments—including the European Union and member countries—were contingent on IMF approval. However, when President Evo Morales was elected (December 2005) and took office in 2006, his government refused to sign any agreements with the IMF. For the first time, Bolivia's other loans and aid were not conditional on an IMF agreement. Washington's leverage was gone, even in a poor country like Bolivia.

When Nicaraguans went to the polls in November of 2006, they were faced with threats of a cutoff of remittances from the United States, warnings from U.S. Commerce Secretary Carlos Gutierrez, and a threat from U.S. Ambassador Paul Trivelli that the United States "would re-eveluate relations" with

Nicaragua if Sandinista candidate Daniel Ortega were to win. But Ortega, who had been the victim of a long, bloody, and expensive U.S.-funded insurgency as president of Nicaragua in the 1980s, won anyway (having lost in the previous election, when the threats were effective). Similarly, Washington was unable to prevent the election of Mauricio Funes as president of El Salvador in 2009. He ran at the head of the ticket for the FMLN (Farabundo Martí Front for National Liberation), the ex-guerillas that Washington had spent billions of dollars fighting in the 1980s.

It is difficult to imagine that governments of even small, poor Latin American countries could exercise this kind of independence even a few years ago without putting their survival at risk. Of course Venezuela did not create the conditions for the political shift in Latin American politics, which in the past 12 years has seen left/populist governments win elections in Argentina, Bolivia, Brazil, Ecuador, El Salvador, Honduras, Nicaragua, Paraguay, Uruguay, and Venezuela—and come very close to winning in Mexico, Costa Rica, and Peru. The majority of South America is now governed by the left, and is more independent of the United States than Europe is.

The major impetus for this shift has come from the unprecedented regional economic growth failure over the last quarter-century. Although most discussion of this subject has focused on Latin America's devastating inequality– the worst in the world—this has not changed much in recent decades. What has changed is that economic growth collapsed in the region. From 1960–1980 in Latin America, per capita GDP—the most basic measure that economists have of economic progress—grew by 82 percent. From 1980–2009—a much longer period loaded with Washington-sponsored neoliberal reforms—it grew by only 18 percent. As noted above, this is the worst long-term economic performance in the region for more than a century. It is difficult to over-emphasize the difference that this economic growth collapse has made. Brazil and Mexico, for example, would have European living standards today if they had simply continued to grow at their pre-1980 rate, which was good but not spectacular for developing countries.

Latin America's long-term economic failure has followed and coincided with the implementation of a particular set of economic reforms, often under pressure from Washington: more conservative monetary policy (including higher interest rates and independent central banks); tighter (and sometimes pro-cyclical) fiscal policies; an indiscriminate opening to international trade and capital flows; massive privatizations of public enterprises (including pension systems); and the abandonment of development planning and industrial policies. While there is plenty of room for debate over which specific policies contributed, and how much, to the economic failure in various countries, it is not surprising that the electorate and most of the new left governments concluded that these policies had failed overall. What we are witnessing now, in a number of countries, is a search for more effective macroeconomic and development policies, as well as ways to deliver on electoral promises to alleviate poverty. Venezuela is very much a part of this regional process, despite Washington's efforts to isolate the Chávez government. In fact, these efforts have mainly served to isolate Washington, as was most sensationally brought home by President Bush's embarrassing trip to Latin America in March of 2007.[31] Chávez continues to enjoy very close relationships with the presidents of Argentina, Bolivia, Ecuador, and Brazil, where Lula has continually reminded the media and the world of his friendship with Venezuela's president.[32]

In addition to a proliferation of bilateral economic agreements that Venezuela has signed with its neighbors, six other countries—Brazil, Argentina, Bolivia, Ecuador, Uruguay, and Paraguay—have joined a Venezuelan-led effort to establish a Bank of the South. This new bank, which was inaugurated on December 9, 2007, is intended to focus on regional integration and poverty alleviation, and unlike the Inter-American Development Bank and World Bank, would operate independently of Washington and of neoliberal principles. The IDB, for example, despite its regional mandate, devotes only about 2 percent of its $8 billion annual lending to regional integration.[33] Although the new bank has been slow in getting off the ground—not least because of the 2008 world recession—it currently has $20 billion of pledges from member countries.

Regional economic integration is a long-term project—it took Europe more than 50 years to get to where it is today. But the alliance that the left-of-center Latin American governments have formed around these general issues is an important part of this process. Even more important in the present and immediate future is the increase in policy space that the region's new independence has enabled. As noted above, Argentina's heterodox policy enabled it to be the fastest-growing economy in the Western Hemisphere for six years; Venezuela's regaining control over its oil industry was key to its own economic growth surge; and Bolivia, the fastest growing economy in the hemisphere for 2008, has benefited enormously from regaining control over its hydrocarbon industry, thereby increasing government revenue by 20 percentage points *annually*.[34] (This is an enormous increase; for comparison, total revenue to the federal government in the United States has averaged 18.7 percent of GDP over the past 40 years).

Washington shows no signs of recognizing that its preferred economic policies have contributed to the region's unprecedented economic failure.

More importantly, the Obama administration, which had raised the hopes of leaders throughout the region—including even Chávez after the famous handshake with President Obama at the April 2009 Summit of the Americas—has continued the Bush administration's policies. This was brought home most forcefully in the aftermath of the military coup that overthrew Honduras President Manuel Zelaya on June 28th of 2009.[35] The White House statement on the day of the coup did not condemn it, merely calling on "all political and social actors in Honduras" to respect democracy. Since U.S. officials acknowledged that they were talking to the Honduran military right up to the day of the coup—allegedly to try and prevent it—they had time to think about what their immediate response would be if it happened. This sent a very strong signal to the diplomatic community as to what the Obama administration would do in the ensuing six months.

Although Washington was soon to join the worldwide condemnation of the coup, it took a series of actions and made a number of statements that clearly demonstrated that it was not on the same page with most of the hemisphere or the United Nations with respect to restoring democracy in Honduras. For example, on September 28, State Department officials representing the United States blocked the Organization of American States (OAS) from adopting a resolution on Honduras that would have refused to recognize Honduran elections carried out under the dictatorship.[36] For at least five months following the coup, Washington also refused to condemn the human rights abuses under the dictatorship, despite widespread condemnation from international and U.S.-based human rights groups, including Amnesty International and Human Rights Watch. And although President Zelaya visited Washington six times during his exile after the coup, President Obama refused to meet with him.

This episode had a profound impact on the region's governments, including Brazil, that were hoping the Obama administration would change at least some of the Bush administration's policies. The administration's decision to expand its military presence in Colombia sowed further distrust, again including the more friendly left-of-center governments such as Brazil and Chile. More than a year into its tenure, the Obama administration also continued the Bush administration's trade sanctions against Bolivia, as well as its predecessor's complaint at the World Trade Organization (WTO) against Bolivia's attempt to exempt its health care sector from being bought by foreign private firms, in accordance with its new constitution. And the Obama administration, in its first year, has made more hostile statements about Venezuela than the Bush administration did in its last year.

These and other indicators of continuity with the widely disliked policies of the Bush administration probably contributed to the decision on February 23, 2010, to form a new regional organization of 32 Latin American and Caribbean countries, excluding the United States and Canada. This was clearly seen as an alternative to the OAS, which has historically been dominated by Washington. Although it will take some time to become a real force, it is another institutional change—like that of UNASUR, ALBA (the Venezuela-led Bolivarian Alliance for the Americas, which includes Antigua and Barbuda, Bolivia, Cuba, Dominica, Ecuador, Nicaragua, Saint Vincent and the Grenadines, and Venezuela), the Bank of the South, and other regional alliances—that will continue the trend toward Latin America's independence from the United States. It is perhaps noteworthy that right-wing President Felipe Calderón of Mexico, one of the Obama administration's best friends in the region, played a leading role in the Cancun summit that formed the new regional organization, provisionally called the Community of Latin American and Caribbean States.

Other global economic developments will reinforce the trend toward increasing Latin American independence: the increasing availability of investment and technology from other countries and regions, especially Asia; the projected decline in the relative importance of the U.S. market for Latin American exports as the U.S. trade deficit inevitably adjusts (it fell by more than half during the recession that began at the end of 2007); the increasing difficulty of securing the standard U.S.-designed "free-trade" agreements in both the U.S. Congress and in Latin American country legislatures; and the breakdown of the multilateral negotiations in the WTO, which will further encourage regional alternatives. Latin America faces many challenges as new governments look for macroeconomic and development policies that can restore sustained growth to the region and redistribute the gains from that growth. But the "long night of neoliberalism," as President Rafael Correa of Ecuador has called it (La Única Vía), is at least approaching an end. As the region increasingly looks for practical alternatives to the failed policies of the last three decades, it will drift further from the United States, and Venezuela will continue to be a part of that process.

## Endnotes

1. For more on Bolivia and its policies during the world recession, see Weisbrot and Ray, "Bolivia: The Economy During the Morales Administration."
2. See Weisbrot, "Restoring Democracy." For more on the role of UNASUR in resolving the crisis, see Volkel, "'Massacre' Designation Strengthens Bolivian Government's Hand," and Vergara, "South American Presidents Back Morales."

3. See, for example, Corrales, "Hugo Boss"; Castañeda, "Latin America's Left Turn"; Shifter, "In Search of Hugo Chávez."

4. Weisbrot, Sandoval, and Rosnick, "Poverty Rates in Venezuela: Getting the Numbers Right."

5. See, for example, Economist Intelligence Unit, "Venezuela Risk: Risk Overview"; Kraul, "Chávez's Grand, Risky Dream"; de Córdoba, "Land Grab: Farmers Are Latest Target in Venezuelan Upheaval."

6. See BCV, quarterly, seasonally-adjusted GDP in 1997 constant prices, available under "Agregados Macroeconómicos."

7. This was noted by Teodoro Petkoff , one of the best-known opposition leaders. He describes an opposition "strategy that overtly sought a military takeover" from 1999–2003, and used the oil industry for purposes of overthrowing the government. See Petkoff, "A Watershed Moment in Venezuela," 5.

8. See IMF, "World Economic Outlook Database." Real, per capita GDP is projected to have grown by 1.5% annually from1999 to 2009 across all of Latin America and the Caribbean.

9. In the United States, the Bureau of Economic Analysis calculates a "Command-Basis Real GDP" which takes into account the difference between changes in export and import prices. See BEA. With the relevant deflators, the same could be done for the Venezuelan economy, and it would capture some of the effects discussed here.

10. 2010 figures are for the first three quarters of the year.

11. For detailed information on government debt and international reserves, see Table 7 (page 214).

12. Ministerio del Poder Popular para la Alimentación 2008. The *Memoria y Cuenta* is an annual report of the Ministry of Food/Nutrition to the National Assembly.

13. The data is only available for the 1994–2005 period (SISOV n.d., "Planteles por dependencia," www.sisov.mpd.gob.ve/indicadores/ED0304100000000/downloads/VarED_Planteles_Total(plantelesporDep).xls) and for the 2006/2007 academic year (from INE (n.d.), "Social: Educación; Planteles y unidades educativas, por nivel educativo, según entidad federal, 2006/07," www.ine.gov.ve/condiciones/educacion.asp).

14. SISOV (n.d.), "Cobertura del sistema. Tasa neta de escolaridad por nivel educativo," www.sisov.mpd.gob.ve/indicadores/ED0106600000000/.

15. Non-oil tax revenue went from 10.8 percent of GDP in 1999 to 12.0 percent in 2007, mostly due to an increase in the collection of income taxes (on individuals and companies) from 2 percent of GDP in 1999 to 3.2 percent in 2006. Data from Venezuela's Ministerio de Economía y Finanzas (n.d.).

16. Schmitt, "Is It Time to Export the US Tax Model to Latin America?"

17. Per capita social spending is a better measure than social spending *per se* because it takes population growth into account.

18. See Weisbrot, Sandoval, and Rosnick, "Poverty Rates in Venezuela," Table 2 and text.

19. The alternative would be to estimate the market value of health care services received, but this would exaggerate the impact of health care on the actual situation of the poor; we have therefore used the conservative estimate described above as a lower bound of the impact of this health care spending on the poor. See Weisbrot, Sandoval and Rosnick "Poverty Rates in Venezuela."

20. It is debt and debt service as a percent of GDP that matters, not the absolute size.

21. For PDVSA debt, see PDVSA "Balance."

22. See Wijnholds and Kapteyn, "Reserve Adequacy in Emerging Market Economies," for a review of the literature on the adequacy of reserves.

23. At the time, these resources included $43.1 billion in official foreign exchange reserves held at the Central Bank as of December 31, 2008 and $828 million in the Macroeconomic Stabilization Fund (see BCV, "Reservas Internacionales," www.bcv.org.ve/excel/2_1_1.xls?id=28); an estimated $33.6 billion in resources available through the National Development Fund ($13.1 billion in bonds and deposits abroad), PDVSA ($5.2 billion in available and restricted cash resources—see PDVSA "Informe") and the National Treasury and other sources ($15.3 billion, including accounts held by the Treasury abroad) (see Tesorería 15) and $16 billion in a Joint Chinese-Venezuelan Fund (see Pretel). There are also other resources, such as the funds held at the National Economic and Social Development Bank (Bandes).

24. All these are monthly year-over-year figures unless otherwise noted.

25. See, for example, Bruno, "Does Inflation Really Lower Growth?"; Easterly and Bruno, "Inflation Crises and Long-Run Growth"; Pollin and Zhu, "Inflation and Economic Growth."

26. This is based on the ratio of Venezuela's cumulative consumer price inflation from February 2003 to January 2010, which is 291.6 percent, to U.S. inflation of 14.8 percent.

27. See Frenkel, "The Sustainability of Sterilization Policy"; Frenkel and Rapetti, "Argentina's Monetary and Exchange Rate Policies."

28. The lending rate is a weighted average of the rates charged on promissory notes and loans made by commercial banks and universal banks.

29. Weisbrot, "Ten Years After: The Lasting Impact of the Asian Financial Crisis."

30. For more on the Argentine recovery, see Weisbrot and Sandoval, "Argentina's Economic Recovery."

31. For more on this trip, see Weisbrot, "President Bush's Trip." See also "Bush Faces Widespread Opposition," and "Mayans to 'Cleanse' Bush Site."

32. See Gosman, "Lula"; Weisbrot, "President Bush's Trip."

33. Culpeper, "Reforming the Global Financial Architecture: The Potential of Regional Institutions."

34. Weisbrot and Ray, "Bolivia: The Economy During the Morales Administration."

35. See Weisbrot, "More of the Same"; Weisbrot, "Obama's Deafening Silence"; and Weisbrot "The High-Powered Hidden Support."

36. Israel and Gutiérrez, "Honduran Police Crack Down, but Pressure Mounts."

# 7

# History Is Not Over: The Bolivarian Revolution, "Barrio Adentro," and Health Care in Venezuela

*Carles Muntaner, Haejoo Chung, Qamar Mahmood, and Francisco Armada*

In March 2003,[1] a group of working class Venezuelans from one of the capital's many impoverished neighborhoods began to plan for the arrival of 50 Cuban physicians.[2] After meeting with government officials and a small Cuban delegation, organizers set out to identify a network of homes able to lodge the doctors, secure space for medical visits, and publicize this new health care program, Barrio Adentro (Inside the Neighborhood).[3] Of the three, they found the last most difficult. After endless broken promises from past governments, the neighborhood was skeptical. But a month later, the local organizers welcomed the 50 Cuban doctors, and the next day, the doctors conducted their first round of free home visits following the schedule developed by the *barrio* organizers, now renamed the Health Committee.[4]

By 2006, over 7,000 such Health Committees worked alongside more than 20,000 Cuban and Venezuelan health professionals in thousands of impoverished *barrios* throughout Venezuela.[5] Unlike most global health programs, Barrio Adentro was shaped by a special set of forces—organized community action, genuine government-community partnership, solidarity between two low- to middle-income countries (Venezuela and Cuba), and no involvement from the main players in the global health arena (World Health Organization, bilateral agencies, World Bank, philanthropies, etc.). In spite of this unusual array of interests and locally driven agenda-setting process, Barrio Adentro has been providing continuous, free, high-quality, community-defined health care to the 70 percent of Venezuelans who previously had no access at all.[6]

As such, Barrio Adentro represents a change in the trend in health care reform in many Latin American countries. Beginning in the early 1990s, health care sector reforms throughout Latin America (indeed, in most of the world) have followed a remarkably similar pattern—a shift to greater private sector involvement from an existing system of public delivery, financing, and ownership.[7] Notwithstanding country-specific differences in modality and process of reform,[8] in most of Latin America, health care has become less of a human right guaranteed by the state and more of a commodity acquired in a marketplace, leaving approximately over 130 million individuals (out of a total population of 450 million) without access to quality health care. How did Barrio Adentro become an exception to this trend? What is this relatively unknown Venezuelan health care model, and how did it develop?

To address these questions, we will explore the Venezuelan health care reform program—Misión Barrio Adentro—that has challenged the seeming inevitability of neoliberal health reforms since 2003. We focus mainly on the period from its founding until 2006. We begin by analyzing the neoliberal models of health care reform in Latin America, and more specifically in Venezuela, within their broader sociopolitical economic contexts. Arguing that neoliberal health care reforms are of benefit mostly, if not exclusively, to transnational capital interests and domestic Latin American elites, we then seek to explain the emergence of Barrio Adentro. We examine the historical, social, and political underpinnings of the program, noting the central role played by popular resistance to neoliberalism. We conclude by suggesting that Barrio Adentro not only provides a compelling health care reform approach for other low- to middle-income "majority-world" countries, but also that it offers relevant policy insights to Western (in this case, Northern) countries.

## Health Care Reform in Latin America from the 1980s until the Bolivarian Revolution

From the end of WWII to the early 1980s, most Latin American countries gradually strengthened their welfare states, primarily reaching urban industrial workers, who had for decades mobilized to improve workplace and social conditions.[9] Welfare state social policy was based partly on the assumption that domestic markets inefficiently and inequitably distributed the gains of economic growth to the population, and the state needed to take an active role in "correcting" these "market failures" in order to secure the welfare of its citizens.[10] Such corrections implied state expenditure and management of health care, social security, education, and other social services. Although inefficiently and inequitably stratified into parallel, hierarchical systems, until the end of the 1970s, social services, including health care, had expanded in most Latin American countries, aiming at greater social equality.

Beginning in the 1970s, a series of important challenges to global capitalism took place that culminated by the early 1980s in a serious threat to the U.S. and European commercial banking sectors' solvency, in turn sparking profound changes in the role of Latin America's welfare states.[11] The first shock came with the introduction of variable exchange rates and a consequent new set of international trading rules as a result of the U.S. government's decision to suspend the fixed-price convertibility of its dollar for gold, thus breaking with the WW II-era Bretton Woods agreement. Coupled with substantial oil price increases in 1973 and 1979 caused by OPEC embargoes, the new international trading system generated large trade deficits for many developing countries. Latin American governments were forced to borrow massively at the relatively low interest rates of the time from IFIs (international financial institutions) and, indirectly, from U.S. and European commercial banks to secure the foreign currency necessary to pay for imports and attenuate the effect of trade imbalances. As Latin American countries' debts rose, a severe recession in OECD countries in the early 1980s led to a rise in international interest rates, leaving many Latin American countries unable to service their rising debts.

The impending collapse of the U.S. and European financial sectors holding most Latin American loans prompted the IFIs, themselves heavily influenced by U.S. and European governments, to shift their lending policies dramatically. The new quid pro quo for securing a loan from the IFIs became guaranteeing national budget surpluses through structural adjustment programs (SAPs), thus allowing countries to service, if not pay back, their foreign debts. Simultaneously, and to justify the severe austerity requirements, an increasingly dominant neoliberal ideology established a new, though unsubstantiated,[12] conventional wisdom: the interventionist welfare state had failed, and an unhindered free market was the best means through which to achieve social and economic prosperity, including the reduction of poverty and social inequality.[13]

The socioeconomic and ideological implications of the changing global economic order described above are increasingly being identified as pathways to detrimental changes in population health status.[14] For Latin American (and many other) welfare states, the changes were drastic: unprecedented cuts to state spending; privatization; deregulation; capital flight due to instability; and new liberalized international trade practices that emphasized the export of primary products at the expense of domestic production.[15]

The period of structural adjustment in Latin America that began in the early 1980s was the first step in what Laurell describes as a two-phase process of destabilization of the welfare state.[16] The erosion of social services such as health care that resulted from the deep funding cuts gradually created conditions that fostered neoliberal reform of those social services. State-administered health care sectors, reeling from the results of structural adjustment—deteriorating quality, greater inefficiency and inequity throughout the 1980s—turned in the 1990s to what appeared to be the only viable option: a shift to greater private sector management and delivery of health care services.

The publication of the World Bank's 1993 *World Development Report: Investing in Health,* marked the second stage in health care's neoliberalization.[17] The *Report* authors advocated two overarching strategies to improve health in low- and middle-income countries: 1) limit state investment in health care to low-cost services that target the poor; and 2) encourage diversity and competition in the financing and delivery of health services by facilitating greater private sector involvement. Throughout the developing world, this meant the introduction of private, for-profit health insurance plans, coupled with the decentralization of service delivery and administration under ever-shrinking budgets.[18] By the time *Investing in Health* was published, the World Bank had become the major international health lender, using its financial and political influence to leverage significant changes to countries' health care systems.[19] In Latin America, the Inter-American Development Bank (IDB) followed the World Bank's lead to provide health-reform loans that favored a shift to greater private sector involvement in health care systems.[20]

Given the increasing evidence of the detrimental effects of these neoliberal reforms on health and well-being,[21] the major, if not the only, beneficiaries seem to have been transnational corporations based mostly in the United States, Europe, and Canada, together with domestic Latin American elites, many of which are linked to the transnationals' subsidiaries.[22] As governments in Latin America privatized health care financing and delivery, several multinational corporations that sell financial, banking, investment, and insurance services entered the new lucrative markets, often by partnering with Latin American companies owned and operated by wealthy Latin Americans. In Mexico and Brazil, the region's two largest countries, neoliberal health care reforms have worsened access to health care services for poor and working-class sectors, stressed the public health care sector with higher risk patients, and further compromised the quality of public services. All the while, private insurance companies, foreign and domestic, have reported significant profits.[23]

Although neoliberal health reforms failed to be fully implemented in most Latin American countries,[24] all but Cuba had undergone some of these changes. Venezuela was no exception.[25]

## Venezuelan Structural Adjustment, Health Care, and the Bolivarian Revolution

Compared to most of its neighbors, Venezuela jumped on the neoliberal bandwagon relatively late. The slower pace of reform may be partially attributed to Venezuela's significant petroleum and natural gas reserves, the largest and second largest in the Western hemisphere, respectively.[26] Indeed, the expanding welfare state common throughout the region in the 1950s and 1960s was bolstered in Venezuela by its steady oil revenues, even if the benefits were never reaped equitably.[27] While its neighbors reeled from the cumulative effects of variable exchange rates and the mid-1970s oil crisis, Venezuela's international reserves exceeded US$11 billion in 1981, helping to resist calls for neoliberal structural adjustment.[28]

Nonetheless, fluctuating oil prices and massive spending to pay for imports and national capital projects led Venezuelan governments to borrow heavily from the late 1970s to the mid-1980s. Rising national debt and decreasing oil revenues in the 1980s contributed to a socioeconomic crisis, with close to 54% of Venezuelans living in extreme or critical poverty in 1989. That same year, Carlos Andrés Pérez was elected president for a second time (his first period in office was during the mid-1970s oil boom), promising jobs, economic growth, and a return to good times.[29]

Following the dominant neoliberal ideology, Pérez committed the country to radical structural adjustment, claiming the need to address rising poverty in Venezuela.[30] The program, dubbed El Paquete, adhered faithfully to SAPs prescribed throughout the region by the World Bank and International Monetary Fund, its major financiers. In return for a US$7 billion extended fund, the Venezuelan government promised deep public spending cuts, privatization, trade liberalization, and social program restructuring to target the poor.[31] However, the zeal to implement the reforms met widespread public opposition and mobilization that helped spark two failed coup attempts and the impeachment of President Pérez in 1993.[32] Yet the reforms continued under his successor.

The health sector was not spared from El Paquete, and in accordance with Laurell's thesis, the erosion of welfare institutions throughout the 1990s fueled increasing calls for health care reform. The new Venezuelan government kept the neoliberal policies intact in all areas, despite a presidential campaign that was run on anti-neoliberal lines. The government, led by President Rafael Caldera, procured two major health reform loans, one from the World Bank, the other from the Inter-American Development Bank.[33] Although these institutions were less explicit about their aims to foster greater private sector involvement in health care (perhaps in deference to the Venezuelan government's reluctance to elicit further public opposition), both generally followed the neoliberal tone set in *Investing in Health*. For example, both loans contained provisions to facilitate or support the restructuring of health sector financing, preferably toward an increased role for private financing. In addition, the loans continued support for a social services decentralization process that had begun in 1989 as part of El Paquete. By the end of the presidential period, the government gained approval from the Congress for a major social security reform that followed the Chilean model both in pensions and health care. This legislation aimed at fully privatizing social security in Venezuela and completed the already neoliberal policies being implemented in the health sector, of under-financing of public health services, progressive deterioration of public primary care clinics and hospitals, and lack of interventions for endemic disease control.[34] Decentralization, coupled with the fiscal austerity measures of the early 1990s, left the newly responsible regional and local levels of government with few options but to carry out an uncoordinated, de facto privatization of many health care services that were high in demand but short on supply.[35] By 1997, 73 percent of health expenditures in Venezuela were private.[36] The introduction of user fees in the public system made the increasingly poor quality health services of that system even less accessible.

The situation became worse leading up to the December 1998 presidential election, when a dramatic drop in oil prices led the Venezuelan government to once again seek loans from IFIs. For the vast majority of poor Venezuelans, who by 1999 comprised nearly three quarters of the population, the only access to health care services was through a precarious public system.

However, the election of Hugo Chávez in December 1998 set the country in a new direction, as the new president had campaigned staunchly against further IFI-prescribed neoliberal reforms. Chávez's overwhelming if surprising victory that month is arguably the political culmination of nearly two decades of increasing popular mobilization against corrupt Venezuelan régimes and their increasingly neoliberal agenda.[37] Once elected, Chávez moved quickly to fulfill one of his most important campaign promises by appointing a cabinet that completely sidelined the traditional political elite and consisted almost exclusively of the progressive Left in Venezuela.[38] He called for a referendum to adopt or reject a new constitution drafted by a special constituent assembly. Following extensive consultation throughout the country of all sectors of society, in December 1999 Venezuelans approved a new Bolivarian Constitution.[39]

## The Bolivarian Alternative to Health Care Reform

The constitutional changes comprehensively covered the health sector.[40] Three constitutional articles in particular have had major implications for health care reform in the country. Article 83 enshrines health as a fundamental human right that the state is obligated to guarantee. Article 84 stipulates the duty of the state to create and manage a universal, integrated public health system providing free services and prioritizing disease prevention and health promotion. In addition, it firmly states that public health care services cannot be privatized. In this norm, community participation in health policy planning, implementation, and evaluation is stated both as a right and duty. Article 85 details that this national public health system must be publicly financed mainly through general revenues and social security contributions; that the state will regulate both the public and private elements of the system; and that that the state will develop a human resource policy to train professionals for the new system. Finally, several other articles also help to shape major health policies: for instance, Article 111 states that "The State assumes responsibility for sports and recreation as an education and public health policy," and Article 122 specifies that "Native peoples have the right to a full health system that takes into consideration their traditional practices and cultures."

Chávez's government introduced several changes in health policy in order to address people's demands for a better quality of life. First, it threw out the neoliberal policies by canceling the process of privatization of the Venezuelan Social Security Institute (the second public health care provider) and by suspending the health and pension bills approved by the Caldera government. Second, it emphasized health promotion policies, particularly in the areas of immunizations, access to essential drugs, and environmental health. Finally, it pursued a comprehensive plan to modernize infrastructure and equipment at primary care clinics.[41] Prior to Barrio Adentro, efforts to reform the health care system in Venezuela during the initial Chávez years were based on the Latin American Social Medicine (LASM) principles. LASM has long endorsed an approach in health that is collective rather than individual in nature, focuses on the political, economic, and social determinants of health, and that emphasizes attention to factors that produce health inequities.[42]

Despite all the initiatives implemented, the gap between people's demands and availability of services remained huge. This led the government to develop alternative redistributive mechanisms to strengthen the Venezuelan welfare state and fulfill the social rights stated in the new constitution. Among them the Misiones figure prominently; these social programs were created as parallel structures either completely outside the scope of government ministries, or in collaboration with them, as a means to increase community participation and meet the new constitutional imperatives more efficiently.

Two factors help explain this parallelism of structures. Despite large oil revenues and relatively large state expenditures on various social programs throughout the 1950s, 1960s, and 1970s, corrupt government bureaucracies failed to breach the social inequity gaps. In addition, despite Chávez's victory and the constitutional reforms, the state bureaucracy initially remained largely opposed to the new president's intended changes. Most of the government structure was designed to keep the nation's power distribution, which concentrated the benefits among few. This situation is of course not peculiar only to Venezuela. Any such major change is beset with challenges. The oft-quoted Brazilian example of participatory budgeting is a case in point. Abers,[43] in her extensive and in-depth study of the challenges that governments face in implementing policies promoting popular participation, mentions the difficulties of implementing such participatory efforts in Brazil. Even if there is commitment from the highest political levels to promote participation by organized community groups, the mid- and lower-level officials may not be willing to relinquish their power to communities. Additionally, a ministerial bureaucracy that opposes the government may hamper its efforts. Participatory budgeting and other participatory initiatives in Brazil started in the 1980s and were facilitated mainly through the election of the Workers' Party (Partido de Trabalhadores) in several municipalities. The changes in Venezuela started much later, and Venezuela learned from the Brazilian experience.[44] Therefore, to counter obstacles presented by some ministerial bureaucracies and as a response to considerable grassroots community organizing, the Misiones were initially largely independent of the ministries.

One of the most popular and successful programs developed under the Chávez administration is Barrio Adentro. Misión Barrio Adentro aims to satisfy the constitutional requirements of health as a social right through a public health care system that spans the primary, secondary, and tertiary levels of care. Moreover, it is underpinned by the principles of equity, universality, accessibility, solidarity, multi-sectorial management, cultural sensitivity, participation, and social justice.[45]

The program's beginnings date to December 1999, when Venezuela suffered torrential rains that caused extensive flooding in the state of Vargas. The most affected were *barrio* dwellers, the marginalized poor living in the hilly periphery of major urban centers. The Cuban government, as part of its international solidarity programs, responded to the tragedy by sending a team of 454 Cuban health care workers, who offered medical care inside the marginalized communities.

Based on this experience, Freddy Bernal, an ally of President Hugo Chávez and the mayor of the Municipality of Libertador (both the largest municipality and home to the largest number of poor people in the metropolitan area of Caracas), later requested the help of Venezuelan physicians, asking them to go into the barrios to attend to the acute needs of the underserviced populace. Most physicians refused, citing security concerns and a lack of infrastructure as their primary reasons. Behind these explicit objections lay an organized opposition by the Venezuelan medical establishment to the health care reform efforts sparked by the Bolivarian government and the country's new Constitution.[46] Undeterred, Mayor Bernal asked the national government for authorization to reach an agreement for a pilot project with the Cuban government, and in April of 2003, 58 Cuban physicians specializing in integral family medicine were sent to various *barrios* in Caracas to practice primary care inside the marginalized neighborhoods.

In September 2003, after witnessing the success of the pilot program, President Chávez officially dubbed the program Misión Barrio Adentro and supported its extension to the states and their municipalities through the coordinated efforts of the Venezuelan Ministry of Health and Social Development (MSDS) and the Cuban Medical Commission in Venezuela. Further cementing Barrio Adentro's institutionalization, in December of 2003 President Chávez created a multi-sectorial Presidential Commission charged with the implementation and coordination of a national Primary Health Care Program. Between April and December of 2003, under a cooperation agreement whereby Cuba would receive a guaranteed preferential price on Venezuelan oil, over 10,000 Cuban physicians, dentists, and ophthalmologists began providing primary health care and dispensing free Cuban-supplied medications for poor Venezuelans in hundreds of *barrios*. Today, over 20,000 Cuban health workers and a growing number of Venezuelan health professionals make up the human resources in Barrio Adentro.[47] To address sustainability, and given the domestic medical establishment's continued though decreasing reluctance to participate in the program, the Venezuelan government has launched a massive training effort to replace, over time, the thousands of Cuban health workers with Venezuelans.

### Table 1.
### Reasons for Not Consulting a Physician, by Household Income Quintile, Venezuela, 1998.

| Income quintile | Not necessary, problem did not justify a medical consultation | Not enough money to pay for visit, medicine, examinations | Health services too far away | Other reasons |
|---|---|---|---|---|
| 1 | 49.3 | 35.3 | 5.9 | 9.5 |
| 2 | 64.9 | 25.9 | 0.6 | 8.7 |
| 3 | 85.4 | 11.1 | 0.6 | 2.9 |
| 4 | 81.4 | 7.7 | 2.6 | 8.4 |
| 5 | 69.6 | 13.1 | 0.5 | 16.8 |
| Total | 70.1 | 19.4 | 2.2 | 8.3 |

Source: Table 3 (Alvarado et al., 2006: 10).

According to the Barrio Adentro planning framework, its goal at the primary care level is to provide round the clock access through health centers inside historically marginalized communities: one for every 250 families.[48] As of 2006, of the over 8,000 planned community health centers, close to 2,000 had been built.[49] A household survey of 270 household heads conducted in various rural and urban areas reported that 51.3% of respondents mentioned that a Barrio Adentro facility was located within a walking distance of 5 minutes.[50] Health centers that are part of the existing primary health care infrastructure also started to be incorporated into Barrio Adentro in 2005.[51] Each community health center has a multi-disciplinary health team consisting of at least one physician specialized in integrated family medicine, a community health worker, and a health promoter. In addition, each center is stocked with medications to be distributed at no cost to patients as required.[52]

The health team personnel live in the *barrios* themselves.[53] Participating Cuban physicians receive free room and board and other necessities. In addition to conducting consultations in the health centers, the health teams are responsible for making daily rounds to survey the residents' living conditions and home visits to those too ill to visit the community health centers.[54] The model of care emphasizes a holistic approach to health and illness through the coordination of Barrio Adentro with other Misiones addressing education, food safety, sanitation, employment, and other social determinants of health. For example, patients lacking potable water who present recurring intestinal infections are not only prescribed the appropriate antibiotics but also encouraged to organize themselves to take advantage of another national program that extends access to potable water.

Health teams and patients are supported by Health Committees comprised of *barrio* residents. Indeed, Misión Barrio Adentro stipulates that the creation of a community health center is contingent upon the establishment of a Health Committee. These are the organizational mechanism through which *barrio* residents participate in primary health care delivery and management. Health Committees are generally made up of 10 people chosen in a meeting of local citizens, and they work with a popular health post.[55] In addition to the plans for 8,000 primary health care clinics, Barrio Adentro Program started the construction of 600 secondary care centers that also included rehabilitation services, and worked to upgrade the existing public tertiary care infrastructure of approximately 300 hospitals nationwide.[56]

Barrio Adentro I, the first primary care center, was established in the poor neighborhood of Libertador in Caracas in March 2003. Since then, the Barrio Adentro system was expanded to II, III, and IV, covering the secondary (clinics), tertiary (general hospitals), and specialized general hospitals.

BA II (Barrio Adentro II) is comprised of 4 distinctive services: popular clinics, comprehensive diagnostic centers (CDCs), high-technology centers (HTCs), and comprehensive rehabilitation centers (CRCs) (See Table 3). Popular clinics are "public establishments whose objective is to promote, protect, and restore health through specialized medical care provided on an outpatient basis."[57] They are capable of treating both medical and surgical cases and are designed to serve a population of about 75,000 people living in the environs.

People's hospitals (BA III) and specialized public hospitals (BA IV) comprise the Hospital Network. Barrio Adentro III seeks to upgrade existing tertiary hospitals and modernize equipment thanks to Venezuela's agreement with Cuba and Argentina and additional public funding.[58] They established priorities based on opinions by community representatives. Community representatives also oversee hospital directors and administrators, who directly administer public resources, to ensure transparency of these processes.

The premier development of Barrio Adentro IV is the Dr. Gilberto Rodríguez Ochoa Latin American Children's Cardiology Hospital, the largest of its kind in the world. This center provides cardiovascular surgeries free of charge to children in all of Latin America. This hospital has treated 1,118 patients in the year 2006 alone.

The foregoing description of Barrio Adentro bears a significant resemblance to the Cuban model of health care that for decades has been a consistent if often ignored successful example for much of Latin America.[59] That said, the distinctiveness of Barrio Adentro is highlighted by Cuban physicians themselves; they note the difference in levels of direct participation

**Figure 1.**
**Medical Visits: 1998–2004, Ministry of Health and Social Development**
**(MSDS) vs. Misión Barrio Adentro (BA).**

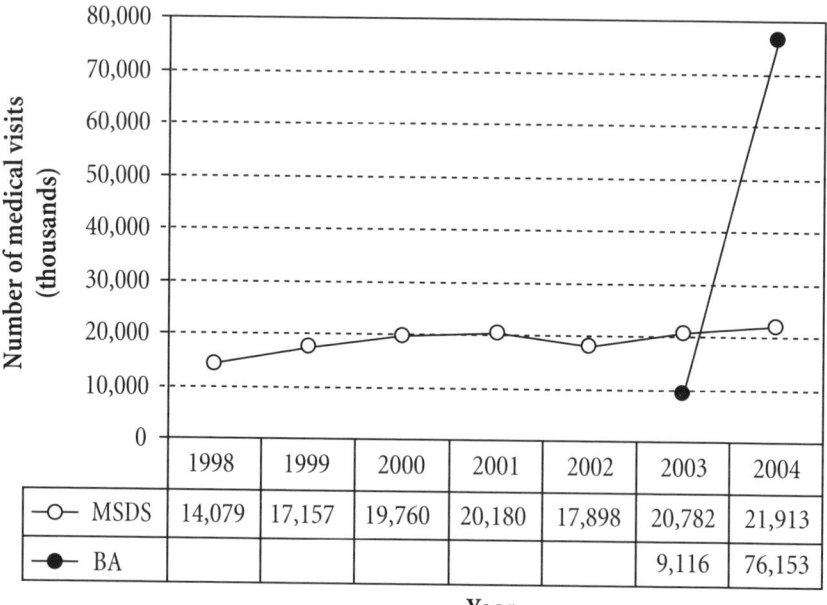

| | 1998 | 1999 | 2000 | 2001 | 2002 | 2003 | 2004 |
|---|---|---|---|---|---|---|---|
| —○— MSDS | 14,079 | 17,157 | 19,760 | 20,180 | 17,898 | 20,782 | 21,913 |
| —●— BA | | | | | | 9,116 | 76,153 |

**Year**

shown by Venezuelans organized in Health Committees.[60] Still, the influence of the Cuban health care is evident, which, given its proven record, should bode well for Barrio Adentro.

As we see in Figure 1, Misión Barrio Adentro has been impressive in terms of expanding access to health care and may well be able to generate a significant improvement in population health status. Indeed, PAHO (Pan-American Health Organzation) data[61] suggest positive health outcomes associated with Barrio Adentro, including a reduction in child mortality from diarrhea and pneumonia. The next years will be critical to evaluate the program and to assess its sustainability over time, with measures including a cost-effectiveness analysis.

Nonetheless, the Barrio Adentro initiative and other major political proposed reforms have elicited opposition from the upper-middle class and elite sectors of Venezuelan society. This opposition resulted in a military coup attempt and a debilitating general strike in 2002 and 2003 and a presidential recall referendum in 2004, all aiming to remove the democratically elected President Chávez from office.[62] The mass mobilization by poor and working-class Venezuelans (the vast majority in the country) in support of the president led to the failure of all three moves.[63] In December 2006, Hugo Chávez was elected for a third term (2007–2012) with 62.84 percent of the votes. The following year, Chávez's proposal to modify 69 articles of the constitution, allowing further presidential re-election among several other changes, was not approved by a slight difference in votes (49.29% in favor versus 50.70% against). Indeed, after nine electoral victories (1998–2006) and one defeat (2007) of the political forces supporting President Chávez, the political struggle continues in Venezuela and will define the conditions for the permanence, consolidation, or suspension of social policies as the one presented here.

## Accomplishments of Barrio Adentro: An Early Appraisal

The Barrio Adentro Mission is a young program: at the time of this writing, it has been only 5 years since its inception. Evaluating its accomplishments is therefore not easy, as it is still too early to observe any significant change in the health of the population. In addition, Barrio Adentro is established as part of an integrated set of social programs, so that it is hard to separate its impact from that of other social programs, for example, Misión Mercal (subsidized food program), Misión Vivienda (housing project), or Misión Robinson (literacy program), which could also have a beneficial effect on people's health. Despite these limitations, the PAHO report on Barrio Adentro provides some insight into what the mission has achieved so far.

### Institutional Achievements

Poor people's access to health care expanded from almost none to an impressive level from 1999 to 2006. Both Barrio Adentro I (primary care clinics) and Barrio Adentro II (secondary care clinics, i.e., Comprehensive Diagnostic Centers or CDC, Comprehensive Rehabilitation Centers, CRC, High-Technology Centers, HTC, and popular clinics) health care services have increased significantly (Table 2).

Table 4 shows us the major achievement of Barrio Adentro I compared to a conventional system. As a matter of fact, during the early years of the Chávez government before the inception of the Barrio Adentro system, the conventional system operated by the Ministry of Health underwent a series of reforms to enhance poor people's access to health services.[64] Despite this effort, what the Barrio Adentro system has achieved compared to the conventional system is outstanding. In 2005, the Barrio Adentro system included almost ten times the number of physicians and covered five times the population of the conventional system. Although the Barrio Adentro

### Table 2.
### Barrio Adentro New Health Centers, July 2006.

| | Built | Under Construction | Total |
|---|---|---|---|
| Primary care centers | 1,612 | 4,618 | 6,230 |
| Comprehensive diagnostic centers (CDCs) | 139 | 461 | 600 |
| Comprehensive rehabilitation centers (CRCs) | 151 | 449 | 600 |
| High technology centers (HTCs) | 6 | 29 | 35 |
| Popular clinics | 10 | 2 | 12 |

Note: Of the 139 CDCs in place, 40 have operating rooms.
Source: Table 8 (Alvarado et al., 2006: 47).

### Table 3.
### Services Offered by Barrio Adentro II: Popular Clinics, Comprehensive Diagnostic Centers (CDCs), High-technology Centers (HTCs), and Comprehensive Rehabilitation Centers (CRCs).

| Type of Facility | Services Offered | | |
|---|---|---|---|
| Popular Clinics | • Pediatrics, internal medicine, surgery, obstetrics<br>• Dentistry: 8 hrs<br>• Emergency service: 24 hrs | • Delivery room: 24 hrs<br>• Laboratory: 24 hrs<br>• Radiology: 24 hrs<br>• Observation: average stay of 48 hrs | • Operating room: same-day surgery<br>• Electrocardiography, ultrasound, endoscopy |
| CDCs | • X-ray<br>• Diagnostic ultrasound<br>• Endoscopy<br>• Electrocardiography<br>• Clinical laboratory | • Ultramicroanalysis (in CDCs with operating room)<br>• Clinical ophthalmology<br>• Emergency, vital support | • Intensive care<br>• Operating room for emergency care (1 in every 4 CDCs) |
| HTCs | • Magnetic resonance imaging<br>• Computerized axial tomography | • Tridimensional ultrasound<br>• Mammography<br>• Bone densitometry<br>• Video endoscopy | • Clinical laboratory<br>• Ultramicroanalysis<br>• Electrocardiography |
| CRCs | • Electrotherapy, ultrasound, and laser therapy<br>• Thermotherapy, infrared heat | • Hydrotherapy/massage pediatric gymnasium<br>• Adult gymnasium<br>• Occupational therapy | • Natural and traditional medicine<br>• Speech therapy<br>• Podiatry |

### Table 4.
### Major Achievements of Barrio Adentro I, 2005.

|  | Conventional System | Barrio Adentro System |
|---|---|---|
| Physicians in primary care | 1,500 | 13,000 |
| Coverage | 3.5 million | 17 million |
| Primary health care centres | 4,400 (1,500 with physicians) | 1,050 (finished) |
| Primary care dentists | 800 | 4,600 |
| Nurses or aides in primary care | 4,400 | 8,500 |
| Ophthalmologists | 0 | 441 |
| Promotion and Prevention Activities | Varies, in the health centre | In the health centre and out in the community |
| Medication dispensing | Varies according to supply | 103 medications for the most common presenting illnesses; Popular Pharmacies |

Source: Alvarado et al., 2006.

system has fewer primary health care centers, the number of planned centers is similar to those with doctors in the conventional system. Barrio Adentro has more primary care dentists and nurses. It also has ophthalmologists, who are scarce in the conventional system. Health promotion and prevention activities occur not only in health care centers but also out in the community, and medications can be obtained at a subsidized price in the Barrio Adentro system. While most nurses and a quarter of the dentists are Venezuelans, the majority of doctors were still Cuban in 2005 (Table 5).

From 2000 to 2007, government health expenditure increased from 6 to around 27 percent of the national budget, showing the government's commitment to providing health care. There can be various reasons for increasing health care expenditure, such as greater privatization in health care delivery or the expense of having an older, more ill population. Since this change happened in a very short period of time and the increase was dramatic, it can hardly be the second reason. And all evidence about political change in Venezuela points to the opposite of privatization.

## Table 5.
## Public Investment in Health as a Percentage of National Budget and GDP, 2000–2006 (millions of VEB.[a]).

| | National budget (Ministerio de Salud 2006) | Regular Ministry of Health Budget (Ministerio de Salud 2006) | Regular health budget as % of the national budget | Regular health budget plus extra-budgetary contributions as % of the national budget | Gross domestic product[b] | Health budget as % of gross domestic product | Regular health budget plus extra-budgetary contributions as % of gross domestic product |
|---|---|---|---|---|---|---|---|
| 2000 | 23,553,561 | 1,435,273 | 6.09 | 6.09 | 79,655,692 | 1.80 | 1.80 |
| 2001 | 28,079,214 | 1,729,247 | 6.16 | 7.34 | 88,945,596 | 1.94 | 2.17 |
| 2002 | 31,687,452 | 2,096,070 | 6.61 | 8.90 | 107,840,166 | 1.94 | 2.63 |
| 2003 | 41,613,125 | 2,644,873 | 6.36 | 11.75 | 134,217,306 | 1.97 | 3.47 |
| 2004 | 60,505,058 | 3,910,674 | 6.46 | 18.81 | 207,599,608 | 1.88 | 5.56 |
| 2005 | 81,805,297 | 4,862,989 | 5.94 | 31.00 | 262,984,000 | 1.85 | 9.17 |
| 2006 | 87,029,741 | 5,010,740 | 5.76 | 26.08 | 285,624,000 | 1.75 | 7.71 |

Note:

a. USD = 2,144.50 VEB (Venezuelan Bolívares) (Live rates at 2008.02.11 19:00:30 UTC).

Source: Tables 4 and 5; Alvarado et al., 2006: 13.

### Participatory Democracy and Health Promotion

One of the most interesting aspects of Barrio Adentro is that it is firmly grounded in participatory democracy, in the shape of the Health Committee (Comité de Salud), which manages the Barrio Adentro program. The number of Health Committees grew from 2,124 in 2003 to 8,951 in 2006, more than four times the number in four years (Figure 2). The graph shows the number of health committees that were elected by popular assemblies. Other, unregistered Health Committees associated with popular medical dispensaries would add up to an even larger number.

The Health Committee is one type of various committees organized starting in 1999 that aim to "promote community development and participative local planning."[65] Its activities aim at the low-income population, and it is comprised of health promoters. A team of professionals, consisting of a physician, a nurse, and a social worker, works with these committees.

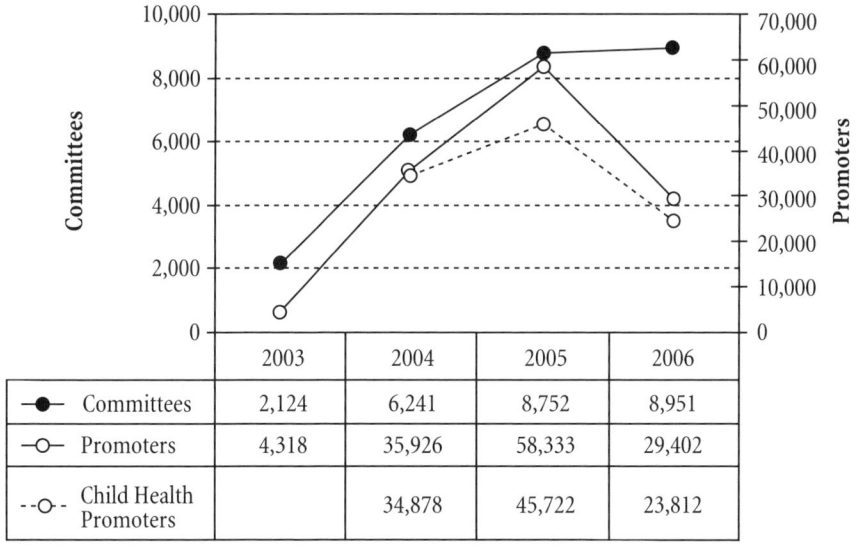

**Figure 2.**
**Number of Health Committees (Comités de Salud),**
**April 2003–May 2006.**

| | 2003 | 2004 | 2005 | 2006 |
|---|---|---|---|---|
| —●— Committees | 2,124 | 6,241 | 8,752 | 8,951 |
| —○— Promoters | 4,318 | 35,926 | 58,333 | 29,402 |
| --○-- Child Health Promoters | | 34,878 | 45,722 | 23,812 |

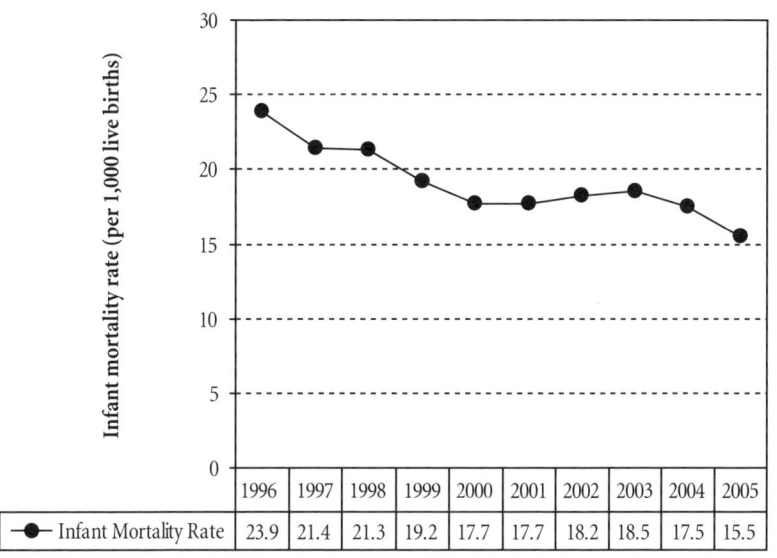

**Figure 3.**
**Infant Mortality in Venezuela, 1996–2005.**

| | 1996 | 1997 | 1998 | 1999 | 2000 | 2001 | 2002 | 2003 | 2004 | 2005 |
|---|---|---|---|---|---|---|---|---|---|---|
| —●— Infant Mortality Rate | 23.9 | 21.4 | 21.3 | 19.2 | 17.7 | 17.7 | 18.2 | 18.5 | 17.5 | 15.5 |

**Table 6.**
**Participants in Various Clubs in Misión Barrio Adentro,**
**April 2003–May 2006.**

|                              | 2003  | 2004  | 2005  | 2006  |
|------------------------------|-------|-------|-------|-------|
| Clubs for pregnant women     | 1,803 | 6,318 | 6,604 | 6,087 |
| Clubs for nursing women      |       | 5,485 | 5,902 | 5,443 |
| Clubs for adolescents        | 3,077 | 7,991 | 8,113 | 7,356 |
| *Clubs for specific diseases:* |     |       |       |       |
| Hypertensives                |       | 5,102 | 5,097 | 4,894 |
| Diabetics                    |       | 1,638 | 1,683 | 1,635 |
| Asthmatics                   |       | 2,438 | 2,476 | 2,397 |
| Smokers                      |       | 3,833 | 3,741 | 3,189 |

Source: Alvarado et al., 2006.

**Table 7.**
**Health Promotion Activities in Primary Health Care Clinics.**

|                              | 2004        | 2005        |
|------------------------------|-------------|-------------|
| **Health education activities** | 43,199,964 | 46,699,477 |
| Circles of adolescents       | 7,991       | 8,116       |
| Number of participants       | 106,942     | 105,370     |
| Circles of grandparents      | 8,126       | 8,474       |
| Number of participants       | 97,444      | 104,110     |
| Circles of pregnant women    | 6,378       | 6,604       |
| Number of participants       | 36,108      | 38,601      |

Source: Alvarado et al., 2006.

Health Committees prepare proposals for health interventions, which are funded by the state government when they are approved.[66] Patients also participate in groups of patients with similar diseases (Table 7).

The Barrio Adentro model stresses health promotion as a comprehensive strategy in contrast to the former model that focused on curative interventions. Tables 7 and 8 describe various health promotion activities that take place in primary health care clinics as a part of Barrio Adentro as a whole.

### Access to Health Care and Health Outcomes
When did Barrio Adentro start achieving better health for the population? We have seen that medical visits have increased through Barrio Adentro system, providing access to health care which was not available before for the

## Table 8.
## Other Health Promotion Activities in the Barrio Adentro System.

| Activities | 2003 | 2004 | 2005 | 2006 |
|---|---|---|---|---|
| Talks | 2,333,409 | 23,961,876 | 13,293,528 | 1,212,085 |
| Public health presentations | 90,798 | 429,485 | 496,489 | 165,096 |
| Face to face conversation | | | 16,960,961 | 10,282,748 |
| *Related activities* | | | | |
| Dance therapy groups | 2,035 | 6,429 | 6,845 | 6,681 |
| Street plans | 1,217 | 5,752 | 5,809 | 2,952 |
| Hygienization days | 2,732 | 7,904 | 7,220 | 3,965 |
| Sports activities | 18,931 | 45,213 | 48,979 | 23,750 |

Source: Alvarado et al., 2006.

underprivileged (Figure 1). Table 9 shows number of new cases and follow-up visits for chronic conditions to conventional and Barrio Adentro systems in 2004–2005. For most diseases, the conventional system treated more of the new cases, but Barrio Adentro I (popular medical dispensaries) accounted for significantly more follow-up visits. In terms of the number of total consultations, the Barrio Adentro system saw 70–90 percent of patients, while the conventional system treated only the rest. The same was true for dental consultations (Table 10). Odontological activities carried out in the popular clinic includes preventive care such as "the application of lacquer of fluorine, early detection of buccal cancer and activities as the adaptation of dental prostheses" for the poor, for the first time in Venezuelan history.[67]

The achievement in Barrio Adentro eye care is widely known as Misión Milagro or Miracle Mission. In 2004, Misión Milagro treated about 1.23 million patients (89%) compared to 0.15 million patients (11%) through the conventional system. The number of eye surgeries conducted from October 2005 to May 2006 was 18,294, including 5,389 cataract and 7,831 pterygium surgeries. Services provided by Barrio Adentro II clinics such as CDCs, CRCs, and HTCs have increased significantly during the period 2007–2010 as well. For example, in the CDCs in the first quarter of 2006, 4,004 patients were treated.[68]

Since just the access to health care is not the principal goal, we need to look at health indicators to see if the provision of health care has any impact on population health. Over the years that the Barrio Adentro system has been in place, the infant mortality rate decreased in Venezuela (Figure 3).

## Table 9.
### Capture of New Cases and Follow-up Consultations for Chronic Diseases: Conventional Network and Popular Medical Dispensaries, 2004–2005 (Ministerio de Salud 2006).

| Type of Chronic Disease | | New Cases | | Return Visits | | Total Consultations | |
|---|---|---|---|---|---|---|---|
| Hypertension | Conventional network | 945,136 | 69.8% | 583,636 | 4.6% | 1,528,772 | 11.4% |
| | Popular medical dispensaries | 408,769 | 30.1% | 11,429,438 | 95.1% | 11,838,207 | 88.5% |
| | Total | 1,353,905 | | 12,013,074 | | 13,366,979 | |
| Diabetes | Conventional network | 213,257 | 68.2% | 218,199 | 8.1% | 431,456 | 14.3% |
| | Popular medical dispensaries | 99,319 | 31.8% | 2,496,240 | 91.9% | 2,595,559 | 85.7% |
| | Total | 312,576 | | 2,714,439 | | 3,027,015 | |
| Ischemic heart disease | Conventional network | 75,033 | 53.3% | 20,547 | 1.9% | 95,580 | 7.9% |
| | Popular medical dispensaries | 65,679 | 46.7% | 1,048,873 | 98.1% | 1,114,552 | 92.1% |
| | Total | 140,712 | | 1,069,420 | | 1,210,132 | |
| Cerebro-vascular disease | Conventional network | 37,723 | 70.3% | 11,668 | 5.1% | 49,388 | 17.4% |
| | Popular medical dispensaries | 15,971 | 29.7% | 218,818 | 94.9% | 234,789 | 82.6% |
| | Total | 53,694 | | 230,483 | | 284,177 | |
| Bronchial asthma | Conventional network | 1,501,924 | 90.7% | 544,112 | 10.4% | 2,046,036 | 29.8% |
| | Popular medical dispensaries | 153,980 | 9.3% | 4,673,842 | 89.6% | 4,827,822 | 70.2% |
| | Total | 1,655,904 | | 5,217,954 | | 6,873,858 | |

## Table 10.
### Number of Odontological Consultations in Venezuela, 2004–2005.

| Odontological Consultations | Number | Percentage |
|---|---|---|
| Conventional network | 5,689,949 | 28.4% |
| Popular physicians' offices | 14,357,331 | 71.6% |
| Total | 20,057,280 | 100% |

Source: Alvarado et al., 2006.

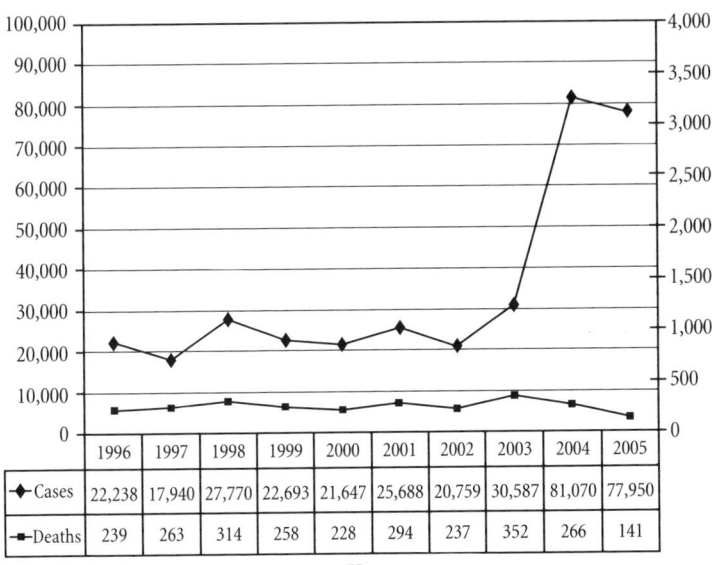

**Figure 4.**
**Cases and Deaths from Pneumonia: Children 1–4 Years of Age, 1996–2005.**

| Year | 1996 | 1997 | 1998 | 1999 | 2000 | 2001 | 2002 | 2003 | 2004 | 2005 |
|---|---|---|---|---|---|---|---|---|---|---|
| Cases | 22,238 | 17,940 | 27,770 | 22,693 | 21,647 | 25,688 | 20,759 | 30,587 | 81,070 | 77,950 |
| Deaths | 239 | 263 | 314 | 258 | 228 | 294 | 237 | 352 | 266 | 141 |

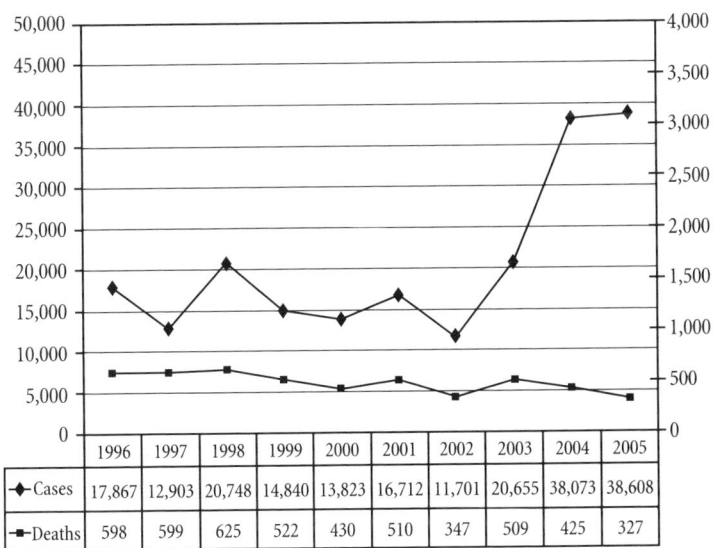

**Figure 5.**
**Cases and Deaths from Pneumonia: Children under 1 Year of Age, 1996–2005.**

| Year | 1996 | 1997 | 1998 | 1999 | 2000 | 2001 | 2002 | 2003 | 2004 | 2005 |
|---|---|---|---|---|---|---|---|---|---|---|
| Cases | 17,867 | 12,903 | 20,748 | 14,840 | 13,823 | 16,712 | 11,701 | 20,655 | 38,073 | 38,608 |
| Deaths | 598 | 599 | 625 | 522 | 430 | 510 | 347 | 509 | 425 | 327 |

### Figure 6.
### Cases and Deaths from Diarrhea: Children 1–4 Years of Age, 1996–2005.

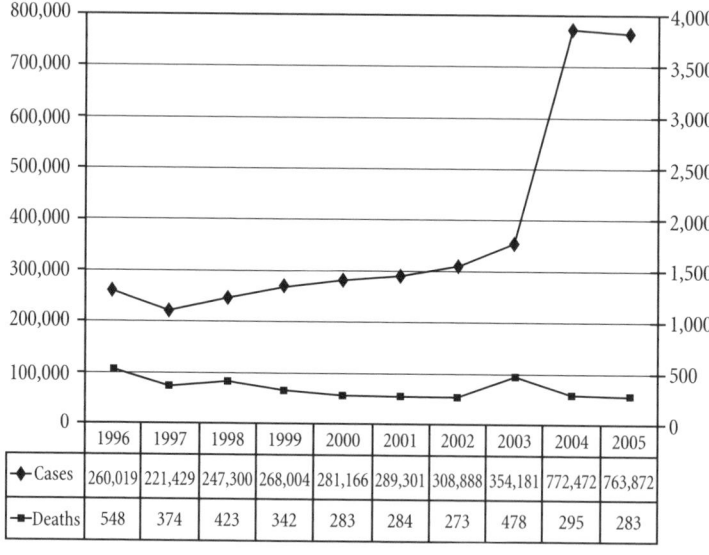

| | 1996 | 1997 | 1998 | 1999 | 2000 | 2001 | 2002 | 2003 | 2004 | 2005 |
|---|---|---|---|---|---|---|---|---|---|---|
| ◆ Cases | 260,019 | 221,429 | 247,300 | 268,004 | 281,166 | 289,301 | 308,888 | 354,181 | 772,472 | 763,872 |
| ■ Deaths | 548 | 374 | 423 | 342 | 283 | 284 | 273 | 478 | 295 | 283 |

Year

### Figure 7.
### Cases and Deaths from Diarrhea: Children under 1 Year of Age, 1996–2005.

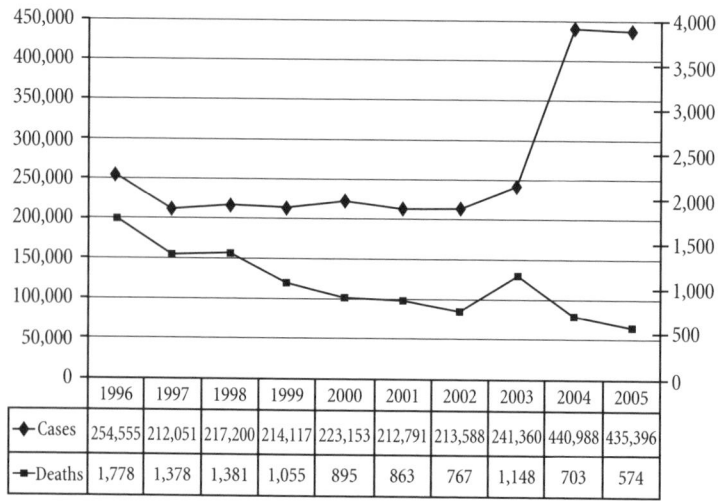

| | 1996 | 1997 | 1998 | 1999 | 2000 | 2001 | 2002 | 2003 | 2004 | 2005 |
|---|---|---|---|---|---|---|---|---|---|---|
| ◆ Cases | 254,555 | 212,051 | 217,200 | 214,117 | 223,153 | 212,791 | 213,588 | 241,360 | 440,988 | 435,396 |
| ■ Deaths | 1,778 | 1,378 | 1,381 | 1,055 | 895 | 863 | 767 | 1,148 | 703 | 574 |

Year

However, this decrease is a general tendency in other Latin American countries as well, so that we need to come up with a new indicator. The examples illustrated in Figure 4 through Figure 7 are more interesting. In these four pediatric conditions, the number of cases increased dramatically after 2002, the beginning year of Barrio Adentro. However, over the same time period, the number of deaths from these diseases has decreased. This may be attributed to increased access to health care due to the Barrio Adentro system, which enabled these child morbidities to be detected and treated widely and relatively early on, so that the deaths due to those conditions decreased significantly. Hence we may conclude that increased access to care through Barrio Adentro actually improves population health status.

### Satisfaction with Misiones

Our last empirical presentation deals with the Venezuelan people's satisfaction with these social programs, or Misiones. Out of 1,300 Venezuelans sampled who are beneficiaries of any one or more of the Misiones, the programs that gave the highest satisfaction were Misión Mercal (subsidized food, 72.8%), Misión Identidad (a national ID that allowed access to several civil rights including voting, 65.7%), and Misión Barrio Adentro I (primary care, 64.6%). A study by Briggs and Briggs[69] reported findings of a household survey where the majority 62 percent rated the services of Barrio Adentro as "excellent" or "good" while only 10 percent considered them to be "average" or "poor." The same study also reported that 77 percent of the individuals surveyed thought that Barrio Adentro has produced "very positive" or "positive changes" while only 3 percent believed that it had produced "negative changes." The mission with the lowest satisfaction rate was Misión Miranda (34.6%), which aims to recruit a voluntary army reserve. Except for this program, satisfaction rates of all missions were larger than the rates of "unsatisfied" and "don't know" responses combined together, ranging between 44.8 and 72.8 percent.

## Participatory Democracy and Barrio Adentro

Besides the achievements of Barrio Adentro in health, its distinctive feature is popular participation. As described, citizen participation is achieved mainly through Health Committees. Such committees exist for other social missions as well. The various committees of social missions are coordinated at the sub-municipality level by Communal Councils. This has been a process of "learning by doing." The committees of various missions including Health Committees originated separately from Communal Councils but now function as working committees of these councils.[70] The Communal Councils

Figure 8.

Level of Satisfaction with the Performance of the Missions or Programs Implemented by the National Government (Sample Size = 1,300).

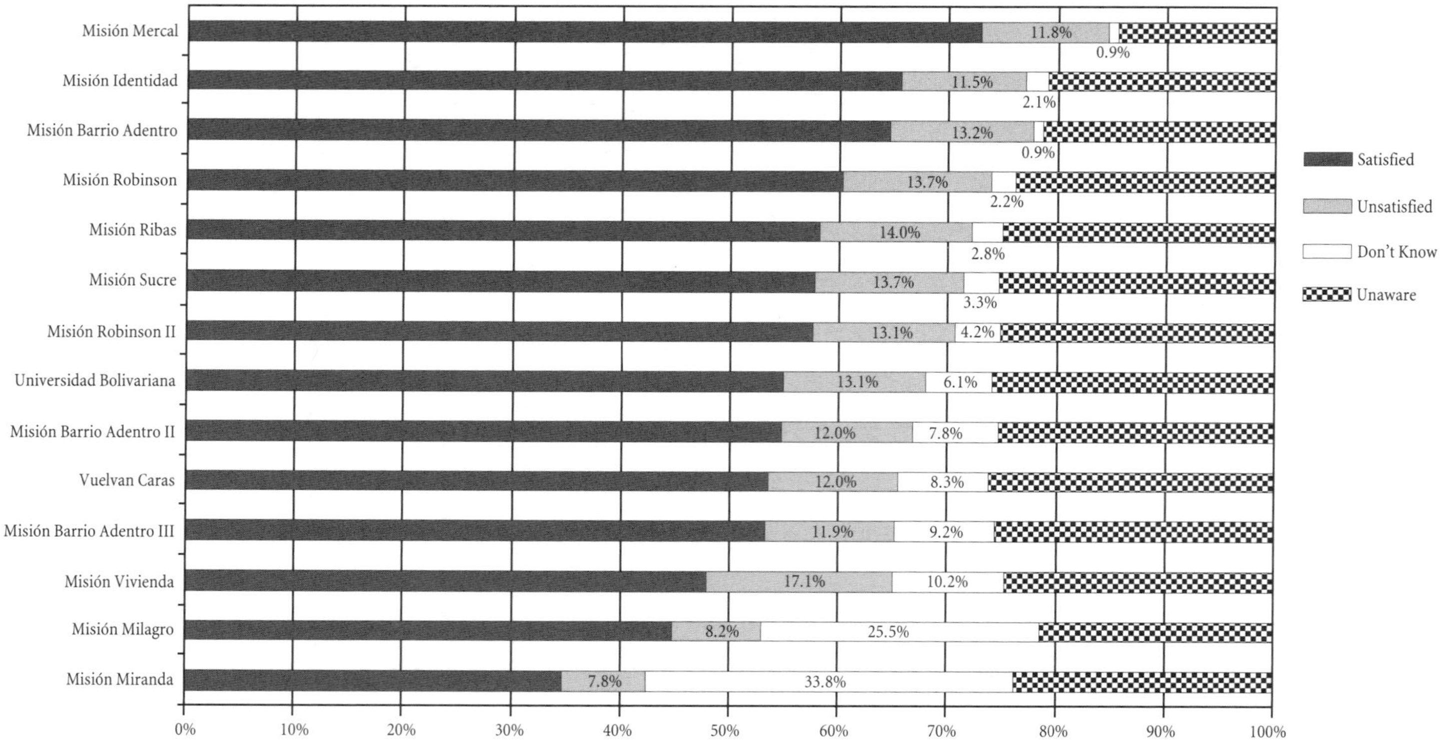

operate at the level of community, representing 200–400 families in the urban areas and 20 families in the rural areas. Communal Councils, along with several other forms of popular participation (such as referenda, social audit/comptrol, citizen assemblies, and cooperatives), serve as institutions of participatory democracy.[71] The working of the councils is regulated by Communal Council Law of 6 April 2006. This law, for example, requires Health Committees to work with other committees affiliated with Communal Councils.[72] These councils, and the ones before them, known as Local Public Planning Councils, were based mainly on the experience of Porto Alegre in Brazil and are involved in activities such as gathering and evaluating community projects, working on development plans, and mapping community needs.[73]

Popular participation is established in the 1999 constitution as a mechanism for the state to enforce health as a social right.[74] Participatory democracy is the fundamental element in the creation of a new health policy.[75] The articles on health in the constitution (Articles 83, 84, 85) have the conceptual underpinning of a "co-responsibility of the triad state-individual-society in social participation, which enables citizens and individuals to become the main actors in the new society."[76] The mandate for the committees of various social missions to work together reflects the importance given to coordination of citizen participation in development projects. In that sense, participatory democracy forms the common thread that serves to weave various sectors of the society together. One analyst views civic participation in decision-making as "a learning process that allows individuals to develop the capabilities necessary to break with psychological barriers that feed the cycle of exclusion."[77] Harnecker, in her study on Venezuelan cooperatives, highlights aspects of participatory democracy that affect collective consciousness and solidarity. She quotes Article 62 of the constitution that relates to this recognition that "participation of the people in the formation, execution, and control of public matters is the means necessary to shape the protagonists who will guarantee the complete development [of the people] both as individuals and collectively."[78]

## Sustainability of Barrio Adentro

While the above account demonstrates that the regime's intention is to bring about positive social change and that health indicators show empirical evidence of improvements, it cannot be denied that there have been several challenges. These concentrate in four main areas: 1) availability of Cuban cooperation; 2) integration with the existing system; 3) increasing accessibility to the health system; and 4) political support.

Community groups in Barrio Adentro conducted a study in 2009 to explore these challenges. A participatory mixed-methods approach was used with 31 participants from Health Committees and Communal Councils representing 5 of 24 states of Venezuela. The main results of the study indicated that implementation was thwarted by political opposition to the reform process, especially in states controlled by the opposition. Also, some mid- or lower-level officials created hurdles for communities in decision-making related to health. However, one of the main difficulties identified was the relations between Cuban and Venezuelan health care providers. For example, many Venezuelan doctors (who are mainly at the tertiary care level) do not accept referrals from Cuban doctors (who are mainly at the primary care level) working within *barrios*.

The results also confirmed the opposition to the reform process by the private health care providers, the Venezuelan Medical Federation, and the private media. Participants indicated that while the opponents thwart the construction of health facilities, they use them later on. As Briggs and Briggs inform us, "Opposition supporters reported that they sometimes used MBA [Mission Barrio Adentro] facilities in emergencies, for example, to avoid a long trip, or when doctors in private clinics prescribed expensive tests or procedures."[79] The opposition has changed its initial stance on Barrio Adentro and has moved to criticizing its perceived failures with a need to improving it.[80] This demonstrates the opposition's tacit approval of the program. Most of the opposition to Barrio Adentro has moved out of the country and appears in opinion pieces in scientific journals or the media. For example, the American and the Venezuela media reported that a group of former Cuban physicians working in Barrio Adentro presented a demand against Venezuela, claiming that the Venezuelan government kept them under unfair working and living conditions, in a sort of "forced labor."[81]

In addition to describing these challenges, which had mainly to do with opposition to Barrio Adentro and generally to the Bolivarian process, the study participants revealed some problems relating to health service delivery and the general infrastructure. Between 2007 and 2009, several news and print media, both politically supportive ones and those in the opposition, reported deficiencies of Barrio Adentro. For example, it was reported that several health facilities lacked physicians, that there were problems with infrastructure in the first and second level facilities, and that Venezuelan personnel complained about working conditions.[82] Such complaints were also reported in the governmental media.[83] Underperformance of Barrio Adentro was recognized by Chávez himself, which led to a relaunching of the program in September 2009.[84] In a cabinet meeting on September 19, 2009, which was also attended by several governors and mayors, it was noted that several medical clinics were not functioning because of "neglect on the part of everyone." In fact, Chávez considered it an emergency situation, citing the abandonment of some 2000 of the total 6700 local medical clinics.[85]

It cannot be denied that a reform process at the national level to bring about social change is a huge task. Moreover, Barrio Adentro, as part of the Bolivarian process, is integral to the Chávez government's commitment to "socialism of the 21st century." Such a commitment not only involves gains in physical indicators such as those of health and quality of life, but a radical transformation of the society to one which is more participatory in nature.

### History Is Not Over: The Bolivarian Process in Barrio Adentro as a Model for the 21st Century

For the past 25 years, the neoliberal ideology that underpins IFI-sponsored health reform initiatives throughout Latin America has been the conventional policy wisdom.[86] Its influence is surprisingly pervasive, given mounting evidence of its ill effects on health and equity throughout the region. Notwithstanding this evidence, numerous countries continue to adhere to neoliberal reform policies. Yet the Venezuelan experience suggests that the neoliberal way is not inevitable. Furthermore, the Venezuelan example supports the thesis that a country's well-being is determined by policy choices closely related to a country's political and ideological power relations rather than its income level.[87]

The Venezuelan government, aided by popular participation as established in its new constitution, has over a short period of time managed to allocate economic and social resources to geographic areas where these can improve the welfare of the population. The process is both planned and implemented by government officials and defended and supported by mass organizations such as Health Committees throughout the country. In addition, as the relationship with Cuba demonstrates, health care reform in Venezuela has been facilitated not by the "policy-based lending" of IFIs, but rather by a novel form of international cooperation based on a bottom-up process of democratic local needs assessments and "South-to-South" mutual aid. Indeed, the unique international cooperation so fundamental to Barrio Adentro suggests a formidable alternative to the principles of conventional international health aid.[88] Just as remarkable as the seeming pervasiveness of the neoliberal paradigm for health reform is Venezuela's ability to break with this paradigm, which, since the 1980s, had dominated the region, though with increasing resistance.

The lessons to be learned from the Venezuelan experience are not exclusive to low- and middle-income countries. The often taken for granted notion that international health knowledge and expertise flow only from core to periphery is questionable, and the Venezuelan case presented here helps to further debunk that myth. Though many of the elements outlined in the 1984 Ottawa Charter for Health Promotion have failed to translate into practice, they are quite evident, on the ground, in Venezuela's Misión Barrio Adentro. The mechanisms and, perhaps more importantly, the social and political context that promotes and fosters community participation in health care management, along with an emphasis on the social determinants of health in Barrio Adentro, may serve as important insights to help marginalized communities in the United States increase their access to quality health services. The future of Barrio Adentro will most likely be a consequence of external factors (the destabilizing efforts of imperialism to topple the Bolivarian Revolution, or the strengthening of a social democratic regional alternative) and internal (the deepening of participatory democracy, the resolution of the contradictions of building socialism and capitalist development simultaneously). For the moment, Venezuela has been able to build a compelling alternative to neoliberalism in community health that serves as a yet little known international health example for all countries. However, it must be realized that Barrio Adentro is no ordinary passive reform process. It is part of an ideological struggle, which in turn is part of the Bolivarian process to create a participatory society whose aim is the development of collective consciousness and solidarity. Social change of that magnitude is not easy. The direction of such social change as observed in Barrio Adentro needs to be such that it produces a more egalitarian society, in the realm of health and in others areas. In spite of several roadblocks (different ministers of health with varying views of primary care, lack of quantitative evaluations , lack of Venezuelan personnel, and, most important, foreign aggression and media campaigns to discredit the Misiones), Barrio Adentro seems thus far to move in that direction because of a broad-based community participation interacting with an often responsive government.

Francis Fukuyama's thesis of the end of history in the early post–Cold War era, which forecast the triumph of liberal democracy and capitalism and the demise of socialism, could not have been more incorrect. In less than a decade history started taking a different turn in much of Latin America, with many center-left political parties gaining state power; these were committed to social equality and implemented policies that promoted broad-based civic participation, especially for groups that had been historically excluded from the political process. Although this swing in the mood on the continent was not initiated by Venezuela, the country is, with Bolivia, leading the way with the most comprehensive reforms in all sectors of society to create a more participatory and egalitarian society. Social change on such a level is of course very difficult, and the outcome is uncertain. But the positive change within Venezuela and the way it has inspired, and in fact facilitated, the change process in many of its neighboring countries and on the continent, resulted in empowerment of people beyond its borders.

## Endnotes

1. The authors would like to thank René Guerra Salazar for his contributions to earlier versions of this manuscript.
2. Laurell, "La política de salud en el contexto de las políticas sociales."
3. Laurell, "Structural Adjustment and the Globalization of Social Policy in Latin America."
4. Ibid.
5. Alvarado et al., *Mission Barrio Adentro.*
6. Ibid.
7. Laurell, "La política de salud en el contexto de las políticas sociales"; Laurell, "Structural Adjustment and the Globalization of Social Policy in Latin America"; Armada, Muntaner, and Navarro, "Health and Social Security Reforms in Latin America"; Birn, Zimmerman, and Garfield, "To Decentralize or Not to Decentralize, Is That the Question?"; Abel and Lloyd-Sherlock, "Health Policy in Latin America: Themes, Trends and Challenges"; Homedes and Ugalde. "Why Neoliberal Health Reforms Have Failed in Latin America"; Iriart, Merhy, and Waitzkin. "Managed Care in Latin America: The New Common Sense in Health Policy Reform"; Schuyler, "Globalization and Health: Venezuela and Cuba."
8. Laurell, "Structural Adjustment and the Globalization of Social Policy in Latin America."
9. Huber, "Options for Social Policy in Latin America." Mesa-Lago, Cruz-Saco, and Zamalloa, "Determinants of Social Insurance/Security Costs and Coverage."
10. Weeks, "The Contemporary Latin American Economies: Neoliberal Reconstruction."
11. Ibid.
12. Ibid.
13. Iriart, Merhy, and Waitzkin, "Managed Care in Latin America: The New Common Sense in Health Policy Reform."
14. Labonte and Schrecker, *Globalization and Social Determinants of Health.*
15. Jaggar, "Vulnerable Women and Neoliberal Globalization."
16. Laurell, "Structural Adjustment and the Globalization of Social Policy in Latin America."
17. Collins and Green, "Decentralization and Primary Health Care."
18. Iriart, Merhy, and Waitzkin. "Managed Care in Latin America: The New Common Sense in Health Policy Reform"; Collins and Green, "Decentralization and Primary Health Care."
19. Homedes and Ugalde. "Why Neoliberal Health Reforms Have Failed in Latin America."

20. Armada, Muntaner, and Navarro, "Health and Social Security Reforms in Latin America."
21. Labonte and Schrecker, *Globalization and Social Determinants of Health*; Jaggar, "Vulnerable Women and Neoliberal Globalization"; Kinman, "Evaluating Health Service Equity at a Primary Care Clinic in Chilimarca, Bolivia"; Manfredi, "Can the Resurgence of Malaria Be Partially Attributed to Structural Adjustment Programmes?"; R. Garfield, "Malaria Control in Nicaragua: Social and Political Influences on Disease Transmission and Control Activities."
22. Armada, Muntaner, and Navarro, "Health and Social Security Reforms in Latin America: The Convergence of the World Health Organization, the World Bank, and Transnational Corporations"; Iriart, Merhy, and Waitzkin. "Managed Care in Latin America: The New Common Sense in Health Policy Reform"; Jasso-Aguilar, Waitzkin, and Landwehr, "Multinational Corporations and Health Care in the United States and Latin America."
23. Armada, Muntaner, and Navarro, "Health and Social Security Reforms in Latin America"; Iriart, Merhy, and Waitzkin. "Managed Care in Latin America";. Jasso-Aguilar, Waitzkin, and. Landwehr, "Multinational Corporations and Health Care in the United States and Latin America."
24. Homedes and Ugalde, "Why Neoliberal Health Reforms Have Failed in Latin America."
25. Naím, *Paper Tigers & Minotaurs*.
26. Ibid.
27. Hellinger, "Democracy Over a Barrel."
28. Naím, *Paper Tigers and Minotaurs*.
29. Ibid.; Buxton, "Venezuela."
30. Tulchin and Bland, eds., *Venezuela in the Wake of Radical Reform*.
31. J. Buxton, "Venezuela"; E. Lander, "The Impact of Neoliberal Adjustment in Venezuela, 1989–1993."
32. Tulchin and Bland, eds., *Venezuela in the Wake of Radical Reform*.
33. World Bank. 2006. *Staff Appraisal Report: Venezuela Health Services Reform Project 2005.*; Inter-American Development Bank. 2006. *Program to Strengthen and Modernize the Health Sector 2006*.
34. Armada, Muntaner, and Navarro, "Health and Social Security Reforms in Latin America"; Feo and Siqueira. "An Alternative to the Neoliberal Model in Health: The Case of Venezuela."
35. Díaz Polanco, "El papel del financiamiento en los procesos de reforma del sector salud: el caso de Venezuela."
36. Lander, "Venezuelan Social Conflict in a Global Context."
37. Ibid.
38. Gregory Wilpert, *Changing Venezuela by Taking Power*.
39. Ministerio de la Secretaría de la Presidencia. *Constitución de la República Bolivariana de Venezuela*. 2000.

40. Gobierno Bolivariano de Venezuela. *Constitución de la República Bolivariana de Venezuela.* http://www.constitucion.ve/. Retrieved May 9, 2008.
41. Chávez, "Discurso del Presidente de la Republica Bolivariana de Venezuela, Hugo Chávez Frias, con motivo del Mensaje Annual de Rendicion de Cuentas ante la Asamblea Nacional. January 15, 2001."
42. Briggs and Mantini-Briggs, "Confronting Health Disparities: Latin American Social Medicine in Venezuela."
43. Abers, *Inventing LocalDdemocracy: Grassroots Politics in Brazil.*
44. Gregory Wilpert, *Changing Venezuela by Taking Power.*
45. Ministerio de Salud y Desarrollo Social (MSDS), *Barrio Adentro: Expresión de Atención Primaria de Salud: Un Proceso de Construcción Permanente*, 2005.
46. Jardim, "Prevention and Solidarity: Democratizing Health in Venezuela."
47. Ministerio de Salud y Desarrollo Social (MSDS) 2006. *Barrio Adentro* 2006.
48. Ministerio de Salud y Desarrollo Social (MSDS), *Barrio Adentro: Expresión de Atención Primaria de Salud: Un Proceso de Construcción Permanente.*
49. Ministerio de Salud y Desarrollo Social (MSDS), *Barrio Adentro* 2006.
50. Briggs and Briggs, "Confronting Health Disparities: Latin American Social Medicine in Venezuela."
51. Ministerio de Salud y Desarrollo Social (MSDS), *Barrio Adentro: Expresión de Atención Primaria de Salud: Un Proceso de Construcción Permanente.*
52. Ibid.
53. Ibid.
54. Ibid.
55. Alvarado et al., "Social Change and Health Policy in Venezuela."
56. Ministerio de Salud y Desarrollo Social (MSDS), *Barrio Adentro* 2006.
57. Alvarado et al., *Mission Barrio Adentro: The Right to Health and Social Inclusion in Venezuela.*
58. Convenio Cuba-Venezuela. 2004. *Declaración Conjunta suscrita el 14 de diciembre de 2004, entre la República Bolivariana de Venezuela y la República de Cuba*; Convenio Argentina-Venezuela. 2004. *Convenio Integral de Cooperación entre la República Bolivariana de Venezuela y la República Argentina, suscrito en Caracas, 8 April 2004.*
59. Spiegel and Yassi, "Lessons from the Margins of Globalization: Appreciating the Cuban Health Paradox."
60. Organización Panamericana de la Salud, *Barrio Adentro: Derecho a la Salud e Inclusión Social en Venezuela.*
61. Ibid.
62. Gott, *Hugo Chávez and the Bolivarian Revolution.*
63. Ibid.
64. Alvarado et al., *Mission Barrio Adentro.*
65. Organización Panamericana de la Salud, *Barrio Adentro: Derecho a la Salud e Inclusión Social en Venezuela.*

66. Ibid.
67. Alvarado et al., *Mission Barrio Adentro.*
68. See pages 105–106 in Alvarado et al., ibid., for more information.
69. Briggs and Briggs, "Confronting Health Disparities: Latin American Social Medicine in Venezuela."
70. Gregory Wilpert, *Changing Venezuela by Taking Power.*
71. Ibid.
72. Organización Panamericana de la Salud, *Barrio Adentro: Derecho a la Salud e Inclusión Social en Venezuela.*
73. Gregory Wilpert, *Changing Venezuela by Taking Power.*
74. Feo and Siqueira, "An Alternative to Neoliberal Model in Health: The Case of Venezuela."
75. Alvarado et al., "Social Change and Health Policy in Venezuela."
76. Feo and Siqueira, "An Alternative to Neoliberal Model in Health: The Case of Venezuela."
77. Harnecker, "Workplace Democracy and Collective Consciousness: An Empirical Study of Venezuelan Cooperatives."
78. Ibid.
79. Briggs and Briggs, "Confronting Health Disparities: Latin American Social Medicine in Venezuela."
80. Ibid.
81. *El Universal*, "Bienes venezolanos en riesgo por demanda de médicos cubanos."
82. *El Universal*, "Barrio Adentro en estado critico"; Gonzáles, "160 Módulos de Barrio Adentro requieren grandes reparaciones," in *El Nacional.*
83. Mijares Espinoza, "Están matando la Misión Barrio Adentro en el estado Carabobo."
84. Janicke, "Chávez Re-launches Venezuela's Flagship Barrio Adentro Healthcare Program."
85. Ibid.
86. Iriart, Merhy, and Waitzkin, "Managed Care in Latin America: The New Common Sense in Health Policy Reform."
87. Navarro and Shi, "The Political Context of Social Inequalities and Health."
88. Birn, *Marriage of Convenience.*

# 8

# The New Balancing Act: International Relations Theory and Venezuela's Foreign Policy

*Mark Eric Williams*

## Introduction

After winning the presidency in 1998, Hugo Chávez unleashed the Bolivarian Revolution, rewrote the federal Constitution, reorganized the Congress and Supreme Court, concentrated power within the executive, and polarized Venezuelan society along sharp class and ideological lines. These events helped raise Venezuela's profile throughout academe.

As the chapters in this volume illustrate, research on Venezuela is now a growth industry. From domestic politics to economics to public policies, all things Venezuelan command increasing scholarly attention. Foreign policy, however, constitutes an important exception. Despite a whirlwind of diplomatic initiatives and high-profile policy ventures by Caracas since Chávez took power—as well as a sharp deterioration in relations between Caracas and Washington—theoretically informed scholarship on Venezuelan foreign policy is exceedingly rare. Since much of this policy revolves around (or seems aimed at) the United States, there is much to study.

Under Chávez, Venezuela has terminated bilateral military programs with Washington, brokered oil deals with states throughout the Caribbean and Latin America that exclude U.S. participation, pursued friendly ties with Cuba, Iran, Libya, and Saddam Hussein's Iraq, purchased military arms from Russia, strongly criticized the U.S. war in Iraq (and civilian deaths in Afghanistan), and worked tirelessly to derail U.S.-sponsored negotiations to create a Free Trade Agreement of the Americas. Under George W. Bush, the United States consistently funded Venezuelan civil society groups that opposed the Chávez government, quietly encouraged and then supported a 2002 coup that deposed Chávez for two days, proposed authorizing the Organization of American States (OAS) to monitor its members' democratic performance (specifically, Venezuela), and make them accountable to the OAS, sought to "inoculate" Latin America from Venezuela's influence via military alliances with Peru and Paraguay, accused Venezuela of failing to cooperate in the wars on drugs and terror, and forbade the sale of U.S. arms to Venezuela.[1]

Sharply divergent visions of global and regional order formed the backdrop to this estrangement. Under Bush, the United States sought to preserve a unipolar world order and promote economic integration among the Western Hemisphere's democratic, market-oriented states. Venezuela preferred a multipolar order (in which it occupied a "small second power" position), and a Latin American integration along more socialist lines which, by excluding the United States, would also serve to balance U.S. power and influence. Despite the increasing animosity and hostile verbal exchange this clash of visions produced, theoretically driven analyses of Venezuela's foreign policy have remained rare.

This chapter makes no normative judgments regarding Caracas' efforts to create a multipolar order, establish ententes with states on unfriendly terms with Washington, or thwart a proposed Free Trade Agreement of the Americas in favor of regional integration based on non-market principles. Instead, the chapter makes several small arguments and one longer one.

First, while Venezuela's foreign policy is antithetical to important U.S. interests, it remains—broadly speaking—a decidedly American-style foreign policy designed to advance the interests of the Venezuelan state as perceived by the Chávez government. For example, like the United States, Venezuela has sought to promote regional integration and trade; and like the United States, it has worked to ensure that friendly governments take power in neighboring and more distant countries. Also like the United States, Venezuela has employed international institutions (or created new institutional instruments) to pursue its interests; and, like the United States, it has even deployed soft power resources (particularly its political values and ideals) to help set the international agenda and alter the behavior of other states in ways that might protect and advance its interests. Such tactics have long been effective staples of U.S. foreign policy, and while the Chávez government might be loath to admit it, Venezuela also has realized gains by taking a page out of the American foreign policy playbook.

Second, whereas few analysts focus on Venezuela's foreign policy, those that do tend to personalize their accounts.[2] That is to say, rather than evaluate Venezuela's policy initiatives through the lens of international relations theory, they stress the primacy of Hugo Chávez's leadership itself. This approach has yielded a largely one-dimensional view of what Venezuela is doing that, while enlightening, invariably casts Chávez as the principal causal agent of its foreign policy and ascribes virtually all Caracas' foreign policy interests to the president and his documented peculiarities. Such a view, I suggest, is not only incomplete, but analytically less useful. On the one hand, it suggests that Venezuela's foreign policy lacks a genuine rational basis owing to Chávez's eccentricities; on the other, it implies that Venezuela and other states with which it makes common cause would behave quite differently (perhaps more "normally"?) in his absence. To be sure, Chávez is clearly the central player in Venezuela's policy initiatives, and his incendiary rhetoric often colors its foreign policy maneuvers. But an excessive focus on one individual can obscure how the broader international context helps shape the country's behavior on the world stage. To gain a fuller understanding of why Venezuela has pursued some of its more high-profile ventures, and the broader implications of these policies, requires an appreciation of how the incentives generated by a U.S.-led, largely unipolar international system can motivate states to behave in certain ways.

My third argument, therefore, is that despite Chávez's bombast and theatricality, and despite the American style his government's foreign policy displays, the intent of Venezuelan policy mirrors the logic one might anticipate given its position in the international system, its desire to play a greater world role, and the dangers it believes emanate from a unipolar world order. In this sense, Venezuela's foreign policy is theoretically understandable, but not revolutionary in conventional terms (even though its policy goals, if fully realized, could have dramatic political effects).[3] Thus, whether it is Caracas' support for ideologically compatible presidential candidates in Bolivia, Ecuador, Mexico, Nicaragua, and Peru, its petro-diplomacy initiatives in the Andean Ridge, Caribbean Basin, or Southern Cone, its anti-neoliberal regional trade and integration schemes, or its quest for a seat on the UN Security Council, these measures are seen as crucial to protecting Venezuela's national security, burnishing its political influence, and countering perceived threats from the United States.

On this latter point in particular, Venezuela's foreign policy exhibits the hallmarks of what international relations theorists term "soft balancing"—a strain of balance of power politics whereby weaker states employ non-military tools to protect their interests, and to delay, frustrate, and undermine a hegemonic state's capacity to impose its preferences. In Venezuela's case, Caracas' efforts to exclude the United States from Latin America's energy sector, compete with the United States in the telecom sector, and work within international institutions to frustrate U.S. political, diplomatic, and economic designs exemplify soft balancing tactics in action.

To illustrate these points I briefly outline the concept of soft balancing and then address those aspects of Venezuela's foreign policy the concept illustrates. Caracas' soft balancing behavior is most evident in: (1) the regional integration scheme it has advanced (including integration via the energy and telecommunications sectors); (2) its use of international institutions to constrain Washington's ability to realize its preferred outcomes (especially within the OAS and the institutional framework of the Summit of the Americas); and (3) its failed quest to obtain a seat on the UN Security Council. The chapter concludes by highlighting the implications its analysis holds for inter-state relations in the Western Hemisphere, U.S. policy in the region, and the potential impact the Obama administration may have on Venezuela's foreign policy calculations.

## Soft Balancing

Historically, states have sought to achieve security and preserve their independence within an anarchic system by balancing the power and perceived threats from stronger states. Whether by means of "internal balancing" (building up one's own military and defensive capacity) or "external balancing" (forging coalitions and alliances to counter more powerful states), the objective is to protect the interests of the weak against the strong or the potentially threatening. However, situations where one state's power exceeds that of a weaker state (or coalition of weaker states) by orders of magnitude make effective hard balancing of either stripe impractical, as evidenced by today's largely unipolar order. Not only does the United States command roughly 30 percent of global production, exercise its influence through a matrix of international organizations like the World Bank, International Monetary Fund, NATO, and United Nations, and enjoy unrivaled military power, it has enjoyed such primacy since the Soviet Union's demise in 1991.[4] Not surprisingly, under these conditions robust, traditional balancing behavior has not emerged against the United States in the post-Cold War era.

What has emerged, however, is "soft balancing," a practice whose logic from a theoretical perspective is straightforward. In an anarchic environment where states confront overwhelming U.S. military dominance, there is little chance of balancing the United States in hard military power. Yet the uncertainties of anarchy ensure that the incentives to balance U.S. influence and offset Washington's ability to impose its will remain; moreover, these incentives grow stronger the more threatening unchecked U.S. power and actions appear to become. Thus, instead of engaging in arms races or forging formal military alliances to counter the United States,[5] weaker states have sought to coordinate their policies in more subtle ways and pursue limited, tacit, or indirect balancing strategies whose explicit goal is to check U.S. power.[6] Such strategies include the use of: (1) "entangling diplomacy" within international institutions to delay or frustrate U.S. policy aims, (2) "territorial denial" to limit U.S. power-projection capabilities, and (3) "economic strengthening" to shift economic power toward weaker states by excluding the United States from regional trade arrangements.[7]

Among the most commonly cited cases of soft balancing behavior are French, German, and Russian efforts in 2002 to entangle the United States within UN institutional procedures and forestall U.S. military action against Iraq; Turkey's 2003 refusal to permit U.S. ground forces to use its territory as a staging area for the invasion of Iraq; and strategic partnerships between Russia, China, and India that have begun to shift the distribution of military power in Asia and were publicly justified, in part, by a shared desire to create a more multipolar world. They also include China and South Korea's diplomatic interventions to avert unilateral U.S. military action against North Korea's nuclear ambitions.[8]

For reasons we need not dwell on here, not all scholars believe these cases reflect genuine instances of soft balancing. Concerning Venezuela's foreign policy, however, what is important are the criteria the skeptics insist any case of soft balancing must meet.

- States must do more than employ the rhetoric of balancing to justify a foreign policy. They must take specific actions to limit U.S. influence, increase constraints on Washington, and/or shift power against the United States; moreover, the link between their actions and attempts to balance U.S. power must be explicit.[9]
- Soft balancing "must reflect the imperative of security seeking under anarchy"—rather than simply a dispute over a particular U.S. policy (for example Iraq)—such that states "see the concentration of power in the United States as a direct security threat, especially if it [Washington] comes to be seen as having malign intentions."[10]
- Soft balancers must be willing to accept the trade-offs between achieving the constraints they seek to impose on Washington and securing other valued objectives, even if the trade-offs jeopardize their relations with the United States.[11]
- Finally, states deemed to be soft balancers must display patterns of behavior that soft balancing theory actually predicts. To quote Stephen Brooks and William Wohlforth: "The prediction is that as other states gain relative capabilities and update their assessments of the U.S. threat, they will begin to take soft-balancing measures. Under the logic

of soft balancing, these measures must plausibly be linked to enhancing these states' security vis-à-vis the U.S. threat."[12]

The question, then, is how well do Venezuela's foreign policy initiatives stack up to these types of benchmarks? The answer, in brief, is, quite well.

## Venezuela: Balancing Softly Against the United States

From 2001 onward, Venezuela's diplomatic and policy initiatives closely followed the soft balancing criteria noted above. Between 2001 and 2003, world oil prices rose sharply while U.S. foreign policy grew more unilateral (Afghanistan, Iraq) and increasingly hostile toward Venezuela. In response, Caracas enhanced its capabilities thanks to windfall oil revenues, and updated its assessment of the U.S. threat. After Washington quietly encouraged (and then supported) the 2002 coup that deposed Chávez for two days, Venezuela began pursuing soft balancing strategies in earnest; it engaged in "economic strengthening" and "diplomatic entanglement," forged informal ententes with other states to coordinate these initiatives, and justified its foreign policy actions precisely in terms of forging a multipolar order and checking U.S. power, influence, and ability to realize preferred outcomes.

### Economic Strengthening: The Bolivarian Alternative for the Americas

Soft balancing theory posits that states seeking to constrain U.S. power might craft economic arrangements and policies that advantage weaker countries, exclude the United States, and/or limit its economic benefits. Venezuela's "Bolivarian Alternative for the Americas" (ALBA) aptly illustrates this strategy.[13]

In December 2004, the Venezuelan president traveled to Cuba, where he unveiled the Bolivarian Alternative as a means to promote Latin America's economic integration. ALBA is not a traditional free trade agreement, nor even a fully developed framework of integration. Rather, it is a philosophical concept of comprehensive integration based on principles at variance with those of the U.S.-backed Free Trade Agreement of the Americas (FTAA): solidarity and complementarity vs. "exploitation," cooperation vs. competition, and cooperative advantage vs. comparative advantage. Under ALBA's banner, regional integration takes the form of bi- or multilateral pacts in areas such as culture, education, energy, health care, and telecommunications. In terms of trade, it takes the form of heterodox People's Trade Agreements reached among regional governments that permit the exchange of goods and services in hard currencies or via trade in kind.

ALBA does not strive to eliminate markets in the sense of the command economies under the old Soviet-style COMECON, but it does prioritize the state's role in development and promoting social welfare over that of the free market or the corporation. In this sense, ALBA competes ideologically with Washington's preferred vision of integration. Indeed, Caracas bills ALBA as a direct challenge to what it describes as U.S. economic domination disguised as market-oriented regional economic integration. By privileging social welfare over deregulated, profit-maximizing corporate opportunities, and resource industrialization over mere commercial export promotion, Venezuela seeks to leverage ALBA as a counterweight to the FTAA's economic policies and goals.

There has been little scholarship on ALBA—perhaps because of its recent advent, its connection to Cuba and Venezuela, and because it lacks the clarity of formal integration schemes like the North American Trade Agreement. Sheila Collins, however, provides a succinct definition.

> The ALBA envisions a regional economic development plan for Latin America and the Caribbean that seeks to develop solidarity with the weakest areas by transferring resources to those weak links so that all can cooperate in exchanging goods in a win-win environment . . . Endogenous development is privileged over export-oriented industry, and agricultural policy would be first focused on indigenous self-sufficiency before turning to profit-making exports. The ALBA . . . rejects any trade agreement that negates the use of public policy instruments to regulate the economy in favor of social redistribution, economic justice, and endogenous development.[14]

ALBA, of course, remains embryonic. Besides Venezuela, its official membership—Antigua and Barbuda, Bolivia, Cuba, Dominica, Ecuador, Honduras (which withdrew in January 2010), Nicaragua, St. Vincent and the Grenadines—includes none of Latin America's more economically advanced countries, and only Bolivia, Cuba, and Nicaragua have signed explicit People's Trade Agreements with Caracas. However, more than 20 other Latin American states have signed onto other Venezuelan initiatives in the energy and telecommunications sectors that fall under the ALBA banner, and which exemplify the soft balancing strategy of economic strengthening: Petrocaribe, Petrosur, and Petroandina in the energy sector, and Telesur in telecommunications.

### Energy
In September 2004, Venezuela and Argentina established Petrosur, an energy alliance comprised of state-owned oil firms in Venezuela (PDVSA),

Argentina (Enarsa), and potentially, Brazil (Petrobras).[15] In practical terms, Petrosur functions to commercialize crude oil and derivative products, facilitate the exploration, exploitation, and processing of oil and natural gas, construct jointly operated refineries, storage facilities, and terminals, manage transportation and logistics, and develop technology and training programs. Beyond these operations, however, lie deeper soft balancing objectives: to unite the region's state petroleum firms, channel a portion of oil revenues into domestic social development projects, and in the process, exclude U.S. and other large multinational oil firms from future energy development within member states.

In June 2005, Caracas created Petrocaribe, an initiative under which eighteen Caribbean Basin states purchase Venezuelan oil at preferential rates, pay a percentage of the market price in hard currency (60 or 50 percent, depending on world oil prices), and convert the remainder to long-term, low-interest loans.[16] Member states may also pay portions of their oil bill in goods and services (trade in kind). Regardless of how states choose to finance their oil purchases, the Venezuelan government transports all shipments at cost; and, because Petrocaribe works only through state-controlled oil companies—not private firms—its operations are deliberately calculated to exclude U.S. and other large multinational oil firms from these transactions.[17] Ostensibly, under the Petrocaribe agreements, the money member states save on energy purchases through this arrangement would then become available to invest in development projects.

Rounding out the energy initiatives is Petroandina, an arrangement between the state oil firms of five Andean Ridge countries.[18] Established in July 2005, its objectives are to coordinate policies and plans within each member's energy sector, ensure adequate energy supplies, strengthen regional integration, and generate funds for anti-poverty programs. As with Petrocaribe, members of Petroandina can purchase Venezuelan oil and finance up to 50 percent of their costs at low-interest loans (2 percent) for up to fifteen years. The agreement also obligates Venezuela to invest in upgrading the oil refining and production capacity of member states. In January 2006, Bolivia became the first to take advantage of this option through a bilateral agreement that commits the two states' national oil firms, Bolivia's Yacimientos Petrolíferos Fiscales Bolivianos (YPBF) and Venezuela's PDVSA to develop infrastructure, processing, and refining projects for gas and petroleum. Four months later, La Paz and Caracas inked another joint venture, under which Venezuela will finance gas exploration, drilling, production, sales, marketing, and training, and YPFB will operate the facilities. In July 2006, Colombia became the second state to embrace this option when Bogotá and Caracas broke ground on a trans-Caribbean pipeline connecting Venezuela and Colombia (plans envision its future extension to Panama), and in January 2007, Ecuador signed a series of similar accords.[19]

Not all Latin American or Caribbean states have joined Venezuela's three energy initiatives; Chile's free trade agreement with the United States, for example, precludes its participation in Petrosur, and Trinidad and Tobago have opted out of Petrocaribe. Still, Caracas continues to encourage the expansion of these ventures toward its ultimate goal of uniting these initiatives into a single entity, Petroamérica—a coalition of Latin American state energy firms that would integrate the region's energy sectors, develop and commercialize its energy resources, upgrade its energy infrastructure, ensure energy self-sufficiency, and generate funds for social welfare programs. In political terms, the end game remains soft balancing: the Venezuelan state sees Petroamérica as nothing short of "a new geoeconomic and geo-political initiative . . . geared towards buttressing both Latin American integration and the conformation of a multipolar world."[20]

A first step toward this broader enterprise is the proposed 7,000-mile, $20 billion Gran Gasoducto del Sur pipeline that Venezuela, Argentina, Bolivia, Brazil, Paraguay, and Uruguay have committed to build. Stretching across South America from Venezuela to Argentina (with branches serving Bolivia and Uruguay), the pipeline is scheduled to go on-line in 2017. Progress on the Gasoducto reflects the tenuous nature of the entire Petroamérica enterprise. In 2006, Chávez described the pipeline as "the end of the Washington Consensus" and "the beginning of the Latin American Consensus,"[21] while other Latin American advocates saw in it a "blueprint for a new era of regional cooperation . . . and *a more prominent voice on the world stage*" (emphasis added). Since then, however, falling global oil prices and the 2008 world economic crisis have cooled this early enthusiasm considerably.

*Telecommunications*

In May 2005, Venezuela launched Telesur, a satellite television network headquartered in Caracas and funded jointly by Argentina (20 percent), Bolivia (5 percent), Cuba (19 percent), Ecuador (5 percent),[22] Uruguay (10 percent), and Venezuela (41 percent). Described as the "first counter-hegemonic telecommunications project known in South America,"[23] Telesur boasts news bureaus stretching from Washington to Mexico City to Buenos Aires. More than a simple commercial venture, the network's mandate is expressly political. Its principal objectives are to counterbalance the "northern bias" emanating from U.S.-dominated satellite broadcasters like CNN,

CNN Español, and other Spanish language broadcasts headquartered in Miami; facilitate regional integration via transnational mass communications exchanges;[24] and, thereby, help promote a multipolar international order to balance U.S. hegemony. Not surprisingly, corporate officials describe Telesur's mission in straightforward political terms. According to the company's director, Uruguayan journalist Aram Ahoronian (formerly of CNN), Telesur is "an initiative against cultural imperialism" and "the only alternative to the hegemonic message with which they bombard us from the North."[25] Jorge Botero, Telesur's director of information, agrees. "The world's unipolarity . . . has to be broken," he explained. "To us, there are many horizons other than those viewed from Washington and that is why our channel's motto is 'Our north is the south.'"[26]

Telesur's overarching goal, then, is to balance Washington's soft power in telecommunications and, potentially, limit the economic benefits it derives from broadcasts to Latin America. In terms of soft power, Telesur seeks to challenge the perceived U.S. capacity to frame political issues (including the official interpretation of its or any other state's foreign policies) in ways that enhance U.S. influence and credibility by controlling the production and flow of information beamed to and consumed by Latin American viewers. With correspondents across the Americas and a broadcast range that blankets the region's 600 million Spanish and Portuguese speakers (along with portions of Western Europe), Telesur aims to challenge U.S. "informational hegemony" in the Western Hemisphere, much as Qatar's Al-Jazeera has done across the Muslim world.[27] Yet Telesur represents more than simply a state propaganda machine, since the more successful it becomes the more advertising it could attract (which, according to its corporate board, is the plan).

Only time will tell the long-term effects of this venture. To date, Telesur has not acquired a wide viewership; most Latin Americans do not have satellite TV, and the network's availability through private cable TV companies has been restricted due to its coverage of sensitive political events in some countries. However, should Telesur become the station of choice for Latin American viewers in the future, the profits it generates would remain in Latin America instead of flowing back to the United States.

While the Bush administration remained mostly silent on the political challenge Telesur represented, legislators in the president's party accurately interpreted the Venezuelan government's intent in establishing the satellite network. As U.S. Congressman Connie Mack (R-FL) exclaimed, Telesur "is a threat to the United States [because it] tries to undermine the balance of power in the western hemisphere."[28]

*Entangling Diplomacy*

According to soft balancing theory, a second way weaker states might constrain Washington's capacity to impose its policy preferences is by entangling the United States within the constraining procedures of international institutions. To the extent such efforts reflect a weaker state's perceived security interests as opposed to mere policy disputes with the United States, they provide prima facie evidence of soft balancing behavior. Here too, Venezuela's foreign policy—particularly within the Organization of American States—exemplifies soft balancing tactics.

Since its founding in 1948, the OAS has served as a multilateral institution for regional governance. As Viron Vaky and Heraldo Muñoz explain, its "Charter and accompanying treaties represented an implicit 'bargain': in return for U.S. nonintervention in their internal affairs, the Latin American countries would support the United States internationally and accept collective responsibility for security in the hemisphere."[29] This bargain swiftly transformed the OAS into a tool by which Washington could advance its broader geostrategic objectives, such as keeping extra-hemispheric powers and ideologies out of the Western Hemisphere, preserving U.S. national security (as when the OAS backed the U.S. naval blockade of Cuba during the 1962 missile crisis), combating drug trafficking, and promoting democracy. As the organization's dominant power and principal funder, the United States exercised enormous influence over OAS operations: its Secretary General was always the preferred U.S. choice, and with a few notable exceptions,[30] the OAS generally deferred to U.S. policy preferences and supported U.S. initiatives.

After Washington badly mishandled Venezuela's 2002 coup, however, its influence within the OAS fell sharply. While the United States had supported the anti-Chávez coup and recognized the new government, the vast majority of OAS members condemned the putsch and denied the new government official recognition—a stance that accorded the Bolivarian Revolution a degree of international legitimacy and thus, greater security. This episode taught Caracas the utility of an OAS that could act independently of U.S. preferences, and made preserving that independence a matter of national security.

To assist OAS independence, in 2005 Caracas worked closely with some of its Petrosur/Petrocaribe/Telesur partners to prevent the election of Washington's preferred candidate as OAS Secretary General—former Salvadoran president Francisco Flores. Politically, Flores was a close U.S. ally and Venezuela had its reasons to oppose his candidacy: under his tenure, El Salvador was the only state in Latin America to recognize the Venezuelan government that seized power briefly in the 2002 coup.[31] Thus, along with Argentina, Brazil, and Uruguay, Venezuela lobbied to elect José Luis Insulza, Chile's foreign minister. While other states backed the candidacy of Mexico's foreign minister, Luis Ernesto Derbez, a majority of Caribbean states (13 of which now belonged to Petrocaribe) sided with Venezuela to support Insulza.[32] Without broad support, in the end, Flores bowed out of the race (as did, eventually, Derbez),[33] and Insulza became the first Secretary General in OAS history who was not the United States' preferred choice. Subsequently, Insulza has worked to maintain a neutral stance, build consensus within the OAS, and distance himself from U.S. positions on several issues, including the extent to which Venezuela threatens regional security.[34]

Shortly after this setback, the United States saw another of its high-priority OAS initiatives fail, after becoming snarled in diplomatic entanglements. At the June 2005 meeting of the OAS General Assembly in Fort Lauderdale, Florida, Washington proposed creating a mechanism within the OAS to monitor the democratic performance of member states and take action against those that failed to govern democratically. In a veiled reference to Venezuela during her opening address, U.S. Secretary of State Condoleezza Rice proclaimed that: "Together we must insist that leaders who are elected democratically have a responsibility to govern democratically . . . governments that fail to meet this crucial standard must be accountable to the OAS."[35] The response to Secretary Rice's proposal from Celso Amorim, Brazil's Foreign Minister, typified the attitude of many delegates: "Madam Secretary, democracy cannot be imposed."[36] Not surprisingly, Venezuela saw the initiative as a direct threat to its security, flatly rejected the proposal, and lobbied hard against it. "The OAS," asserted its then Foreign Minister, Ali Rodríguez, "should be an organization promoting democracy, not an organ for intervention in the internal affairs of our countries."[37]

In the end, over 80 percent of the membership voted down the proposal. Publicly, some members justified their vote because, they argued, the proposal violated the principle of nonintervention enshrined in the OAS Charter; some expressed fears that it could eventually be turned against them; and many others believed (correctly) that it was a thinly disguised effort to weaken the Venezuelan government and intervene in its domestic affairs.[38] Most states simply found U.S. insistence that the proposal was not "some kind of effort to isolate Venezuela"[39] unpersuasive: as Argentina's OAS delegate noted, this proposition was "impossible to sell to any adult human being."[40]

Prior to the vote, Venezuela cast the contest over the U.S. initiative in explicit anti-hegemonic terms (accusing Washington of seeking to impose a "global dictatorship"), and predicted its ultimate defeat. "The times in which the OAS was an instrument of the government in Washington," President Chávez asserted, "are gone."[41] In the wake of the decisive vote, his then Vice President, José Vicente Rangel, maintained the anti-hegemonic drumbeat. The OAS decision, he said, "was a defeat for Bush and Rice, who could not impose the point of view that they brought: this monitoring, this type of disguised intervention that they proposed and that was rejected by the majority."[42]

Working within the institutional context of the Summit of the Americas, Caracas pursued a similar entanglement strategy to thwart U.S. efforts to realize a Free Trade Agreement of the Americas. Since its 1994 inception in Miami, the United States and other governments had used the summit framework—under which leaders of the 34 members of the OAS convene—to advance the FTAA agenda. The Chávez government termed such efforts a "colonialist project" based on an "imperialist and neocolonial model" of integration,[43] whose implementation would institutionalize U.S. economic domination over western hemispheric states. Although one might question the objectivity of Caracas' views regarding the FTAA, Nicola Phillips' analysis suggests that the manner by which Washington has pursued free trade in the Americas reveals that the accord's "political and economic objectives . . . are intrinsically informed and molded by the broader ideological—neoliberal—foundation of U.S. hegemony," and are designed to "ensure that the regional economic regime takes a form consistent with U.S. interests and preferences."[44]

After talks bogged down in 2003, Washington tried to resuscitate negotiations at the November 2005 Summit, held at Mar del Plata, Argentina. From the beginning, though, it faced strong opposition from some states, including the host, Argentina.[45] Venezuela quickly joined other opponents (Argentina, Brazil, Paraguay, and Uruguay) to deny the United States the consensus needed to craft a final Summit Declaration that would commit the 34 states to restarting the trade talks, and predictably, of those opposed, Venezuela's objections contained the most critical tone and "anti-hegemonic" intent. Caracas not only rejected the entire concept of U.S.-style market-oriented economic integration, it pitched ALBA as the remedy for U.S. "imperialist" aspirations.[46] With the prospects of a consensus dead, President Bush left the Summit early rather than suffer the humiliation of witnessing the final vote.

Venezuela's failed campaign to represent the Latin American/Caribbean region on the UN Security Council as a non-permanent member reflects yet another way that soft balancing logic informed its foreign policy. Caracas sought a Security Council seat precisely to help expand its anti-U.S. influence beyond the Western Hemisphere (the ultimate goal was to "balance against hegemonic trends, in favor of the interests of countries from the South with an independent position").[47] Besides providing a vote and platform in Council deliberations on issues critical to U.S. interests, this position would have afforded Venezuela new opportunities to pursue diplomatic entanglement strategies. Even as a non-permanent member, in "close vote" situations Venezuela could well have undermined the preferred U.S. response to a range of issues. Given the potential leverage it could have exerted from within the Security Council, the vigorous lobbying campaign Washington mounted to deny Venezuela this position is no surprise (the surprise, perhaps, was the unexpected assistance Chávez may have provided the United States by likening President Bush to the devil in his September 2006 address to the General Assembly).[48]

Summing up, in recent years Venezuela has coordinated its efforts with other Latin American governments to resist U.S. initiatives and constrain America's ability to realize its preferred outcomes. To some degree, soft balancing incentives have influenced the behavior of some states, as reflected in Telesur's anti-hegemonic mandate, the People's Trade Agreements reached between Bolivia, Cuba, Nicaragua, and Venezuela, and much of the opposition to the U.S.-backed candidate for the OAS secretary generalship. In a region long subject to repeated U.S. interventions and political slights (real and imagined), it is no surprise that states might gravitate to soft balancing, especially when such measures are unlikely to elicit Washington's focused enmity. That said, there is no doubt that other factors besides soft balancing mattered too. For example, the opposition to restarting FTAA negotiations from Southern Cone Market states like Argentina, Brazil, and Uruguay was mostly the stuff of standard policy disputes—e.g., disagreement over agricultural subsidies and market access—within the context of a general consensus on market-oriented free trade.

The same cannot be said, however, for Venezuela, whose efforts to limit U.S. influence within the Western Hemisphere, OAS, and Summit of the Americas fell well outside of simple policy disputes. As shown, Caracas not only sought to constrain Washington's ability to impose its preferences, then justified these actions as a means to balance U.S. influence and promote a more multipolar order; it also advanced these measures notwithstanding the damage they caused to U.S.-Venezuelan relations.

Looking back, the point at which Caracas stepped onto the path of soft balancing seems clear. Prior to 2001, U.S.-Venezuelan relations were appropriate, although not warm. True, in 1999 Caracas took steps that resembled the soft balancing tactic of "territorial denial," when it denied U.S. jets permission to over-fly Venezuelan airspace in pursuit of drug traffickers, and in 2000, it also spoke of the virtues of a multipolar world.[49] However, the government justified its 1999 decision not on the need to constrain U.S. influence or actions (indeed, it continued to cooperate with Washington's anti-drug campaign), but rather, on a desire to preserve its national sovereignty; moreover, while its leaders may have lauded multipolarity, the Venezuelan state took no concrete measures to promote it. Between 2001 and 2003 things changed, as bilateral relations soured, hostility deepened, and Venezuela's sense of insecurity grew. In 2001, Caracas criticized civilian casualties in the U.S. war against Afghanistan's Taliban regime. This, plus Chávez's admonishment that President Bush not respond to terror with more terror (implicitly equating America's self-defense actions to the 9/11 terrorist attacks) led Washington to recall its ambassador to Venezuela. Seven months later, the United States supported the ill-fated 2002 coup, and Venezuela began to embrace soft balancing in earnest.

## Conclusion

While Venezuela's soft balancing policies are not revolutionary in a conventional sense, they do constitute a form of state behavior quite distinct from more generic patterns of foreign policy. Major incentives to engage in this behavior sprang from the unprecedented context of global politics in the early 21st century: an apparent unipolar world where unrivaled U.S. military power seemed to provide the United States with extraordinary degrees of freedom. In this context, the uncertainties of anarchy generated incentives for some weaker states—including Venezuela—to balance U.S. influence indirectly via non-military means.

Despite some theorists' concerns that soft balancing could be a prelude to more traditional hard balancing policies,[50] the ententes Caracas has forged with other Latin American states seem unlikely to evolve in this direction. The economic, financial, military, and political asymmetries inherent in the overall U.S.-Latin American relationship render the prospects of a formal, efficacious anti-U.S. military alliance exceedingly remote.

Although Venezuela's policy initiatives display clear elements of soft balancing, the totality of its foreign policy stems from more than rational incentives to soft balance. Anti-imperialist ideology, Caracas' quest for a larger world role, domestic political calculations, and Hugo Chávez's vaulted ambitions and propensity to pick verbal fights have influenced Venezuela's foreign policy too. These factors help to account for some of Caracas' more incendiary and wildly exaggerated allegations of Washington's malign intentions, such as routine cries of an imminent U.S. invasion and plans to assassinate the Venezuelan president.

Caracas' foreign policy agenda has broader implications for inter-state relations in the Western Hemisphere, as well as for U.S. policy in the region. For Latin America, the short-term success of Venezuela's initiatives could help deepen and institutionalize a split between what we might call its regionalists (Argentina, Brazil, Bolivia, Cuba, Ecuador, Paraguay, and Venezuela) and its globalists (Chile, Central America, Colombia, Mexico, and Peru). The former generally prefer independence from the United States and greater multipolarity; the latter prefer closer political and economic relations with Washington. The result could be a gradual political realignment (foreshadowed by the regional split for and against the U.S. position over the OAS secretary generalship), and ironically, weaker ties among some Latin American states—an outcome at variance with Venezuela's vision of a comprehensive, ALBA-style regional integration. At the same time, though, unity among regionalists themselves is not guaranteed. Venezuela's drive to achieve regional leadership places it on a collision course with Brazil, which has long aspired to the same position.

In terms of U.S. policy interests, while the United States is unlikely ever to face a serious military threat from this region, it does confront an ideological competitor in Venezuela. Without putting too fine a point on it, Caracas' agenda represents the most significant ideological challenge to U.S. hemispheric interests that Washington has faced in perhaps 50 years. The extent to which Venezuela can achieve multipolarity by forging market-diversifying strategic partnerships with oil-hungry states outside of Latin America (for example China) is debatable.[51] But even if ALBA initiatives like Telesur, Petroamérica, and People's Trade Agreements are only moderately successful, they could permanently foreclose the type of hemispheric integration that Washington has envisioned, restrict the economic benefits the United States might otherwise derive from free trade and regional energy development, further weaken U.S. influence in the region, and promote an alternative pole of influence (though not hard military power) with Venezuela at its epicenter.

During the George W. Bush administrations, U.S. policy-making toward Latin America lacked the sustained focus and dexterity required to meet Caracas' challenge. This was partly due to Washington's preoccupation with the Middle East and South Asia, and partly because the alacrity and skill with which Venezuela pursued soft balancing were masked by Chávez's bombastic theatricality, and at times, Washington's inclination to dismiss him simply as a buffoon or oddball regional threat. With U.S. attention diverted elsewhere, Venezuela—despite missteps—executed its soft balancing policy with aplomb, and by design or happenstance, followed short, medium, and long-term strategies that bolster its prospects of success.

In the short term, Caracas responded nimbly to U.S. maneuvers (for example within the OAS) and exploited nearly every opportunity to make its case for multipolarity in international forums (the United Nations, the Summit of the Americas, and the World Social Forum).[52] It built its foreign policy around several strategic themes that in the medium term, (1) offered a relatively coherent direction for political action; (2) articulated its policy objectives effectively; and (3) helped brand Venezuela as an anti-hegemonic champion. These themes—multipolarity, regional integration, materially beneficial cooperation—are embedded in what Caracas hopes other Latin American states will perceive as a wider positive agenda for the region's future, and one quite distinct from U.S. preferences. A good example is regional integration, which Venezuela embraced via ALBA, but defined in anti-neoliberal, anti-free market terms. For the long term, Venezuela has floated additional proposals to promote multipolarity and deepen the integration process. Among these are a Bank of the South (formally inaugurated on December 3, 2007) to finance infrastructure and development programs, and help states escape the clutches and conditionality of U.S.-influenced international financial institutions,[53] and a potential University of the South—replete with cultural exchange programs and thousands of scholarships—to train a new generation of technical and professional leaders.

Of course, the extent to which Caracas' soft balancing tactics yield the results it desires depends on other factors, including concerns and resentment that other governments harbor toward the United States, the resources Venezuela can command, its economic interdependence with the United States, and the U.S. response to Venezuela's challenge. For most of the Bush years, these factors tilted in Venezuela's favor. Resentment and insecurity bred potential allies with whom it could coordinate its soft balancing actions. The financial and political resources derived from oil helped Caracas leverage those concerns into informal ententes and concrete institutions. Economic interdependence (Venezuela exports 60 percent of its oil to the United States, accounting for 15 percent of total U.S. oil imports) limited the prospects of Washington employing military force against Caracas, despite its provocations. And through the first part of Bush's second administration, the clumsy U.S. responses to Venezuela—support for the failed coup, the proposed OAS democracy monitoring project, and the unrealized Paraguayan-Peruvian-American military alliance—merely helped Caracas make its anti-American case.

Except for bilateral economic interdependence, however, none of the factors that facilitated Venezuela's policy successes should be considered a constant in the short to medium term. Resentment toward the United

States—always more than a product of historic U.S.-Latin American tensions—has surged or fallen in response to contemporary U.S. policies. Thus, anti-Americanism rose sharply across most of Latin America after the onset of the Iraq War, but has declined more recently. Similarly, the rise of world oil prices between 2001 and 2007 inflated Venezuela's resource base handsomely; but its oil revenues have dropped since petroleum prices began falling in 2007, and the 2008–2009 global economic crisis further dampened demand in oil consuming countries. In short, this variability leaves Venezuelan policy subject to some external limitations.

Might the presidency of Barack Obama and the promise of less unilateral U.S. foreign policy produce warmer U.S.-Venezuelan relations? Probably not soon. True, Obama pledged to take American foreign policy in a different direction—one premised on engagement, multilateralism, and adherence to international norms of conduct. His administration quickly sought to reverse two highly controversial Bush policies (Guantánamo, torture). It did not try to block an OAS effort that Venezuela supported to rescind the 1962 resolution that cost Cuba its OAS membership. It also condemned the 2009 coup against Honduran president José Manuel Zelaya (an ALBA advocate), called for his reinstatement, and levied sanctions on the post-coup government. Both the administration's general philosophy and specific policy stances signal the possibility of warmer ties.

Yet, more cordial bilateral relations or an end to Venezuela's multipolarity enterprise seem unlikely. The latter seems poised to continue not because of any real security threats from the Obama White House, but simply because Caracas is already well invested financially and politically in its multipolarity project (which, in some ways, has become Venezuela's signature foreign policy item). These sunk costs provide powerful incentives to maintain policy continuity. Opposition to the United States and its initiatives is unlikely to change much either, based on early evidence. In 2009, Venezuela was quick criticize a Colombia-U.S. agreement that would give American forces access to Colombian military bases, and at the December UN Climate Change Summit in Copenhagen, it rejected U.S.-supported, multilateral climate initiatives and sharply attacked the United States and its president (whom Chávez likened to a warmonger).

What could change, though, is how the Chávez government's policies and diplomatic barbs play outside Venezuela. Because genuine soft balancing is triggered by a hegemonic state's actions and penchant for unilateralism that (at least indirectly) threaten another state's security, the Obama administration's aversion to robust unilateralism could forestall the expansion of Venezuela's regional, informal ententes. Moreover, because the new

U.S. administration is harder to caricature than its predecessor and seems less prone to rise to Caracas' verbal taunts, it is likely to be a less useful political foil. Yes, wild allegations against the Obama administration might still resonate with Chávez's domestic loyalists, but they also are more likely to be seen in most other Latin American countries as a contrivance.

For the time being, a useful approach for the United States to adopt toward Venezuela would be simply to ignore Caracas' verbal outbursts (which may not always be easy), deal with Venezuela on issues of common interest, and work toward resolving one or two high-profile, regional issues that would enhance its regard among other Latin American states. Rescinding the ineffective economic embargo against Cuba, for example, would bring the United States back in line with its hemispheric neighbors and send a powerful signal that Washington was attentive to their concerns. Reforming U.S. immigration policy would also be quite well received (especially in the Caribbean, Central America, Colombia, and Mexico). To be sure, progress on these fronts would be difficult due to U.S. domestic political factors; but successful policy shifts on either one would help blunt Venezuela's anti-American campaign, deflate its momentum, and bolster the U.S. image across the region.

## Endnotes

1. Weinstein, "Intelligence Brief: Rumsfeld Visits Paraguay and Peru"; Bachelet, "Washington: Cuba, Venezuela Not Helping in War on Terrorism"; Bright, "US Slaps Arms Sale Ban on Venezuela."

2. Such personalization is evident whether the analyses seem favorably disposed toward Chávez or not. See, for example, Ellner, "Venezuela: Defying Globalization's Logic"; and Shifter, "In Search of Hugo Chávez." Only rarely have analysts examined Venezuela's foreign policy through an international relations lens. For example, see Corrales, "Using Social Power to Balance Soft Power: Venezuela's Foreign Policy."

3. A revolution denotes a rapid transformation of a country's basic economic, political, and social institutions, and revolutionary foreign policies are designed to effect such changes. To date, Venezuela's foreign policy falls quite short of seeking such wholesale transformations in most countries with which it interacts.

4. Walt, *Taming American Power*, 31–37; Mandelbaum, *The Case for Goliath*.

5. Although Venezuela's arms purchases from Russia (ostensibly to defend against a potential U.S. invasion) do constitute traditional balancing, it is hardly robust. On the general lack of hard balancing against the United States, see Lieber and Alexander, "Waiting for Balancing."

6. Paul, "Soft Balancing in the Age of U.S. Primacy"; Pape, "Soft Balancing against the United States"; Joffe, "Defying History and Theory: The United States as the "Last Superpower"; and Walt, "Keeping the World 'Off Balance': Self-restraint in U.S. Foreign Policy."

7. Pape, "Soft Balancing against the United States," 36–37.
8. Paul, "The Enduring Axioms of Balance of Power Theory"; Paul, "Soft Balancing in the Age of U.S. Primacy"; Pape, "Soft Balancing against the United States"; and Joffe, "Defying History and Theory."
9. Brooks and Wohlforth, "Hard Times for Soft Balancing," 76.
10. Ibid., 78.
11. Ibid., 82, 84.
12. Ibid., 80.
13. For information on ALBA see its principal web site at http://www.alternativabolivariana.org.
14. Collins, "Breaking the Mold? Venezuela's Defiance of the Neoliberal Model," 392.
15. Brazil signaled its interest in the alliance in 2004, but has yet to ratify its participation; Argentina and Venezuela became founding signatories in September 2004.
16. The Caribbean states are Antigua and Barbuda, the Bahamas, Belize, Cuba, Dominica, the Dominican Republic, Grenada, Guyana, Haiti, Jamaica, Suriname, St. Lucia, St. Kitts and Nevis, and St. Vincent and the Grenadines. Petrocaribe's pricing formula works on a sliding scale that reflects global oil prices. When oil prices exceed $50/bl, member states pay 60 percent of that price (the remaining 40 percent becomes a 2-year, 1 percent interest loan), and if prices exceed $100/bl, they would pay 50 percent of the market price with the remaining 50 percent converting to long-term loans.
17. Owing to infrastructure gaps in the Caribbean states, the energy agreements brokered between Caracas and Petrocaribe members permit some private firm participation, but limit that participation solely to "the necessary logistics" required to "physically move the volumes of hydrocarbons purchased" for internal consumption. However, under Petrocaribe, even this limited private sector participation will end as Venezuela upgrades the infrastructure of member states. See Article II of the *Energy Co-Operation Agreement Petrocaribe Between the Government of the Bolivarian Republic of Venezuela and the Government of Jamaica*, August 23, 2005.
18. The members are Bolivia, Colombia, Ecuador, Peru, and Venezuela.
19. See "Uribe, Torrijos y Chávez inician construcción de gasoducto transcaribeño," July 7, 2006, retrieved from: telesur.net; "Venezuela, Colombia, start building gas pipeline," July 8, 2006, retrieved from: http://money.cnn.com/2006/07/08/news/venezgas_reut/index.htm; and Mather, "Venezuela and Ecuador Sign Energy Agreements," January 17, 2007, retrieved from: http://www.venezuelanalysis.com/news/2180.
20. "Rendering Account," *The New PDVSA Contact*, 5.
21. Reel, "A Latin American Pipe Dream," A 24; "Bolivia, Paraguay y Uruguay se suman al Gran Gasoducto del Sur," July 21, 2006, retrieved from: http://www.pdvsa.com/index.php?tpl=interface.sp/design/salaprensa/readnew.tpl.html&newsid_obj_id=2835&newsid_temas=1.

22. Ecuador bought into Telesur in August 2007. "Ecuador Signs Deal with Venezuela's Telesur Network, Acquires 5 Percent."

23. Petrich, "Alistan *proyecto contrahegemónico* de televisión que sea opción real en AL."

24. According to Andrés Izarra, Telesur President and Venezuela's former Minister of Communication and Information, Latin American governments created Telesur "to integrate through communication the different countries of the region. It's a window, so we can get to know each other better." See Bruce, "Venezuela Sets up 'CNN Rival.'"

25. Adams, "Latin America's Balanced/Biased Voice"; Kirk, "Media-Latin America: Telesur Goes on the Air Under Fire from US."

26. Quoted in Copley, "Telesur Is Constructing Another View."

27. By presenting news "from an Arab perspective"—especially during the run-up to, and prosecution of, the Iraq war—Al Jazeera earned a credibility that eluded Western media. Ultimately, it dethroned U.S. and other Western media outlets as the primary source of "official" news for its 35 million viewers. Venezuela and other Latin American states seek the same type of credibility for Telesur. See Seib, "Hegemonic No More," 602–604.

28. Dos Reis, "The Al Jazeera of the South."

29. Vaky and Muñoz, *The Future of the Organization of American States*, 9–10.

30. For example, during the 1979 Nicaraguan Revolution the OAS refused a U.S. proposal to authorize sending a multilateral peacekeeping force to restore order and create a mission that would negotiate a political transition from the dictatorship of Anastasio Somoza to a new government. See Muñoz, "The Rise and Decline of the Inter-American System: A Latin American View," 31.

31. By contrast, Colombia did not support the coup but it did give Pedro Carmona—the businessman who briefly took power while Chávez was under military detention—temporary asylum until he fled to Miami.

32. Haiti, Petrocaribe's fourteenth member, did not join the alliance until May 2006. Caribbeannetnews.com, "Chile leads race for OAS top post with backing from 11 CARICOM members," April 4, 2005, retrieved from: http://www.caribbeannetnews.com/cgi-bin/GPrint2002.pl?file+2005–04–04/oas.shtml.

33. Sheridan, "In OAS Election, U.S. Favorite Bows Out," A23.

34. Bachelet, "OAS Leader Charts an Independent Course."

35. Gindin, "Whose Democracy? Venezuela Stymies U.S. (Again)."

36. Sojo, "Venezuela, OAS Countries Reject US Proposal to Monitor Democracies."

37. Gindin, "Latin America Defies US Over Venezuela at OAS."

38. Brinkley, "Latin States Shun U.S. Plan to Watch Over Democracy," 8.

39. So said Roger Noriega, Assistant Secretary of State for Western Hemisphere Affairs, and the proposal's chief architect. Brinkley, "U.S. Proposal in the O.A.S. Draws Fire as an Attack on Venezuela."

40. Ibid.

41. "Rice, Chávez Clash as OAS Meeting Opens."

42. Gregory Wilpert, "Venezuela Hails OAS Meeting As Great Success."

43. Chávez, "Capitalism Is Savagery."
44. Phillips, "U.S. Power and the Politics of Economic Governance in the Americas."
45. "Palabras del presidente de la República Argentina, Dr. Nestor Kirchner durante la inauguracion de la IV Cumbre de las Americas, en Mar del Plata."
46. Upon his arrival in Argentina, Chávez told the international press that he had come to the summit "to bury the FTAA," and was "determined to defeat neo-liberalism"; later during a speech at the alternative People's Summit, he charged activists with "a double task: bury [the FTAA] and...be the initiators of a new time, the initiators of a new history, the initiators of ALBA...for the peoples of the Americas, a real liberating integration, for liberty, for equality, for justice and for peace." See Gregory Wilpert, "Chávez Says Americas Summit Will Serve to Bury FTAA"; and Fuentes, "Argentina: A President, A Soccer Star, and the Dreams of Millions."
47. See Charles and Bachelet, "Venezuela Gets Backing for U.N. Council Seat"; and "Venezuela's Candidacy for the UN Security Council Appears on Track."
48. On the anti-Venezuela lobbying campaign by the United States, see CNN News, "U.S. Opposes Venezuela Bid for U.N. Council Seat." On Chávez's "devil speech," see CNN News, "Chávez: Bush 'devil'; U.S. 'on the way down.'"
49. Rohter, "A Man with Big Ideas, a Small Country . . . and Oil."
50. Brooks and Wohlforth, "Hard Times for Soft Balancing."
51. See, for example, Corrales, "Looking for an Alternative Market for Venezuelan Oil: Will China Help?"
52. At both the 2005 and 2006 World Social Forums (hosted in Brazil and Venezuela respectively), Chávez used the occasion to denounce the Free Trade Agreement of the Americas (and U.S. "imperialism" in general), and rally participants behind a drive to promote a multipolar world order. See Sojo, "Venezuela's Chávez Closes World Social Forum with Call to Transcend Capitalism"; and Hernández Navarro, "Caracas: Sixth World Social Forum."
53. The Bank of the South began with a $2 billion Venezuelan-Argentine Bond of the South initiative in July 2006; the same month Mercosur formally endorsed creating a Bank of the South. By October 2007, Bolivia, Ecuador, Paraguay, and Uruguay had endorsed the project explicitly, while Brazil and Colombia had done so implicitly. See Hearn, "S. American Nations Eye Alternative to IMF"; Harvey, "The Fifth Element: A South American Trade Bloc Shifts Left as Venezuela Becomes Its Fifth Member State"; Barrionuevo, "Chávez's Plan for Development Bank Moves Ahead"; and "Bank of the South Opening Delayed until December," *MercoPress*, October 26, 2007, retrieved from: http://www.mercopress.com/vernoticia.do?id=11727&formato=HTML.

# Conclusion: The Conceptual Revolution in Venezuela

*Thomas Ponniah*

> *Overcoming injustice means dismantling institutionalized obstacles that prevent some people from participating on a par with others, as full partners in social interaction.*
>
> —Nancy Fraser

## Introduction

Perceptions of the Chávez government tend to the Manichaean, with the president seen by some as the shining knight of twenty-first century socialism, and by others as an avenging Stalinist *caudillo*.[1] Despite the passion on different sides of the divide, the overall Bolivarian process, as the essays in this volume demonstrate, will not be captured by one interpretation or ideology, nor can it easily be placed in a seamless fable of emancipatory or authoritarian history. "El Proceso" is an impermanent blend of antinomies that resists monolithic narration[2]; some ardently contend that the government is increasingly autocratic, and from this perspective, the steady augmentation of state control over the economy and society presage a dictatorship.[3] Others fervently state that the government is more committed to economic redistribution than any administration before it—pointing to the numerous policies implemented over the last decade. As the diversity of viewpoints in this volume makes evident, the Bolivarian process embodies both centralized forms of decision-making and socially egalitarian courses of action. However, if we approach the analysis from a third lens, we see something quite novel that transcends standard left-right distinctions: the process constitutes a conceptual revolution in the categories by which social change, development, and modernity have been traditionally understood. The revolution in Venezuela, at its most experimental, is a transformation of the standard discourse: from a unidimensional focus on "socialism versus capitalism" to a multidimensional project anchored in participatory democracy.

In this volume various authors have considered the nature of social change across a number of domains in contemporary Venezuela. The first four chapters cover political conflict, culture, and contestation during the

Chávez years, revealing a diversity of views about the forms of contention over the last decade. The initial essay, by Fernando Coronil, situates the Bolivarian Revolution in its broader sociocultural context, examining the relationship between the state's social body (its population) and its natural body (its oil reserves), demonstrating how the interaction between the two potentially allows the state to renew its legitimacy. The author also describes the coup d'état, the "coup within a coup," and the crucial civil society mobilization that occurred between April 11–14, 2002, which allowed Chávez to return to power. The second essay, by Javier Corrales, describes some of the reasons for Venezuela's political polarization; rather than focus on structural factors, Corrales looks at the Chávez government's strategic intentions in fomenting political polarization, noting that intentionally produced divisions can lead to favorable electoral results for the incumbent. The next piece, by Gregory Wilpert, takes an opposing view of political polarization, pointing to the obduracy of the opposition as the source of the country's political divisions. As well, Wilpert contends that the government's commitment to participatory democracy is a more profound reflection of the government's intentions than are any of its centralist actions. The chapter by Margarita López-Maya and Luis Lander analyzes Chávez's decisive victory in the 2006 electoral campaign and his subsequent loss in the 2007 constitutional reform proposal. The authors significantly note the shift in the opposition's tactics: prior to 2006, large and loud parts of the opposition appeared to favor extra-legal strategies; however, this changed to a concentration on electoral politics.

The second set of chapters focuses on specific features and projects of the Chávez government, in which, according to the government's supporters, great changes have been made: gender relations, poverty reduction, public health, and foreign affairs. In their chapter, Cathy Rakowski and Gioconda Espina note the complexities underlying the successes of the Chávez government's gender policies; they point out that while the Bolivarian process has moved an anti-sexist agenda forward, it has marginalized many of the civil society actors who initially proposed these projects in the years prior to Chávez's 1998 election. Notably, they also highlight that there is in some cases a gap between symbolic declarations and concrete results. In the next essay Mark Weisbrot examines the government's economic decisions, demonstrating Venezuela's impressive economic performance beginning in 2003 and arguing that the crisis of 2009–2010 is not an indication of the weaknesses of the government's policies. In addition, Weisbrot highlights the innovative international economic alternatives that the government has proposed, documenting the effectiveness of its efforts at poverty reduction. Following his analysis, Muntaner, Chung, Mahmood, and Armada note that the Bolivarian solution to the public health dilemmas produced by neoliberalism has substantially improved the country's overall well-being. Last, Mark Williams examines the government's international political strategies, noting that they are not random, impulsive, or irrational, but instead follow a "soft balancing" strategy that aims to produce a multipolar world. On the one hand, if successful, this would involve an important transformation of the geopolitical order, yet on the other hand, as Williams stresses, it is "revolutionary" neither in methods or goals. Together, the various chapters embody many of the diverse political positions and interpretations concerning the nature of the social transformation that is taking place in Venezuela. The picture they reveal is one of considerable change but not a clear revolution in the traditional sense. Rather, as I have suggested, they give evidence of the possibility that the Chávez government may be advancing a "revolution" of the conception of development. I will utilize various ideas from the different chapters to propose that the government, at its most innovative, is pushing forward a novel discursive revision of how we imagine progress, development, and modernity.

As mentioned in the Introduction, the government's practice does not fit the standard social science definitions of revolution.[4] Nor could the Bolivarian process be simply equated with a state-led "revolution from above," along the lines of Egypt under Nasser, Turkey under Ataturk, or Peru under Velasco. If there is a revolution in Venezuela, it is first a conceptual one in our thinking about development. The Bolivarian discourse is oriented to a multidimensional paradigm that embodies an inventive re-articulation of the discourse of social change. This new narrative unifies three leftist agendas concerning redistribution, recognition, and representation.[5] This novel synthesis is having a catalytic impact on individuals, social movements, political parties, and practitioners across Latin America.

Social theorist Richard Peet has noted that the development process, in its broadest sense, aims to build another, better world for all, especially the most marginalized.[6] Such a project necessarily involves an attempt to make sense of social life; Charles Taylor has argued that "making sense" intrinsically involves an orientation of the self in relation to some idea of what is "the good." The value horizons within which we live include strong qualitative discriminations, that is, moral frameworks that anchor our conception of progress.[7] There are numerous principles to which we aspire, such as "equality," "non-discrimination," and "freedom of assembly"; these values are standpoints from which we weigh, judge, and decide other ones.[8] Revised versions of these principles now guide Venezuela's attempt at unraveling various forms of social stratification. While past generations of progressives have placed primary emphasis on income distribution or cultural status as driving mechanisms for social change, the Bolivarian process emphasizes an experimental concept of reform that includes past goals tethered to class and identity, as well as new ones focused on democracy.

Alternatives to the dominant conceptions of development and modernity have generally been aligned with class or income redistribution. Prominent themes concern the issues of poverty alleviation, resource redistribution, and reducing economic inequality.[9]

## Class and Redistribution

As Laclau and Mouffe point out, political movements are never one-dimensional, but braid together numerous concerns into a chain of equivalence that links their various interests via one overarching theme.[10] While redistribution was certainly not the only goal of leftist states—many aimed at transforming cultural and political relations as well—economic change was generally their primary aspiration. At its most apparent level the question of redistribution is: how can we ensure that every citizen has equal capacity to intervene in social life when there are significant income differentials between various groups in society?[11] Jorge Castañeda has noted that Venezuela's poverty rate tripled from the 1970s to the 1990s, while Latin America has become the world's most unequal region in terms of income.[12] In such a context development policy makers in the region and elsewhere have inquired: how do we transform societies that are profoundly economically stratified?

In terms of this first dimension of development, theorists and policy makers over the last generation have debated the role of state versus market-oriented development. The dominant trend has emphasized the role of market-led economic growth as the solution to the problems of poverty, inequality, and unemployment. These analysts argue that the level of economic output has to increase in order to have enough goods to redistribute. Advocates of the unregulated market have claimed that state intervention distorts market activity and therefore impedes the full potential of the market to create greater prosperity for all.[13] Despite some countervailing processes, the overriding tendency of development policy makers at the IMF and the World Bank has been to advocate for substantial reduction of protectionism in all sectors.[14] In contrast, other policy makers have disagreed with such neoliberal policies, proposing instead that various forms of state planning will encourage growth and re-allocation:[15] state-led redistribution has been the principal strategy for left-oriented conceptions of development, whether social democratic, communist, or national liberationist, throughout the twentieth century.[16] Social democrats and welfare state liberals emphasized an incremental approach to redistribution, whereas radicals aimed at a revolutionary transformation of economic production and allocation. In each case the state was the pivotal agent—thus it is not surprising that recent leftist governments in Latin America have called for a more equitable allotment of resources via government intervention.

Venezuela is the most prominent contemporary example of a Latin American call for state-driven re-allocation, and it has delivered substantial poverty reduction since Chávez entered power in 1998.[17] The government has, over the last decade, presented the public with an avalanche of concepts, statements, and policies;[18] some of these proposals have been ephemeral, but one constant principle has been a focus on poverty alleviation. As Mark Weisbrot observes in his chapter in this volume, the country in 1998 had a poverty rate of 60.9 percent.[19] The Venezuelan government has tried to redistribute resources via a number of means: as several chapters here have demonstrated, a key strategy to reduce poverty has been through the *misiones*. As Muntaner, Chung, Mahmood, and Armada point out, these missions are "social programs created as parallel structures either completely outside the scope of government ministries, or in collaboration with them, as a means to increase community participation and meet the new constitutional imperatives more efficiently."[20] For example, the Mercal mission is a network of places for the distribution of food and other basic consumer items; these markets, located in poorer areas, sell basic foods such as rice, beans, and milk substantially cheaper than the typical commercial food chain would. The Mercal program serves over half of the Venezuelan population.[21] Along with this program, another way that the government has tried to redistribute resources is via the Barrio Adentro ("Inside the Neighborhood) mission, which offers on-site free health services that include medicine, house calls, and 24-hour services.[22] Many of the poor are receiving free medical care for the first time.[23] Over this time period, according to Weisbrot, the poverty rate dropped from 60.9 percent in 1997 to 23.8 percent in 2009;[24] extreme poverty meanwhile dropped from 29.5 percent in the first half of 1997 to 5.9 percent in 2009.[25] Consistent with the above, Lopez-Maya and Lander point out in their chapter that the Human Development Index (the UN composite measure which combines statistics on life expectancy, adult literacy rate, educational enrolment, and GDP per capita) has advanced to a high level of development in Venezuela.[26] The country has demonstrated an impressive decrease in poverty and increase in human development over the last decade.

What has been intriguing about this version of state-led development is that it has placed prominent conceptual emphasis on public participation. Article 62 of the 1999 Constitution states:

> The participation of the people in forming, carrying out and controlling the management of public affairs is the necessary way of achieving the involvement to ensure their complete development, both individual and collective. It is the obligation of the State and the duty of society to facilitate the generation of optimum conditions for putting this into practice.[27]

Supporters of the government refer to Venezuela's political system as a "participatory democracy."[28] The government has tried to involve the public in decision-making. For example, for the redistribution of rural and urban land, citizens are encouraged to form committees that help governmental institutions measure land that is to be redistributed and decide how plots are allotted.[29] Similarly, Caracas' water company, Hidrocapital, has encouraged communities to set up "technical water committees" that help the water company determine where there is a need to improve service and how best to organize it. As a result of this community consultation process, it was possible, according to government statistics, for the water company to significantly expand its service from 60% of the population to over 90% in six years.[30] Other remarkable examples of community involvement in public services have been, as Muntaner, Chung, Mahmood, and Armada point out, the seven thousand health committees that have helped shape the Barrio Adentro program, which provides "continuous, free, high quality, community-defined health care to the 70% of Venezuelans who previously had no access at all."

This emphasis on participation, meaning the creation of a democracy that is more direct, self-representative, and expressive has been popular in Venezuela. The Bolivarians' implicit underlying theory is that in a participatory society individuals can represent themselves more completely when they are both personally and collectively involved in building a society that is an organic whole rather than simply an aggregate of atomized spectators. The call for novel forms of self-representation expresses a desire for a society that enriches the quality of democracy while augmenting its compass of intervention. The explicit argument is that this modality is in contrast to a strictly representative democracy in which citizens are represented by often distant others. The demand for greater deliberation is not simply, as with past statist interventions, a response to the perception of a neoliberal system as a volatile, indifferent market that could be improved by a rationally planned economy. This desire also emerges from contemporary leftist criticism of past statist projects such as the welfare state, the Soviet Union, and Third World national liberation projects:[31] the unintended consequences of centralized planning undermined past revolutionaries' anticipated goals. Hence the Bolivarians are not only critics of right-wing neoliberalism but also of traditional left-wing statism: the government aspires to a new type of democratized administration that relies on the public's information, experience, and insight.[32]

This unprecedented focus on deliberation has been expressed by the call for regular participation and numerous referenda. The Chávez government has, to the time of this writing, gone to the public eleven times for elections and referenda, winning all except for the 2007 constitutional referendum. Regular consultation has been welcomed by the public: as Gregory Wilpert notes in the conclusion to his chapter, studies by the polling agency Latino-barómetro show that the appreciation for Venezuelan democracy has grown in Venezuela to a larger extent than in any other country in the Americas in recent years. In Latin America, Venezuelans are a population that has on the whole grown increasingly more satisfied with its democracy.[33]

To summarize, the first obvious development commitment in Venezuela is to dismantle inequality via the redistribution of resources. What is striking about this emphasis is that it proposes a participatory democracy as an integral factor for genuine equitable allocation to take place. Thus Venezuela is an example of a novel type of state-driven development vision that includes new forms of political representation as a means to genuine redistribution. Most of the progressive governments in Latin America are state-driven, redistribution-oriented, and emphasize citizen deliberation, but Venezuela has gone farthest along this trajectory.

Numerous criticisms can be made of the Bolivarian government's economic project. The government's management has been inconsistent and often inefficient[34]: while government policy has generally produced high economic growth that reduces poverty and unemployment, it is not clear that the growth is sustainable. Oil dependency, as Karl contends, leads to a "paradox of plenty" that has never produced a durable development project.[35] Imposing Karl's analysis onto Venezuela suggests that the increase in social spending could simply be a transitory reflection of the growth in oil prices.[36] The current levels of social investment could be a repetition of the state redistribution enacted during the last major oil boom under the first Carlos Andrés Pérez government (1974–79). The government's programs have been financed by exceptionally high income; the new improved capacity to access oil in the Orinoco basin does herald the possibility of even more redistributive options for the state, but without necessarily being a more sustainable re-allocation.[37]

## Status and Recognition

One of the major theoretical criticisms of the economic redistribution model in more general terms, often advanced by post-modern and post-developmental theorists, has come from the vantage point of questions of identity.[38] Economic growth does not necessarily transform status relations such as those existing around race, ethnicity, gender, or sexuality; therefore some have contended that attempts at social change should place primacy, or at least equal emphasis, on the politics of difference. Correspondingly, the second dimension within the Bolivarian development vision consists of questions of status, identity, and recognition. The challenge of status is: how can everyone in society be able to intervene with equal capacity when there are such significant differentials in the recognition that we allot to different identities in society? Critics of development over the past generation have argued that the emphasis on economic redistribution, by either advocates of the market or the state, has ignored the crucial role that identity and diversity play in society.[39] Economic re-allocation does not end discrimination; redistribution does not end the identity hierarchies that place indigenous groups at a lower rung on the status ladder throughout the Americas.[40] Chávez himself, citing the United Nations, has noted that 70% of impoverished people are women and children.[41] Rather than a horizontal diversity, critics of standard development claim that we have a vertical mosaic with some identities at the highest rung and others at the lowest. An example of the government's emphasis on the question of recognition is the issue of gender equality:[42] as numerous writers over the past generation have noted, women's experience and knowledge have been historically devalued.[43]

Political philosopher Nancy Fraser has contended that advocates of cultural diversity implicitly begin from the proposition that our identity is developed in interaction with others.[44] Our self-esteem is constructed in relation to receiving acknowledgment from others and providing recognition to them; therefore if members of a group are regularly presented with negative images of themselves, then their self-esteem suffers. Non-recognition, or mis-recognition, produces psychological injury: one's self-perception becomes distorted. A number of social movements have countered cultural discrimination by calling for collective celebration of one's identity with other members of one's group.[45] Such affirmation is meant to produce a new recognition from others within the group and from people outside the group.

This logic has underpinned the call for transformation of the identity hierarchies that dominate the Americas—if not the rest of the world.

Implicit in the emphasis on diversity is the understanding that the lack of recognition for many groups is a form of social domination; that is to say, cultural discrimination does not simply encourage groups to devalue themselves but prevents them from participating as equals in social life.[46] Therefore the solution to the problem of discrimination is not simply cultural affirmation, but a strategy of facilitating each person's entry into society as a citizen with equal rights. To be mis-recognized in society is not simply to be perceived negatively, as unworthy of esteem, but for that perception to be institutionalized such that one is denied full voice as a member of society.[47] In order for groups to achieve full recognition from the self and from others, civil society actors maintain that there is a need to establish a system in which all actors can be full partners in social life. Feminists, both within and outside the Bolivarian process, advocate policies that encourage equal participation in all social institutions.[48]

In their chapter, Rakowski and Espina note many progressive changes that the Chávez government has implemented, the most prominent example being the explicitly anti-sexist 1999 constitution. The constitution was the result of cooperation amongst members of the constitutional assembly's Committee on Family and Women, the National Women's Council (Conamu), and women's civil society organizations. The constitutional assembly's committee consulted women from every political sector: legal rights, international agencies, academics, labor unions and small business leaders.[49] The constitution guarantees women's right to work, to health services, to social security and pensions.[50] Most innovatively it recognizes the monetary value of housework by, in principle, supporting housewives' right to pensions.[51]

In the case of women's rights, the Bolivarians are explicit about the need for new forms of democracy as an integral condition for genuine recognition to take place. They insist that marginalized groups have to be able to qualitatively participate in order to create a genuinely fair society. Full respect for diversity will only emerge through an expressive, as opposed to rationalized, democracy. Representative democracy, they contend, is too focused on quantity: the winner is the one who gets the majority of votes every four years; thus such detached, numbers-based democracy contributes to erasing the experience of most of society. Therefore the essential, implicit, message of feminist and progressive civil society conceptions of social change is that decision-making has to be informed by a self-representative, expressive democracy.

While the commitment to more egalitarian gender relations has been impressive, Rakowski and Espina raise some key criticisms. They note that the government has made tremendous discursive advances in terms of women's rights, yet it is not clear which advances have been materially accomplished. As they indicate, while the notion of pensions for house-wives is a pioneering project, there is no proof that any housewives have received them.[52] In addition, while the government has been consulting women's groups, it has also steadily incorporated women's civil society into the state, while taking credit for the policies. Rather than simply frame itself as a vehicle for the struggle for women's rights, the government could be using gender issues as a means toward expanding its control over new sectors of society.

The issue of identity in terms of gender, ethnicity, race, and sexuality has been a key framework for a range of collective mobilizations over the past generation. This second generation of leftists often considered questions of class, but in alignment with issues of diversity. The theory and practice of identity movements has clearly had a significant influence on the Bolivarian conception of an alternative form of development: for example, the planned 2007 constitution contained a reform prohibiting discrimination based on sexual orientation. However, redistribution and recognition are not the only two progressive tendencies that have been incorporated into the Bolivarian proposal for an alternative modernity. There is a new wave of social movements, which have emerged in the era of globalization, that deals with the question of democratizing representation.

## Power and Representation

The most recent criticism of the standard modernist development model has focused on the challenge that political power poses to democracy. The question is: how can everyone in society be equally capable of intervention in social life in light of modern society's representational hierarchies? Some groups' interests are less likely to be politically represented than others. The Bolivarians do not simply criticize neoliberal economics, or the traditional status hierarchies that have devalued the contribution of women or citizens of indigenous or African descent; they also question the system of governance. Rather than see representative democracy, the quintessential institution of political modernity, as a neutral or even progressive form of administration, the advocates of the Bolivarian process hold that Venezuela's traditional form of representative democracy has favored political-economic elites.[53] Thus many of the various functionaries, movements, and individuals that make up the Bolivarian process explicitly state that new, participatory forms of democracy need to have the same weight as representative democracy, or even, in some cases, replace it.[54]

The constitution's "Elucidation of Reasons" for promoting a new politics reads as follows:

> This regulation [in favor of participatory democracy] responds to a felt aspiration of organized civil society that strives to change the political culture, which so many decades of state paternalism and the dominance of party heads generated and that hindered the development of democratic values. In this sense, participation is not limited to electoral processes, since the need for the intervention of the people is recognized in the in the processes of formation, formulation, and execution of public policy, which would result in the overcoming of the governability deficits that have affected our political system due to the lack of harmony between state and society.
>
> To conceive public administration as a process in which a fluid communication between governed and the people is established, implies a modification of the orientation of state-society relations, so as to return to the latter its legitimate protagonism.

Examples of this participatory democracy are referenda, communal councils, cooperatives, forms of social auditing, and the aforementioned inclusion of civil society in state decision-making. We can define these new forms of political representation proposed in the constitution as self-representative for obvious reasons: they are attempts at directly facilitating public input. However, these new forms are also what we would term "expressive" in the Romantic sense of giving individuals the opportunity to collectively articulate their own, original contribution to society.[55] Rather than imagine democracy simply as a rationalized process, the Bolivarians perceive democracy to be an act of human self-fulfillment. Participation in the democratic process enables the citizen to articulate his or her individual and collective political potential: the public is given the opportunity to express its ingenuity in tackling the most important questions that society faces. The implicit philosophical anthropology of Venezuela's participatory democracy is that through the process of public deliberation, each individual becomes an agent, not a spectator, a self-conscious subject, not an instrumentalized object of social life. In the Bolivarian imaginary the relationship of political engagement to "human nature" could be compared to the relationship between language and thought: the former articulates and completes the potential of the latter. Thus, for the revolutionaries in government, "expressive" democracy is essentially a form of interdependent self-realization that incorporates the rational, affective, and inter-subjective character of human experience.

Participatory democracy is not a new or simply Western phenomenon. As John Markoff has noted, democracy has global roots.[56] Participatory democracy's best known European manifestation was the ancient Athenian polis, where every citizen over the age of 18, excluding women and slaves who were not considered citizens, was allowed to participate in directly, democratically debating the city-state's major decisions. The Greek social formation inspired many Enlightenment thinkers as a model of the ideal democratic society, especially because of the "ethical community" exemplified by the polis.[57] The implicit belief of the ethical community was that moral self-determination could only fully manifest itself in political self-government.[58] This conception of the ideal society, often linked to Rousseau, was later picked up by activists in the 1960s, most prominently by Students for a Democratic Society.[59] More recently, new deliberative forms of democracy have emerged again in the consciousness of social movements, such as the example of the city of Porto Alegre in Brazil. Since 1989, Porto Alegre has run an annual participatory budget that takes place over ten months and regularly involves over 10,000 citizens from a city with a population of one million people.[60] The success of this innovative budget process has reactivated the aspiration for citizen-driven governance; Porto Alegre has become a reference point for the newest cycle of leftist social movements—that is, the "global justice" movements that have called for a deeper local and universal democracy.[61]

The most prominent meeting space for social movements committed to the search for alternatives has been the World Social Forum. The Forum has been an annual event that pulls together civil society movements from around the world to debate proposals for an alternative globalization. Anywhere from 20,000 to 150,000 participants have attended each of the Forums.[62] Four of the nine World Social Forums have been held in Porto Alegre, and William Fisher and I have contended that the dominant alternatives proposed at these meetings been novel forms of participatory democratic representation.[63] Porto Alegre and the World Social Forum are the most obvious contemporary influence on the Bolivarian project:[64] it was at the 2005 World Social Forum held in Porto Alegre where Chávez announced that he was pursuing 21st century socialism.[65]

The implicit Bolivarian theory of development suggests that new forms of governance are integral to tackling questions of class and status. The Bolivarians do not interpret redistribution, recognition, and representation as equal, interpenetrating dimensions of an alternative modernity, but instead see the last as the integrative dimension of all three.[66] Thus the significance of the Bolivarian project is not simply, as some suggest, that it represents the immoderate rather than the moderate left[67]; rather, the meaning of the process lies in the reconceptualization of the categories by which we understand what constitutes progress, and thus what could be construed as moderate or immoderate. The Venezuelan government is proposing that new forms of democracy are an integral condition for tackling the obstacles posed by economic, cultural, and political hierarchies; thus social development has to be assessed according to these three elements, with the last being the integral agent. This multidimensional concept of development, this convergence of three leftist discourses, rests not simply on the basis of "needs," but on a reconstruction of how freedom is conceived: for the Bolivarians it is the right to participate in society without being inhibited by obstacles associated with class, status, or power.

As mentioned earlier, the issue of participation in Venezuela has been crucial in terms of ensuring access to water, to land, and to health care. Meanwhile, in terms of gender, there is a fundamental belief that the policies of the past, whether driven by the state or the market, did not allow for the full expression of human experience. In the case of women, for example, individuals should be encouraged to explain their experience and use that knowledge to directly, democratically deliberate on questions of public policy. Whether the focus is on class or status, a new vision of development is emerging. The Bolivarian process is not simply the rebirth of a radical populist left led by a charismatic leader,[68] but—at its most idealistic—it is the eruption of novel, experimental forms of democracy that aspire to facilitate the public's ability to deliberatively regulate market, cultural, and state forces.

The attempt at producing new forms of democracy in order to enhance redistribution, recognition, and representation is genuinely novel. In past decades the call for greater public participation, though not necessarily the practice, has been heard in numerous countries such as Tanzania in the 1970s and Zimbabwe, Mozambique, and Nicaragua during the 1980s. However, the previous goals for participation were not embedded within a three-dimensional development project. None of the earlier projects placed as much emphasis on local autonomy, cultural diversity, and regular referenda; this combination of factors makes the Venezuelan experiment unique.

Yet despite its innovation, numerous critics as well as writers from within the Bolivarian process have noted that the personalist organization of power around the president subverts the government's aspirations to building an engaged democracy.[69] There are many examples of decisions that demonstrate overly centralized governance; one factor that has contradicted the government's aspiration for a new democracy is its carousel of cabinet ministers. Javier Corrales has pointed out, when discussing "power grabs," that while previous governments, from 1959 to 1998, have in total changed cabinet members anywhere from 28 to 90 times, the current one, from 1998–2007, changed ministers 153 times.[70] Although there may have been substantive reasons for replacing each minister at each conjuncture, the overall result is a concentration of institutional memory in the hands of the president, or simply a loss of information leading to institutional inefficiency. This centralization of knowledge and power is a political landmine: it is the central obstacle to the long-term viability of the Bolivarian process. While the process is made up of elites, supporters, and ideologues, it is disproportionately centered on President Chávez. History shows us that a political movement evolves as it is structured: personalist, charismatic governance subverts its own capacity to cultivate democracy.[71] The primary internal restraint to the government's innovative conceptual revolution lies in its inability, or unwillingness, to fully follow its stated commitment to democratizing governance. The perpetual fluidity within the cabinet is symptomatic of a government that is not only propelling a participatory democracy but also advancing a highly centralized, personalized, state apparatus that threatens representative democracy.[72]

## Closing Thoughts

When the supporters and critics of the government argue, with the former affirming that Venezuela's social policy is substantial and the quasi-authoritarianism superficial, while the latter claim the exact opposite, we are faced with a phenomenon that defies an unequivocal analysis. The advocates contend that the wealth of the country is being used to implement a radical democratization, whereas the opponents maintain that it is being used to dismantle representative democracy. This political debate has a historical scholarly analogue with those who argue that the discourse of participation is often one aspect of an overall "governmentality," that is, a strategy of increasing state control over more spheres of society.[73] In this case, the reasons proffered by the government could be interpreted as disingenuous claims that ultimately legitimate state expansion by means of a sophisticated form of clientelism. Jennifer McCoy, among numerous others, has noted that participatory democracy is actually leading to the unraveling of representative democracy: the government's imposition of a new democracy is reducing the pluralism of political debate because of its erosion of the separation of powers.[74] The Venezuelan government thus clearly provokes understandable criticism. Both its supporters and its opponents point to the two elephants in the room in any discussion of the Bolivarian process: detractors rightly criticize the quasi-authoritarianism of the government with infamous internal and external examples such as "la Lista Tascón"[75] and the decision to embrace the nefarious Ahmadjinedad of Iran; meanwhile, advocates reply that an autocratic government would not have instituted numerous democratic experiments over the last decade, nor respected the result of the 2007 constitutional referendum. In such a context, where the contest is as much over truth as it is of politics, the challenge for the analyst is not simply to denounce or defend but to document the coexistence, even complementarity, of antagonistic interpretations of the Chávez presidency.

While the Bolivarian discourse is lofty, the practice is less pristine: it is veined with destabilizing contradictions, making the future uncertain. The process may follow the historical pattern once discerned by Hegel, namely, that the political process that embodies a new universal impulse often perishes while its principle persists.[76] As the Bolivarians' institutional project ebbs and flows, the conceptual innovation spreads, rippling throughout Latin America and further. The aspiration for an alternative form of development in which humanity deliberatively, directly, and democratically shapes society, is spilling across the borders of Venezuela through the continent and across global civil society. Thus while the future of the national process is unclear, the principle elaborated by the Chávez government is helping articulate a new Latin American left. The concept of an expressive, multidimensional project— the real meaning of the phrase "21st century socialism"—is helping inform a new generation of political parties and social movements.[77] The dream of a participatory democracy is the seed of an alternative modernity even if the prospects of its most prominent advocate, the Chávez government, rest imperiled not only by relentless external forces but also by its own evident internal contradictions.[78] Whether this vision is generalizable, that is, whether other governments can implement this newest left discourse while lacking the prodigious oil supplies that have always funded Venezuela's "magical state,"[79] is a question whose answer perhaps best lies in Antonio Gramsci's famous epigram about the optimism of the will in the context of the pessimism of the intellect.

In his chapter, Mark Eric Williams concludes by making a number of notable suggestions for future U.S. administrations to adopt when dealing with the left in Latin America.[80] We can add that global development institutions that wish to remain relevant—such as the International Monetary Fund, the World Bank, and the World Trade Organization—need to be reinvented. The lesson from the past decade in Venezuela is that the key to being effective lies in conceiving of development as a participatory process that has to take account of economic redistribution, cultural recognition, and political representation. Empowering the citizenry's capacity to directly, locally, and consistently influence the direction of the state, social relations, and the market may be the key to revitalizing development. The global governance institutions need to learn from the conceptual revolution in Venezuela, to re-imagine progress as an expressive, publicly driven process rather than one that is primarily determined by economic, cultural, political, or personalist elites.

## Endnotes

1. Thanks to Jon Eastwood, Merilee Grindle, Steve Levitsky, Richard Tuck, Richard Peet, Robert Ross, Fernando Coronil and a number of anonymous reviewers for their helpful comments.

2. My analysis builds on the analytic paradigms found in Nancy Fraser's "Reframing Justice in a Globalizing World" and Max Weber's "Class, Status and Party." The epigraph of this Conclusion is found in the above Fraser article. Unlike Fraser and Weber, my analysis goes beyond the social and adds an explicit expressivist philosophical anthropology to the argument.

3. One of the best known articles advancing the "authoritarianism" reading of Chávez is Corrales' "Hugo Boss." Another interesting essay along these lines is by Corrales and Penfold, "Venezuela: Crowding out the Opposition." For further discussion of authoritarianism see Levitsky and Way "The Rise of Competitive Authoritarianism."

4. Skocpol, "Explaining Social Revolutions: First and Further Thoughts."

5. I define the left, according to Bobbio's definition, as committed to egalitarianism. Dr. Bobbio defines the right as committed to inequality or hierarchy. I would suggest that the right is committed to social cohesion and therefore will often defend traditional hierarchical institutions. See Bobbio, *Left and Right: The Significance of a Political Distinction.*

6. Peet with Hartwick, *Theories of Development.*

7. Taylor, *Sources of the Self.*

8. Ibid, 63.

9. Peet with Hartwick, *Theories of Development.*

10. Laclau and Mouffe, *Hegemony and Socialist Strategy,* vii-xix.

11. For research that looks at how Venezuelan class relations shape political narratives, see Cannon, "Venezuela, April 2002: Coup or Popular Rebellion? The Myth of a United Venezuela." For substantial discussion on the question of capability see Sen, *Development as Freedom.*

12. http://www.foreignaffairs.org/20060501faessay85302/jorge-g-castaneda/latin-america-s-left-turn.html. (Site visited on April 4, 2008). For another explanation

for the rise of the left in Latin America, see Foster, "The Latin American Revolt: An Introduction."

13. For the best known pro-market position, see von Hayek, *The Road to Serfdom.*

14. For example, see the Muntaner, Chung, Mahmood and Armada's chapter on the World Bank's position on the privatization of health care. This dominant trend has contained countermovements within it: business interests in Southern countries may be structurally predisposed to support protectionism if they are in a fixed-asset, non-internationally competitive sector or if they prioritize access to the state in terms government contracts—especially in a context where they distrust the opposition.

15. For a definition of neoliberalism I use MacEwan, *Neo-liberalism or Democracy?* 4: "The policy calls for reducing the economic roles of government in providing social welfare, in managing economic activity at the aggregate and sectoral levels, and in regulating international commerce. The ideas at the foundation of this policy are not new. They come directly from the classical economic liberalism that emerged in the nineteenth century and they proclaimed 'the market' as the proper guiding instrument by which people should organize their economic lives. As a new incarnation of these old ideas, this ascendant economic policy is generally called 'neo-liberalism.'"

16. See Polanyi, *The Great Transformation;* Prebisch, *International Economics and Development;* and Stiglitz, *Globalization and Its Discontents.*

17. See Weisbrot, "Poverty Reduction in Venezuela: a Reality-Based View?"

18. I am indebted to Gerver Torres for this phrase.

19. See Weisbrot's chapter in this volume.

20. See Muntaner, Chung, Mahmood and Armada's in this volume.

21. See Weisbrot's chapter in this volume for Mercal statistics.

22. See Muntaner, Chung, Mahmood, and Armada's chapter.

23. For an analysis of the proposals advanced by the health sector in Venezuela during the framing of the 1999 Constitution, see Feo and Siquiera, "An Alternative to the Neoliberal Model in Health: The Case of Venezuela."

24. See Weisbrot's chapter.

25. For an interesting discussion concerning the government's commitment to poverty alleviation, see the debate between Francisco Rodríguez and Mark Weisbrot. See Rodríguez, "An Empty Revolution" and "How Not to Defend the Revolution: Mark Weisbrot and the Misinterpretation on Venezuelan Evidence." Weisbrot, "An Empty Research Agenda: The Creation of Myths About Contemporary Venezuela" and "How Not to Attack An Economist (and An Economy): Getting the Numbers Right."

26. See López-Maya's chapter in this book.

27. Quoted in Wilpert's chapter in this volume.

28. Ibid.

29. For more information on the urban land committees, see Wilpert, *Changing Venezuela by Taking Power: The History and Policies of the Chávez Government.*

30. Kuiper and Wilpert, "Interview with Jacqueline Faria, Minister for the Environment: The Many Tasks of Environmental Protection in Venezuela."

31. For an analysis of the breakdown of these three statist projects, see Wallerstein, *After Liberalism*.

32. For an article that argues that participatory democracy is a key element in the Bolivarian struggle against neoliberalism, see Gibbs "Business as Unusual: What the Chávez Era Tells Us About Democracy Under Globalization." For research on the government's search for an alternative participatory economic model see Parker, "Chávez and the Search for an Alternative to Neoliberalism."

33. See Wilpert's chapter in this book and see http://www.latinobarometro.org/ (site visited April 4, 2008).

34. See Ellner, "Hugo Chávez's First Decade in Office: Breakthroughs and Shortcomings."

35. See Karl, *The Paradox of Plenty: Oil Booms and Petro-States*.

36. For further discussion of this point see López-Maya, "After the Referendum: Reading the Defeat," and Coronil, "Chávez's Venezuela: A New Magical State?"

37. For further research on the relationship between oil and governance, see Daniel Hellinger, "Venezuelan Oil: Free Gift of Nature or Wealth of a Nation?"

38. Escobar, *Encountering Development*; Rahnema with Bawtree, *The Post-Development Reader*.

39. Ibid.

40. For excellent research that examines the situation of indigenous people in Venezuela, see Briggs and Mantini-Briggs, "'Bad Mothers' and the Threat to Civil Society: Race, Cultural Reasoning, and the Institutionalization of Social Inequality in a Venezuelan Infanticide Trial." For research on indigenous movements and constitutional transformation in Venezuela see Van Cott, "Andean Indigenous Movements and Constitutional Transformation: Venezuela in Comparative Perspective."

41. Janicke, Kiraz, "Chávez Swears in New Venezuelan Minister for Women's Affairs," in Venezuelanalysis.com (site visited April 27, 2008). For a well-known analysis of the lives of street children in Caracas in the pre-Chávez era, see Márquez, *The Street Is My Home: Youth and Violence in Caracas*.

42. The challenge of racism and anti-racism could have also been used to help explain the government's policies on issues of identity, status, and recognition. Chávez often boasts of being a "zambo," that is, someone of both African and indigenous descent. As well see Coronil's chapter in this volume for pertinent anecdotes concerning racism. Also, see the work of Briggs mentioned above.

43. Numerous writers have noted this. See, for example, Lloyd, *The Man of Reason*; Harding, *The Science Question in Feminism*; and Mohanty, "Under Western Eyes."

44. Fraser, Nancy, "Rethinking Recognition."

45. Ibid.

46. Ibid.

47. Ibid.

48. Ibid.

49. Ibid.

50. Ibid. See also Rakowski, "Women's Coalitions as a Strategy at the Intersection of Economic and Political Change in Venezuela."

51. For research on how the 1999 constitution encompasses not only political and civil rights but also economic, social/cultural, environmental, indigenous, and national sovereignty rights, see Collins, "Breaking the Mold?"

52. See Rakowski and Espina's chapter in this book.

53. For research on the political reasons for the emergence of Chávez and the Bolivarian process, see the edited volume by Ellner and Salas, *Venezuela: Hugo Chávez and the Decline of an Exceptional Democracy*. For research from a theorist who has had significant influence on Chávez see Meszaros, "Bolívar and Chávez."

54. See Wilpert's chapter in this volume.

55. See Taylor, *Sources of the Self*.

56. See Markoff, "Where and When Was Democracy Invented?"

57. Avineri, *Hegel's Theory of the Modern State*.

58. See ibid., 21. Notably, Hegel did not think that an Athenian type participatory democracy could be extended across the length or character of the modern state.

59. Port Huron statement (http://www2.iath.virginia.edu/sixties/HTML_docs /Resources/Primary/Manifestos/SDS_Port_Huron.html) Site visited 23/05/10.

60. Baiocchi, "Participation, Activism and Politics: the Porto Alegre Experiment." See also Abers, *Inventing Local Democracy: Grassroots Politics in Brazil*.

61. These movements have also been termed "anti-globalization," "alternative globalization," and "global justice." See Klein, *No Logo*, and Hardt and Negri's *Empire* and *Multitude* for influential interpretations of these movements. No doubt many of the prominent activists of the 1960s who believed in participatory democracy have had a substantial impact on the current global justice movements. If anything, as Robert Ross has insightfully pointed out, the global justice movements began as a mobilization of both older 1960s activists and younger 1990s activists. See Ross, "From Antisweatshop to Global Justice to Antiwar: How the New New Left Is the Same and Different from the Old New Left."

62. Santos, *The Rise of the Global Left*.

63. Ponniah and Fisher, "The World Social Forum, or, the Reinvention of Democracy."

64. For articles on the 2006 World Social Forum held in Caracas see Nineham, *"The World Social Forum in Chávez Venezuela"* and Pallister, "Continuity and Change: An Eyewitness Account of the World Social Forum – Caracas 2006."

65. There are a number of works debating 21st century socialism. Two influential books are Wilpert, *Changing Venezuela by Taking Power*, and Leibowitz, *Build It Now*.

66. Nancy Fraser argues that redistribution, recognition, and representation are three semi-autonomous interpenetrating dimensions of justice. I argue that the

Bolivarians implicitly emphasize the third dimension as having greater constitutive weight and it is therefore integral to the achievement of the other two.

67. Castañeda, Jorge. "Latin America's Left Turn." See (http://www.foreignaffairs .org/20060501faessay85302/jorge-g-castaneda/latin-america-s-left-turn.html), Site visited 08/12/08.

68. For an analysis of Chávez's populism see Ellner, "Revolutionary and Non-Revolutionary Paths of Radical Populism"; "The Contrasting Variants of the Populism of Hugo Chávez and Alberto Fujimori"; and "The Radical Potential of Chavismo in Venezuela."

69. For a criticism of the Bolivarian process from within, see Lander, "Party Disciplinarians," as well as Wilpert, *Changing Venezuela by Taking Power.*

70. See Corrales, "Database on Cabinet Members in Venezuela." Table 3 in his chapter in this book.

71. For articles on the relationship between charisma and democracy, see Hawkins, "Populism in Venezuela: The Rise of Chavismo."

72. See López-Maya and Lander's chapter in this volume.

73. See Foucault, *Security, Territory, Population.*

74. McCoy, "From Representative to Participatory Democracy?" Other scholars, such as Erik Olin Wright and Archon Fung, note that participation can be used as a tool by civil society to exert regulatory control over the state, thereby empowering the public. See Fung and Olin Wright, *Deepening Democracy.*

75. In December 2003, many Venezuelans signed a petition in favor of holding a recall referendum. The list was publicized by the National Assembly deputy Luis Tascón, who posted the list on his website in 2004. The media noted numerous cases where those who had signed the petition were denied government services such as receiving a passport or government employment.

76. Hegel, *Political Writings,* 264.

77. For examples of the proliferation of the discourse of participatory democracy among the Latin American and global left, see Fisher and Ponniah, *Another World Is Possible*; Santos, *The Rise of the Global Left*; and Olin Wright, "Compass Points: Towards a Socialist Alternative."

78. Over the last generation we have witnessed claims for the end of history, the end of the state, and the end of any substantial difference between the left and the right. One area of research worth pursuing would be to examine the discursive impact of the Venezuelan process on the apocalyptic "end of" discourse.

79. Coronil, *The Magical State: Nature, Money and Modernity in Venezuela.*

80. For a view that criticizes Venezuela's foreign aid programs, see Naim, "Rogue Aid." For an interesting piece on Washington's loss of legitimacy in Latin America see Hakim, "Is Washington Losing Latin America?" For further analysis of the relationship between the UN and the U.S. see Lander, "Venezuelan Social Conflict in a Global Context." For another argument calling on the U.S. to adopt a sounder policy towards Venezuela see Shifter, "In Search of Hugo Chávez."

# Bibliography

Abel, C., and P. Lloyd-Sherlock. "Health Policy in Latin America: Themes, Trends and Challenges." In *Healthcare Reform & Poverty in Latin America*, edited by P. Lloyd-Sherlock. London, UK: Institute of Latin American Studies, 2000.

Abers, Rebecca N. *Inventing Local Democracy: Grassroots Politics in Brazil*. Boulder: Lynne Rienner, 2000.

Abrams, Philip. "Notes on the Difficulty of Studying the State." *Journal of Historical Sociology*, 1, 1 (March 1988): 58–89.

Adams, David. "Latin America's Balanced/Biased Voice," *St. Petersburg Times*, August 8, 2005.

Adelman, Jeremy. "Andean Impasses," *New Left Review*, 18 (Nov.–Dec., 2002): 41–72.

———. "Unfinished States: Historical Perspectives on the Andes." In *State and Society in Conflict: Comparative Perspectives on Andean States*, edited by Paul Drake and Eric Hershberg, 41–74. Pittsburgh: University of Pittsburgh Press, 2006.

Agencia Bolivariana de Noticias (ABN). "Banmujer ha entregado más de 100 mil crédito en más de ocho años." Oct. 31, 2009. Published at http://generoconclase.blogspot.com/. Accessed on Feb. 21, 2010.

Agüero, Felipe. "Crisis and Decay of Democracy in Venezuela: The Civil-Military Dimension." In *Venezuelan Democracy under Stress*, edited by Jennifer McCoy, William C. Smith, Andrés Serbin, and Andrés Stambouli, 215–35. New Brunswick: North-South Center/Transaction Press, 1995.

Alexander, Robert J. *Rómulo Betancourt and the Transformation of Venezuela*. New Brunswick: Transaction Publishers, 1982.

Alford, John R., and John Hibbing. "The Origins of Politics: An Evolutionary Theory of Political Behavior," *Perspectives on Politics* 2, 4 (2004): 707–711.

Aló Presidente Web site, http://www.alopresidente.gob.ve/.

Alvarado, Carlos, et al. *Mission Barrio Adentro: The Right to Health and Social Inclusion in Venezuela*. Caracas: PAHO/Venezuela, 2006.

Alvarado, C. H., María E. Martínez, Sarai Vivas-Martínez, Nuramy J. Gutiérrez, and Wolfram Metzger. "Social Change and Health Policy in Venezuela," *Social Medicine*, 3, 2 (2008): 95–109.

Alvarez, Angel E. "State Reform Before and After Chávez's Election." In *Venezuelan Politics in the Chávez Era: Class, Polarization, and Conflict*, edited by Steve Ellner and Daniel Hellinger, 147–160. Boulder, CO: Lynne Rienner, 2003.

———. "Venezuela 2007: Los Motores del Socialismo se alimentan con petróleo," *Revista de Ciencia Política*, special vol. (2007): 265–289.

Alvarez, Bernardo."Letter to The Honorable Nancy Pelosi, Speaker of the House, U.S. House of Representatives, Washington, D.C., May 30, 2007," retrieved Dec. 5, 2007, from http://www.iacenter.org/Venezuela/venez_media0607.html.

Anderson, Benedict. *Imagined Communities: Reflections on the Origin and Spread of Nationalism.* New York: Verso, 1991.

Arendt, Hannah. *On Revolution.* New York: Viking Press, 1963.

Armada, F., C. Muntaner, and V. Navarro. "Health and Social Security Reforms in Latin America: The Convergence of the World Health Organization, the World Bank, and Transnational Corporations." *International Journal of Health Services,* 31, 4, (2001): 729–768.

Asamblea Nacional Constituyente. *Constitución de la República Bolivariana de Venezuela.* Caracas, *Gaceta Oficial* N° 36.860, December 30, 1999.

Avineri, Shlomo. *Hegel's Theory of the Modern State.* Cambridge, UK: Cambridge University Press, 1972.

Avritzer, Leonardo. "Civil Society, Public Space and Local Power: A Study of the Participatory Budget in Belo Horizonte and Porto Alegre." 2000. http://www.chs .ubc.ca/participatory/docs/avritzer.pdf.

Bachelet, Pablo. "Washington: Cuba, Venezuela Not Helping in War on Terrorism,"*Miami Herald,* April 9, 2006.

———. "OAS Leader Charts an Independent Course," *Miami Herald,* June 9, 2006.

Baiocchi, Gianpaolo. *Militants and Citizens: The Politics of Participatory Democracy in Porto Alegre.* Stanford, CA: Stanford University Press, 2005.

———. "Participation, Activism, and Politics: The Porto Alegre Experiment," in *Deepening Democracy: Institutional Innovations in Empowered Participatory Governance,* edited by Archon Fung and Erik Olin Wright. New York: Verso, 2003.

Banco Central de Venezuela (BCV). www.bcv.org.ve, Nov. 2006.

———."Indicadores." Online database. Retrieved 2 Mar. 2010. <http://www.bcv .org.ve/c2/indicadores.asp>.

Banmujer Web site: http://www.banmujer.gob.ve/.

———. Newsletter of the Communications Team at Banmujer, Year 5, No. 10, June 2006.

———. Newsletter of the Communications Team at Banmujer, Year 5, No. 11, Oct. 2006.

Baptista, Asdrúbal. *El Relevo del Capitalismo Rentístico. Hacia un Nuevo Balance de Poder.* Caracas: Fundación Polar, 2004.

Baptista, Asdrúbal, and Bernard Mommer. "Renta petrolera y distribución factorial del ingreso." In *Adios a la Bonanza? Crisis de la Distribución del Ingreso en Venezuela,* edited by Hans-Peter Nissen and Bernard Mommer, 15–40. Caracas: ILIS-CENDES, Editorial Nueva Sociedad, 1989.

Barrionuevo, Alexei. "Chávez's Plan for Development Bank Moves Ahead," *New York Times,* October 22, 2007.

Benford, Robert, and David A. Snow. "Framing Processes and Social Movements: An Overview and Assessment," *Annual Review of Sociology,* 26 (2000): 611–639.

Berlin, Isaiah. "Two Concepts of Liberty," in Isaiah Berlin, *The Proper Study of Mankind: An Anthology of Essays.* New York: Farrar, Straus, and Giroux, 1998.

Bermeo, Nancy. *Ordinary People in Extraordinary Times: The Citizenry and the Breakdown of Democracy.* Princeton, NJ: Princeton University Press, 2003.

Biardeau, Javier R. "Del Árbol de las Tres Raíces al 'Socialismo Bolivariano del Siglo XXI' ¿Una Nueva Narrativa Ideológica de Emancipación?" *Revista Venezolana de Economía y Ciencias Sociales*, 15, 1 (enero-abr. 2009): 57–113.

Birn, A. E. *Marriage of Convenience: Rockefeller International Health and Revolutionary Mexico*. Rochester: University of Rochester Press, 2006.

Birn, A. E., S. Zimmerman, and R. Garfield. "To Decentralize or Not to Decentralize, Is That the Question? Nicaraguan Health Policy under Structural Adjustment in the 1990s." *International Journal of Health Services* 30, 1 (2000): 111–128.

Bisbal, Marcelino. "Los medios en Venezuela ¿Dónde estamos?" In *Anuario Iberoamericano de la Comunicación Social*. Madrid: Fundación Telefónica, 2007.

Blanco, Carlos. "Chávez and the Fate of the Left," Paper Presented at the conference "The Politics of Regime Change" held at Harvard University's David Rockefeller Center for Latin American Studies, Dec. 14, 2007.

———. *Revolución y desilusión. La Venezuela de Hugo Chávez*. Madrid, Catarata, 2002.

Blanco, Jessie. 2007a. "Al debate feminismo revolucionario y socialismo. En el marco de la construcción del socialismo del siglo XXI (Venezuela)," *Revista Venezolana de Economía y Ciencias Sociales* 13, 2.

———. 2007b. "Nuestro socialismo ¿feminista?" *Revista Venezolana de Estudios de la Mujer* 12, 28. Accessed online on December 30, 2009.

———. 2009. "Al debate feminismo revolucionario y socialismo. En el marco de la construcción del socialismo del siglo XXI (Venezuela)." Posted online at www.sociologando.org.ve, Nov. 25. Accessed on Jan. 1, 2010.

Bobbio, Norberto. *Left and Right: The Significance of a Political Distinction*. Trans. and introduced by Allan Cameron. Chicago: University of Chicago Press, 1997.

"Bolivia, Paraguay, y Uruguay se suman al Gran Gasoducto del Sur," July 21, 2006, retrieved from http://www.pdvsa.com/index.php?tpl=interface.sp/design /sala-prensa/readnew.tpl.html&newsid_obj_id=2835&newsid_temas=1.

Bolívar, Simón. "Discurso ante el Congreso de Angostura." In *Textos Fundamentales de Venezuela*, edited by Rafael Arráiz and Edgardo Mondolfi, 23–53. Caracas: Fundación para la Cultura Urbana, 2001.

Borgucci, Emmanuel. "Representaciones y discurso en los procesos de descentralización administrativa en Venezuela," *Revista de Ciencias Sociales*, 9, 3 (Sept.–Dec., 2003): 405–430.

Briceño-León, Roberto. "La expectativa de futuro del venezolano y la crisis," *Espacio Abierto: Cuaderno Venezolano de Sociologia*, 15, 1–2 (Jan.–Jun., 2006): 7–19.

———. "Violencia Urbana en América Latina: Un modelo sociológico de explicación," *Espacio Abierto: Cuaderno Venezolano de Sociologia*, 16, 3 (July–Sept., 2007): 541–574.

Briggs, Charles L., and Clara Mantini-Briggs. "Bad Mothers and the Threat to Civil Society: Race, Cultural Reasoning, and the Institutionalization of Social Inequality in a Venezuelan Infanticide Trial," *Law & Social Inquiry* 25, 2 (Spring 2000): 299–354.

———. "Confronting Health Disparities: Latin American Social Medicine in Venezuela," *American Journal of Public Health*, 99, 3 (March 2009): 549–555.

Bright, Arthur. "US Slaps Arms Sale Ban on Venezuela," *Christian Science Monitor*, May 17, 2006.

Brinkley, Joel. "Latin States Shun U.S. Plan to Watch Over Democracy," *New York Times*, June 9, 2005, 8.

———. "U.S. Proposal in the O.A.S. Draws Fire as an Attack on Venezuela," *New York Times*, May 22, 2005.

Brinton, Crane. *Anatomy of Revolution*. New York: Prentice-Hall, Inc., 1952.

Brooks, Stephen G., and William C. Wohlforth. "Hard Times for Soft Balancing," *International Security*, 30, 1 (Summer 2005): 72–108.

Bruce, Iain. *The Porto Alegre Alternative: Direct Democracy in Action*. London: Pluto Press, 2004.

———. "Venezuela Sets up 'CNN Rival,'" *BBC News*, June 8, 2005. Retrieved from http://newsvote.bbc.co.uk/mpapps/pagetools/print.news.bbc.co.uk/2/hi/americas/4620411.stm.

———. *The Real Venezuela: Making Socialism in the 21st Century*. London: Pluto Press, 2009.

Bruno, Michael. "Does Inflation Really Lower Growth?" *Finance and Development*, 32 (Sept. 1995): 35–38.

Bulmer-Thomas, Victor. *The Economic History of Latin America Since Independence*, 2nd ed. New York: Cambridge University Press, 2003.

Bureau of Economic Analysis (BEA). "Table 1.8.6. Command-Basis Real Gross National Product, Chained Dollars." National Income and Product Accounts Tables. Feb. 26, 2010. U.S. Department of Commerce. Retrieved Mar. 9, 2010 <http://www.bea.gov/national/nipaweb/TableView.asp?SelectedTable=46&Freq=Qtr&FirstYear=2007&LastYear=2009>.

Burgess, Katrina, and Steven Levitsky. "Explaining Populist Party Adaptation in Latin America: Environmental and Organizational Determinants of Party Change in Argentina, Mexico, Peru, and Venezuela," *Comparative Political Studies*, 36, 8 (Oct. 2003): 881–911.

Bush, George W. Remarks on 6 November 2001, as cited in the White House press release at http://www.whitehouse.gov/news/releases/2001/11/20011106-4.html "Bush Faces Widespread Opposition in Latin America." CNN 9 Mar. 2007. Retrieved 9 Mar. 2010. <http://www.cnn.com/2007/WORLD/americas/03/08/bush.latinamerica/index.html>.

Buxton, Julia. *The Failure of Political Reform in Venezuela*. Burlington: Ashgate, 2001.

———. "Venezuela." In *Case Studies in Latin American Political Economy*, edited by J. Buxton and N. Phillips, 246–270. New York: Manchester University Press, 1999.

———. "Venezuela's Contemporary Political Crisis in Historical Context," *Bulletin of Latin American Research*, 24, 3 (2005): 328–347.

Caballero-Arias, Hortensia. "(Post)desarrollo, Antropología y Estado en Venezuela. La nueva lógica de la participación local." *Espacio Abierto* 16, 1 (Jan.–Mar. 2007): 135–162.

Calvert, Peter. *Revolution and Counter-Revolution*. Minneapolis: University of Minnesota Press, 1990.

Canache, Damarys. "Urban Poor and Political Order," in *The Unraveling of Representative Democracy in Venezuela*, edited by Jennifer McCoy and David Myers, 33–49. Baltimore: Johns Hopkins University Press, 2004.

Cannon, Barry. "Venezuela, April 2002: Coup or Popular Rebellion? The Myth of a United Venezuela," *Bulletin of Latin American Research*, 23, 3 (2004): 285–302.

———. "Class/Race Polarization in Venezuela and the Electoral Success of Hugo Chávez: A Break with the Past or the Song Remains the Same?" *Third World Quarterly*, 29, 4 (2008): 731–748.

Carlson, Chris. "What Is Venezuela's Constitutional Reform Really About?" Retrieved Nov. 24, 2007, from www.venezuelanalysis.com.

Carosio, Alba. 2007. "Feminismo en el socialismo del siglo XXI." Article posted at www.rebelion.org (accessed Feb.12, 2007).

Castañeda, Jorge G. "Latin America's Left Turn," *Foreign Affairs*, 85, 3 (May/June 2006): 28–43.

Castro, Pedro. "El caudillismo en América Latina, ayer y hoy," *Politica y Cultura*, 27 (Spring, 2007): 9–29.

Cedeño, Jeffrey. "Venezuela in the Twenty-First Century: New Men, New Ideals, New Procedures," *Journal of Latin American Cultural Studies*, 15, 1 (March 2006): 93–109.

Centeno, Miguel Ángel. *Democracy Within Reason: Technocratic Revolution in Mexico*. University Park, PA: The Pennsylvania State University Press, 1994.

CEPAL. *Social Panorama of Latin America 2007*. Retrieved from: http://www .cepal.org/cgi-bin/getProd.asp?xml=/publicaciones/xml/9/30309/P30309 .xml&xsl=/dds/tpl/p9f.xsl&base=/comercio/tpl/top-bottom.xslt.

Charles, Jacqueline, and Pablo Bachelet. "Venezuela Gets Backing for U.N. Council Seat," *Miami Herald*, July 2, 2006.

Chávez, Hugo. "Capitalism Is Savagery: Speech at 2005 World Social Forum," *Third World Traveler*, April 10, 2005, Retrieved on July 17, 2008 from: http://www .thirdworldtraveler.com/South_America/CapitalismSavagery_Chavez.html.

———. "Discurso del Presidente de la Republica Bolivariana de Venezuela, Hugo Chávez Frias, con motivo del Mensaje Annual de Rendición de Cuentas ante la Asamblea Nacional." In *Despacho de la Presidencia; 2001 Año de las Leyes Habilitantes. Selección de Discursos del Presidente de la Republica Bolivariana de Venezuela, Hugo Chávez Frias*. Caracas, Venezuela: Ediciones de la Presidencia de la Republica, Jan. 15, 2001.

———. "Discurso en el encuentro de solidaridad en la revolución Bolivariana Efectuado en el marco del foro social mundial." In *El golpe fascista contra Venezuela*. La Habana: Ediciones Plaza, 2003.

———. *Palabras antimperialistas*. Caracas: Ministerio de Comunicación e Información, 2005.

———. *Revolución Bolivariana, Año de Logros*. Caracas: Ministerio del Poder Popular para la Comunicación y la Información, 2008.

"Chile leads race for OAS top post with backing from 11 CARICOM members," April 4, 2005, retrieved from: http://www.caribbeannetnews.com/cgi-bin /GPrint2002.pl?file+2005-04-04/oas.shtml.

CNN News. "U.S. Opposes Venezuela bid for U.N. Council Seat," July 20, 2006, retrieved from: http://www.cnn.com/2006/WORLD/americas/07/20/venezuela .un.ap/index.html.

————. "Chávez: Bush 'devil'; U.S. 'on the way down.'" Retrieved from: http://www .cnn.com/2006/WORLD/americas/09/20/chavez.vn.ap.index.html.

Cohen, Youssef. *Radicals, Reformers, and Reactionaries: The Prisoner's Dilemma and the Collapse of Democracy in Latin America*. Chicago: University of Chicago Press, 1994.

Colectiva Alejandra Kollontai. 2009. "A propósito de la exclusión de las peticiones feministas y la sexodiversidad en la discusión de la Ley Orgánica de Equidad e Igualdad de Género." Circulated on feminist e-mail networks on August 13, 2009. Accessed January 16, 2010.

Collier, Paul, and Anke Hoeffler. *Greed and Grievance in Civil War*. Policy Research Working Paper Series 2355, The World Bank, 2002.

Collier, Ruth Berins, and David Collier. *Shaping the Political Arena: Critical Junctures, the Labor Movement, and Regime Dynamics in Latin America*. Princeton, NJ: Princeton University Press, 1991.

Collins, C., and A. Green. "Decentralization and Primary Health Care: Some Negative Implications in Developing Countries," *International Journal of Health Services* Vol. 24, No. 3 (1994): 459–476.

Collins, Sheila D. "Breaking the Mold? Venezuela's Defiance of the Neoliberal Agenda," *New Political Science*, Vol. 27, No. 3 (2005): 367–395

Comaroff, Jean, and John Comaroff. *Christianity, Colonialism, and Consciousness in South Africa*, Vol. 1 of *Revelation and Revolution*. Chicago: University of Chicago Press, 1991.

Comisión de Enlace para la Internacionalización de las Misiones Sociales (CEIMS). "Misión Robinson I, II." Ministerio del Poder Popular para las Relaciones Exteriores. Retrieved 9 Mar. 2010. <http://ceims.mre.gob.ve/index.php?option =com_content&view=article&id=51>.

Conaghan, Catherine, and James Malloy. *Unsettling Statecraft: Democracy and Neoliberalism in the Central Andes*. Pittsburgh and London: University of Pittsburgh Press, 1994.

CONAPRI. Informe de Inversiones, 2006, http://www.conapri.org/download /Informe_Inversiones_2006.pdf.

Congreso de la República de Venezuela. *Ley Orgánica del Sufragio y Participación Política*. Caracas, Gaceta Oficial extraordinaria N° 5.223, May 28, 1998.

Constitución de la República Bolivariana de Venezuela. 1999. Published in *Gaceta Oficial* No. 36,860, Thursday, December 30.

Contreras, Joseph, and Michael Isikoff. "Hugo's Close Call," *Newsweek*, April 29, 2002.

Convenio Argentina-Venezuela. Convenio Integral de Cooperación entre la República Bolivariana de Venezuela y la República Argentina, suscrito en Caracas, 8 April 2004. Caracas, 2004.

Convenio Cuba-Venezuela. *Declaración Conjunta suscrita el 14 de diciembre de 2004, entre la República Bolivariana de Venezuela y la República de Cuba.* Caracas, 2004.

Cooper, Andrew, and Thomas Legler. "A Tale of Two Mesas: The OAS Defense of Democracy in Peru and Venezuela," *Global Governance*, 11 (2005): 425–444.

Copley, Florencia. "Telesur Is Constructing Another View," retrieved from http://www.venezuelasolidarity.org.uk/ven/web/articles/Telesur_another_view.html.

Coppedge, Michael. "Explaining Democratic Deterioration in Venezuela through Nested Inference." In *The Third Wave of Democratization in Latin America: Advances and Setbacks,* edited by Scott Mainwaring and Frances Hagopian, 289–319. New York: Cambridge University Press, 2005.

———. *Strong Parties and Lame Ducks: Presidential Partyarchy and Factionalism in Venezuela.* Stanford, CA: Stanford University Press, 1994.

———. "Venezuela: Popular Sovereignty versus Liberal Democracy." In *Constructing Democratic Governance in Latin America,* edited by Jorge Dominguez and Michael Shifter, 165–192. Baltimore: Johns Hopkins University Press, 2003.

———. "Venezuelan Parties and the Representation of Elite Interests." In *Conservative Parties, The Right, and Democracy in Latin America,* edited by Kevin Middlebrook, 110–136. Baltimore: The Johns Hopkins University Press, 2000.

Coronel, Gustavo. *Corruption, Mismanagement, and Abuse of Power in Hugo Chávez's Venezuela.* Washington, D.C.: The Cato Institute, 2006.

Coronil, Fernando. "After Empire: Rethinking Imperialism from the Americas." In *Imperial Formations and Their Discontents,* edited by Ann Stoler, Carole McGranahan and Peter Purdue, 241–271. Santa Fe: SAR: Santa Fe. School of American Research Press, 2007.

———. *El estado mágico. naturaleza, dinero y modernidad en Venezuela.* Caracas: Nueva Sociedad, 2002.

———. *The Magical State: Nature, Money, and Modernity in Venezuela.* Chicago: University of Chicago Press, 1997.

———. "Chávez's Venezuela: A New Magical State?" 2008. *ReVista: Harvard Review of Latin America* 8, 1 (Fall 2008): 3–4.

Coronil, Fernando, and Julie Skurski. "Dismembering and Remembering the Nation: The Semantics of Political Violence in Venezuela," *Comparative Studies in Society and History,* 33, 2 (2001): 288–337.

Corrales, Javier. "Explaining Chavismo," Paper prepared for book project by Ricardo Hausmann and Francisco Rodríguez. Amherst, MA, Amherst College, 2007.

———. "Hugo Boss: How Chávez Is Refashioning Dictatorship for a Democratic Age," *Foreign Policy* (Jan./Feb. 2006): 32–40.

———. "In Search of a Theory of Polarization," *European Review of Latin American and Caribbean Studies,* 79 (2005): 105–108.

———. "Looking for an Alternative Market for Venezuelan Oil: Will China Help?" Working Paper. Amherst, MA: Amherst College, September 15, 2005.

———. *Presidents without Parties: The Politics of Economic Reform in Argentina and Venezuela in the 1990s.* University Park, PA: Penn State University Press, 2002.

————. "Strong Societies, Weak Parties: Regime Change in Cuba and Venezuela in the 1950s and Today," *Latin American Politics and Society*, 43, 2 (2001): 81–113.

————. "Why Citizen-Detached Parties Impaired Economic Governance," *ReVista: Harvard Review of Latin America*, Retrieved on July 17, 2008 from: http://drclas .fas.harvard.edu/revista/articles/view/479.

————. "Using Social Power to Balance Soft Power: Venezuela's Foreign Policy," *The Washington Quarterly*. 3, 4 (Oct. 2009): 97–114.

————. "Polarización y oposición en Venezuela: ¿Existe evidencia de aprendizaje político?" in Manuel Hidalgo, ed., *Revolución en Venezuela* (forthcoming).

————. "The Repeating Revolution: Chávez's New Politics and the Old Economics," in Kurt Weyland, Raúl L. Madrid, and Wendy Hunter, eds., *Leftist Governments in Latin America: Successes and Shortcomings*. New York: Cambridge University Press, 2010.

————. "Venezuela: A Setback for Chávez," *Journal of Democracy*, January, 2011.

Corrales, Javier and Michael Penfold, "Venezuela: Crowding Out the Opposition," *Journal of Democracy,* 18, 2 (April 2007): 99–113.

————. *Dragon in the Tropics: Hugo Chávez and the Political Economy of Revolution in Venezuela*. Washington, D.C.: Brookings Institution Press, 2011.

Cress, Daniel, and David Snow. "The Outcomes of Homeless Mobilization: The Influence of Organization, Disruption, Political Mediation, and Framing." *The American Journal of Sociology* 105, 4 (2000): 1063–1104.

Crisp, Brian. "Lessons from Economic Reform in the Venezuelan Democracy," *Latin American Research Review*, 33, 1 (1998): 7–41.

Crisp, Brian. Daniel Levine, and Juan Carlos Rey. "The Legitimacy Problem." In *Venezuelan Democracy under Stress,* edited by Jessica McCoy, William C. Smith, Andrés Serbin, and Andrés Stambouli, 139–170. New Brunswick: North South Center/Transaction Press, 1995.

Culpeper, Roy. "Reforming the Global Financial Architecture: The Potential of Regional Institutions." Seminar on Regional Financial Arrangements, UN-ECLAC and UN-DESA. New York, 14–15 July 2004. Retrieved 9 Mar. 2010. <http://www.un.org/esa/ffd/regionalcommissions/seminar2004/0704-RFA-Culpeper-paper.pdf>.

Datanálisis. "Monitoreo exploratorio del mercado de productos con precios regulados por el Estado." Caracas, October 16, 2007.

————. "¿Cómo evalúa usted la labor del Presidente HChF por el bienestar del país? Results of Public Opinion Polls, Power Point Presentation," Caracas, 2003.

Dávila, Luis Ricardo. "New Times, Old Procedures: Elections and Political Developments in Venezuela," *Revista Europea de Estudios Latinoamericanos y Del Caribe,* 70 (April 2001): 89–98.

De Códoba, José. "A Bid to Ease Chávez's Power Grip; Students Continue Protests in Venezuela; President Threatens Violence," *Wall Street Journal*, June 8, 2007.

————. "Land Grab: Farmers Are Latest Target in Venezuelan Upheaval." The Wall Street Journal. 17 May 2007.

De la Cruz, Rafael. "Decentralization: Understanding a Changing Nation." In *The Unraveling of Representative Democracy in Venezuela*, edited by Jennifer McCoy and David Myers, 181–202. Baltimore: Johns Hopkins University Press, 2004.

De Sousa Santos, Boaventura. "Participatory Budgeting in Porto Alegre: Toward a Redistributive Democracy," *Politics & Society,* 26, 4 (Dec. 1998): 461–510.

D'Elia, Yolanda, and Luis Francisco Cabezas. *Las Misiones Sociales en Venezuela.* Caracas: Instituto Latinoamericano de Investigaciones Sociales, 2008. Accessed at http://www.ildis.org.ve, May 31, 2010.

Deering, Ben. "Chávez's Populism Threatens the Economic Engine of His Revolution," *SAIS Review,* 27, 1 (Winter–Spring, 2007): 159–160.

Derham, Michael. "Undemocratic Democracy: Venezuela and the Distorting of History," *Bulletin of Latin American Research*, 21, 2 (2002): 270–289.

Diamond, Larry. *The Spirit of Democracy: The Struggle to Build Free Societies Throughout the World.* New York: Times Books, 2008.

Díaz Polanco, J. "El papel del financiamiento en los procesos de reforma del sector salud: el caso de Venezuela." In *La Reforma de Salud de Venezuela: Aspectos Políticos e Institucionales de la Decentralización de la Salud en Venezuela*, edited by J. Díaz Polanco. Caracas: Fundación Polar, 2001.

Dietz, Henry A., and David J. Myers. "From Thaw to Deluge: Party System Collapse in Venezuela and Peru," *Latin American Politics and Society,* 49, 2 (Summer 2007): 59–86.

DiJohn, Jonathan. "Economic Liberalization, Political Instability, and State Capacity in Venezuela." *International Political Science Review,* 26, 1 (Jan, 2005): 107–124.

"Discutir un Tema Tabú," published in *Tal Cual* (Caracas), March 31, 2009, and reprinted at www.guia.com.ve.

Domhoff, G. William. *The Power Elite and the State: How Policy Is Made in America.* New York: A. de Gruyter, 1990.

Domínguez, Jorge, ed. *Technopols: Freeing Politics and Markets in Latin America in the 1990s.* University Park, PA: The Pennsylvania State University Press, 1997.

Dos Reis, Flávio Américo. "The Al Jazeera of the South," *World Press Organization*, August 22, 2005, retrieved from http://www.worldpress.org/Americas/2136.cfm.

Drake, Paul, and Eric Hershberg. "The Crisis of State-Society Relations in the Post-1980s Andes." In *State and Society in Conflict: Comparative Perspectives on Andean States*, edited by Paul Drake and Eric Hershberg, 3–63. Pittsburgh: University of Pittsburgh Press, 2006.

Duina, Francesco. *The Social Construction of Free Trade.* Princeton: Princeton University Press, 2006.

Easterly, William. *The Elusive Quest for Growth.* Cambridge, MA: MIT Press, 2001.

Easterly, William, and Michael Bruno. "Inflation Crises and Long-Run Growth." Journal of Monetary Economics. 41, 1 (1998): 3–26.

Eastwood, Jonathan. *The Rise of Nationalism in Venezuela.* Gainesville: University Press of Florida, 2006.

"Ecuador Signs Deal with Venezuela's Telesur Network, Acquires 5 Percent," Associated Press Financial Wire, August 30, 2005, retrieved from Lexis-Nexis.

Eckstein, Susan, ed. *Power and Popular Protest: Latin American Social Movements*, updated and expanded ed. Berkeley: University of California Press, 2001.

Economist Intelligence Unit. "Venezuela Risk: Risk Overview," Risk Briefing Select, April 27, 2007.

Edwards, Sebastian. *Left Behind: Latin America and the False Promise of Populism*. Chicago: University of Chicago Press, 2010.

Ellner, Steve. "Introduction: The Search for Explanations." In *Venezuelan Politics in the Chávez Era*, edited by Steve Ellner and Daniel Hellinger, 7–26. Boulder: Lynne Rienner, 2003.

———. "Las estrategias 'desde arriba' y 'desde abajo' del movimiento de Hugo Chávez." *Cuadernos del CENDES*, 23, 62 (May–August 2006): 73–93.

———. "Revolutionary and Non-Revolutionary Paths of Radical Populism: Directions of the *Chavista* Movement in Venezuela," *Science and Society*, 69, 2 (April 2005): 160–190.

———. "The Radical Potential of Chavismo in Venezuela: The First Year and a Half in Power," *Latin American Perspectives*, 28, 5 (2001): 5–32

———. "Venezuela: Defying Globalization's Logic," *NACLA Report on the Americas*, 39, 2 (Sept.–Oct. 2005).

———. "The Constrasting Variants of the Populism of Hugo Chávez and Alberto Fujimori." *Journal of Latin American Studies*, 35, 1 (Feb., 2003): 139–162.

———. *Rethinking Venezuelan Politics: Class, Conflict, and the Chávez Phenomenon*. Boulder: Lynne Rienner, 2008.

———. "A 'Revolutionary Process' Unfolds in the Absence of a Well-Defined Plan," *ReVista: Harvard Review of Latin America* (Fall 2008): 14–16.

———. "Hugo Chávez's First Decade in Office: Breakthroughs and Shortcomings," *Latin American Perspectives*, 37,1 (Jan. 2010): 77–96.

Ellner, Steve, and Daniel Hellinger, eds. *Venezuelan Politics in the Chávez Era: Class, Polarization, and Conflict*. Boulder: Lynne Rienner, 2003.

Ellner, Steve, and Miguel Tinker Salas, eds. *Venezuela: Hugo Chávez and the Decline an 'Exceptional Democracy.'* Lanham MD: Rowan and Littlefield, 2007.

*El Universal*: "Barrio Adentro en estado crítico." Caracas, July 18, 2009. Retrieved from: http://www.eluniversal.com/2009/07/18/ccs_art_barrio-adentro-en-es_1477530.shtml.

———. "Bienes venezolanos en riesgo por demanda de médicos cubanos" Caracas, Feb. 24, 2010. Retrieved from: http://politica.eluniversal.com/2010/02/24/pol_art_bienes-venezolanos-e_1772452.shtml.

Encarnación, Omar G. "Venezuela's 'Civil Society Coup,'" *World Policy Journal*, 19, 2 (Summer 2002): 38–48.

Energy Information Administration (EIA). *Energy Co-Operation Agreement Petrocaribe Between the Government of the Bolivarian Republic of Venezuela and the Government of Jamaica*. August 23, 2005.

———. "Annual Energy Outlook 2010," Dec. 2009. U.S. Department of Energy. Retrieved 9 Mar. 2010.

———. "Short-Term Energy Outlook," July 10th, 2007. Retrieved on July 17, 2008: http://www.eia.doe.gov/emeu/steo/pub/contents.html.

"Entrevista con María León." 2002. *Tribuna Popular,* 86, 8, posted to www.tribuna-popular.org/, former website of the Communist Party of Venezuela (accessed March 2007).

Escobar, Arturo. *"Encountering Development: the Making and Unmaking of the Third World.* Princeton: Princeton University Press, 1995.

España, Luis P. *Detrás de la Pobreza.* Caracas: Universidad Católica Andrés Bello, 2004.

———. "Programas Sociales y Condiciones de Vida en Venezuela 1999–2007." Powerpoint presentation at the *Venezuelan Forum: Social Factor in the Bolivarian Republic,* Washington, D.C.: Center for Strategic and International Studies, 12 Dec. 2007.

———. "The Social Policy of the Bolivarian Revolution: Mission Tricks," *ReVista: Harvard Review of Latin America* (Fall 2008): 48–50.

Espina, Gioconda. "Ley habilitante y reforma constitucional previa: Propuestas de feministas y sexodivers@s reunid@s hace varias semanas con este propósito." Manifesto circulated on the e-mail lists of Gioconda Espina and Gladis Parentelli on April 9, 2007.

———. "Las mujeres del presidente y la pensión al ama de casa que no llega." Paper presented to Fundamul (Fundación por los Derechos de la Mujer Latinoamericana), June 16, 2006.

———. "Entre sacudones, golpes y amenazas. Las venezolanas organizadas y las otras." In *Mujeres y Participación Política,* edited by Magdalena León, 167–180. Bogotá: Tercer Mundo Editores, 1994.

———. "Más allá de la polarización, las venezolanas organizadas y su agenda mínima de trabajo." *NACLA Report on the Americas,* 40 (2007): 20–24.

———. "El inconsciente saboteador y las políticas públicas: Venezuela," coord. Alicia Girón, *Género y Globalización,* 253–269. Buenos Aires: Clacso Latin American Council of Social Sciences, 2009.

Espina, Gioconda, and Cathy A. Rakowski. "¿Movimiento de mujeres o mujeres en movimiento? El caso de Venezuela." *Cuadernos del Cendes,* 49 (2002): 31–48.

"Fall of the Boligarchs: Banking in Venezuela," *The Economist,* Dec. 10, 2009.

Fearon, J. D. "Primary Commodity Exports and Civil War," *Journal of Conflict Resolution,* 49, 4 (2005): 483–507.

Feo, O., and C. E. Siqueira. "An Alternative to the Neoliberal Model in Health: The Case of Venezuela," *International Journal of Health Services: Planning, Administration, Evaluation,* 34, 2 (2004): 365–375.

Ferguson, Niall. *Empire: The Rise and Demise of the British World Order.* New York: Basic Books, 2003.

———. *Colossus: The Price of America's Empire.* New York: Penguin Press, 2004.

Fernandes, Sujatha. *Who Can Stop the Drums? Urban Social Movements in Chávez's Venezuela.* Durham: Duke University Press, 2010.

Fernández, S., María Eugenia. "Cooperatives: Social Economic Organizations and Instruments for Citizen Participation," *Revista de Ciencias Sociales*, 12, 2 (May–Aug., 2006): 237–253.

FIDES Web site: http://www.fides.gob.ve/.

Figueroa, Victor M. "The Bolivarian Government of Hugo Chávez: Democratic Alternative for Latin America?" *Critical Sociology*, 32, 1 (2006): 187–211.

Figueroa-Clark, Liza. "Venezuela's Electoral Council Rules Referendum Petition Signatures to Be Kept Secret." *Venezuelanalysis.com*, Feb. 8, 2007. Retrieved July 17, 2008 from: http://www.venezuelanalysis.com/news.php?newsno=2213.

Fleischer, Ari. "Remarks as Transcribed in an Official Press Release." 12 April 2002. Retrieved on July 17, 2008, from: http://www.whitehouse.gov/news/releases /2002/04/20020412-1.html.

Foran, John. "Theories of Revolution Revisited: Toward a Fourth Generation?" *Sociological Theory*, 11, 1 (March 1993): 1–20.

———. *Taking Power: On the Origins of Third World Revolutions*. New York: Cambridge University Press, 2005.

Foster, John Bellamy. "The Latin American Revolt: An Introduction." *Monthly Review*, 59, 3 (July–Aug., 2007): 1–7.

Foucault, Michel. *Security, Territory, Population*. New York: Picador, 2009.

Fraser, Nancy. "Reframing Justice in a Globalizing World." *New Left Review*. 36 (Nov./Dec. 2005): 69–88. (Oxford, UK: Alden Press.)

———. "Rethinking Recognition." *New Left Review* (May–June 2000): 107–120.

French, John D. "Understanding the Politics of Latin America's Plural Lefts (Chávez/Lula): Social Democracy, Populism and Convergence on the Path to a Post-neoliberal World," *Third World Quarterly*, 30, 2 (2009): 349–370.

Frenkel, Roberto. "The Sustainability of Sterilization Policy." Sept. 2007. Center for Economic and Policy Research. Retrieved 9 Mar. 2010. <http://www.cepr.net /documents/publications/RF_MW_SterilizationPolicyPaper.pdf>.

Frenkel, Roberto, and Martín Rapetti. "Argentina's Monetary and Exchange Rate Policies after the Convertibility Regime Collapse." Apr. 2007. Center for Economic and Policy Research. Retrieved 9 Mar. 2010. <http://www.cepr.net/documents/publications/argentina_2007_04.pdf>.

Frieden, Jeffrey. *Debt, Development and Democracy: Modern Political Economy and Latin America, 1965–1985*. Princeton: Princeton University Press, 1991.

Friedman, Elisabeth J. *Unfinished Transitions: Women and the Gendered Development of Democracy in Venezuela, 1936–1996*. University Park: Pennsylvania State University, 2000.

Fuentes, Federico. "Argentina: A President, a Soccer Star, and the Dreams of Millions," *Green Left Weekly*, Nov. 16, 2005. Retrieved from http://www.greenleft .org.au/back/2005/649/649p17.htm.

Fukuyama, Francis. *The End of History and the Last Man*. New York: Free Press, 1992.

Fundación CEPS. 2010. "Venezuela. La Discriminación de la Mujer en el Actual Código Penal. Informe de la Fundación CEPS. Caracas, January 8. Published online by La Revolución Vive, a news outlet at www.larevolucionvive.org.ve /spip.php?articles1203&lang=es. Accessed Feb. 1, 2010.

Fung, Archon, and Erik Olin Wright. *Deepening Democracy: Institutional Innovations in Empowered Participatory Governance, the Real Utopias Project IV.* New York: Verso, 2003.

Gamson, William. *Talking Politics.* New York: Cambridge University Press, 1992.

García, Carmen Teresa, and Morelba Jiménez. "Proceso constituyente, identidad femenina y ciudadanía." *Revista Venezolana de Estudios de la Mujer*, 5 (2000): 89–122.

García, Carmen Teresa, and Magdalena Valdivieso. "Las mujeres venezolanas y el proceso bolivariano: Avances y contradicciones." *Revista Venezolana de Economía y Ciencias Sociales*, 15 (2009): 133–153.

García-Guadilla, Maria Pilar. "Civil Society: Institutionalization, Fragmentation, Autonomy." In *Venezuelan Politics in the Chávez Era: Class, Polarization, and Conflict*, edited by Steve Ellner and Daniel Hellinger, 179–214. Boulder: Lynne Rienner, 2003.

———. "Democracy, Decentralization, and Clientelism: New Relationships and Old Practices," *Latin American Perspectives*, 29, 5 (Sept. 2002): 90–109.

———. "Ciudadanía y autonomía en las organizaciones sociales bolivarianas: los Comités de Tierra Urbana como movimientos sociales," *Cuadernos de Cendes*, 24, 66 (sep.–dic. 2007): 47–73.

———. "Social Movements in a Polarized Setting: Myths of Venezuelan Civil Society," in *Venezuela: Hugo Chávez and the Decline of an 'Exceptional Democracy'.* Edited by Steve Ellner and Miguel Tinker Salas, 140–154. Lanham, MD: Rowman and Littlefield, 2007.

García Prince, Evangelina. "Impacto de las leyes de igualdad en América Latina: El caso de Venezuela." Report prepared for Instituto Interamericano de Derechos Humanos, San Jose, Costa Rica, 2007.

Garfield, R. "Malaria Control in Nicaragua: Social and Political Influences on Disease Transmission and Control Activities." *Lancet*, 354 (1999): 414–418.

Garzón, Aníbal, and Roosevelt Barboza. "En Venezuela no hay Revolución. Es un modelo de economía mixta y de conciliación de clases" (interview with Douglas Bravo). http://www.kaosenlared.net/noticia/Venezuela-no-hay-revolucion-modelo-economia-mixta-conciliacion-clases. Accessed May 28, 2010.

Gates, Leslie C. "The Business of Anti-Globalization: Lessons from Venezuela's 1998 Presidential Elections." *Research in Political Sociology*, 15 (2006): 101–137.

———. *Electing Chávez: The Business of Anti-Neoliberal Politics in Venezuela.* Pittsburgh: University of Pittsburgh Press, 2010.

Giacalone, Rita. "The Impact of Neo-Populist Civilian-Military Coalitions on Regional Integration and Democracy: The Case of Venezuela," *Journal of Political and Military Sociology*, 33, 1 (Summer 2005): 25–38.

Gibbs, Terry. "Business as Unusual: What the Chávez Era Tells Us about Democracy under Globalisation," *Third World Quarterly*, 27, 2 (2006): 265–279.

Gil, Gustavo. "Mujeres bajo la violencia." *Tal Cual* (Caracas), Dec. 13, 2007.

Gil Yepes, José Antonio. "Public Opinion, Political Socialization, and Regime Stabilization." In *The Unraveling of Representative Democracy in Venezuela*, edited by Jennifer McCoy and David Myers, 231–263. Baltimore: Johns Hopkins University Press, 2004.

Gindin, Jona. "Latin America Defies US over Venezuela at OAS," June 7, 2005, retrieved from: www.venezuelanalysis.com/news.php?newsno=1649.

———. "Whose Democracy? Venezuela Stymies U.S. (Again)," June 8, 2005, retrieved from: www.venezuelanalysis.com/articles.php?artno=1475.

Giordani, Jorge C. *La Transición Venezolana, y la Búsqueda de su Propio Camino*. Caracas: Vadell Hermanos, 2007.

Gobierno Bolivariano de Venezuela. *Constitución de la República Bolivariana de Venezuela*, http://www.constitucion.ve/. Retrieved May 9, 2008.

Goffman, Erving. *Frame Analysis*. New York: Harper, 1974.

Goldman Sachs. *Latin America Economic Analyst*, 07/14, July 13, 2007.

———. *Latin America Economic Analyst*, 07/23, Dec. 3, 2007.

Goldstone, Jack. "Analyzing Revolutions and Rebellions: A Reply to the Critics." In *Debating Revolution*, edited by Nikki Keddie, 178–199. New York: New York University Press, 1995.

———. *Revolution and Rebellion in the Early Modern World*. Berkeley: University of California Press, 1993.

———. "Toward a Fourth Generation of Revolutionary Theory," *Annual Review of Political Science*, 4 (June 2001): 139–187.

Gonzales, S. "160 Módulos de Barrio Adentro requieren grandes reparaciones." *El Nacional*, C2, Nov. 11, 2008.

González Plessman, Antonio J. "La Desigualdad en la Revolución Bolivariana. Una Década de Apuesta por la Democratización del Poder, La Riqueza y la Valoración del Estatus," *Revista Venezolana de Economía y Ciencias Sociales*, 14, 3 (sep.–dic. 2008): 175–199.

González de Pacheco, Rosa Amelia. "Encuestas, cacerolazos, y marchas." In *En Esta Venezuela*, edited by Patricia M. Márquez and Ramón Piñango. Caracas: Ediciones IESA, 2004.

Gosman, Eleonara. "Lula: 'Nadie Hará que Discute con Chávez, es mi Amigo,'" Clarín. 7 Jul. 2007. Retrieved 9 Mar. 2010. <http://www.clarin.com/diario/2007/07/07/elmundo/i-04401.htm>.

Gott, Richard. *Hugo Chávez and the Bolivarian Revolution*. New York: Verso, 2005.

———. *In the Shadow of the Liberator: Hugo Chávez and the Transformation of Venezuela*. New York: Verso, 2000.

Government of Venezuela website: http://www.mem.gob.ve/index.php.

Greenfeld, Liah. *Nationalism: Five Roads to Modernity*. Cambridge, MA: Harvard University Press, 1992.

———. "Russian Nationalism as Medium of Revolution." Paper written for the National Council on Soviet and Eastern Research July, 1994.

Grindle, Merilee. *Audacious Reforms: Institutional Invention and Democracy in Latin America*. Baltimore: Johns Hopkins University Press, 2000.

Grusky, David, ed. *Social Stratification: Race, Class, and Gender in Sociological Perspective*, 2nd ed. Boulder: Westview Press, 2000.

Guerra, Claudia. "Ley sobre los Derechos de la Mujer a la altura de la Constitución Bolivariana de Venezuela." Article based on an extensive interview with Gabriela Ramírez, president of the Asamblea Nacional's Committee on Family, Women and Youth (Dec. 5, 2006). Published online at cguerra@minci.gob.ve.

Gurr, Ted. *Why Men Rebel*, Princeton: Princeton University Press. 1970.

———. "The Revolution-Social Change Nexus: Some Old Theories and New Hypotheses," *Comparative Politics*, 5, 3 (April, 1973): 359–392.

Habermas, Jürgen. *Between Facts and Norms*. Cambridge, MA: MIT Press, 1996.

Hakim, Peter. "Is Washington Losing Latin America? *Foreign Affairs*, 85, 1 (Jan.–Feb., 2006): 39–53.

Harding, Sandra. *The Science Question in Feminism*. Ithaca: Cornell University Press, 1986.

Hardt, Michael, and Antonio Negri. *Empire*. Cambridge MA: Harvard University Press, 2000.

———. *Multitude: War and Democracy in the Age of Empire*. New York: Penguin Press, 2004.

Harnecker, C. P. "Workplace Democracy and Collective Consciousness: An Empirical Study of Venezuelan Cooperatives," *Monthly Review*, 59, 6 (2007): 27–40.

Harnecker, Marta. "After the Referendum: Venezuela Faces New Challenges," *Monthly Review*, 56, 6 (Nov. 2004): 34–48.

———. "The Venezuelan Military: The Making of an Anomaly," *Monthly Review*, 55, 4 (Sept. 2003): 14–21.

Harris, Jerry. "Bolivia and Venezuela: The Democratic Dialectic in New Revolutionary Movements," *Race & Class*, 49, 1 (2007): 1–24.

Harvey, Nelson. "The Fifth Element: A South American Trade Block Shifts Left as Venezuela Becomes Its Fifth Member State," *The American Prospect* (web exclusive), July 27, 2006, retrieved from http://prospect.org/web/printfriendly-view.ww?id=11778.

Hawkins, Kirk. "Populism in Venezuela: The Rise of Chavismo," *Third World Quarterly*, 24, 6 (2003): 1137–1160.

———. *Venezuela's Chavismo and Populism in Comparative Perspective*. New York: Cambridge University Press, 2010.

Hawkins, Kirk A., and David R. Hansen. "Dependent Civil Society: The Circulos Bolivarianos in Venezuela" *Latin American Research Review*, 41, 1 (Feb. 2006): 102–32.

Hearn, Kelly. "S. American Nations Eye Alternative to IMF," *The Washington Times*, July 24, 2006.

Heath, Oliver. "Explaining the Rise of Class Politics in Venezuela," *Bulletin of Latin American Research*, 28, 2 (2009): 185–203.

Hegel, G. W. F. *Political Writings* Trans. T. M. Knox, with an introductory essay by Z. A. Pelczynski. Oxford: Oxford University Press, 1964.

Held, David. *Models of Democracy*, 2nd ed. Stanford: Stanford University Press, 1996.

Hellinger, Daniel. "When 'No' Means 'Yes to Revolution': Electoral Politics in Bolivarian Venezuela." In *Venezuela: Hugo Chávez and the Decline of an 'Exceptional Democracy,'* edited by Steve Ellner and Miguel Tinker Salas, 157–184. Lanham: Rowan and Littlefield, 2007.

―――. *Venezuela: Tarnished Democracy.* Boulder: Westview Press, 1991.

―――. "Democracy over a Barrel: History through the Prism of Oil." *NACLA,* 27, 5 (1994): 35–41.

―――. "Political Overview: the Breakdown of Puntofijismo and the Rise of Chavismo." In *Venezuelan Politics in the Chávez Era: Class, Polarization, and Conflict,* edited by Steve Ellner and Daniel Hellinger, 27–53. Boulder: Lynne Rienner, 2003.

―――. "Tercermundismo and Chavismo," *Espacio Abierto: Cuaderno Venezolano de Sociologia,* 15, 1–2 (Jan.–June 2006): 323–342.

―――. "Venezuelan Oil: Free Gift of Nature or Wealth of a Nation?" *International Journal,* 62, 1 (Winter 2006): 55–67.

Hernández Navarro, Luis. "Caracas: Sixth World Social Forum," *Americas Program Report,* March 30, 2006. Retrieved on July 17, 2008 from: http://www.americas.irc-online.org.

Herrera Salas, Jesus María. "Ethnicity and Revolution: The Political Economy of Racism in Venezuela" *Latin American Perspectives,* 32, 2 (Mar. 2005): 72–9.

Hillman, Richard. "Intellectuals: An Elite Divided." In *The Unraveling of Representative Democracy in Venezuela,* edited by Jennifer McCoy and David Myers, 115–130. Baltimore: Johns Hopkins University Press, 2004.

Hinterlaces. "Monitor socio-político. Tendencias de coyuntura." 16a investigación. Retrieved on July 17, 2008 from: http://www.hinterlaces.com.

Hobsbawm, Eric, and Terence Ranger, eds. *The Invention of Tradition.* New York: Cambridge University Press, 1983.

Homedes, N., and A. Ugalde. "Why Neoliberal Health Reforms Have Failed in Latin America." *Health Policy,* 71 (2005):83–96.

Horowitz, Irving Louis, and Jaime Suchlicki, eds. *Cuban Communism,* 10th ed. New Brunswick: Transaction Publishers, 2001.

Huber, E. "Options for Social Policy in Latin America: Neoliberal Versus Social Democratic Models." In *Welfare States in Transition,* edited by G. Esping-Andersen, 141–191. London: Sage, 1996.

Human Rights Watch. "Venezuela: Proposed Amendments Threaten Basic Rights." Nov. 29, 2007. Retrieved Dec. 13, 2007, from: http://hrw.org/doc/?t=americas&c=venezu.

―――. "A Decade Under Chávez: Political Intolerance and Lost Opportunities for Advancing Human Rights in Venezuela." Sept. 18, 2008, in www.hrw.org (http://www.hrw.org/en/reports/2008/09/18/decade-under-ch-vez).

Humphreys, Macartan, Jeffrey D. Sachs, and Joseph E. Stiglitz, eds. *Escaping the Resource Curse.* New York: Columbia University Press, 2007.

Huntington, Samuel. *Political Order in Changing Societies.* New Haven: Yale University Press, 1968.

Immigration and Refugee Board of Canada. 2008. "Venezuela: Implementation and Effectiveness of the 2007 Organic Law on the Right of Women to a Life Free of Violence." Report published on April 3, VEN10202784.E. Accessed at www.unhcr.org/refworld/docid/49b92b1cc.html on March 7, 2010.

Inamujer Web site: http://www.inamujer.gob.ve/.

Inamujer. "Document prepared for the Trigésima Novena Reunión de la Mesa Directiva de la Conferencia Regional sobre la Mujer de América Latina y el Caribe (CEPAL)." Mexico City, May 11–12, 2006. Retrieved from: http://www .inamujer.gob.ve/.

Informe para la Segunda Discusión. Proyecto de Ley Orgánica para la Equidad e Igualdad de Género. Circulated for comments and feedback by the electronic network of REUVEM, Red Universitaria Venezolana de Estudios de las Mujeres, Nov. 1, 2009.

Instituto Nacional de la Estadística (INE). www.ine.gov.ve, noviembre, 2006.

———. "Indicadores." Ministerio del Poder Popular para la Planificación y Desarrollo. Retrieved 2 Mar. 2009. Retrieved 9 Mar. 2010. <http://www .ine.gov.ve/>.

Inter-American Development Bank. *Program to Strengthen and Modernize the Health Sector, 2006*. Retrieved on Feb.15, 2006, from: http://www.iadb.org/projects/Project.cfm?project=VE0091&Language=English.

International Monetary Fund (IMF). "World Economic Outlook Database." Retrieved 2 Mar. 2009. <http://www.imf.org/external/pubs/ft/weo/2009/02/weodata/index.aspx>.

Iriart, C., E. E. Merhy, and H. Waitzkin. "Managed Care in Latin America: The New Common Sense in Health Policy Reform," *Social Science and Medicine,* 52 (2001): 1243–1253.

Israel, Esteban, and Miguel Angel Gutiérrez. "Honduran Police Crack Down, but Pressure Mounts." *Reuters.* 30 Sept. 2009. Retrieved 9 Mar. 2010. <http://www.reuters.com/article/idUSN3095905>.

Jaggar, A. M. "Vulnerable Women and Neoliberal Globalization: Debt Burdens Undermine Women's Health in the Global South." In *Recognition, Responsibility, and Rights: Feminist Ethics and Social Theory*, edited by R. N. Fiore and H. Lindemann Nelson, 425–440. Lanham: Rowman and Littlefield, 2003.

Janicke, Kiraz. "Without Workers Management There Can Be No Socialism." Oct. 30, 2007. Retrieved on July 17, 2008 from: http://www.venezuelanalysis .com/analysis/2784.

———. *Chávez Re-launches Venezuela's Flagship Barrio Adentro Healthcare Program*. Online. Accessed: 26 February 2010. http://www.zcommunications.org /chavez-re-launches-venezuela-s-flagship-barrio-adentro-healthcare-program -by-kiraz-janicke.

Jardim, C. "Prevention and Solidarity: Democratizing Health in Venezuela." *Monthly Review,* 56, 8 (2005): 35–39.

Jasso-Aguilar, R., H. Waitzkin, and A. Landwehr. "Multinational Corporations and Health Care in the United States and Latin America: Strategies, Actions, and Effects," *Journal of Health and Social Behavior,* 45, extra issue (2004): 136–157.

Jatar, Ana Julia. *Apartheid del siglo XXI*. Caracas: Publications Monfort, 2006.

Jiménez, Morelba, ed. *Mujeres Protagonistas y Proceso Constituyente en Venezuela*. Caracas: Nueva Sociedad, 2000.

Joffe, Josef. "Defying History and Theory: The United States as the 'Last Superpower.'" In *America Unrivaled: The Future of the Balance of Power*, edited by G. John Ikenberry, 155–180. Ithaca: Cornell University Press, 2002.

Kantorowicz, Ernst. *The King's Two Bodies: A Study in Mediaeval Political Theology*. Princeton: Princeton University Press, 1957.

Karl, Terry Lynn. *The Paradox of Plenty: Oil Booms and Petro-States*. Berkeley: University of California Press, 1997.

———. "The Venezuelan Petro-State and the Crisis of 'Its' Democracy." In *Venezuelan Democracy Under Stress*, edited by Jennifer McCoy, William C. Smith, Andrés Serbin, and Andrés Stambouli, 33–55. New Brunswick: North-South Center/Transaction Press, 1995.

———. "Petroleum and Political Pacts: The Transition to Democracy in Venezuela," *Latin American Research Review*, 22, 1 (1987): 63–94.

Katz, Mark N. *Revolutions and Revolutionary Waves*. New York: St. Martin's Press, 1999.

Keller, Alfredo. "Las Fortalezas Aparentes: El Caso de los Actores Políticos Venezolanos frente a los Procesos de Democratización y de Reformas Económicas." In *Los Actores Sociales y Políticos en los Procesos de Transformación en América Latina*, edited by Manuel Mora y Araujo. Buenos Aires: CIEDLA, 1997.

Keller, Alfredo y Asociados. "Estudio de la opinión pública nacional: Consultoría en Asuntos Públicos. Estudio de la Opinión Pública Nacional. 1er. Trimestre de 2008." Caracas, Marzo 2008.

Kelly, Janet, and Pedro A. Palma. "The Syndrome of Economic Decline and the Quest or Change." In *The Unraveling of Representative Democracy in Venezuela*, edited by Jennifer McCoy and David Myers, 202–230. Baltimore: Johns Hopkins University Press, 2004.

Kinman, E. "Evaluating Health Service Equity at a Primary Care Clinic in Chilimarca, Bolivia." *Social Science and Medicine*, 49 (1999): 663–678.

Kirk, Alejandro. "Media-Latin America: Telesur Goes on the Air under Fire from US," *Inter Press News Service Agency*, July 22, 2005.

Klein, Naomi. *No Logo: Taking Aim at the Brand Bullies*. Toronto: Random House, 2000.

Kornblith, Miriam. "Elections versus Democracy." *Journal of Democracy*, 16, 1 (2005): 124–137.

———. "Public Sector and Private Sector: New Rules of the Game." In *Venezuelan Democracy under Stress*, edited by Jennifer McCoy, William C. Smith, Andrés Serbin, and Andrés Stambouli, 77–103 New Brunswick: North-South Center/Transaction Press, 1995.

———. "The Referendum in Venezuela: Elections versus Democracy." *Journal of Democracy*, 16, 1 (Jan. 2005): 124–137.

———. "Venezuela: de la democracia representativa al socialismo del siglo XXI." In *La nueva encrucijada en los países andinos. Política y sociedad a inicios del siglo XXI*, edited by Martín Tanaka. Lima: Instituto de Estudios Peruanos, forthcoming.

Kozloff, Nikolas. *Hugo Chávez: Oil, Politics, and the Challenge to the U.S.* New York: Palgrave Macmillan, 2007.

Krastev, Ivan. "Democracy's 'Doubles.'" *Journal of Democracy*, 17, 2 (April 2006): 52–62.

Kraul, Chris. "Chávez's Grand, Risky Dream." *Los Angeles Times.* 23 June 2007. Retrieved 9 Mar. 2010. <http://articles.latimes.com/2007/jun/23/business/fi-works23>.

Kuiper, Jeroen, and Gregory Wilpert. "Interview with Jacqueline Faria, Minister for the Environment: The Many Tasks of Environmental Protection in Venezuela." 2005. Retrieved on July 18, 2008 from: http://www.venezuelanalysis.com/articles.php?artno=1508.

Kumar, Krishan. *1989: Revolutionary Ideas and Ideals.* Minneapolis: University of Minnesota Press, 2001.

———. "Revolution." In Maryanne Horowitz, ed., *The New Dictionary of the History of Ideas*, Vol. 5. Detroit: Charles Scribner's Sons, 2005.

———. "The Future of Revolutions." In *Revolution in the Making of the Modern World: Social Identity, Globalization, and Modernity*, edited by John Foran, David Lane, and Andreja Zivkovic, 222–235. New York: Routledge, 2008.

———. "The Revolutionary Idea in the Twentieth-Century World." In *1989: Revolutionary Ideas and Ideals*, edited by Krishan Kumar, 215–238. Minneapolis: University of Minnesota Press, 2001.

Krugman, Paul. *The Return of Depression Economics and the Crisis of 2008.* New York: W.W. Norton, 2009.

"La Única Vía Posible es la Constituyente." *El Comercio*, 27 Nov. 2006. Retrieved 9 Mar. 2010. <http://www.elcomercio.com/solo_texto_search.asp?id_noticia=50426&anio=2006&mes=11&dia=27>.

Labonte, R., and T. Schrecker. "Globalization and Social Determinants of Health." Analytic and Strategic Review Paper. Ottawa: Globalization Knowledge Network, Institute of Population Health, University of Ottawa, 2006.

Laclau, Ernesto. "Populism: What's in a Name?" in *Empire and Terror: Nationalism/Postnationalism in the New Millennium*, edited by Begoña Aretxaga, Dennis Dworkin, Joseba Gabilondo, and Joseba Zulaika, 103–114. Reno: University of Nevada Press, 2004.

Laclau, Ernesto, and Chantal Mouffe. *Hegemony and Social Strategy: Towards a Radical Democratic Politics,* 2nd ed. New York: Verso, 2001.

Lander, Edgardo. "The Impact of Neoliberal Adjustment in Venezuela, 1989–1993." *Latin American Perspective,* 23, 3 (1993): 50–73.

———. "Venezuelan Social Conflict in a Global Context." In *Venezuela: Hugo Chávez and the Decline of an 'Exceptional Democracy,'* edited by Steve Ellner and Miguel Tinker Salas, 16–32. Lanham: Rowan and Littlefield, 2007.

———. "Venezuelan Social Conflict in a Global Context." *Latin American Perspectives,* 32, 2 (2005): 20–38.

———. http://redpepper.blogs.com/venezuela/2007/10/the-threat-to-d.html. Accessed 8/12/08.

————. "Presentación: Diez Años de la Revolución (Segunda Parte)." *Revista Venezolana de Economía y Ciencias Sociales*, 15, 1 (enero–abr. 2009): 51–56.

Lander, Luis E., and Margarita López-Maya. "Referendo revocatorio y elecciones regionales en Venezuela: Geografía electoral de la polarización." *Revista Venezolana de Economía y Ciencias Sociales*, 11, 1 (enero–abril 2005): 43–58.

Latinobarómetro: http://www.latinobarometro.org.

Laurell, A. C. "La política de salud en el contexto de las políticas sociales." In *Salud, Cambio Social y Política: Perspectivas Desde América Latina*, edited by M. Bronfman and R. Castro. México, D.F.: EDAMEX, 1999.

————. "Structural Adjustment and the Globalization of Social Policy in Latin America." *International Sociology*, 15, 2 (2000): 306–325.

Legler, Thomas. "Venezuela 2002–2004: The Chávez Challenge." In *Promoting Democracy in the Americas*, edited by Thomas Legler, Sharon F. Lean, and Dexter S. Boniface, 204–225. Baltimore: Johns Hopkins University Press, 2007.

Leibowitz, Michael A. *Build It Now: Socialism for the Twenty-First Century*. New York: Monthly Review Press, 2006.

León, Magdymar. "Informe sobre observaciones del Movimiento Amplio de Mujeres al proyecto de reforma de la Ley Sobre la Violencia contra la Mujer y la Familia propuesto por la Asamblea Nacional." Unpublished report. Caracas, July 18, 2005.

Lerner, Josh. "Communal Councils in Venezuela: Can 200 Families Revolutionize Venezuela?" *Z Magazine* (Feb. 2007). Retrieved on July 18, 2008 from: http://venezuelanalysis.com/print.pht?artno=1975

Levine, D. H. "Civil Society and Political Decay in Venezuela." In *Civil Society and Democracy in Latin America*, edited by Richard Feinberg, Carlos H. Waisman, and Leon Zamosc, 169–192. New York: Palgrave Macmillan, 2006.

————. "The Decline and Fall of Democracy in Venezuela: Ten Theses." *Bulletin of Latin American Research*, 21, 2 (2002): 248–269.

Levine, Daniel H., and Brian F. Crisp. "Venezuela: The Character, Crisis, and Possible Future of Democracy." *World Affairs*, 161, 3 (Winter 1999): 142–143.

Levitsky, Steven, and Lucan A. Way. *Competitive Authoritarianism: Hybrid Regimes after the Cold War*. New York: Cambridge University Press, 2010.

————. "Elections without Democracy: The Rise of Competitive Authoritarianism." *Journal of Democracy*, 13, 2 (April 2002): 51–65.

Ley Orgánica de la Administración Pública. *Gaceta Oficial* de la República Bolivariana de Venezuela, 17 de octubre de 2001, No. 37.305. Caracas: Imprenta Nacional.

Ley Orgánica de Planificación Pública. *Gaceta Oficial* de la República Bolivariana de Venezuela, No. 5.554 (extraordinaria), 13 de noviembre del 2001. Caracas: Imprenta Nacional.

Ley de los Consejos Comunales. *Gaceta Oficial* de la República Bolivariana de Venezuela, No. 5.806 (extraordinaria), 10 de abril del 2006. Caracas: Imprenta Nacional.

Ley de los Consejos Locales de Planificación Pública. *Gaceta Oficial* de la República Bolivariana de Venezuela, No. 37.463, 6 de diciembre de 2002. Caracas: Imprenta Nacional.

Ley Orgánica de la Contraloría General de la República y del Sistema Nacional de Control Fiscal. *Gaceta Oficial* de la República Bolivariana de Venezuela, No. 37.347, 17 de diciembre de 2001. Caracas: Imprenta Nacional.

Lichbach, Mark Irving. *The Rebel's Dilemma.* Ann Arbor: University of Michigan Press, 1995.

Lieber, Keir A., and Gerard Alexander. "Waiting for Balancing: Why the World Is Not Pushing Back." *International Security*, 30, 1 (Summer 2005): 109–139.

Linares, Gilcely. "Gobierno apuesta por abolir discriminación feminina." Article published online at www.analitica.com/global/xvas/xvade/ on Oct. 13, 2009.

Lijphart, Arend. *Democracy in Plural Societies: A Comparative Exploration.* New Haven: Yale University Press, 1977.

Lindholm, Charles, and José Pedro Zuquete. *The Struggle for the World: Liberation Movements for the 21st Century.* Stanford: Stanford University Press, 2010.

Lloyd, Genevieve. *The Man of Reason: "Male" and "Female" in Western Philosophy.* London: Methuen, 1984.

"Lolita" (pseudonym of Edith Franco). "María León: 'El Socialismo del Signo XXI es el Comunismo.'" Extensive interview dated Sept. 5, 2005, published in *Jóven Guardia* and posted at www.jotaceve.org (accessed March 15, 2007).

Lombardi, John. "Prologue: Venezuela's Permanent Dilemma." In *Venezuelan Politics in the Chávez Era: Class, Polarization, and Conflict,* edited by Ellner and Hellinger, 1–6. Boulder: Lynne Rienner, 2003.

López, Edgar. "Lucha contra la violencia de género venció la polarización." *El Nacional* (Caracas), Friday, April 30, 2010. Accessed online at www.elnacional.com.

———. "Movimiento de mujeres reclamará ante el TSJ." *El Nacional* (Caracas), Thursday, April 29, 2010. Accessed online at www.elnacional.com.

López, Nina, and Selma James. *Creando una Economía Solidaria. Nora Castañeda y el Banmujer.* London: Crossroads Books, 2006.

López-Maya, Margarita. *Del viernes negro al referendo revocatorio.* Caracas: Alfadil Ediciones, 2005.

———, ed. *Ideas para debatir el socialismo del siglo XXI.* Caracas: Editorial Alfa, 2007.

———. "Insurrecciones de 2002 en Venezuela: causas e implicaciones." En *Movimientos sociales y conflictos en América Latina,* compilado por José Seoane, 23–40. Buenos Aires, Clacso-Asdi, 2003.

———. "La protesta popular venezolana entre 1989 y 1993 (en el umbral del neoliberalismo)." In *Lucha popular, democracia, neoliberalismo: protesta popular en América Latina en los años de ajuste,* edited by Margarita López-Maya, 209–235. Caracas: Editorial Nueva Sociedad, 1999.

———. "The Venezuelan *Caracazo* of 1989: Popular Protest and Institutional Weakness." *Journal of Latin American Studies,* 35, 1 (Feb. 2003): 117–137.

———. "Venezuela 2001–2004: actores y estrategias." *Cuadernos del Cendes,* 56 (mayo-agosto 2004): 105–130.

———. "Venezuela after the *Caracazo*: Forms of Protest in a Deinstitutionalized Context." *Bulletin of Latin American Research,* 21, 2 (2002): 199–218.

————. "After the Referendum: Reading the Defeat," *ReVista: Harvard Review of Latin America*, 8, 1 (Fall 2008): 5–7.

López-Maya, Margarita, and Luis E. Lander. "El gobierno de Chávez: democracia participativa y políticas sociales." Ponencia presentada en el XXVI Congreso de LASA celebrado en San Juan, Puerto Rico, 15–18 de marzo, 2006.

————. "The Struggle for Hegemony in Venezuela: Poverty, Popular Protest, and the Future of Democracy." In *Politics in the Andes: Identity, Conflict, and Reform*, edited by J.M. Burt and P. Mauceri. Pittsburgh: University of Pittsburgh Press, 2004.

————. "Venezuela. La Victoria de Chávez. El polo patriótico en las elecciones de 1998." *Nueva Sociedad*, 160 (1999): 4–19.

López-Maya, Margarita, David Smilde, and Keta Stephany. *Protesta y cultura en Venezuela: los marcos de acción colectiva en 1999*. Caracas: FACES-UCV, CENDES, FONACIT, 2002.

Lupi, Juan Pablo, and Leonardo Vivas. "(Mis)Understanding Chávez and Venezuela in Times of Revolution." *Fletcher Forum of World Affairs*, 29, 1 (Winter 2005): 81–102.

Lupu, Noam. "Who Votes for *Chavismo*? Class Voting in Hugo Chávez's Venezuela." *Latin American Research Review*, 45, 1 (2010): 7–32.

MacEwan, Arthur. *Neo-Liberalism or Democracy? Economic Strategy, Markets and Alternatives for the 21st Century*. London: Zed Books, 1999.

Mainwaring, Scott, and Frances Hagopian. "Introduction: the Third Wave of Democratization in Latin America." In *The Third Wave of Democratization in Latin America: Advances and Setbacks*, edited by Frances Hagopian and Scott Mainwaring, 1–14. New York: Cambridge University Press, 2005.

Mainwaring, Scott, and Anibal Pérez-Liñan. "Latin American Democratization Since 1978: Democratic Transitions, Breakdowns, and Erosions." In *The Third Wave of Democratization in Latin America: Advances and Setbacks*, edited by Frances Hagopian and Scott P. Mainwaring, 14–63. New York: Cambridge University Press, 2005.

Mandelbaum, Michael. *The Case for Goliath: How America Acts as the World's Government in the Twenty-first Century*. New York: Public Affairs, 2005.

Manfredi, C. "Can the Resurgence of Malaria be Partially Attributed to Structural Adjustment Programmes?" *Parasitologia*, 41 (1999): 389–390.

Mangon, Thais, Carmen Pérez Baralt, and Heinz R. Sonntag. "La batalla por una nueva Constitución para Venezuela," *Revista Mexicana de Sociologia*, 62, 4 (Oct.–Dec. 2000): 91–124.

Marcano, Cristina, and Alberto Barrera Tyszka. *Hugo Chávez*, trans. Kristina Cordero. New York: Random House, 2007.

Markoff, John. "When and Where Was Democracy Invented?" *Comparative Studies in History and Society*, 41, 4 (Oct. 1999): 660–690.

Markoff, John, and Verónica Montecinos. "The Ubiquitous Rise of Economists," *Journal of Public Policy*, 13, 1 (Jan.–Mar. 1993): 37–68.

Marquez, Patricia. "The Hugo Chávez Phenomenon: What Do 'the People' Think?" In *Venezuelan Politics in the Chávez Era: Class, Polarization, and Conflict*, edited by Steve Ellner and Daniel Hellinger, 197–215. Boulder: Lynne Rienner, 2003.

———. "Vacas flacas y odios gordos: la polarización en Venezuela." In *En esta Venezuela,* edited by Patricia Marquéz and Ramón Piñango, 29–46. Caracas: Ediciones IESA, 2003.

———. *The Street Is My Home: Youth and Violence in Caracas.* Stanford: Stanford University Press, 1999.

Martinez, C., M. Fox, and J. Farrell. *Venezuela Speaks! Voices from the Grassroots.* Oakland, CA: PM Press, 2010.

Martz, John. *Acción Democrática: The Evolution of a Modern Political Party.* Princeton: Princeton University Press, 1966.

Marx, Karl. *The Eighteenth Brumaire of Louis Bonaparte.*" In *The Portable Karl Marx,* edited by Eugene Kamenka, 287–325. New York: Penguin, 1983.

———. "Manifesto of the Communist Party." In *The Marx-Engels Reader,* edited by Robert Tucker, 473–491. New York: W.W. Norton, 1978.

"Mas fondos para consejos comunales," *El Universal*, Jan. 12, 2007. (http://buscador.eluniversal.com/2007/01/12/eco_art_138895.shtml.

Mather, Steven. "Venezuela and Ecuador Sign Energy Agreements," Jan.17, 2007. Retrieved on July 17, 2008 from: http://www.venezuelanalysis.com/news/2180.

———. "Venezuelan Government Announces $5 Billion for Communal Councils in 2007," Jan. 10, 2007. Retrieved on July 18, 2008 from: http://www.venezuelanalysis.com/news.php?newsno=2188.

"Mayans to 'Clean' Bush Site." CNN. 12 Mar. 2007. Retrieved 9 Mar. 2010. <http://www.cnn.com/2007/WORLD/americas/03/12/bush.guatemala/index.html>.

McCarthy, Michael. The Practice of Institutionalizing Ideas: Institutionalizing 'Popular Power' in Venezuela (2010). APSA 2010 Annual Meeting Paper. Available at SSRN: http://ssrn.com/abstract=1643696.

———. "Ordering Chavismo from Above and Below: Institutional Complexity and Endogenous Organizational Change in Venezuela," 2010, unpublished manuscript.

McCoy, Jennifer. "From Representative to Participatory Democracy? Regime Transformation in Venezuela." In *The Unraveling of Representative Democracy in Venezuela,* edited by Jennifer McCoy and David Myers, 263–296. Baltimore: Johns Hopkins University Press, 2004.

———. "One Act in an Unfinished Drama," *Journal of Democracy*, 16, 1 (Jan. 2005): 109–123.

McCoy, Jennifer, and David J. Myers, eds. *The Unraveling of Representative Democracy in Venezuela.* Baltimore: Johns Hopkins University Press, 2004.

McCoy, Jennifer, William C. Smith, Andres Serbin, and Andres Stambouli, eds. *Venezuelan Democracy under Stress.* New Brunswick: North-South Center/Transaction Press, 1995.

Mead, George Herbert. *Mind, Self, and Society: From the Standpoint of a Social Behaviorist.* ed. Charles W. Morris. Chicago: University of Chicago Press, 1962.

Mesa-Lago, C., M. A. Cruz-Saco, and L. Zamalloa. "Determinants of Social Insurance/Security Costs and Coverage: An International Comparison with a Focus on Latin America." In *Welfare, Poverty and Development in Latin America*, edited by C. Abel and C. Lewis. New York: Macmillan, 1993.

Meszaros, Istvan. "Bolívar and Chávez: The Spirit of Radical Determination." *Monthly Review,* 59, 3 (July–Aug., 2007): 55–84.

Mijares Espinoza, L. E. "Están matando la Misión Barrio Adentro en el estado Carabobo." Oct. 12, 2007, *Aporrea.* Retrieved from: http://www.aporrea.org /regionales/a42484.html.

Mills, Melinda. "Globalization and Inequality," *European Sociological Review,* 25, 1 (2009): 1–8.

Ministerio de Educación, *La Educación Bolivariana. Políticas, Programas y Acciones.* Caracas: Ministerio de Educación, 2003.

Ministerio de Energía y Petróleo, www.mem.gob.ve. Dic. 2006.

Ministerio de Planificacion y Desarrollo. "Logros, febrero 2007, SISOV." Feb. 2007. Retrieved on July 17, 2008 from: http://www.sisov.mpd.gob.ve/estudios/.

———. "Cobertura del sistema. Tasa bruta de escolaridad por nivel educativo." SISOV, Retrieved on Dec. 15, 2007 from: http://www.sisov.mpd.gob.ve /indicadores/ED0105800000000/.

———. "Planteles por dependencia." SISOV. Retrieved on Dec. 15, 2007 from: http://www.sisov.mpd.gob.ve/indicadores/ED0304100000000/downloads/VarE _Planteles_Total(plantelesporDep).xls.

Ministerio del Poder Popular para la Alimentación. *Memoria y Cuenta 2008.* Retrieved 9 Mar. 2010.<http://www.minpal.gob.ve/portal/index.php?option=com _docman&task=doc_download&gid=47>.

Ministerio del Poder Popular para Economía y Finanzas. "Estadísticas de las Finanzas Públicas." Retrieved 2 Mar. 2009. <http://www.mf.gov.ve/inicio /info/estadisticas-fiscales/estadisticas-de-las-finanzas-publicas>.

Ministerio del Poder Popular para la Educación. "Más de 4 millones de niños reciben atención alimentaria en Venezuela." Press release, 23 Dec. 2008. Retrieved 9 Mar. 2010. <http://www.me.gob.ve/noticia.php?id_contenido=16106>.

Ministerio del Poder Popular para la Energía y Petróleo: http://www.mem.gob.ve.

Ministerio del Poder Popular para las Finanzas (Venezuela): http://www.mf.gov.ve/.

Ministerio de Salud. *Epi 15 y Reporte Misión Médica Cubana.* Caracas: Ministerio de Salud, 2006.

———. *Presupuesto de gastos nacionales del Ministerio de Salud.* Caracas: Dirección de Planificación y Presupuesto, 2006.

Ministerio de Salud y Desarrollo Social (MSDS). *Barrio Adentro: Expresión de Atención Primaria de Salud: Un Proceso de Construcción Permanente.* Caracas: MSDS, 2005.

———. *Barrio Adentro.* 2006. Retrieved on February 15, 2006 from: http://www .msds.gov.ve/msds/modules.php?name=Content&pa=showpage&pid=239.

Misiones Bolivarianas: http://www.misionesbolivarianas.gob.ve.

Mohanty, Chandra. "Under Western Eyes: Feminist Scholarship and Colonial Discourses." In *Third World Women and the Politics of Feminism,* edited by C. Mohanty, A. Russo, and L. Torres. 51–80. Bloomington: Indiana University Press, 1991.

Molina, Jose. "The Unraveling of Venezuela's Party System: From Party Rule to Personalistic Politics and Deinstitutionalization." In *The Unraveling of Representative Democracy in Venezuela*, edited by Jennifer McCoy and David Myers, 152–180. Baltimore: Johns Hopkins University Press, 2004.

Mommer, Bernard. "Petróleo subversivo." In *Poder y Petróleo en Venezuela*, edited by Luis Lander, 19–39. Caracas: Faces-Universidad Central de Venezuela, 2003.

———. "Subversive Oil." In *Venezuelan Politics in the Chávez Era: Class, Polarization, and Conflict*, edited by Steve Ellner and Daniel Hellinger, 131–145. Boulder: Lynne Rienner, 2003.

Monaldi, Francisco, Rosa Amelia González, Richard Obuchi, and Michael Penfold. *Political Institutions, Policymaking Process, and Policy Outcomes in Venezuela*. Washington, D.C.: Inter-American Development Bank, 2005.

Morillo, Miriam. "Un avance hacia la igualdad." *Ultimas Noticias*, Jan. 19, 2007, and posted at www.analitica.com/mujeranalitica/noticias.

Movimiento Ampliado de Mujeres (MAM). "Agenda del Movimiento Ampliado de las Mujeres para el Trabajo Parlamentario y Legislativo. Noviembre 2005." *Otras Miradas*, 5, 1 (2005).

Mufson, Steven. "AES to Sell Utility Stake to Venezuela; Chávez's State-Control Plan Nets Electric Firm," The Washington Post, 9 Feb. 2007. Retrieved 9 Mar. 2010. <http://www.washingtonpost.com/wp-dyn/content/article/2007/02/08/AR2007020802261.html>.

Mujeres independientes, movimientos sociales y organizaciones de mujeres. "Ciudadana María León, Ministra del Poder Popular para la Mujer y la Igualdad de Género." Letter dated Nov. 3, 2009, signed by 143 individuals (113 women, 30 men) and 13 organizations. Published online by Insurrectas y Punto, Por Género con Clase at the website of the Observatorio Género y Equidad www.observatoriogeneroyliderazgo.cl/ Accessed Feb. 21, 2010.

Muñoz, Boris. "Rosales disputa la política territorial." *Éxxito*, 28 (2006): 23–28.

Muñoz, Heraldo. "The Rise and Decline of the Inter-American System: A Latin American View." In *Alternative to Intervention: A New U.S.-Latin American Security Relationship*, edited by Richard J. Bloomfield and Gregory F. Treverton, 27–37. Boulder: Lynne Rienner, 1990.

Myers, David. "Perceptions of a Stressed Democracy." In *Venezuelan Democracy under Stress*, edited by Jennifer McCoy, William C. Smith, Andrés Serbin, and Andrérs Stambouli, 107–139. New Brunswick: North-South Center/Transaction Press, 1995.

———. "The Normalization of Punto Fijo Democracy." In *The Unraveling of Representative Democracy in Venezuela*, edited by Jennifer McCoy and David Myers, 11–33. Baltimore: Johns Hopkins University Press, 2004.

Naím, Moisés. *Paper Tigers and Minotaurs: The Politics of Venezuela's Economic Reforms*. Washington, D.C.: The Carnegie Endowment for International Peace, 1993.

———. "The Real Story Behind Venezuela's Woes," *Journal of Democracy*, 12, 2 (April 2001): 17–31.

————. "Rogue Aid," *Foreign Policy* (Mar.–Apr., 2007): 159.

Naím, Moisés, and Antonio Francés. "The Venezuelan Private Sector: From Courting the State to Courting the Market." In *Lessons of the Venezuelan Experience,* edited by Luis W. Goodman, Johanna Mendelson Forman, Moisés Naím, Joseph S. Tulchin and Gary Bland, 165–192. Washington, D.C. and Baltimore: The Woodrow Wilson Center Press and Johns Hopkins University Press, 1995.

Naím, Moisés, and Ramón Piñango, eds. *El Caso Venezuela: Una Ilusión de Armonía.* Caracas: Ediciones IESA, 1984.

National Institute of Statistics (INE): http://www.ine.gob.ve/sintesisestadistica /estados/miranda/index.htm).

Navarro, Juan Carlos. "In Search of the Lost Pact: Consensus Lost in the 1980s and 1990s." In *Venezuelan Democracy under Stress,* edited by Jennifer McCoy, William C. Smith, Andrés Serbin, and Andrés Stambouli, 13–33. New Brunswick: North-South Center/Transaction Press, 1995.

Navarro, V., and L. Shi. "The Political Context of Social Inequalities and Health." *Social Science and Medicine,* 52 (2001): 481–491.

Nelson, Brian. *The Silence and the Scorpion: The Coup against Chávez and the Making of Modern Venezuela.* New York: Nation Books, 2009.

Nietzsche, Friedrich. *On the Genealogy of Morality: A Polemic.* Trans. Maudemarie Clark and Alan J. Swensen. Indianapolis: Hackett Publishing, 1998.

Nineham, Chris. "The World Social Forum in Chávez Venezuela," *Radical Philosophy,* 138 (July–Aug., 2006): 60–62.

Njaim, Humberto. "Financiamiento Político en los Países Andinos: Bolivia, Colombia, Ecuador, Perú y Venezuela." In *De las Normas a las Buenas Prácticas,* edited by Steve Griner and Daniel Zovatto. San José, Costa Rica: Organización de los Estados Americanos/IDEA, 2004.

Norden, Deborah. "Party Relations and Democracy in Latin America," *Party Politics,* 4, 4 (1998): 423–443.

O'Donnell, Guillermo, and Phillipe Schmitter. *Transitions from Authoritarian Rule: Tentative Conclusions about Uncertain Democracies.* Baltimore: Johns Hopkins University Press, 1986.

Ojo Electoral. *Boletín No. 2,* Dec. 4, 2006. www.ojoelectoral.org.ve, diciembre, 2006.

————. *Elecciones Presidenciales diciembre 2006. Resumen Informe Final.* Caracas, 2007. Retrieved from www.ojoelectoral.org.ve.

Olin Wright, Erik. "Compass Points: Towards a Socialist Alternative," *New Left Review,* 41 (Sept.–Oct. 2006). Oxford: Alden Press.

Olivo de Celli, Virginia, and Isolda Heredia de Salvatierra. (writing as "Foro por la Equidad de Género"). 2006. *Informe a la 34ᵃ Sesión CEDAW.* Report delivered to CEDAW, New York, Jan. 23–27.

————. *Informe a la 34ᵃ Sesión CEDAW.* Report delivered to CEDAW, New York, January 23–27, 2006.

Olson, Mancur. *The Logic of Collective Action.* Cambridge MA: Harvard University Press, 1965.

Organización Panamericana de la Salud. *Barrio Adentro: Derecho a la Salud e Inclusión Social en Venezuela*. Caracas: OPS/OMS, 2007.

Ortega, Daniel, and Francisco Rodríguez. "Freed from Illiteracy? A Closer Look at Venezuela's *Misión Robinson* Literacy Campaign." *Economic Development and Cultural Change*, 57, 1 (Oct. 2008): 1–30.

Ortiz, Nelson. "Entrepreneurs: Profits without Power?" In *The Unraveling of Representative Democracy in Venezuela*, edited by Jennifer McCoy and David Myers, 71–92. Baltimore: Johns Hopkins University Press, 2004.

"Palabras del presidente de la República Argentina, Dr. Néstor Kirchner durante la inauguración de la IV Cumbre de las Américas, en Mar del Plata," Nov. 4, 2005. Retrieved from: http://www.summit-americas.org/NextSummit_eng.htm.

Pallister, Elizabeth. "Continuity and Change: An Eyewitness Account of the World Social Forum – Caracas, 2006." *Globalizations*, 3, 2 (June 2006): 270–272.

Palmer, R. R. *The Age of Democratic Revolutions*. Vol. 2. Princeton: Princeton University Press, 1964.

Pape, Robert A. "Soft Balancing against the United States." *International Security*, 30, 1 (Summer 2005): 7–45.

Parker, Dick. "Chávez and the Search for an Alternative to Neoliberalism." *Latin American Perspectives*, 23, 2 (Mar. 2005): 39–50.

Pateman, Carole. *Participation and Democratic Theory*. Cambridge: Cambridge University Press, 1970.

Patruyo, Thanalí. *El estado de las misiones sociales: balance sobre su proceso de implementación e institucionalización*. Caracas: Instituto Latinoamericano de Investigaciones Sociales, 2008, accessed at http://www.ildis.org.ve, May 31, 2010.

Paul, T. V. "Soft Balancing in the Age of U.S. Primacy." *International Security*, 30, 1 (Summer 2005): 46–71.

———. "The Enduring Axioms of Balance of Power Theory." In *Balance of Power Revisited: Theory and Practice in the Twenty-first Century*, edited by T. V. Paul, James J. Wirtz, and Michel Fortmann, 1–25. Stanford, CA: Stanford University Press, 2004.

Pearson, T. "Venezuelan President Designates New Caracas Head and Communications Minister" in Venezuelanalysis.com, April 17, 2009. (http://www.venezuelanalysis.com/news/4371).

———. "Venezuela Expands Outlets for Denunciations of Violence against Women." Article published on Internet, 2009, at www.venezuelanalysis.com. Accessed Feb. 20, 2010.

Peet, Richard, with Elaine Hartwick. *Theories of Development*. New York: The Guilford Press, 1999.

Penfold-Becerra, Michael. "Clientelism and Social Funds: Empirical Evidence from Chávez's Misiones Programs." *Latin American Politics and Society*, 49, 4 (2007): 63–84.

———. "Federalism and Institutional Change in Venezuela." In *Federalism and Democracy in Latin America*, edited by Edward L. Gibson, 197–226. Baltimore: Johns Hopkins University Press, 2004.

Petkoff, Teodoro. *Checoslovaquia: el socialismo como problema.* Caracas: MonteÁvila, 1969, 1990.

———. *Dos izquierdas.* Caracas: Alfa Grupo Editorial, 2005.

———. "A Watershed Moment in Venezuela." July 2008. Inter-American Dialogue. Retrieved 9 Mar. 2010. <http://www.thedialogue.org/PublicationFiles/A Watershed Moment in Venezuela - Teodoro Petkoff %28July 2008%29.pdf>.

———. *El Chavismo Como Problema.* 3rd ed. Caracas: Editorial Libros Marcados, 2010.

Petrich, Blanche. "Alistan *proyecto contrahegemónico* de televisión que sea opción real en AL." *La Jornada,* Feb. 27, 2005.

Petróleos de Venezuela, S.A. (PDVSA). Summary of Financial Problems: http://www.pdvsa.com/interface.sp/database/fichero/publicacion/1792/76.PDF.

———. "Balance de la Deuda Financiera Consolidada al 31-12-2009." *Informes Financieros.* Retrieved 9 Mar. 2010. <http://www.pdvsa.com/interface.sp /database/fichero/free/5431/843.PDF>.

———. "Informe Operacional y Financiero al 30 de Junio de 2009." *Informes Financieros.* Retrieved 9 Mar. 2010. <http://www.pdvsa.com/interface.sp /database/fichero/free/5332/800.PDF

Phillips, Nicola. "U.S. Power and the Politics of Economic Governance in the Americas." *Latin American Politics and Society,* 47, 4 (Winter 2005): 1–25.

Pincus, Steven. "Rethinking Revolutions: A Neo-Tocquevillian Perspective." In *Oxford Handbook of Comparative Politics,* edited by Carles Boix and Susan Stokes, 397–415. New York: Oxford University Press, 2007.

Piñango, Ramón. "Muerte de la armonía." In *En esta Venezuela,* edited by Patricia. Márquez and Ramón Piñango, 15–28. Caracas: Ediciones IESA, 2003.

Piñero Harnecker, Camila. "The New Cooperative Movement in Venezuela's Bolivarian Process." 2005. Retrieved on July 17, 2008 from: http://www.venezuelanalysis.com/analysis/1531.

Polanyi, Karl. *The Great Transformation.* Boston: Beacon Press, 1944.

Pollin, Robert, and Andong Zhu. "Inflation and Economic Growth: A Cross-Country Non-linear Analysis." 27 Oct. 2005. Political Economy Research Institute, University of Massachusetts. Retrieved 9 Mar. 2010. <http://www.peri.umass.edu /236/hash/ae49da3487/publication/185>.

Ponniah, Thomas, and William F. Fisher. "The World Social Forum, or, the Reinvention of Democracy." In *Another World Is Possible: Popular Alternatives to Globalization at the World Social Forum,* edited by William F. Fisher and Thomas Ponniah. London: Zed Books, 2003.

Prada, Lizardi, and James Suggett. "Venezuela's Homemakers Union: An Interview with Founder and Coordinator Lizardi Prada." Published in Venezuelanalysis .comon, July 7, 2009. Accessed Feb. 28, 2010.

Prebisch, Raul. *International Economics and Development.* New York: Academic Press, 1972.

Prensa Presidencial: http://www.minci.gob.ve/noticias-prensa-presidencial/.

Pretel, Enrique Andrés. "Chávez busca ampliar fondo China a 20.000 mln dlr" Reuters. 25 Feb. 2010. Retrieved 9 Mar. 2010. <http://www.reuters.com/article/idARN2510846120100225>.

Programa Vuelvan Caras: http://www.vuelvancaras.gov.ve/home.php

"Propondrán despenalizar la interrupción del embarazo producto de una violación," *El Nacional* (Caracas), Jan. 22, 2010.

"Proyecto de ley establece 'control obrero' en empresas," *El Universal*, Jan. 13, 2007 (http://buscador.eluniversal.com/2007/01/13/pol_art140072.shtml.

Purcell, Mark. "Urban Democracy and the Local Trap." *Urban Studies*, 43, 1 (Oct. 2006): 1921–1941.

Rahnema, Majid, with Victoria Bawtree. *The Post-Development Reader*. London: Zed Books, 1997.

Rakowski, Cathy A. "Women's Coalitions as a Strategy at the Intersection of Economic and Political Change in Venezuela." *International Journal of Politics, Culture, and Society*, 16, 3 (Spring 2003): 387–405.

Rakowski, Cathy A., and Gioconda Espina. "Institucionalización de la lucha feminista/femenina en Venezuela: Solidaridad y fragmentación, oportunidades y desafíos." In *De lo Privado a lo Público: 30 Años de lucha ciudadana de las mujeres en América Latina*, edited by Nathalie Lebon and Elisabeth Maier, 310– 330. New York: Unifem and Siglo XXI Editores, 2006.

Ramírez, Cristobal Valencia. "Venezuela's Bolivarian Revolution: Who Are the Chavistas?" In *Venezuela: Hugo Chávez and the Decline of an 'Exceptional Democracy*,' edited by Scott Ellner and Miguel Tinker Salas, 121–140. Lanham: Rowan and Littlefield, 2007.

Rawls, John. *A Theory of Justice*, Cambridge, MA: Harvard University Press, 1971.

Reel, Monte. "A Latin American Pipe Dream," *Washington Post*, Feb. 12, 2006.

"Rendering Account," *The New PDVSA Contact*. Caracas: Ministerio de Energía y Petróleo, August 2005.

República Bolivariana de Venezuela. *Indicadores de la Fuerza de Trabajo*. Caracas: Instituto Nacional de Estadística, 1999–2006.

———."Ley de los Consejos Comunales," *Gaceta Oficial* 5805, April 10, 2006.

Revolucionarias a favor del Socialismo Feminista. "¿Somos o no somos?" Proclamation directed to the National Assembly demanding rights for lesbians, homosexuals, transgender and transexual persons. Dated July 23, 2009. Posted to Insurrectasypunto, the website of the Colectivo de Lesbianas Feministas Josefa Camejo. Accessed August 2, 2009.

"Rice, Chávez Clash on OAS Meeting Opens," *Financial Times*, June 7, 2005.

Roberts, Kenneth. "Populism, Political Conflict, and Grass-roots Organization in Latin America." *Comparative Politics*, 38, 2 (Jan. 2006): 127–148.

———. "Social Correlates of Party System Demise and Populist Resurgence in Venezuela." *Latin American Politics and Society*, 45, 3 (2003): 35–57.

———. "Social Polarization and the Populist Resurgence in Venezuela." In *Venezuelan Politics in the Chávez Era: Class, Polarization, and Conflict*, edited by Steve Ellner and Daniel Hellinger, 55–72. Boulder: Lynne Rienner, 2003.

Rodríguez, Francisco. "An Empty Revolution: The Unfulfilled Promises of Hugo Chávez." *Foreign Affairs* (March/April 2008).

―――. "How Not to Defend the Revolution: Mark Weisbrot and the Misinterpretation of Venezuelan Evidence." *Wesleyan Economics Working Papers*, Wesleyan University, March 25, 2008.

Rodríguez, Francisco, Chang-Tai Hsieh, Edward Miguel, and Daniel Ortega. "The Price of Political Opposition: Evidence from Venezuela's Maisanta," April 2009, available at http://frrodriguez.web.wesleyan.edu/docs/working_papers/maisanta _april2009_final.pdf.

Rohter, Larry. "A Man with Big Ideas, a Small Country ... and Oil," *New York Times*, Sept. 24, 2000.

Romero, Juan Eduardo. "El discurso político de Hugo Chávez." *Espacio Abierto: Cuaderno Venezolano de Sociologia*, 10, 2 (Apr.–Jun. 2001): 21–38.

Romero Salazar, Alexis. "Al ascensor detenido. La crisis de la movilidad social a través de la titulación." *Espacio Abierto: Cuaderno Venezolano de Sociologia*, 15, 1–2 (Jan.–June 2006): 99–113.

Rosnick, David, and Mark Weisbrot. "Political Forecasting? The IMF's Flawed Growth Projections for Argentina and Venezuela." Washington, D.C.: Center for Economic and Policy Research, 2007. Retrieved from: http://cepr.net/index .php?option=com_contents&task=view&id=1107.

Ross, M. L. "Does Oil Hinder Democracy?" *World Politics*, 53, 3 (2001): 325–361.

―――. "How Do Natural Resources Influence Civil War? Evidence from Thirteen Cases," *International Organization*, 58, 1 (2004): 35–67.

Ross, Robert J. S. "From Antisweatshop to Global Justice to Antiwar: How the New New Left Is the Same and Different from the Old New Left." *Journal of World Systems Research*, 10, 1 (2004): 287–319.

Sabatini, Christopher. "Decentralization and Political Parties." *Journal of Democracy*, 14, 2 (April 2003): 138–150.

Sainz Borgo, Juan Carlos, and Guadalupe Paz. "Venezuela: Revolutionary Changes under Chávez." In *The Andes in Focus: Security, Democracy, and Economic Reform*, edited by Russell Crandall, Guadalupe Paz, and Riordan Roett, 91–120. Boulder: Lynne Rienner, 2005.

Saiz, Mónica. *Bolivarianas: El protagonismo de las mujeres en la Revolución Venezolana*. Vol. 1. Caracas: Ediciones Emancipación, 2004.

Salamanca, Luis. "Civil Society: Late Bloomers." In *The Unraveling of Representative Democracy in Venezuela*, edited by Jennifer McCoy and David Myers, 93–115. Baltimore: Johns Hopkins University Press, 2004.

―――. "The Venezuelan Political System: A View from Civil Society." In *Venezuelan Democracy Under Stress*, edited by Jennifer McCoy, William C. Smith, Andrés Serbin, and Andrés Stambouli, 197–215. New Brunswick: North-South Center/Transaction Press, 1995.

Samuels, David. "Money, Elections, and Democracy in Brazil." *Latin American Politics and Society*, 43, 2 (2001): 27–48.

Sanderson, Stephen K. *Revolutions: A Worldwide Introduction to Political and Social Change.* Boulder: Paradigm Publishers, 2005.

Sanjuán, Ana María. "La Revolución Bolivariana en Riesgo, La Democratización Social en Cuestión. La Violencia Social y la Criminalidad en Venezuela Entre 1998–2008." *Revista Venezolana de Economía y Ciencias Sociales*, 4, 3 (sept.–dic. 2008): 145–173.

Santeliz Granadillo, Andrés. "1999–2009, La Economía en Diez Años de Gobierno Revolucionario." *Revista Venezolana de Economía y Ciencias Sociales*, 14, 3 (sept.–dic. 2008): 83–119.

Santos, Boaventura de Souza. *The Rise of the Global Left: The World Social Forum and Beyond.* London: Zed Books, 2006.

Sartori, Giovanni. *Parties and Party Systems: A Framework for Analysis.* New York: Cambridge University Press, 1976.

Sassen, Saskia. *Territory, Authority, Rights: From Medieval to Global Assemblages.* Princeton: Princeton University Press, 2006.

Schalom, Steven. "ParPolity: Political Vision for a Good Society," *Znet*, 2005. Retrieved from: http://www.zmag.org/shalompol.htm.

Schamis, Hector E. *Re-forming the State: The Politics of Privatization in Latin America and Europe.* Ann Arbor: University of Michigan Press, 2002.

Scheler, Max. *Ressentiment.* New York: Schocken Books, 1972.

Schmitt, John. "Is It Time to Export the US Tax Model to Latin America?" Apr. 2003. Center for Economic and Policy Research. Retrieved 9 Mar. 2010. <http://www.cepr.net/documents/publications/latin_america_2003_04.pdf>.

Schumpeter, Joseph A. *Imperialism and Social Classes*, trans. Heinz Norton. New York: Augustus M. Kelley, 1951.

Schuyler, G. W. "Globalization and Health: Venezuela and Cuba," *Canadian Journal of Development Studies,* 23, 4 (2002): 687–716.

Schwartzman, Kathleen. *The Social Origins of Democratic Collapse: The First Portuguese Republic in the Global Economy.* Lawrence, Kansas: University Press of Kansas, 1989.

Seib, Philip. "Hegemonic No More: Western Media, the Rise of Al-Jazeera, and the Influence of Diverse Voices," *International Studies Review*, 7 (2005): 602–604.

Selbin, Eric. *Latin American Revolution.* Boulder: Westview Press, 1998.

Sen, Amartya. *Development as Freedom.* New York: Alfred A. Knopf, 1999.

Serrano, Pascual. "Venezuelans See Economy and Democracy More Positively Than Other Latin Americans," trans. from Rebelion.org, posted on Venezuelanalysis.com, Jan. 17, 2008, accessed at: http://www.venezuelanalysis.com/analysis/3075.

Shadlen, Kenneth. *Democratization without Representation: The Politics of Small Industry in Mexico.* University Park: The Pennsylvania State University Press, 2004.

Sheridan, Mary Beth. "In OAS Elections, US Favorite Bows Out," *Washington Post*, April 10, 2005. A23.

Shifter, Michael. "In Search of Hugo Chávez." *Foreign Affairs*, 85, 3 (May/June 2006): 45–59.

Shils, Edward. "Deference." In Shils, *The Constitution of Society,* 143–178. Chicago: University of Chicago Press, 1982.

Silva, Eduardo. *The State and Capital in Chile: Business Elites, Technocrats, and Market Economics.* Boulder: Westview Press, 1996.

Silva R., Jesús. "Hablar de Equidad de Género es hablar de Socialismo." Speech on the occasion of International Women's Day. Caracas, March 7, 2008. Retrieved from Inamujer web site on July 27, 2008.

Sistema Integrado de Indicadores Sociales de Venezuela (SISOV). "Logros Sociales." 2007. Ministerio del Poder Popular para la Planificación y Desarrollo. Retrieved 2 Mar. 2009. <http://www.sisov.mpd.gob.ve/estudios/158/LOGROS_AGOSTO2007.pdf>.

————. "Indicadores." Ministerio del Poder Popular para la Planificación y Desarrollo. Retrieved 2 Mar. 2009. <http://www.sisov.mpd.gob.ve/>.

Skocpol, Theda. "Explaining Social Revolutions: First and Further Thoughts." In *Social Revolutions in the Modern World,* edited by Theda Skocpol, 3–25. New York: Cambridge University Press, 1994.

————. *States and Social Revolutions: A Comparative Analysis of France, Russia, and China.* New York: Cambridge University Press, 1979.

Skurski, Julie. "The Ambiguities of Authenticity in Latin America: *Doña Bárbara* and the Construction of National Identity." *Poetics Today,* 15, 4 (Winter 1994): 605–642.

Smilde, David. "The Social Structure of Hugo Chávez." *Contexts,* 7, 1 (2008): 38–43.

————. *Reason to Believe: Cultural Agency in Latin American Evangelicalism.* Berkeley: University of California Press, 2007.

Smith, B. "Oil Wealth and Regime Survival in the Developing World, 1960–1999." *American Journal of Political Science,* 48, 2 (2004): 232–246.

Smith, William C., and Jennifer McCoy. "Venezuelan Democracy under Stress." In McCoy et al., eds., *Venezuelan Democracy under Stress,* 1–9. New Brunswick: Transaction Publishers, 1995.

Sojo, Cleto. "Venezuela, OAS Countries Reject US Proposal to Monitor Democracies." June 8, 2005. Retrieved from: www.venezuelanalysis.com/news.php?newsno=1651.

————. "Venezuela's Chávez Closes World Social Forum with Call to Transcend Capitalism," January 31, 2005. Retrieved from: http://www.venezuelanalysis.com/news.php?newsno=1486.

Spiegel, J., and A. Yassi. "Lessons from the Margins of Globalization: Appreciating the Cuban Health Paradox." *Journal of Public Health Policy,* 25, 1 (2004): 85–110.

Stiglitz, Joseph. *Globalizaiton and Its Discontents.* New York: W.W. Norton, 2003.

Students for a Democratic Society (SDS). "Port Huron Statement." http://www2.iath.virginia.edu/sixties/HTML_docs/Resources/Primary/Manifestos/SDS_Port_Huron.html (Site visited 23/05/10).

Subcomandante Marcos. "La 4e guerre mondiale a commencé." *Le Monde diplomatique,* August 1997, 4–5.

Suggett, J. "Venezuela Transfers Administration of Ports and Airports to National Government," in Venezuelanalysis.com, March 16, 2009 (http://www.venezuelanalysis.com/news/4297).

Sylvia, Ronald, and Constantine P. Danopoulos. "The Chávez Phenomenon: Political Change in Venezuela," *Third World Quarterly*, 24, 1 (Feb. 2003): 63–76.

Talmon, J. L. *The Origins of Totalitarian Democracy*. New York: Praeger, 1961.

Tarrow, Sidney. *Power in Movement: Social Movements and Contentious Politics*, 2nd ed. New York: Cambridge University Press, 1998.

Taylor, Charles. *Sources of the Self: The Making of the Modern Identity*. Cambridge MA: Harvard University Press, 1989.

Tesorería (Oficina Nacional del Tesoro). "Informe Anual Gestión 2009." Ministerio del Poder Popular para Economía y Finanzas. Retrieved 9 Mar. 2010. <http://www.ont.mf.gov.ve/OntWeb/descarga/download.action?id=23&file=115>.

Thacker, Strom. *Big Business, the State, and Free Trade: Constructing Coalitions in Mexico*. Cambridge: Cambridge University Press, 2000.

Tilly, Charles. *European Revolutions, 1492–1992*. Boston: Blackwell, 1995.

Tinker Salas, Miguel. "Culture, Power and Oil: Oil Camps and the Construction of Venezuelan Citizenry." *Espacio Abierto*, 15, 1–2 (Jan.–June, 2006): 343–367.

———. *The Enduring Legacy: Oil, Culture, and Society in Venezuela*. Durham: Duke University Press, 2009.

Tocqueville, Alexis. *Democracy in America*. Trans. George Lawrence; ed. J. P. Mayer. New York: Perennial Classics, 2000.

———. *Old Regime and the French Revolution*. Trans. Stuart Gilbert. New York: Anchor Books, 1983.

Torres, Gerver. "21st Century Socialism: Old Names, New Ideas?" Paper presented at the conference "The Politics of Regime Change, Continuity, and Stability in Venezuela," David Rockefeller Center for Latin American Studies, Harvard University, Dec. 14, 2007.

Tovar, Marianela. "Ley Orgánica para la Equidad e Igualdad de Género en Venezuela: Se les ve el bojote." Article posted online at www.insurrectasypunto.org, with multiple comments following, April 9, 2009.

Trinkunas, Harold. *Crafting Civilian Control of the Military in Venezuela: A Comparative Perspective*. Chapel Hill: University of North Carolina Press, 2005.

———. "What Is Really New about Venezuela's Bolivarian Foreign Policy?" *Strategic Insights*, 5, 2 (Feb. 2006).

Tulchin, J. S., and G. Bland, eds. *Venezuela in the Wake of Radical Reform*. Boulder: Lynne Rienner, 1993.

Turner, Victor W. *The Forest of Symbols: Aspects of Ndembu Ritual*. Ithaca: Cornell University Press, 1967.

———. *The Ritual Process: Structure and Anti-Structure*. Chicago: Aldine Publishing, 1969.

Unifem: http://www.unifem.org/.

Unión Europea: Misión de Observación Electoral Venezuela 2006. *Informe Final.* Caracas, feb. 2007.

United Nations Development Programme. *Human Development Report 2001, Making New Technologies Work for Human Development,* http://hdr.undp.org/en /media/completenew1.pdf, Accessed on June 1, 2010.

———. *Human Development Report 2009, Overcoming Barriers: Human Mobility and Development,* accessed at http://hdr.undp.org/en/media/HDR_2009_EN _Complete.pdf, accessed on June 1, 2010.

United States Geological Survey (USGS). "An Estimate of Recoverable Heavy Oil Resources of the Orinoco Oil Belt, Venezuela." World Petroleum Resources Project. Oct. 2009. Department of the Interior, Fact Sheet 2009–3028. Retrieved 9 Mar. 2010. <http://pubs.usgs.gov/fs/2009/3028/pdf/FS09-3028.pdf>.

"Uribe, Torrijos, y Chávez inician construcción de gasoducto transcaribeño," July 7, 2006, retrieved from Telesur.net.

Vaky, Viron L., and Heraldo Muñoz. *The Future of the Organization of American States.* New York: Twentieth Century Fund Press, 1993.

Vallenilla-Lanz, Laureano. *Caesarismo Democrático.* Caracas; Monte Ávila, 1990.

Van Cott, Donna. "Andean Indigenous Movements and Constitutional Transformation: Venezuela in Comparative Perspective." *Latin American Perspectives,* 30, 1 (Jan. 2003): 49–69.

Van Gennep, Arnold. *Rites of Passage.* Chicago: University of Chicago Press, 1960.

Varianzas de opinión. "Resultados Estudio de Opinión." Caracas, Venezuela, 2008.

Vásquez Barquero, Antonio. "Desarrollo endógeno: Interacción de las fuerzas que gobiernan los procesos de crecimiento económico." In *En la frontera del desarrollo endógeno,* edited by E. Vergara and Von Baer. Temuco, Chile: Ediciones Universidad de la Frontera, 2004.

Veneconomía. "Daily Report," Veneconomía. Caracas. April 30, 2008. Retrieved from: http://www.veneconomia.com/site/.

"Venezuela, Colombia, Start Building Gas Pipeline," July 8, 2006, retrieved from http://money.cnn.com/2006/07/08/news/venezgas_reut/index.htm.

Venezuelalibre: http://venezuelalibre.noblogs.org/post/2007/01/30/trueque-y-moneda-social.

"Venezuelan Government Announces $5 Billion for Communal Councils in 2007," Venezuelanalysis.com, January 10, 2007. (http://www.venezuelanalysis.com /news.php?newsno=2188).

"Venezuelan Risk: Risk Overview." Economist Intelligence Unit. 30 Oct. 2007. Retrieved 9 Mar. 2010. <http://www.eiu.com/index.asp?layout=RKArticleVW3 &article_id=1642722349>.

"Venezuela's Candidacy for the UN Security Council Appears on Track," Press Release, Washington, D.C.: Council on Hemispheric Affairs, August 10, 2006.

"Venezuela's Electoral Council Rules Referendum Petition Signatures to be Kept Secret," Venezuelanalysis.com, Feb. 8, 2007. (http://venezuelanalysis.com/news .php?newsno=2213).

Vergara, Eva. "South American Presidents Back Morales." Associated Press. 16 Sept. 2008.

Volkel, Christian. "'Massacre' Designation Strengthens Bolivian Government's Hand Against Opposition Prefects." World Markets Research Center. Global Insight, 4 Dec. 2008.

Von Hayek, Friedrich. *The Road to Serfdom.* Chicago: University of Chicago Press, 1956.

Wagner, Sarah. "Problems and Opportunities for Citizen Power in Venezuela." 2004. Retrieved from: http://www.venezuelanalysis.com/analysis/825.

———. "The Bolivarian Response to the Feminization of Poverty in Venezuela." Feb. 5, 2005. Retrieved from: http://www.venezuelanalysis.com.

———. "Women and Venezuela's Bolivarian Revolution." Jan. 15, 2005. Retrieved from: http://www.venezuelanalysis.com.

———. "Coloring Venezuela's Gender Debate." Article published online by Venezuelanalysis.com, June 17 2005.

Wallerstein, Immanuel. "Semi-Peripheral Countries and the Contemporary World Crisis." *Theory and Society,* 3, 4 (1976): 461–483.

———. "Class Formation in the Capitalist World Economy," In *The Capitalist World Economy,* edited by I. Wallerstein, 222–230. New York: Cambridge University Press, 1979.

———. *After Liberalism.* New York: The New Press, 1995.

Walt, Stephen M. "Keeping the World 'Off Balance': Self-restraint in U.S. Foreign Policy." In *America Unrivaled: The Future of the Balance of Power,* edited by G. John Ikenberry, 121–154. Ithaca: Cornell University Press, 2002.

———. *Taming American Power: The Global Response to U.S. Primacy.* New York: W. W. Norton, 2005.

———. *The Origins of Alliances.* Ithaca, NY: Cornell University Press, 1987.

Weber, Max. *The Theory of Social and Economic Organization.* New York: The Free Press, 1947.

———. "Politics as Vocation." In *From Max Weber,* edited by H. H. Gerth and C. Wright Mills, 77–128. London: Routledge, 1999.

———. "Class, Status and Party" (1924). In ibid.

Weeks, J. "The Contemporary Latin American Economies: Neoliberal Reconstruction." In *Capital, Power, and Inequality in Latin America,* edited by S. Halebsky and R. L. Harris. Boulder: Westview Press, 1995.

Weingast, Barry R. "Constructing Self-Enforcing Democracy in Spain." In *Politics from Anarchy to Democracy: Rational Choice in Political Science,* edited by E. L. Morris, J. A. Oppenheimer, and K. E. Soltan, 161–196. Stanford, CA: Stanford University Press, 2004.

Weinstein, Michael A. "Intelligence Brief: Rumsfeld Visits Paraguay and Peru," *Power and Interest News Report,* August 23, 2005.

Weisbrot, Mark. "Ten Years After: The Lasting Impact of the Asian Financial Crisis." In *Ten Years After: Revisiting the Asian Financial Crisis,* edited by Bhumika

Muchhala, 105–118. Washington, D.C.: Woodrow Wilson International Center for Scholars, 2007. Retrieved 9 Mar. 2010. <http://www.cepr.net/documents /publications/tenyearsafter_2007_11.pdf.>.

———. "President Bush's Trip to Latin America Is All about Denial." McClatchy-Tribune Information Services, 5 Mar. 2007. Retrieved 9 Mar. 2010. <http://www .cepr.net/index.php/op-eds-&-columns/op-eds-&-columns/president-bushs-trip-to-latin-america-is-all-about-denial/>.

———. "An Empty Research Agenda: The Creation of Myths about Contemporary Venezuela." Center for Economic and Policy Research Issue Brief, March 2008, http://www.cepr.net/index.php/publications/reports/an-empty-research-agenda-the-creation-of-myths-about-contemporary-venezuela/.

———. "How Not to Attack an Economist (and An Economy): Getting the Numbers Right." *CEPR Research Issue Brief*, April, 2008.

———. "Poverty Reduction in Venezuela: A Reality-Based View." *ReVista: Harvard Review of Latin America* (Fall 2008): 36–39.

———. "More of the Same in Latin America." *New York Times,* 11 Aug. 2009. Retrieved 8 Mar. 2010. <http://www.nytimes.com/2009/08/12/opinion/12iht-edweisbrot.html.

———. "Obama's Deafening Silence on Honduras." *The Guardian.* 21 Aug. 2009. Retrieved 8 Mar. 2010. <http://www.guardian.co.uk/commentisfree/cifamerica/2009/aug/21/honduras-coup-us-foreign-policy>.

———. "Restoring Democracy in Honduras: Hillary Clinton's Attempts to Resolve the Crisis in Honduras Have Failed. It's Time for Latin America to Take the Lead." *Guardian Unlimited.* 30 June 2009. Retrieved 8 Mar. 2010. <http://www .guardian.co.uk/commentisfree/cifamerica/2009/jul/30/honduras-hillary-clinton-zelaya>.

———. "The High-Powered Hidden Support for Honduras' Coup." *Los Angeles Times.* 23 July 2009. Retrieved 9 Mar. 2010. <http://articles.latimes.com/2009/jul /23/opinion/oe-weisbrot23>.

Weisbrot, Mark, and Luis Sandoval. "Argentina's Economic Recovery: Policy Choices and Implications." Oct. 2007. Center for Economic and Policy Research. Retrieved 8 Mar. 2010. <http://www.cepr.net/documents/publications/argentina _recovery_2007_10.pdf>.

———. "Update: The Venezuelan Economy in the Chávez Years." Feb. 2008. Center for Economic and Policy Research. Retrieved 8 Mar. 2010. <http://www.cepr .net/documents/publications/venezuela_update_2008_02.pdf>.

Weisbrot, Mark, Luis Sandoval, and David Rosnick. "Poverty Rates in Venezuela: Getting the Numbers Right." May 2006. Center for Economic and Policy Research, Retrieved 8 Mar. 2010. <http://www.cepr.net/documents/venezuelan_poverty_rates_2006_05.pdf>.

Weisbrot, Mark, and David Rosnick, "A Shrinking Market: Projections for U.S. Imports." Washington, D.C.: Center for Economic and Policy Research, July 2006. Retrieved from: http://www.cepr.net/documents/import_market_2006 _07.pdf.

Weisbrot, Mark, and Rebecca Ray. "Bolivia: The Economy During the Morales Administration." Dec. 2009. Center for Economic and Policy Research. Retrieved 8 Mar. 2010. <http://www.cepr.net/documents/publications/bolivia-2009-12.pdf>.

Weyland, Kurt. "Clarifying a Contested Concept." *Comparative Politics*, 34, 1 (2001): 1–22.

———. "Economic Voting Reconsidered: Crisis and Charisma in the Election of Hugo Chávez." *Comparative Political Studies*, 36, 7 (Sept. 2003): 822–848.

———. "The Politics of Corruption in Latin America." *Journal of Democracy*, 9, 2 (1998): 108–21.

———. "Will Chávez Lose His Luster?" *Foreign Affairs* (Nov./Dec. 2001).

———. "The Performance of Leftist Governments in Latin America: Conceptual and Theoretical Issues." In *Leftist Governments in Latin America: Successes and Shortcomings*, edited by Kurt Weyland, Raúl L. Madrid, and Wendy Hunter, 1–27. New York: Cambridge University Press, 2010.

Wijnholds, J. Onno de Beaufort, and Arend Kapteyn. "Reserve Adequacy in Emerging Market Economies." Sept. 2001. International Monetary Fund, Working Paper WP/01/143. Retrieved 8 Mar. 2010. <http://www.imf.org/external/pubs/ft/wp/2001/wp01143.pdf>.

Williams, Mark. "Escaping the Zero-Sum Scenario: Democracy versus Technocracy in Latin America." *Political Science Quarterly*, 121, 1 (2006): 119–140.

———. "U.S. Policy in the Andes: Commitments and Commitment Traps." In *The Andes in Focus: Security, Democracy & Economic Reform*, edited by Russell Crandall, Guadalupe Paz, and Riordan Roett, 151–172. Boulder: Lynne Rienner, 2005.

Williamson, John. "What Washington Means by Policy Reforms." In *Latin American Adjustment: How Much Has Happened?* Edited by John Williamson. Washington, D.C.: Institute for International Economics, 1990.

Wilpert, Bernhard. "A View from Psychology." In *Organizational Participation: Myth and Reality*, edited by Frank Heller, Eugen Pusic, George Strauss, and Bernhard Wilpert, 40–64. Oxford: Oxford University Press, 1998.

Wilpert, Gregory. *Changing Venezuela by Taking Power: The History and Policies of the Chávez Government*. New York: Verso, 2007.

———. "Chávez Announces Nationalizations, Constitutional Reform for Socialism in Venezuela." Jan. 8, 2007. Retrieved from: http://www.venezuelanalysis.com/news.php?newsno=2187.

———. "Chávez Says Americas Summit Will Serve to Bury FTAA." Nov. 4, 2005. Retrieved from: http://www.venezuelanalysis.com/news.php?newsno=1806.

———. "Venezuela's Quiet Housing Revolution: Urban Land Reform." 2005. Retrieved from: http://www.venezuelanalysis.com/analysis/1355.

———. "Poll: Venezuelans Have Highest Regard for Their Democracy." Dec. 20, 2006. Retrieved from: http://venezuelanalysis.com/news.php?newsno=2179.

———. "Making Sense of Venezuela's Constitutional Reform." 2007. Retrieved from: http://www.venezuelanalysis.com/analysis/2943.

———. "Venezuela Hails OAS Meeting As Great Success." June 9, 2005. Retrieved from: www.venezuelanalysis.com/news/php?newsno=1654.

————. "Venezuela: Revolution Checked," *Le Monde Diplomatique,* Jan. 2008.

————. "Smoke and Mirrors: An Analysis of Human Rights Watch's Report on Venezuela," in Venezuelanalysis.com, Oct. 17, 2008 (http://www.venezuelanalysis.com/analysis/3882).

Wimmer, Andreas, and Nina Glick Schiller. "Methodological Nationalism and Beyond: Nation-State Building, Migration, and the Social Sciences." *Global Networks,* 2, 4 (2002): 301–334.

World Bank. *Staff Appraisal Report: Venezuela Health Services Reform Project 2005.* Retrieved Feb.15, 2006 from: http://www-wds.worldbank.org/servlet/WDSContentServer/WDSP/IB/1999/04/28/000009265_3961007072638/Rendered/PDF/multi0page.pdf.

————. "World Development Indicators Online." Retrieved 8 Mar. 2010. <http://go.worldbank.org/6HAYAHG8H0>.

————. "Doing Business 2008," from www.doingbusiness.org.

World Social Forum: http://allies.alliance21.org/fsm/.

Wright, Winthrop. *Café con leche: Race, Class, and National Image in Venezuela.* Austin: University of Texas Press, 1990.

Wynter, Coral. "Nora Castañeda and the Women's Development Bank of Venezuela." (Originally from *Green Left Weekly,* Feb. 21, 2006). Retrieved from: http://www.venezuelanalysis.com.

YKVE Mundial. "Banmujer entregará 567 créditos a cooperativas y microempresas del país," Sept. 17, 2007. Published at http://www.radiomuncial.com.ve/yvke/noticia.php?32487. Accessed on Feb. 21, 2010.

Zapata, Juan Carlos. *Los Ricos Bobos.* Caracas: Alfadil Ediciones, 1995.

————. *Plomo más Plomo es Guerra: Proceso a Chávez.* Caracas: Alfadil Ediciones, 2000.

# Editors and Contributors

## Editors

**Jonathan Eastwood** is Associate Professor of Sociology at Washington and Lee University in Lexington, VA, and the author of *The Rise of Nationalism in Venezuela* (2006).

**Thomas Ponniah** is a Lecturer, Assistant Director of the Social Studies Program, and Faculty Associate of the Project on Justice, Welfare and Economics at Harvard University in Cambridge, MA. He is the co-editor of *Another World Is Possible: Popular Alternatives to Globalization at the World Social Forum* (2003) and the author of the forthcoming *Global Civilization: Civil Society Proposals for an Alternative Globalization* (2012).

## Contributors

**Francisco Armada** was Minister of Health and Social Development in Venezuela from 2004 to 2007 and is now Technical Officer, Health Governance Research, WHO Centre for Health Development, Kobe, Japan.

**Haejoo Chung** is Assistant Professor in Health Policy, Department of Health Care Management, College of Health Sciences, Korea University, Seoul, Korea.

**Fernando Coronil** is Presidential Professor of Anthropology at the Graduate Center of the City University of New York, New York City.

**Javier Corrales** is Professor of Political Science at Amherst College, Amherst, MA.

**Gioconda Espina** is Professor of Feminist Theory in the Women Studies Program in the Faculty of Economic and Social Sciences at the Universidad Central de Venezuela, Caracas.

**Luis Lander** is Professor of Political Science at the Universidad Central de Venezuela, Caracas.

**Margarita López-Maya** is Professor of Political Science at the Universidad Central de Venezuela, Caracas.

**Qamar Mahmood** is a Postdoctoral and Canadian Institutes of Health Research CIHR Public Health Policy Fellow at the University of Toronto.

**Carles Muntaner** is Professor at the Bloomberg faculty of Nursing and Dalla Lana School of Public Health, University of Toronto.

**Cathy Rakowski** is Associate Professor in the Rural Sociology Program of the School of Environment and Natural Resources and in the Department of Women's, Gender and Sexuality Studies at The Ohio State University, Columbus, Ohio.

**Mark Weisbrot** is Co-Director of the Center for Economic Policy Research in Washington, D.C., and has a Ph.D. in Economics from the University of Michigan, Ann Arbor, MI.

**Mark Williams** is Professor of Political Science at Middlebury College, Middlebury, VT.

**Gregory Wilpert** is an Adjunct Professor at Brooklyn College's Graduate Center for Worker Education and is co-founder and one of the editors of Venezuelanalysis.com.